The Ethical Dimension of Psychoanalysis

A Dialogue

W. W. Meissner, S.J.

STATE UNIVERSITY OF NEW YORK PRESS

Published by
State University of New York Press, Albany

For information, address State University of New York Press,
90 State Street, Suite 700, Albany, NY 12207

Production by Christine L. Hamel
Marketing by Patrick J. Durocher

Library of Congress Cataloging in Publication Data

Meissner, W. W. (William W.), 1931–
    The ethical dimension of psychoanalysis : a dialogue / W. W. Meissner.
    p. cm. — (SUNY series in psychoanalysis and culture)
    Includes bibliographical references and index.
    ISBN 0-7914-5689-7 (alk. paper) — ISBN 0-7914-5690-0 (pbk. : alk. paper)
    1. Psychoanalysis—Moral and ethical aspects. I. Title. II. Series.

BF173.M3592 2003
150.19'5—dc21   2002029218

10 9 8 7 6 5 4 3 2 1

Contents

Preface

Psychoanalysis intersects with many areas of human interest, especially with disciplines concerned with understanding the organization and functioning of the human mind. Psychoanalysts have endeavored to engage in interdisciplinary dialogue with a wide range of scientific and humanistic disciplines seeking to explore areas of interaction between analytic understanding and these other areas. It has found such mutual ground for exploration in interaction with psychology, neurosciences, anthropology, sociology, art, literature, history, biography, and so on. One salient though relatively neglected area is ethics. The conjunction of ethical and psychoanalytic perspectives is a natural by-product of the inherent nature of the two disciplines, each dedicated in its own fashion to understanding the mental processes and behaviors contributing optimally to the betterment of the human condition, both in terms of the inner well-being of the individual subject and in terms of adaptation to the outside world, including both intimate personal relations as well as broader societal and communal relations. My objective in this study is to explore and explicate some of these areas of interaction and common interest.

Such interdisciplinary efforts encounter pressures for mutual adaptation, assimilation, and internal modification created by the transformative influence of each upon the other. This has certainly been my experience in pursuing this inquiry, and the reader may find himself or herself encountering similar pressures for rethinking basic issues in either discipline in order to take into account the data and perspectives engendered by the other discipline. This process involves both reshaping certain ethical considerations in a form more congruent with analytic conceptualization on one hand, and a corresponding rethinking of certain tenets of analytic theory on the other to allow greater integration with ethical perspectives.

One of the critical points of revision in the analytic perspective involves reformulation of the concept of drives as causal components of human decision and action. Postulation of an independent source of causality for human actions within the ethical agent undercuts components of choice, free will, and responsibility to name just a few. Without these elements, ethical decision-making and judgment become impossible or severely compromised. But rethinking the drive component leaves open questions of how aspects of behavior formerly explained by appeal to drives and drive-derivatives are to be accounted for. And on the ethical side, articulation of unconscious sources of motivation and unconscious mental processes as inherent in any meaningful ethical reflection brings complementary aspects of ethical reflection, deliberation, decision, and judgment into question. One hand washes the other! Both the analytic and the ethical perspectives must undergo mutually reinforcing modulation in the process of interdisciplinary dialogue.

The basic question addressed in these pages is the following: "Does psychoanalysis have anything to contribute to ethical understanding and reflection?" Some analysts, and no doubt some ethicians as well, would respond with a resounding "No!" Others, however, might answer with an unqualified "Yes!" And then again, a good many might hedge their bets and offer a qualified response. My argument would challenge the naysayers, since I will maintain that analysis unavoidably involves issues that have ethical implication. But my allegiance to the yeasayers is muted by my agreement with the naysayers that analysis does not contain an ethical doctrine in any formal sense. Any attempt to articulate an understanding of the ethical relevance of psychoanalysis cannot approach the issues with a black-and-white mental set, but must be prepared to work in the muted shadings of gray expressed in terms of more-or-less, and plus-and-minus, without ever being able to shake free of the ambiguities posed by unconscious motivations and mental processes. If we are to answer the basic question with a "Yes!" then, it must be a qualified "Yes," one that can be asserted only in nuanced, limited, and proportional terms and must continually be framed in reference to individual dynamics and diversifying contexts.

But I would submit that this enterprise is entirely consistent with the spirit of Sigmund Freud's own attitudes in this regard. In his preface to Putnam's addresses on psychoanalysis (1921b), after lauding James Putnam's ethical character, he noted that Putnam "bore witness to the fact that the physician who makes use of analysis understands far more about the sufferings of his patients and can do far more for them than was possible with the earlier methods of treatment; and finally how he began to extend beyond the limits of analysis, demanding that as a science it should be linked on to a particular philosophical system, and that its practice should be openly associated with a particular set of ethical doctrines" (p. 270).

Such an interdisciplinary study points in more than one direction. While one might expect the primary audience to be ethicians or any students of human behavior concerned with the ethical dimensions of the human condition, these issues and concerns are also relevant to the interests of psychoanalysts or psychotherapists who work personally and intensely with individual patients. Ethical issues pervade the therapeutic process: if they come into play in salient ways in analysis, they assuredly do so in other therapeutic approaches as well. I have tried throughout these reflections to keep in mind the relevant audiences for whom these reflections would be of interest.

My own competency in ethics is limited, based on a half-dozen years of course work in which I was exposed to a wide spectrum of ethical viewpoints and principles of ethical reflection. But my interest in ethical issues has been persistent, if peripheral, but in no sense represents anything like professional competence in the study of ethics. Specialists in ethics may find my efforts to be little more than amateurish infringements on a privileged terrain, but I can find no other vantage point from which to enter a dialogue across the divide separating (or uniting) psychoanalysis and ethics. My reflections here are generated from a primarily analytic stance and represent no more than tentative and exploratory probings into this complex and difficult terrain. Throughout this book, the prevailing modality is subjunctive, even when the expression may seem to take an indicative or declarative form. But the merit in the venture, as I see it, is in the hope and expectation that others more expert than myself will find the issues sufficiently challenging and provocative to merit further reflection, discussion, and even debate.

I would like to express my appreciation to the library staff at the Boston Psychoanalytic Institute and the research librarian staff at the O'Neill Library at Boston College for their assistance in checking and cross-checking references. I would also like to thank Miss Elfriede Banzhaf, my executive assistant, for her valuable contribution to this manuscript in various stages of its development.

CHAPTER ONE

Freudian and Postfreudian Ethics

INTRODUCTION

Sigmund Freud, the father of psychoanalysis, was not slow in expressing his ethical views, often based on arguments developed on the basis of his psychoanalytic perspective. I will begin this exploration with a considera-tion of his ethical views and those of some of his followers. Early psycho-analytic contributions to ethical reflection were rooted in Freud's thinking, but were subsequently elaborated and diversified by both his immediate fol-lowers and by subsequent generations of analysts.[1]

We can imagine the conflicting perspectives in Freud's mind as he sat listening to his patient on the couch. On the one hand, he had discovered a level of mental functioning that was unconscious and, as he thought, driven inexorably and in predetermined fashion by instinctual drives that acted as mental forces demanding immediate discharge. Such drive-derivative expressions acted beyond the range of conscious awareness and left no room for discretion, decision, reflection, or choice. On the other hand, he knew very well that there had to be something in the patient that would enable him to come to terms with these forces and to integrate them with the conscious personality in order for the patient to escape from instinctu-ally driven conflict and attain some degree of adaptive self-regulation. Freud knew the value of autonomy as a central component of psychic health and maturity. The patient had to come to a point of self-awareness, self-determinism, and choice in order to free himself from the grasp of unconscious and neurotic entanglements. The puzzle and the problem was how to help the patient find his or her way through this maze of interlock-ing complexities. It still is!

The prevailing view of freudian ethics emphasizes his deterministic, egoistic, and antimoral stance. This interpretation focuses on the role of the

1

superego in the development of ethical attitudes, especially conscience; on the role of libidinal and aggressive drives and narcissism; on dominance of the pleasure principle; repression; and in general on the effects of unconscious dynamics on human thought and action. In sum, the freudian perspective, so conceived, was charged with undermining the very foundations of ethical choice and morality. Ernest Wallwork (1991), however, drew a contrasting picture of Freud's ethics:

> The theory is naturalistic, grounded in a concept of human flourishing and regard for others, critical of exclusively Kantian-based ethics, yet respectful of certain Kantian emphases (such as the centrality of respect for autonomy), and concerned with the common good and special relations, as well as with individual rights. Significantly, this new understanding of Freud's ethic challenges postmodernist readings of Freud that find in him a model of the radically pluralistic self. Although it recognizes the decentering implications of the workings of the unconscious it allows for a self with sufficient cohesiveness and structure to counter the ethical relativism of much postmodernist thought. At the same time Freud's ethic acknowledges tensions between the private self and public responsibilities, impersonal moral reasoning and personal concerns and commitments. (p. x)

If we can fractionate the meaning of "ethics" into directives for a general pattern of life, a set of rules or codes governing right and wrong behavior, or an inquiry into the basis of rules of conduct (metaethics), Freud touched on all of these areas, although his primary focus fell on the second (Wallace 1986b).

READING FREUD

One reading of Freud (Klein 1976b) distinguished between experience-remote metapsychology and experience-near clinical theory. Much of Freud's thinking about ethical or moral issues was only loosely connected to his metapsychology. Much of contemporary analytic thinking has distanced itself from the mechanistic aspects of Freud's drive-derived theory. The dynamic hypothesis, conceived as the energy-driven and drive-derivative apparatus of the mind, can be read interpretively rather than mechanistically: mechanistically it deals with conflicting psychic forces (energically powered), while interpretively it is more a matter of "purposeful intentions working concurrently or in mutual opposition" (Freud

1916–1917, p. 67). Drive influences can thus be understood in terms of motives and reasons (Meissner 1995a,b,c; 1999a,b; Rapaport 1960; Sherwood 1969).[2]

The tension between energic and hermeneutical dimensions of analytic concepts led Paul Ricoeur (1970) to suggest an integration of metapsychological and hermeneutic concerns by reading the patient's productions in the analytic hour as a text to be interpreted; and viewing the analytic effort as "limited to restoring the integral, unmutilated and unfalsified text" (p. 260). But this did not cover the demands of either psychoanalytic praxis or theory: "As I see it," wrote Ricoeur,

> the whole problem of Freudian epistemology may be centralized in a single question: How can the economic explanation be *involved* in an interpretation dealing with meanings; and conversely, how can interpretation be an *aspect* of the economic explanation? It is easier to fall back on a disjunction: either an explanation in terms of energy, or an understanding in terms of phenomenology. It must be recognized, however, that Freudianism exists only on the basis of its refusal of that disjunction. (p. 66, italics in original)

In subsequent years, the ground has shifted somewhat to allow for the possibility of an economic metapsychology without reliance on outdated energic models and for closer connection of a revised metapsychology with hermeneutical and informational models (Meissner 1995a,b,c).[3]

However impelled Freud might have felt to make his theory acceptable to the mechanistic scientific world of his day, he also allowed room for concepts that spoke to ordinary experience and to his own clinical experience. Ernest Wallwork (1991) notes:

> For the fact is that the metapsychology makes liberal use of bridge concepts such as "instinct" and "the dynamic point of view" that have clinically interpretable referents that must be appreciated on the level of ordinary folk psychology in order for the metapsychology itself to be properly understood. With these bridge concepts, Freud was struggling to do justice to both nonteleological and teleological explanations of human mental life that we have yet to reach consensus about how to combine theoretically. (p. 34)

Freud's writing indulges in shifting perspectives that introduce inevitable tensions, even at times contradictions, in his theorizing. He was not unaware of this aspect of his work, writing (1915b), somewhat apologetically:

> The extraordinary intricacy of all the factors to be taken into consideration leaves only one way of presenting them open to us. We must select first one and then another point of view, and follow it up through the material as long as the application of it seems to yield results. Each separate treatment of the subject will be incomplete in itself, and there cannot fail to be obscurities where it touches upon material that has not yet been treated; but we may hope that a final synthesis will lead to a proper understanding. (pp. 157–158)

This inherent looseness of freudian theory has yet to be adequately integrated. There is still an unresolved debate whether psychoanalysis is a more-or-less unified theory or an aggregate of multiple theoretical perspectives, only loosely and problematically interconnected (Wallerstein 1992).

The ambiguity between mechanistic and more personal experiential formulations was present from the beginning of Freud's enterprise. Even in the *Project for a Scientific Psychology* (1895), the helmholtzian dictates of all-embracing materialism did not prevent Freud from leaving an island of personal agency in the form of the decidedly unmechanistic "I" capable of registering signals of pleasure and displeasure, evaluating qualitative differences, and deciding on remedial action—"a prime mover, the willer and ultimate knower, and thus a vitalistic homunculus with some degree of autonomy" (Holt 1965, pp. 99–100). The issues of personal agency in psychoanalytic theory remain unsettled, but in my view demand a theoretical accounting that goes beyond efforts of ego psychology to center personal agency in an impersonal and systemic ego (Meissner 1993).

FREUD'S ETHICS

Freud's profoundly humanistic interests and his sense that he was uncovering aspects of human behavior not previously well understood led him to reevaluate on his own terms matters that had long been prerogatives of philosophy and ethics. But he made little distinction between ethics and morality and spoke of ethics in more-or-less generic, even at times naive, terms: "What is moral is always self-evident. I believe that in a sense of justice and consideration for one's fellow men and in discomfort in making others suffer or taking advantage of them, I can compete with the best men I have known";[4] or ethics was "a kind of highway code for traffic among mankind";[5] or ideas "which deal with the relations of human beings to one another are comprised under the heading of ethics" (1930, p. 142). And as Heinz Hartmann (1960) noted, "He had no urge to go deeper into the question of the 'validity' of moral feelings or judgments" (p. 15). He wrote to Oskar Pfister at one point, somewhat cynically and condescendingly:

> "Ethics are remote from me. . . . I do not break my head very much about good and evil, but I have found little that is "good" about human beings on the whole. In my experience most of them are trash, no matter whether they publicly subscribe to this or that ethical doctrine or to none at all. . . . If we are to talk of ethics, I subscribe to a high ideal from which most of the human beings I have come across depart most lamentably. (Meng and Freud 1963, pp. 61–62)

In his assessment of such matters, there was much he could endorse and support in more traditional viewpoints, but also much he felt compelled to critique and condemn. He accepted the necessity for moral codes and regarded conscience as a necessity whose lack could only lead to the greatest conflicts and dangers potentially undermining human society. Among the motivational underpinnings of repression, shame and morality were early targets of criticism (Freud 1950 [1892-1899]), and somewhat later ethical and aesthetic standards (Freud 1909b, 1923b). Subsequent institutionalization of the superego gave the moral perspective a locus and function within the structural theory. The terms *moral* and *immoral* found consistent application respectively to repressing and repressed mental contents. Parapraxes, for example, were attributed to "compliant tolerance of the immoral" (Freud 1901, p. 276), and again in discussing one of his patients, the Rat Man (Freud 1909c), "He had only to assimilate this new contrast, between a moral self and an evil one, with the contrast . . . between the conscious and the unconscious. The moral self was the conscious, the evil self was the unconscious" (p. 177). This evil was further specified: "Repression invariably proceeded from the sick person's conscious personality (his ego) and took its stand on aesthetic and ethical motives; the impulses that were subjected to repression were those of selfishness and cruelty, which can be summed up in general as evil, but above all sexual wishful impulses, often of the crudest and most forbidden kind" (Freud 1924c [1923], p. 197).

Despite the strains of puritanical conscience in his own private life, he was often critical of traditional moral stances, but his condemnations were "hardly ever condemnation of the traditional principles but rather, in the name of these principles, a critique of actual behavior deviating from them" (Hartmann 1960, p. 18). A particular target of his criticism was attitudes toward sexual behavior, advocating greater understanding and tolerance of sexual deviation. In the previously cited letter to James Putnam, he wrote: "I interpret morality, such as we speak of it here, in the social, rather than the sexual sense. Sexual morality as society—and at its most extreme, American society—defines it, seems very despicable to me. I stand for a much freer sexual life. However, I have made little use of such freedom, except in so far as I was convinced of what was permissible for me in this area."[6]

DEVELOPMENTAL CONSIDERATIONS

His reinterpretation of immorality in terms of infantile developmental residues, universal bisexuality, and the emergence in childhood and persistence in adulthood of perverse modes of sexual experience provided the framework for his modified ethical attitudes. He regarded infantile sexuality as polymorphous perverse and asserted that "this disposition to perversions of every kind is a general fundamental human characteristic" (Freud 1905c, p. 191). His intent seems to have been to withdraw these aspects of human behavior from moral consideration and thereby increase the level of tolerance for them (Wallace 1986b).

Freud developed a more-or-less systematic view of the childhood origins of morality. The infant's total dependence on parents and early threats of the loss of love provided the basis for internalizing parental moral attitudes and led to further sublimation and reaction formation of perverse instinctual impulses. Much of character formation arose on the basis of defensive modifications of relatively perverse preoedipal drives and impulses (Freud 1905c). Morality, along with shame and disgust, were defined as forms of reaction formation (Freud 1908a) contributing to sphincter morality. This was followed in the oedipal phase by formation of the superego, the regulatory agency for establishing moral control over disordered and perverse instinctual drives. Basic to these considerations was the question of how much of apparently virtuous and consciously well-intentioned ethical behavior was based on such repressive and other defensive responses to unconscious wishes and impulses that had a very different character. In some cases, dispositions to generosity, goodness, and kindness were found to be riding on a substratum of selfish, sadistic, envious, and hateful impulses.

UNCONSCIOUS GUILT

Unconscious guilt played a central role in Freud's thinking about morality and about the pathology of conscience. His thinking about unconscious guilt found expression in his analysis of depressive processes following loss of a loved object. The basic mechanisms were identification with the lost object and turning of aggression toward the ambivalently held object against the self. He (1917) wrote: "The patient represents his ego to us as worthless, incapable of any achievement and morally despicable; he reproaches himself, vilifies himself, and expects to be cast out and punished" (p. 246). Thus all the reproaches and hostility, directed originally toward the lost object, are directed against that portion of the self identified with that object. This channeling of destructive impulses into the "conscience" was the basis for depressive reactions and states (Freud 1917b) and contributed to motivations of obsessional doubts and rituals (Freud 1907), and to forms of character pathology (Freud 1916). In ensuing years, Freud increasingly emphasized the role of unconscious guilt in the genesis of neurosis—even calling it "perhaps the most powerful bastion in the subject's (usually composite) gain from illness—in the sum of forces which struggle against his recovery and refuse to surrender his state of illness" (Freud 1924b, p. 166).

I would note that Freud was concerned with "neurotic guilt" operating in pathological contexts in which moral judgment was distorted and subject to neurotic needs and wishes. This neurotic sense of guilt focused more on fantasies than on facts or deeds, more specifically with unconscious fantasies. In Freud's (1913b) view, morality was a matter of action rather than fantasy:

> This creative sense of guilt still persists among us. We find it operating in an asocial manner in neurotics, and producing new moral precepts and persistent restrictions, as an atonement for crimes that have been committed and as a precaution against the committing of new ones. If, however, we inquire among these neurotics to discover what were the deeds which provoked these reactions, we shall be disappointed. We find no deeds, but only impulses and emotions, set upon evil ends but held back from their achievement. What lie behind the sense of guilt of neurotics are always *psychical* realities and never *actual* ones. (p. 159, italics in original)

The tension between unconscious and conscious motivation, between psychic and actual reality, and between neurotic and real guilt remain points of confusion and controversy.

INSTINCTS VS. MORALITY

The charge of sexual libertinism, leveled against Freud on the basis of his tolerance for sensual and sexual wishes and criticism of restrictive and punitive attitudes toward instinctual derivatives, seems to misread his position. He took up the challenge in his lectures at Clark University (1909b), arguing that the alternative was not simply acting out sexual impulses without restraint, but rather that neurotic restraints imposed through repression or other defenses could be replaced with conscious moral restraints:

> If what was repressed is brought back again into conscious mental activity . . . the resulting psychical conflict, which the patient had tried to avoid, can, under the physician's guidance, reach a better outcome than was offered by repression. There are a number of such opportune solutions, which may bring the conflict and the neurosis to a happy end, and which may in certain instances be combined. The patient's personality may be convinced that it has been wrong in rejecting the pathogenic wish and may be led into accepting it wholly or in part; or the wish itself may be directed to a higher and consequently unobjectionable aim (this is what we call its "sublimation"); or the rejection of the wish may be recognized as a justifiable one, but the automatic and therefore inefficient mechanism of repression may be replaced by a condemning judgement with the help of the highest human mental functions—conscious control of the wish is attained. (pp. 27–28)

The refrain is sounded again in the last lecture:

> On the other hand, the final outcome that is so much dreaded—the destruction of the patient's cultural character by the instincts which have been set free from repression—is totally impossible. For alarm on this score takes no account of what our experiences have taught us with certainty—namely that the mental and somatic power of a wishful impulse, when once its repression has failed, is far stronger if it is unconscious than if it is conscious; so that to make it conscious can only be to weaken it. An unconscious wish cannot be influenced and it is independent of any contrary tendencies, whereas a conscious one is inhibited by whatever else is conscious and opposed to it. Thus the work of psychoanalysis puts itself at the orders of precisely the highest and most valuable cultural trends, as a better substitute for the unsuccessful repression. (p. 53)

Freud's claim, then, is not that psychoanalysis drives moral and ethical considerations from the field, but precisely the opposite—that successful analysis brings underlying unconscious conflicts within the range of conscious ethical judgment and decision-making, thus undercutting the neurotic process and leading toward greater ethical maturity. In his words, "Analysis replaces the process of repression, which is an automatic and excessive one, by a temperate and purposeful control on the part of the highest agencies of the mind. In a word, analysis replaces repression by condemnation" (1909a, p. 145).[7]

ETHICAL CRITICISMS

But Freud was far from acting as a moral advocate. He wrote, "We can present society with a blunt calculation that what is described as its morality calls for a bigger sacrifice than it is worth and that its proceedings are not based on honesty and do not display wisdom" (1916–1917, p. 434). A decade later (Freud 1925a [1924]), he proclaimed:

> Psychoanalysis has never said a word in favour of unfettering instincts that would injure our community; on the contrary it has issued a warning and an exhortation to us to mend our ways. But society refuses to consent to the ventilation of the question, because it has a bad conscience in more than one respect. In the first place it has set up a high ideal of morality—morality being restriction of the instincts—and insists that all its members shall fulfil that ideal without troubling itself with the possibility that obedience may bear heavily upon the individual. (p. 219)

This state of affairs Freud did not hesitate to describe as "cultural hypocrisy" (1925a, [1924] p. 219).

At the same time, he staunchly resisted any effort to enlist psychoanalysis in the service of any ethical system, insisting on its ethical neutrality (Freud 1921a). There was undoubtedly good reason for insisting on this neutrality in the clinical context, yet the essential neutrality of the consulting room seems often enough to have yielded to more value-ladened and judgmental stances beyond those confines. Freud's many disclaimers on the undue restraints and moral rigidities of traditional views and societal norms are far removed from neutrality. If analysis itself was to remain neutral, the same constraints did not apply vis-à-vis society.

By the same token, he held back from any claim that analysis contributed to the moral betterment of patients. He wrote Putnam: "The unworthiness of human beings, including the analysts, always has impressed me deeply, but why should analyzed men and women in fact be better. Analysis makes for integration but does not of itself make for goodness."[8] But his somewhat ambiguous position on this score stands revealed in other texts. For example, "We tell ourselves that any one who has succeeded in educating himself to truth about himself is permanently defended against the danger of immorality, even though his standard of morality may differ in some respect from that which is customary in society" (Freud 1916–1917, p. 434). Other letters to Putnam make similar claims: "Our art consists in making it possible for people to be moral and to deal with their wishes philosophically. Sublimation, that is striving toward high goals, is of course one of the best means of overcoming the urgency of the drives. . . . Whoever is capable of sublimation will turn to it inevitably as soon as he is free of his neurosis. Those who are not capable of this at least will become more natural and more honest."[9] And nearly three years later: "The great ethical element in psycho-analytic work is truth and again truth and this should suffice for most people. Courage and truth are of what they are mostly deficient".[10] And much later: "the analytic relationship is based on a love of truth—that is on a recognition of reality . . . it precludes any kind of sham or deceit" (Freud 1937, p. 248). The honesty and truth he had in mind was not merely that between analyst and analysand, but that of the analysand to and about himself. This was the essential "ethic of honesty" of analysis (Rieff 1959).

Edwin Wallace (1986b) has offered a summary statement of Freud's ethic:

> a Stoic-Epicurean notion of balance between self-expression and fulfillment on the one hand and self-restraint and renunciation on the other; governance of one's life by the reality principle; adaptation—the optimal fit between a well-equilibrated psyche and its environment; empowering the ego in its negotiations with id, superego, and external reality; the independence of ethical principles from religious foundations; an increased tolerance for certain aspects of self and others (especially regarding the private fantasy and sexual lives) and for a more understanding approach to certain types of human frailty and disability (particularly that related to psychopathology and to certain universal and enduring psychological features of humankind); a premium on individuation, independence, and autonomy; strong allegiance to Eros (particularly as manifested in altruistic, aim-inhibited libido and in ties based on mutual identifications) in the war against Thanatos; an emphasis on the value of sublimation and work to the individual and to society; "endurance with resignation" (1927a, p. 50) of that which cannot be changed; and emphasis (with the exception

of his equation of Eros with *caritas*) on "prudential" (prudence, wisdom, justice, and fortitude) rather than Christian (faith, hope, and charity) values. (pp. 118–119, italics in original)

POSTFREUDIAN DEVELOPMENTS

In the more than three score years since Freud's final comment on ethical concerns, ethical issues have not been a primary focus for analytic reflection. Yet it may also be said that the seeds Freud cast fell on somewhat fertile ground and stimulated a generation of meaningful developments in psychoanalytic thinking about these complex questions. These developments largely reflect theoretical evolution within psychoanalysis itself— beginning with the development of ego psychology, complemented by the emergence of object relations theory, and still later by development of hermeneutical and linguistic approaches and various forms of self-psychology. These developments led not only to an increasingly sophisticated understanding of the origins and functions of the superego, as involved in moral or ethical functions, but also to a deepening grasp of the extent to which ethical issues were linked to not only personality development but to effective adult functioning as well.

For the most part, these post-freudian writers were concerned more with implications of psychoanalytic findings than with ethical theory as such. As Ernest Wallwork (1991) notes: "Most of the literature on psychoanalysis and morality comes from psychoanalysts and sociologists whose primary concern has been to draw normative implications out of psychoanalysis for evaluating modern culture and personality formation . . . not with understanding how psychoanalytic findings relate to the deepest questions of philosophical ethics" (pp. 1–2). We can take this as a caution not to look for more than is offered in these efforts, but at the same time not to overlook the complex of analytic perspectives emerging from the work of these thinkers.

Flugel

Flugel's (1945) book marked a point of departure for more extensive study of implications of analytic ideas for ethical and moral questions. Fully aware of anxieties created by efforts to bring psychological insights to bear on ethical issues, he emphasized the role of psychology, including psychoanalysis, in describing and explaining mental phenomena rather than evaluating or establishing norms. At the same time, values can be examined psychologically. For the most part, psychologists study instrumental rather than intrinsic values, the former related as means to the latter as ends. Investigation and understanding of intrinsic values belong more properly to ethics, but within this dichotomy, the intricate relations of means and ends provide gray areas, in which the interests of psychologists and ethicists overlap and intersect, resulting in deeper appreciation of the influence of psychological understanding even on intrinsic values.

Following Freud, Flugel argued that at root much ethical behavior is biologically determined and influenced by instinctive factors. Ethical discipline and constraint, however, must be learned and developed. This view is complemented by analytic discoveries that unconscious (often pathogenic) derivatives tend to have an "immoral" cast contravening accepted moral standards of either the individual or society, and are usually connected with sexual or aggressive impulses not tolerated by cultural conventions. Intrapsychically, these forces were opposed by counterforces acting in the interests of order and morality, giving rise to conflict and defense. Flugel reinforced Freud's view that repressive and defensive forces are essentially ethical in character.

These controlling forces, however, associated with conscience, could at times and under pathogenic conditions become harmful rather than positive. At times, allowing repressed impulses a degree of ventilation achieved more positive results than enforcing repressive controls. Indeed, analytic experience brought more clearly to light the often infantile, crude, and archaic rudiments of conscience, bringing its reliability as a moral guide increasingly into question. The analytic effort was directed toward replacing this often rigid and repressive tendency with a more discriminating and realistic capacity for conscious and reasonable deliberation and decision. The psychoanalyst, in this difficult terrain, tried to set a course between unregulated gratification of instinctual impulses and excessive submission to the dictates of moral authority, opening the way to the exercise of reason, conscious decision, adaptive self-restraint, and self-determination.

Flugel also sketched a schematic overview of moral progression reflecting some of the moral assumptions of the psychoanalytic view. Morality, in the form of ideals, restraints, guilt, and punishment, was deeply embedded in the human mind. Man was fundamentally a moral animal, but much of mankind's morality was crude and primitive, poorly adapted to reality, and often at variance both with understanding and higher conscious aspirations. Moral development progressed from egocentricity to sociality; from egoistic to altruistic motives; from unconscious to conscious needs and motivations: from autism to realism; from prevalence of the pleasure principle to regulation by the reality principle; from narcissism to object-related care and concern; from moral inhibitions to spontaneous "goodness," reflecting diminution of the guilt dynamic and allowing freer use of instinctual energy in the service of individual and social adaptation; from destructiveness to tolerance and love, including superego destructiveness, whether turned against the self or directed against external scapegoats; from fear to security; from heteronomy to autonomy, implying development of autonomous moral judgment, and replacing superego control with ego regulation; and from moral to cognitive (psychological) judgment, reflecting Flugel's faith that reason and scientifically informed judgment would provide a better basis for ethical decision than anger and moral condemnation.

And as his final dictum on the superego, Flugel wrote:

> In so far as its basis is fundamentally sound . . . the super-ego can also be entrusted with the enforcement of what might be called moral routine. But it is clearly unsuited to serve (as it is often expected to do) as the supreme court of moral appeal. If, as seems indeed to be the case, man is by his very nature doomed to conflict, we must seek the ultimate solution of conflict at the higher level of reason rather than at the lower one of conscience or tradition. (p. 260)

Fromm

For Erich Fromm man was unique in nature, a freak of evolution, embedded in nature yet transcending it (Fromm 1955). Man alone among animals has the capacity for self-creation and self-realization. This capacity is embedded in his *freedom*—both *freedom from* and *freedom to* (Fromm 1941). But the ability of contemporary men to achieve negative freedom, freedom from constraint whether internal or external, left them isolated, alienated, anxious, suffering from a sense of loneliness and separation, powerless, and driven to seek new submissions, largely due to the effects of modern capitalistic society and culture that turns men into commodities and alienated automatons (Fromm 1956).

Hope can be found in positive freedom, in the freedom for self-realization, and in the achievement of intellectual, emotional, and sensuous potential. But such freedom brings with it a threat and a burden from which men are often driven to escape (Fromm 1941). Fromm located his ethical considerations in forms of character and character pathology resulting from the need to escape from existential isolation. As a counterpoise to Hartmann's (1960) effort to separate ethical from analytic issues, Fromm and other neo-Freudians took the position that neurosis had moral implications insofar as neurotic mechanisms alienated man from himself as well as from his fellowmen and interfered with his productivity and creative potential. For Karen Horney (1950), neurotic forces impeded man's natural striving for psychic growth and self-realization. Among the Kleinians, Roger Money-Kyrle (1961) even held out the utopian ideal of a better humanity to be achieved through psychoanalysis (Eckhardt 1996).

Fromm proposed a humanistic ethical theory opposed to authoritarian forms of ethics. Authoritarian ethics were based on forms of irrational authority, as found in the authoritarian character, whereas rational authority was based on competence and reason and open to scrutiny and criticism. Authoritarian ethics negates man's power to discriminate right from wrong, good from bad, addressing these questions in terms of the interest of rulers rather than the ruled. In contrast, humanistic or rational ethics views man alone as determining the criteria of good and evil, in virtue of his capacity for reason, and not any transcendent authority. The ultimate criterion is thus man's inherent self-interest and individual welfare, not in any purely egoistic sense since self-interest can only be achieved in relation to others. Vice in this sense is indifference to authentic self-interest and virtue the affirmation of one's truly human self. Thus self-love stands in opposition to selfishness and self-renunciation assumes a valued place in humanistic ethics (Fromm 1947, 1955).

The role of psychoanalysis in this scheme is critical, since it was the first psychological system in modern times to study the total personality, thus making character the focus of ethical study rather than isolated virtues or vices. He faulted orthodox freudians for turning conscience into an internalized irrational authority and seeing morality as no more than a reaction formation to evil inclinations, claiming that his humanistic ethics were antithetical to Freud's ethics (Fromm 1947, 1955). The only satisfying vehicle for overcoming isolation and alienation and gaining sanity and satisfaction was productive love, i.e., love that is active, creative, caring, responsible, respectful, and based on knowledge and truth. From this platform, Fromm developed his criteria for judging right and wrong, and good and evil. Action was good insofar as it tended toward fulfilling basic needs, enabling maturation of human potentialities and attaining mature functioning, and thus becoming an authentic self.

Hartmann

Hartmann's *Moral Values in Psychoanalysis* (1960) was his seminal contribution to psychoanalysis and ethics. He drew moral issues to the forefront of analytic interest and gave them a legitimacy they previously lacked. His reappraisal of the relation of the pleasure principle to moral issues not only softened the impact of Freud's antinomian bent, but undercut any purely hedonistic ethical theory. He described three grades of satisfaction:

> It appears that the three types of satisfaction . . . cannot completely be substituted for one another. Instinctual gratification can often take the place of the other two types of gratification—of ego gratification and of moral or aesthetic gratification—although not fully nor under all conditions. Moral satisfaction, on the other hand, can replace even less completely, in most people, the gratification of instinctual demands. (pp. 36–37)

Thus, any "widespread expectation that a maximal consideration of self-interest would provide solutions most satisfactory from all points of view . . . is not borne out by psychoanalytic experience and is unlikely to prove true" (Hartmann 1960, p. 33).

By implication the economic demands of the pleasure principle or regulatory and moral agencies can be ignored only at a certain cost. He commented that the misperception, common among analysts, that "deep interpretations, the broad range of communication, unlimited self-revelation, widest permissiveness, the discarding of every consideration which stands in the way of full psychological understanding . . . the avoidance of what we consider moral judgement" were the only right course for dealing with personal relations was well worthy of challenge. He was critical of tendencies to elevate technical analytic considerations to moral principles and to extrapolate permissive and nonjudgmental attitudes of the consulting room to the world at large. Freud's ethic of honesty was never intended as normative beyond the walls of the consulting room and provided no endorsement of any and every form of self-expression and gratification.[11]

Hartmann argued that morality and mental health were not synonymous. Moral codes served a certain integrative function in mental economy, but the connections between morality and mental health were not straightforward, since many neurotics can be highly moral and socially productive, and many healthier people are neither. Where moral difficulties are rooted in neurotic causes, analytic treatment may have a role in remedying it by fortifying the ego, by modifying the harshness or archaic attitudes of superego, or by increasing awareness of moral values and their dynamic components, allowing for more consistent and integrated moral behavior. Hartmann was thus one of the first to focus on the possibility of an adaptive and reality-based ethics, as a function of the ego and not restrictively of the superego.

The confusion of moral values with mental health values ran the risk of equating badness with mental dysfunction. Freud had argued firmly that his neurotic patients were not morally inferior—a common misconception of the time. But the insistence on health ethics can harbor illusions; as Hartmann (1960) commented: "As a matter of fact, 'health ethics' can be as 'moralistic' as any other type of ethics. The strictness and rigidity which are so often found in moral demands are displaced onto another field. Some wishful thinking, too, may well have a part in this form of 'ethics': the hope that in attacking neurosis individual therapy can do away also with everything that is considered 'bad' in human nature" (p. 70).

Hartmann (1960) insisted on the status of analysis as value-free—a technology that minimizes evaluation and value-conflicts. He proposed that analysis could properly include the study of values as important aspects of mental life. He insisted, however, that values were to be regarded on the same basis as any other piece of mental content or fact. Analysis explores their form, content, and origin, assesses the degree of strength and authority they exercise and their influence on the individual's attitudes, beliefs, and behavior, without passing judgment on them or subjecting them to any moral evaluation. At the same time, he warned against "hidden preachers" who "actually preach their own philosophies, their own old or new values, or old or new religions (camouflaged with analytic terminology), while pretending to teach analysis, and present what are their own 'Weltanschauung' as logically derived from analysis" (pp. 23–24)—possibly aimed at Fromm's then current ethical constructions.

The contrast between Hartmann's approach and that of Fromm raises some questions. Hartmann was much closer to Freud, although his theorizing was intended and generally accepted as creatively developing Freud's view of the ego in the structural theory and elaborating it into a fully developed ego psychology. The essay on moral values was part of this program. The focus remained intrapsychic, reflecting on the intrapsychic qualities of moral valuation, ethical decision-making, and the authentic aspects of moral behavior as reflected in, processed through, and developed as a result of analytic therapy. Throughout, the ethical neutrality of the analytic situation was emphasized. Despite his emendations of Freud, Hartmann remained within the line of more-or-less orthodox freudianism. In contrast, Fromm followed a more "deviant" path, or so it was viewed in analytic circles at the time. He was more interested in confronting and challenging the implicit morality of the freudian system and locating the sources and causes of moral inclinations and behavior in social and cultural determinants. He proclaimed the inherent morality of the analytic situation, suggesting a very different role of the analyst in therapy. His concept of character served a mediating function between society and social influences and the individual personality. Analysts of the freudian tradition were not at that point ready to accept and integrate social input, which was declared nonanalytic and labeled as *sociological*. Curiously, it was only after the work of Erikson on psychosocial crises and the development of identity that social and cultural influences began to find a place in analytic thinking.

Rieff

In the outcropping of ethically oriented works and opinions, contrary to Hartmann's defense of ethical neutrality, Philip Rieff also argued that there was an ethical, both normative and prescriptive, core of psychoanalytic thought that found its way into, not only Freud's cultural and social think-ing, but was evident even in psychoanalytic therapeutic praxis. Psycho-analysis presented a moral challenge to the neurotic patient, and in this sense was a treatment for those prepared to render the sacrifices necessary to achieve psychological health. As Rieff (1959) put it, "For those who seek, through analysis, to avoid the sacrifice, therapy must inevitably fail" (p. xiii). Freud, he asserted, had no message to preach, no ideology, no morality, but his thinking contained an implicit set of ideas and ethical con-notations that could be shaped into such a message. He sought shrewd com-promises with the human condition, not its transformation or salvation. Rieff saw the impact of Freud's morality as sketched more on the larger canvas of cultural and social values than on the sketchpad of individual eth-ical behavior. If we live in the age of psychological man, it is in good meas-ure due to Freud that that image has come to replace the older image of economic man.

Even so, Freud's view of humanity reflected not merely a sense of moral conflict at the source of his neurotic symptomatology, but moral issues at the level of character (not unlike Fromm). As Rieff (1959) com-mented, "It was not simply the objective symptoms manifested by the patient but was, beyond that, an element of *character,* identical with the patient himself. It was the host himself—or rather his moral character—that must be treated" (p. 11, italics in original). Thus, Freud's views echo stoic themes of emotional disturbance causing physical sickness, the need for rational regulation of the passions, and the place of virtue in moral character. However, Freud also diverged from the stoic path by elevating the aristotelian ethos above pathos—if the development of character (ethos) was determinative, such that character was to become destiny, the vagaries of time and experience also had to have their say. But there also had to be room for pathos, the passions that reflect the play of circumstance, experi-ence, and life history.

Rieff regarded Freud's theory, cast in metaphors of energy and mental mechanisms, as thinly veiled masks for the essentially ethical direction of his thought. The inner voices of the tripartite theory were reminiscent of the good and bad counselors of old morality plays—id speaking with the voice of desire, ego steering and directing with the voice of reason, and superego exhorting and scolding. In his effort to grasp the meaning of symptoms and behaviors, Freud had to rely not only on metaphors rather than on measurements, but also on intuition, interpretation, and evaluation—implicitly reflecting the moral cast of his thought. Thus, evaluation was essential to the understanding of conflict and defense—"Certain crucial events of the past may, at the behest of the ego, which does not want to remember them, be at some time repressed. Repression thus becomes an infallible index of ethical import. What is too imperative to be remembered suffers the compliment of being forgotten" (Rieff 1959, p. 40).

In Rieff's reading of Freud, morality was centered in the superego such that superego and conscience were regarded as synonymous. Insofar as the therapeutic task was to reduce the degree of conflict and defense in the ego and to draw it in the direction of greater integration and adaptive functioning, the separation of ego functioning from moral judgment left a vacuum of ethical reassurance. As Rieff (1959) put it, "But this integration of self is no harbinger of goodness. It is possible to become more sound of mind and yet less good—in fact, worse" (p. 65). This interpretation drove a wedge between therapeutic and ethical concerns, a view of Freud leaving a trail of uncertainty with regard to the rest of Rieff's argument pointing to the inherent ethicality of Freud's argument.[12]

An essential component of Freud's view of man was his emphasis on self-deception. As part of the hermeneutic of suspicion, Freud cast doubt on the role of intellect and self-understanding. As Rieff (1959) observed: "Against the conventional assumption that each knows himself best in his own heart, Freud supports the nietzschean assumption that each is farthest from his own self and must journey through experience in search of it. He surpasses even the Romantics in his deprecation of mere intellect. He calls into question all self-insight, intuitive as well as intellectual" (p. 75). The freudian answer is to submit self-knowledge to the analytic other—to "know thyself" is to be known by another. The great promoter of self-deception and enemy of self-understanding was the superego, taken as Freud's repository of conscience and moralistic self-criticism. In Rieff's (1959) terms, "Conscience, not passion, emerges as the last enemy of reason. True self-awareness is impossible until the moralizing voice is restrained, or at least controlled. Freud presumes it is impossible otherwise to be truly self-aware" (p. 78).

Freud's penetration of the conscious and manifest to reach the level of the latent and unconscious often led him to seek the source of distortion in repressed sexuality—even though, as Rieff (1959) noted, there may have been no necessary connection. But the reason lay in an underlying ethical imperative to chastise ethical aspirations insofar as they reflect varying degrees of self-deception—"we are really natural beings, irrational, capricious, limited" (p. 161). But by the same token, Freud was no advocate of unbridled sex; his message of reform, familiar enough to the nineteenth century, sought "a lifting of the ascetic barrier, a relaxation of the moral fervor that created more hypocrites than saints, more sick minds than healthy souls" (p. 164). Thus the quantitative metaphors of the *Three Essays on the Theory of Sexuality* (1905c) can be read in ethical terms, pleading for greater sexual latitude and picking at the repressive order by underlining the relation of perverted and normal sexuality as differentiated quantitatively rather than qualitatively.

Freud did not intend psychoanalysis as an ethic of social adjustment, although the prudential course he envisioned might support submission to social demands out of considerations of expediency and personal need. Psychoanalysis cautions against social enthusiasms and overinvestments and proposes the grounds for skepticism of all ideologies, even its own. In Rieff's (1959) terms, "Psychoanalysis is the doctrine of the private man defending himself against public encroachment. He cultivates the private life and its pleasures, and if he does take part in public affairs it is for consciously private motives" (p. 278).[13] And further: "Like those who worked for shorter hours but nevertheless feared what men might do with their leisure, Freud would have welcomed more constructive releases from our stale moralities, but did not propose to substitute a new one. Our private ethics were his scientific problem: he had no new public ethics to suggest, no grand design for the puzzle of our common life" (Rieff 1968, p. 38).[14]

Rieff (1959) was among the first to stake a claim for psychoanalysis as a form of moral teaching: "Psychoanalysis cannot disclaim its influence on the day-to-day consciousness of our age by calling itself simply a science. All the issues which psychoanalysis treats—the health and sickness of the will, the emotions, the responsibilities of private living, the coercions of culture—belong to the moral life" (p. 329). But whatever moral teaching it had to render was distilled into a critique of social and cultural mores that Freud regarded as repressive and that he counted among major contributing factors to the development of neuroses. In his view, the advantages of civilization and culture were purchased at too high a cost—the repression of fundamental instinctual drives and resulting intrapsychic conflict. As Rieff commented:

Freud found the essential lie upon which culture is built in its zeal-
ous but faltering repressions. His way of mitigating them was,
first, through rational knowledge, and, second, through a prudent
compromise with the instinctual depths out of which rational
knowledge emerges. He proposes that "certain instinctual
impulses, with whose suppression society has gone too far, should
be permitted a certain amount of satisfaction; in the case of certain others *the inefficient method of suppressing them by means of
repression should be replaced by a better and securer procedure*
(Freud, 1925a, [1924] p.171, in *Collected Papers V*) (pp.
345–346, italics in Rieff)

Rieff labeled this the *ethic of honesty* that Freud regarded as essential
to his therapy, as well as potentially reformative of culturally reinforced tendencies to do violence to natural desires and needs. Freud's reliance on a
view of social and cultural processes as repressive and restrictive remain
open to question, and call for consideration of ways in which these same
institutions are essential to the enhancement and preservation of human life
and culture—a point to which Freud gave ambivalent and grudging
acknowledgment. Nor does the freudian critique necessarily endorse current social and cultural settings fostering greater permissiveness and tolerance of deviance, thus elevating psychological health and normality to the
status of moral indexes (Rieff 1968). But, if Freud could stringently critique
society and culture, neither did he proclaim himself the prophet of pleasure.
As Rieff (1959) noted: "He believed no more in instinct than in culture; for
his day and age he sought only to correct the imbalance between these two
main categories of the moral life. He is the architect of a great revolt against
pleasure, not for it. Rather he exhibited its futility. It is toward the reality
principle that Freud turns us, toward the sober business of living and with
no nonsense about its goodness or ease" (p. 355).[15]
   But having reached this point, Rieff (1959) argues that the freudian
ethic runs out of gas—"Being honest, admitting one's nature, does not
resolve specific issues of choice. The Freudian ethic emphasizes freedom at
the expense of choice. To achieve greater balance within the psyche, to shift
the relative weights of instinct and repression, instills no new substantive
rules of decision" (p. 352). Thus, openness and honesty about oneself and
one's needs offers no guarantee of validly ethical outcomes. In Rieff's
(1959) terms: "Openness of character may well elicit more, not less, brutality. Unaided by the old transcendental ethics of guilt, or by the rational-
ist ethics of a future harmony through knowledge, the Freudian lucidity
may pierce the deepest shadows of the self without dispelling one degree of
gloom" (p. 353). This perspective on the freudian ethic leaves several ques-

tion unanswered—as I shall argue. To my reading, Rieff's rendering of the freudian ethic is truncated and relatively simplistic, since it leaves aside issues of moral integrity and value formation as essential components of the psychoanalytic (if not freudian) ethical perspective. More of this later![16]

Winnicott

Donald Winnicott gave us a view of psychological development as an aspect of moral development. Insofar as healthy psychic development contributes to healthy moral growth, psychic development involves assimilation of moral attitudes and orientations derived from caretaking figures, parents, educational influences, and the surrounding culture. Winnicott spoke to the conditions of care and nurturance in the mother-child interaction that provide essential components for this process (1960a). To the degree that the process is successful, the basic elements are put in place enabling the individual to pursue a path of ethical self-realization. In this context we seek to understand what goes right in healthy and adaptive ethical adjustment and what goes wrong when development of the personality seems to lead to character flaws and ethical deficits. What influences come into play when individuals need to flaunt or ignore ethical concerns, or conversely when they are overly conformist or turn to authoritarian submission?

The moral or ethical sense Winnicott had in mind was not simply taught or instilled, but was the by-product of normal development and an expression of well-formed and stable human identity. The issue, therefore, was not moral judgment, but moral character and the psychic structure of the moral agent. The patterns of behavior inclining to moral goodness and the courses of life leading toward greater happiness and self-fulfillment were facilitated by authentic personal development and by achievement of mature identity—the basic building blocks of which Winnicott was to identify in the very first stages of human experience. He drew our attention to issues fundamental to all ethical concern, the task of establishing an authentic sense of self and the capacity to relate meaningfully and productively with others—both other persons and society. Without a belief in oneself and in one's personal value, moral issues are devoid of meaning. Without such a sense of self, the individual has few resources with which to withstand guilt for destructive impulses and to undertake reparative initiatives. Winnicott (1963) wrote:

> In the same way it is no answer to the problem of moral values to expect a child to have his or her own, and for the parents to have nothing to offer that comes from the local social system. And there

is a special reason why a moral code should be available, namely, that the infant's and the small child's innate moral code has a quality so fierce, so crude, and so crippling. Your adult moral code is necessary because it humanizes what for the child is subhuman. The infant suffers talion fears. The child bites in an excited experience of relating to a good object, and the object is felt to be a biting object. The child enjoys an excretory orgy and the world fills with water that drowns and with filth that buries. These crude fears become humanized chiefly through each child's experiences in relation to the parents, who disapprove and are angry but who do not bite and drown and burn the child in retaliation related exactly to the child's impulse or fantasy. (p. 101)

But where the rudiments for a purposeful moral sense are lacking, due to early failures of development, society imposes a moral code—but the effect is not the same since it lacks the quality of authenticity and results in little more than false-self conformity and unstable socialization. The impulse to implant a moral code in the interest of compliance and conformity is not only counterproductive, but may end in disaster:

> Compliance brings immediate rewards, and adults too easily mistake compliance for growth. The maturational processes can be by-passed by a series of identifications, so that what shows clinically is a false, acting self, a copy of someone perhaps; and what could be called a true or essential self becomes hidden, and becomes deprived of living experience. This leads many people who seem to be doing well actually to end their lives which have become false and unreal; unreal success is morality at its lowest ebb. (Winnicott 1963, p. 102)

The worst sin for Winnicott, then, is forcing a child into a pattern of compliance, in the process aborting discovery of the true self, driving that self into hiding and substituting a form of conformity that falsifies its whole life experience. The essence of moral growth lies in development of the true self—that is, an authentic self to which one can lay claim as truly one's own and as the root of a mature and productive identity (1960b).

Erikson

These themes concerning development of the moral sense found their self-conscious elaboration in the work of Erik H. Erikson. From his study of psychic development in children to his discussions of social and cultural forces and complexities, Erikson centered his argument on the need for mutuality and loving acceptance as essential for growth to mature identity and ethical integrity. Even his schema of psychosocial crises, tracing the epigenetic pattern of development leading to the formation of identity and beyond, was tinged with ethical import (Meissner 1970a).

He distinguished between morality and ethics. Moral rules were based on a relatively immature and primitive level of development. They derived from fear, responding to threats of abandonment, punishment, exposure, or inner threats of guilt, shame, or isolation. Ethical rules, however, were based on ideals to be striven for. Moral and ethical senses are different in their development and in their psychodynamics. This does not mean, however, that the primitive morality of fear and retribution can be bypassed developmentally. They exist in the adult mind as remnants of childhood. The child's morality precedes the adult's ethical sense not only developmentally but in the sense that the earlier stage is necessary for the emergence of the later.

In his *Childhood and Society* (1950), Erikson laid out a program of ego development from birth to death: the individual passed through phases of the life cycle by meeting and resolving a series of developmental psychosocial crises. In the earliest stage of infancy, at the mother's breast, the child developed either a sense of basic trust or mistrust. In later infancy the child had to achieve a sense of autonomy or, failing that, he would be left with some degree of shame and doubt. In early childhood the child developed a sense of initiative hopefully without guilt. In latency the issue was a sense of industry without a sense of inferiority. The adolescent crisis saw the crystallization of the residues of preceding crises into a more-or-less definitive sense of personal identity, as opposed to a diffusion of identity and to a confusion of roles. For the young adult the question was development of a capacity for intimacy rather than isolation. For the older adult the issue was generativity, as a concern for establishing and guiding the next generation. And finally, in the twilight of life, the crisis to be resolved was that of ego integrity in the face of death and ultimate despair.

Finally, Erikson's treatment of these crises as specifically psychosocial brought into focus the fact that the development of the ego was not merely a matter of intrapsychic vicissitudes of inner psychic states. It was that, certainly, but it was also a matter of interaction and "mutual regulation" between the developing human organism and significant persons in its environment. Even more strikingly, it was a matter of mutual regulation evolving between the growing child and the culture and traditions of his or her society. Erikson made the sociocultural sphere an integral part of the developmental matrix out of which the personality emerges.

The ethical concern runs as a slender thread through the entire epigenetic schema. Erikson saw adolescence as a traditional psychosocial stage
between childhood and adulthood. The individual must pass from the
morality of the child to the ethics of the adult. The adolescent mind then is
prone to ideology, where the outlines of what is best and most valuable can
be most clearly delineated. There is danger in harnessing human ideals to
such overriding ideologies, whether they be communist, capitalist, religious,
or whatever. The young adult, emerging from the search for, and need for,
identity, is ready for intimacy, the capacity to commit himself to concrete
partnerships and affiliations, and to develop the ethical strength to abide by
such commitments regardless of personal sacrifice. The adult phase is dominated by the ethics of generativity—regulated by what is required to promote and guide the emergence of the coming generation to the fulness of
identity and productivity. All institutions codify the ethics of generative suc-
cession. This extends beyond the demands of genitality as such; even where
spiritual tradition might propose renunciation of the right to procreation,
there is care for creatures of this world along with concern for spiritual
values and for charity that meets, as it transcends, this world.

Adult moralism is easily subverted to moral vindictiveness. There is a
violence inherent in the moral sense. We violate children and arouse them
to an inner rage when we keep from them the guidance and support without which they cannot develop fully. Nonviolence means more than preservation of another's physical inviolacy; it means protection of the human
essence as developing person and personality. Erikson (1969) wrote: "Non-
violence, inward and outward, can become a true force only where ethics
replaces moralism. And ethics, to me, is marked by an insightful assent to
human values, whereas moralism is blind obedience; and ethics is transmitted with informed persuasion, rather than enforced with absolute inter-
dicts" (p. 251).

Erikson (1964) made the ethical dynamism in his thought more explicit
and specific. He wrote

> that the collective life of mankind, in all its historical lawfulness,
> is fed by the energies and images of successive generations; and
> that each generation brings to human fate an inescapable conflict
> between its ethical and rational aims and its infantile fixations.
> The conflict helps drive man toward the astonishing things he
> does—and it can be his undoing. It is a condition of man's human-
> ity—and the prime cause of his bottomless inhumanity. For when-
> ever and wherever man abandons his ethical position, he does so
> only at the cost of massive regressions endangering the very safe-
> guards of his nature. (p. 45)

Man's basic ethical sense was in turn contingent on the inner strengths that supported and sustained it.

Lacan

Jacques Lacan, despite his obscurities and ambiguities, can be counted among those who view psychoanalysis as not merely a psychology or as a system of therapeutics, but as an inherently ethical view of man's nature. As he put it, "We are concerned here with the Freudian experience as an ethics, which is to say, at its most essential level, since it directs us towards a therapeutic form of action that, whether we like it or not, is included in the register or in the terms of an ethics" (1992, p. 133). His views are set forth primarily in his seminars on the ethics of psychoanalysis, delivered in 1959–1960. He stated his basic position clearly enough:

> Moral experience as such, that is to say, the reference to sanctions, puts man in a certain relation to his own action that concerns not only an articulated law but also a direction, a trajectory, in a word, a good that he appeals to, thereby engendering an ideal of conduct. All that, too, properly speaking constitutes the dimension of ethics and is situated beyond the notion of a command, beyond what offers itself with a sense of obligation . . . one can, in short, say that the genesis of the moral dimension in Freud's theoretical elaboration is located nowhere else than in desire itself. It is from the energy of desire that the agency is detached which at the end of its development will take the form of the censor. (p. 3)

The connection of desire and the good occupies a central position in Lacan's analysis, interestingly enough with a strong linkage to Aristotle's vision of the good as an end of human desire found in the *Nichomachean Ethics*. Lacan makes the firm point that moral experience is not limited to the dictates of the superego; rather the burden of analytic experience is that the command of the superego is to be opposed as the analytic process uncovers and reveals its jurisdiction.

Analysis is thus not without its ideals. Lacan lists three: the first is human love that analysis places at the heart of the ethical experience. The second is the ideal of authenticity, as a norm and valued end product of analysis, and finally the third is the ideal of nondependence, more in tune with what we would call "autonomy." In similar terms, Lacan calls our attention to the matter of virtues and values that form such a predominant focus of the aristotelian reflection but that have been notably neglected by psychoanalysts. Ethical experience in Aristotle's view was also a matter of character, not merely of attitudes or behavior.

The aristotelian problematic was that of the good, ultimately the sovereign good. This led Lacan to explore the problem of pleasure and its role in the mental economy of ethics. In analytic terms, pleasure and reality are interconnected, especially in the form of regulatory principles connected with primary and secondary process. The reality principle plays a central role in the modification and satisfaction of desires governed by the pleasure principle. The scope and nature of those desires is what separates psychoanalysis from Aristotle and from most philosophical approaches to ethics. But moral action is inexorably tied to reality as one of the channels through which we can enter the real.

To further explore this thesis, Lacan returns to a rereading of Freud's *Project for a Scientific Psychology* (1895), where the issues of the regulatory principles and their interrelations are considered in some detail. He recast these reflections in an ethical framework rather than in the familiar economic one. The problem of neurosis he contends was cast in ethical terms from the beginning—a matter of the conflict of wills and desires. The paradox is that moral insistence on the real is opposed to mere pleasure, but it is only through the dynamic of desire and its connection with the pleasure principle that the ultimate good guiding ethical action can be achieved. His lengthy and circuitous exploration of the *Project for a Scientific Psychology,* then, was concerned with uncovering the traces of ethical thought masquerading as the economics of impersonal psychic systems.

With this review of some analytic approaches to ethical issues behind us, we can turn in chapter 2 to a consideration of some ethical systems with an eye to their relevance and implications in relation to psychoanalytic perspectives.

CHAPTER TWO

Psychoanalysis and Ethical Systems

INTRODUCTION

My purpose in this chapter is to draw psychoanalysis into closer dialogue and engagement with ethical systems. Rather than scrutiny or critique of ethical systems, I hope to explore implications, points of congruence and consensus, tensions, ambiguities, and areas of conflict, even contradiction. Psychoanalysis for its part is far from a monolithic enterprise, but rather presents a variety of points-of-view and theoretical emphases. Much the same can be said of ethical discourse in its differential emphases and in the variety and complexity of its viewpoints. The effort to bring these respective areas of discourse about the human condition into conjunction, therefore, has its difficulties and pitfalls. The heterogeneity on both sides makes comparison and contrast more uncertain and complex. Moreover, there is always the danger that viewpoints become polarized and the dichotomizing logic of good versus bad, truth versus falsity, and reason versus unreason, will afflict the dialogue. I will do my best to avoid such dichotomous thinking.

ETHICAL FACTS

We can assume some basic facts about ethical decision-making, for example the distinction between good-bad or right-wrong actions. The decision to pursue a course of action is often accompanied by a sense of obligation to do what we think right and good and to avoid what seems wrong and bad. In making the choice to act one way or another, we often have a sense of freedom, that is, we do not feel forced to accept any one option. Furthermore, we have a sense of responsibility for our choices and resulting actions, and correspondingly hold others responsible for their actions. But problems arise in considering the meaning of right and wrong. Are good and right synonymous, or can good be reduced to right or right to good? Various ethical theories provide different answers. Some would argue that good-bad or right-wrong are irrelevant to the moral act, since they are little more than expressions of feelings or attitudes of approval or disapproval of the act in question. In what sense, then, might "good" have any meaning beyond the emotive? Furthermore, we can ask what sort of necessity is implied in the "ought" associated with the sense of obligation. The necessity is not physical certainly, but is it absolute and categorical, or is it hypothetical and, if so, on what presuppositions does it rely? And furthermore, whence arises this obligation? Does it come from God, as some have said, or from our own reason, from conscience, from social conditioning? And what role does the unconscious play, if any?

ETHICAL THEORIES

Ethical theories can be broadly divided into cognitive and noncognitive types. Cognitive theories claim objective reference—some actions are objectively right or wrong; noncognitive approaches lean toward empiricism and positivism. David Hume, for example, distinguishing between factual knowledge and moral feeling, allowed no objective right or wrong; they were matters of feeling and could not be analyzed rationally or scientifically. Modern logical positivists and analytic philosophers follow a similar path.

Beyond this, classification is not easy. One possible division is into naturalist, intuitionist, and metaphysical systems. Naturalist views are rooted in this world and present experience and admit no transcendent moral values: morality cast in terms of God and the afterlife are out. This group includes hedonists, utilitarians, and pragmatists of various descriptions. Intuitionists appeal to a special moral sense operating independently of any utilitarian correlation of means-and-ends or any metaphysical view of human nature. For them the nature of the good is less important than the way we know it, emphasizing psychological factors more than objective considerations. Metaphysical views seek to orient the good and human nature in general terms relating them to the universe and to the last end of human life. Aristotle stressed the virtuous life, Thomas Aquinas union with God, and G. W. F. Hegel the self-realization of the Spirit. For all these, ethics derives from metaphysics and reflects the values inherent in that orientation to reality.

Another set of distinctions is made between axiological and deontological theories. Axiology derives the sense of obligation from a theory of value: actions involve obligation to the extent that they have value or goodness, a view found in Aristotle, medieval schoolmen, and some moderns. Deontology views right and wrong as independent of consequences or of any connection with metaphysical views of the good or pleasure; this approach can be found in formalists like Immanuel Kant or intuitionists like Lord Shaftesbury or Joseph Butler. None of these categories provide much help in organizing ethical theories, but they offer at least a schematic framework that will allow us to survey particular approaches.

INTUITIONISM

Despite variations on the theme, intuitionists base moral judgments on feelings rather than on intellectual discernments of objective right and wrong—subjective attitudes are determinative rather than the results of action. In contrast to formalists like Kant, who ascribed the feeling of moral rectitude to what is reasoned and known, advocates of the moral sense contend that knowledge of right and wrong depends on what is felt. This leads to a psychological analysis of moral activity rather than searching for reasons as to why actions may be objectively right or wrong. Shaftesbury, for example, tried to answer Thomas Hobbes's view of rugged individualism and the doctrine of *Homo homini lupus* by an appeal to the moral sense. In Hobbes's view, in the state of nature people would hardly rise above sheer animal brutality, so that certain ground rules were required to avoid mutual destruction. The basic motivation was self-interest—if I wish to live I must let others live; if I desire to insure my possession of property I must allow the same security to others.

In contrast, Shaftesbury emphasized man's capacity for unselfishness and generosity rather than his selfishness. These qualities allowed man to participate in the order of creation with balance and harmony. Selfish investment in one's own good had to be balanced by generous investment in the good of others. This was essential to man's social nature and altruism. In his optimism, the wish-fantasy held sway that the good always prevail, but, whatever its appeal, had to run afoul of reality. If individual happiness is linked to that of one's fellow men, it is a truth too often ignored. For Shaftesbury, the guiding norm of choice of the good lie in one's own affections, so that the truly moral man must be capable of knowing and weighing his affections and evaluating their claims.

The psychoanalytic view of human nature would diverge considerably from this benign assessment. Freud resonated to a degree with Hobbes's view of social antipathy, at least to the extent of envisioning opposition between instinctual desires and the constraints of civilization. Love, interpreted as sexual desire, was egotistic and therefore incongruent with social cohesion and compatibility. Certainly, the classic model, based on instinctual drives conceived as determining human choice and behavior, would pay more attention to the inherent destructiveness and selfishness of human motives, particularly of aggression and narcissism. Yet, if Freud had sympathies with the hobbesian assessment of human life, he could not endorse it fully. He wrote: "In consequence of this primary mutual hostility of human beings, civilized society is perpetually threatened with disintegration. The interest of work in common would not hold it together; instinctual passions are stronger than reasonable interests" (1930, p. 112). Civilization, therefore, could not rely on necessity alone to preserve itself, but requires Eros or love. Civilization was "a process in the service of Eros, whose purpose is to combine single . . . individuals, and after that . . . peoples and nations, into one great unity. . . . These collections of men are to be libidinally bound to one another. Necessity alone, the advantages of work in common, will not hold them together" (p. 122).

If he found reason to retrench from the hobbesian alternative, he could move in Shaftesbury's direction only with reservation. If we envision Shaftesbury's emphasis on willing the good as an expression of rational ego-functioning, as reasoned and deliberate choice, it might resemble one form of analytic ideal—where id was, ego shall be—but it seems to underestimate the powerful motivational influences operating unconsciously to determine choice of good or evil. There is also the issue of what is the good. Intuitionists often write as though that were not an issue, as though the course of good action were simply intuited and known. But we also know that goods are often in conflict, that one man's good can be another man's evil, and so on. In other words, the circumstances and contexts of ethical decision-making are rarely so clear-cut or decisive that one is confronted with an unambiguous choice. Psychoanalysis has made us considerably more aware of the complexity of influences that come to bear on choices of all kinds, not only ethical. For the intuitionist model to be effective, motives, other contributing factors, and issues would all have to be on a conscious and explicit level. But for analysts, this would be by far the exception and not the rule.

Shaftesbury's thinking was extended by Joseph Butler—primarily attacking Hobbes's psychological egoism. Conscience was central to his version of the moral sense, occupying the highest level of the moral sense. Conscience judges right from wrong, exercising authority over other mental faculties, particularly affections and passions on the lowest level, and self-love and benevolence on the next, judging their claims and determining good and evil. Self-love looked to personal happiness and well-being, regulating affections and appetites in terms of enlightened self-interest. Benevolence, on the other hand, looked to the well-being of others. Conscience ruled over all. Butler left no room for conflict between demands of conscience and self-love or benevolence. He regarded enlightened self-love as entirely consistent with directives of conscience. Neither Butler nor Shaftesbury expended much effort on issues of obligation, since they saw no need to go beyond enlightened self-interest. Critics have described this approach as a form of moral aesthetics emphasizing beauty of the moral sense rather than any sense of moral law imposing obligation. A morally good person did not obey laws or fulfill obligations, but had developed a character structure endowed with harmony and uniformity with the moral sense. The intuitionist moral aesthetic left little room for reason in making moral judgments, allowing it little more than advisory status helping to sort out the balance of pleasure.

The emphasis on the role of affect and appetite as determiners of ethical choice and the corresponding devaluation of reason and judgment would not fit well with an analytic perspective. But analytic experience bears witness to the extent to which desires and affections, both conscious and unconscious, can lead to behaviors that are self-defeating and not in the individual's best interest. But by the same token, an appeal to reason and reality, the domain of the ego, does not always result in optimal or unambiguous courses of behavior. However well reason plays its role, it is not omniscient nor omnipotent. Our capacity to think, plan, analyze, understand, and determine the benefit or disadvantage of any course of action is quite limited. On the other hand, there is ample room for the individual to be attuned to, recognize, and respect his affects as guides to self-understanding and as a form of vital communication about himself and his experience. But they do not and cannot act as determiners of the morality of action without processing and evaluation by the thinking and judging capacities of the rest of the psychic organization—including both ego and superego. Reliance on an autonomous moral sense seems in this view simplistic and naive.

FORMALISM

If moral sense theorists are empiricists, formalists are rationalists more concerned with principles than with psychological experience. The archformalist was Kant, who laid the foundations for his approach to practical reason and moral philosophy in his *Critique of Pure Reason* (1781). His ethics was largely a reaction against hedonism, especially in its egoistic forms—the moral criterion was not happiness or unhappiness, or consequences of action, but the nature of the action itself. If practical reason was to have any necessity or universality, it had to derive from a priori principles that in turn could not be drawn from experience that remains contingent and particular. Thus we could know a priori that we should not lie, even if we would still need empirical knowledge to know what was true and what not, and how to say it so as not to be misunderstood (Ewing 1962). Like the synthetic a priori judgment of pure reason, the universality and necessity of practical reason did not require proof, but was a recognized fact. This was borne out by the universal experience of obligation to obey the moral law, regardless of how we explain that law or its precepts. Furthermore, this obligation is absolute, not relative to desires. As Richard Rorty (1986) commented: "Kant tried to make morality a nonempirical matter, something that would never again have anything to fear from religion, science, or the arts, nor have anything to learn from them" (p. 13). George Moore (1903) regarded the attempt to base ethical principles on some metaphysical view of the nature of the real as another variant of the naturalistic fallacy.

The notion of duty was central to Kant's ethical thought—the will was good only to the extent that it acted out of a sense of duty. Good intentions would not carry the freight; the intention to conform to duty was essential.[1] And duty itself was binding by reason of man's rationality, not by reference to any good man might desire, even the absolute good fulfilling man's nature and ultimate desire. This principle of morality imposed the obligation to act as a universal law, so that the maxim governing action could apply to all men, as though given by a lawgiver of a universal kingdom in which each person could achieve self-fulfillment without infringing on that of others. In this sense, the moral imperative implied treating all men, whether himself or others, always as ends and never as merely means.[2] Such a general principle of morality was objective and universal, purely formal, and imposed by autonomous practical reason. Consequently, the categorical imperative was the basic principle of all morality and depended on autonomy of the will in conjunction with the a priori guidance of practical reason. The will, then, was a law unto itself, not heteronomously deriving its principles from any principle outside itself, for instance, God and happiness. The categorical imperative was thus distinct from hypothetical imperatives telling us to act in a certain way if we desire the result of the action. These conditional imperatives are not strictly ethical, but at best prudential. Mere desire does not oblige under the moral law (Ewing 1962).[3]

The capacity to act in accord with the moral law and the duty to observe it requires that man be free. If he is responsible for moral choices, has obligations, and is accountable for his moral decisions, he must be free—otherwise morality becomes nonsense. But the phenomenal world follows laws of cause and effect in which the present is the effect of the past. The world of appearance is constructed in categories of space and time, so that freedom must be found in the noumenal world beyond appearances. Kant affirmed action in the phenomenal world and freedom in the noumenal, although he was not clear about how this worked. But postulates of practical reason dictate this conclusion, especially since, were it not so, morality would become unthinkable, irrational, and self-contradictory. The assertion of speculative reason that man *may* be free is not enough; morality requires the assertion of practical reason that man *is* free.

The formalist reliance on reason opposes the intuitionist reliance on affect. Just as the psychoanalyst might have difficulties with the latter, he might well have difficulties with the former. The insistence on the role of reason carries a note of the apodictic or imperative and the categorical that analysis would find alien. The judgments of reason alone are too uncertain, too fraught with complexity and difficulty, to serve as the sole basis for arbitration of moral issues. Not only does the inherent complexity of things compromise this view, but the discourse of reason can lead in many directions—one man's reasonable analysis is another man's misguided error, as history attests. Analytic experience would demand that greater consideration be given to the immense capacity of the human mind for self-deception and for the role of hidden motives that becloud men's minds and carry the potential for misguided judgment and error.[4] As Heinz Hartmann (1960) commented:

> Rather intolerant of and impatient with our empirically minded endeavor to trace objectively the psychological givens of morality are those also who attempt to erect an artificial system of moral values on heterogeneous grounds. Ethical systems based on an image of man as a totally rational being are an example. That image is then used to decide what man "ought" to value. But, from our point of view, this particular picture of man is a distortion of reality. Also, analysts try to keep apart what man actually values from what, according to this or that philosophy, he ought to value. (pp. 44–45)

Freud might have agreed with Kant's phenomenology of conscience, but the effort to separate practical reason from sensuality as a presumption for moral life he would have found both impossible and morally self-defeating. Far from isolating conscience from desire, Freud (1923a) saw it as developmentally grounded in desire—rooted in derivatives of oedipal attachments and involvements; later analysts would have extended this to preoedipal levels. For Freud, divorcing ethical reasoning from desire was impossible. This runs counter to the kantian view of conscience as a law unto itself and as posing the sense of duty and respect for the moral law as the basis of moral decision to the exclusion of any other purpose, especially any dictated by pleasure whether self- or other-directed. Ernest Wallwork (1991) captures this tension nicely:

> In contrast to Kant, who views all inclinations, including benevolent ones, as "pathological" when they intrude into what ought to be a "pure" realm of unmotivated moral duty, Freud recognizes that other-regarding sentiments from deep within the self are more reliable than cognitive decisions divorced from affect. Freud sees dispositions as providing a far more genuine basis on which to ground morality than categorical imperatives, since they express the self more authentically than disembodied cognitive judgments. Absolutist principles are often not particularly trustworthy in complex moral situations because, too often, they lead their duty-bound devotees to sacrifice people to principles; their rigidity leads to the neglect of important subtleties; and the unacknowledged unconscious motives they repudiate tend to erupt without warning to cancel the alleged superiority of the stability of principles over sentiments in moral life. (p. 239)

To this we can add Jacques Lacan's (1992) observation that Kant's radical revision of practical reason dictated a morality "that detaches itself purposefully from all reference to any object of affection, from all reference to what Kant called the *pathologisches Objekt,* a pathological object, which simply means the object of any passion whatsoever" (p. 76). On the contrary, Freud stressed the closeness and dependence of the superego on instinctual drives or motives. As Wallwork (1991) observes, "For Freud, the moral imperative cannot be categorical, in the sense of being explained by itself. In reality, it is motivated by desire. It is only by understanding the subtle unconscious connections between conscience and desire that we can begin to find that degree of distance from desire that is optimal for practical reason" (p. 234).

From a more contemporary perspective, the sense in which both desire and conscience can still be regarded as instinctual drive derivatives remains open to question, but regardless, the psychoanalytic perspective would find itself at odds with the categorical imperative as the basis of moral thought. Moreover, the desire for moral perfection based on respect for the moral law is itself partly motivated by narcissistic investments in the ego-ideal (Freud 1914a, 1921a). Thus self-interest can never be excluded and absolute adherence to the categorical imperative must be qualified accordingly. Freud (1933a), then, could not follow Kant in elevating conscience to the starry heavens—as he commented in respect to the kantian simile: "The stars are indeed magnificent, but as regards conscience God has done an uneven and careless piece of work" (p. 61).

The formalist critique tends to a polarized conceptualization that disallows influence of other aspects of the mind in moral matters, as though somehow the mind could exist independently of social and historical contexts and personal motives. Analysis would look for a more balanced and integrated account of the mind in moral decision-making. Freud took the position that in some sense genuine morality had to be instinctually grounded. Inauthentic morality was, in contrast, driven by narcissistic or neurotic needs to avoid punishment or to gain rewards. Morality required more than rational dictates opposed to affects and desires. The categorical imperative also carried the burden of obligation and moral duty. Whether this imperative embodied superego dictates, or whether it represented something more complex, remains to be seen. But the implication that it operated independently of other psychic influences and exercised absolute validity and authority would not resonate with analytic perspectives. Some ethicists have pointed out that the kantian imperative had to be complemented by consideration of utilitarian consequences, at a minimum, to decide between conflicting alternative precepts (Ewing 1962).

Conscience, characterized by strict dictates and not subject to the constraints and influences of other aspects of human nature, had to carry the seeds of its own demise. The very autonomy that Kant sought to sustain by his doctrine of the transcendental ego would be inevitably subverted by a categorical conscience in two senses: one that the presumably autonomous ego becomes the subservient slave to dictates of an uncompromising moral master, and second, that unconscious desires alienated from the realm of conscience can become a subversive influence undermining the autonomy and freedom of the self from within—a kind of moral fifth column. This issue will return in further considerations of the development and functioning of conscience. The bottom line, however, is that a psychoanalytic approach to moral issues would have to weave a path between the Scylla of intuitionism and the Carybdis of formalism in order to find its own authentic way.

UTILITARIANISM

Among more empirically minded ethicists reacting against kantian formalism, utilitarians looked to consequences of the act—if consequences are desirable, the act is good, if not, bad. But what consequences count? Kant contended that reliance on consequences would render rational morality impossible. But utilitarian thought marched to a very different drummer, proclaiming that the greatest happiness or pleasure of the greatest number was the first principle of moral judgment. The advantages could be measured in terms of the benefit to the individual acting (egoistic utilitarianism) or to the plurality of others affected (universal utilitarianism). English moralists of the eighteenth and nineteenth centuries, particularly Jeremy Bentham and John Stuart Mill, adopted a deterministic position in which pleasure became the only good in itself and pleasant consequences the criterion of morality.

Bentham proposed pain and pleasure as sovereign governing principles of ethical choice, indicating not only what we ought to do, but determining our doing it. Every action was calculated to seek pleasure or avoid pain—specifically of one's own. Bentham thought of this as a kind of hedonic calculus, in which pleasurable or painful consequences could be measured and compared, based on considerations of intensity, duration, certainty, the extent to which it led to other pleasures or pains, whether there was an admixture of pain and pleasure and to what extent, and of course the extent to which pleasure or pain might be shared by others—the greater the number the greater the pleasure or pain. This last provision seems somewhat at odds with his idea that we should seek our own greatest pleasure. But, he argued, to the extent that we ignore the general welfare, we may open ourselves to painful consequences that act as naturally and socially imposed sanctions on selfishness and self-interest. In some degree our own happiness was contingent on the well-being and happiness of others.

Mill expanded Bentham's principle of greatest happiness, arguing that the validity of this first ethical principle could not be demonstrated. Whatever conduces to the ultimate end of moral action is good, but demonstrating what that end is or that it is good is beyond us. According to the greatest happiness principle, happiness is both the ultimate and only end for which all actions are carried out. Acts are morally good insofar as they produce happiness or means to achieve it, and morally evil if they do not. Like Bentham, Mill regarded unselfishness as essential to happiness, arguing that the standard of conduct is not merely the good of the agent but of all concerned. Ethical judgments are best made when the agent is impartial and objective, a disinterested and benign observer determining whether this or that action will bring the greatest happiness to the greatest number and not just to himself.

Morality of an act was judged by the end of happiness and not by motives or moral condition of the agent. Faced with the objection that he was ignoring the motive, Mill replied that the action he had in mind was not the interior act of choosing, but the external act. There is no difference in saving a drowning man out of a sense of duty or for pay—the consequence was the same. But subjectivity did enter the picture. The most important sanction obligating us to act morally is internal, the conscience. In his view, conscience was a feeling or affective state of sympathy or fellow-feeling joining us to our fellow creatures. This feeling was secondary to self-interest and desire, but was nurtured by education and social influences to become a powerful source of the desire to be in harmony with others and to respect their interests. Violation of this tendency draws an affliction of remorse from conscience that is painful. This for Mill was the ultimate sanction for moral action and the explanation of obligation as based on "the conscientious feelings of mankind."

The utilitarian view has significant appeal to psychoanalysts. In a sense, analysts are outcome-oriented. We tend to measure outcomes by consequences—the successful analysis is one that results in optimal or beneficial consequences. The successful interpretation is one that leads to meaningful and productive insight. We often lay ourselves open to the *post hoc propter hoc* fallacy, since the demonstrable link between input and output is not always specifiable. In addition, the hedonistic calculus finds echoes in the similar psychoanalytic calculus of pleasure-and-pain as determining principles of psychic functioning, at least in Freud's early economic formulations. But utilitarian perspectives on pleasure-pain and the psychoanalytic regarding the pleasure principle may not be synonymous. The question is complicated by the extent to which the pleasure principle functions as a regulatory principle as opposed to an experiential determinant (Meissner 1995b). Pleasure in the utilitarian scheme translated into happiness, that is, into an experiential state or condition. Also the utilitarian principle allowed freedom to pursue personal pleasure as long as it did not interfere with the pleasure-seeking of others. Freud set a more rigid standard by restricting pleasure according to the limits imposed by the reality principle. The reluctance to surrender pleasures in the face of the real or in the interest of greater freedom are constant themes in neurotic disturbance.

However, the utilitarian credo is not necessarily one that analysts can endorse unreservedly. Despite its empirical orientation, the principle of greatest happiness carries as absolute and peremptory a quality as ever did the kantian categorical imperative—the sense of obligation is as apodictic and absolute. Both principles survive on the basis of logical justifications with which psychoanalysis would have little sympathy. Both resort to some degree of sleight of hand in trying to explain the origins of conscience and the sense of obligation—Kant by appeal to an inherent moral imperative

and utilitarians by a circular argument based on fellow feeling. The absolutist ring to the utilitarian principle forms another variant of superego
imperative that can and often does set a standard of conduct well beyond
the reasonable capabilities of limited and conflicted individuals. We might
well ask, Why the standard has to be first of all the greatest good, and
second why to the greatest number? Is this a reasonable and realistic standard for ordinary mortals? Why not a more amenable standard—let us say
of what seems useful, contributory to one's personal good without imposing excessively on others or prejudicing the good of others?

In clinical work, we find ourselves frequently faced with neurotic
propensities to sacrifice one's own good excessively, unnecessarily, unrea-
sonably, in favor of someone else—the situation of the masochistic patient
who readily offers self-interest up on the altar of capitulation to the desires
or wishes of another—usually for the sake of retaining the goodwill, love,
or acceptance of that other. No less frequently do we encounter the opposite scenario—the patient whose narcissism, entitlement, and even grandiosity, leads him to disadvantage, take advantage of, and even deprive or
humiliate others in favor of his own self-enhancement or self-aggrandizement. For such patients, the utilitarian principle might serve a salutary purpose, but only in the service of tempering otherwise excessive neurotic
needs and tendencies.

But for many patients, whether because of their perfectionism or other
narcissistic traits or out of an hypertrophied sense of obligation and duty,
who are drawn to the excesses of an absolute standard of self-criticism or
self-evaluation impinging on their self-esteem, achieving a more realistic
and reasonable norm of behavior is a difficult therapeutic goal. Within this
analytic perspective, it is better to seek a goal that accomplishes some good,
whether for oneself or for others, within reasonable and realistic limits,
than to answer to a higher call of the greatest and best. While the psychoanalytic perspective would be respectful of consequences, it would take a
less peremptory and demanding approach to the evaluation of such consequences and would aim at a meaningful and productive balancing of the
good of the individual and the good of others.[5]

NATURALISTIC ETHICS

Naturalism seeks to define moral good in terms of ordinary experience,
especially in terms of something outside itself—personal well-being, happiness, pleasure, conformity with human nature, conformity to God's will, or
whatever. More strictly conceived, it bases ethical reflection on empirical,
scientific, and nonsupernatural considerations. It pays special attention,

then, to ordinary experience and to the data of science, particularly social science. In other words, naturalism contends that the *ought* of ethical obligation can be derived from the *is* of natural knowledge, that values are based on facts.

Consequently, for him, nothing exists beyond the scope of scientific inquiry and discovery, which is beyond the material world. The status of moral values and value judgments in this perspective is problematic. Are values natural? Nonnatural? Neither? Those who assert the natural status of value saw it as a natural quality like color, sound, or shape found in the world of experience in much the same way as other natural qualities. The nonnatural claimants had to resort to some principle separate from the world of experience, appealing to a spiritual realm—the details remain obscure, usually claiming no more than that these qualities are not natural. Many others disavow this disjunction and appeal to a more subjective theory of value as located in the subject's response to a given situation, making value equivalent to the agent's subjective reaction or attitude.

For the most part, naturalists reject the nonnatural option as contradicting naturalistic presuppositions, but controversy remains over the status of moral value. The subjectivist option finds little favor, since most naturalists would not go to the extreme of holding that, for example, murder is wrong because it evokes a negative feeling in me. They would tend to regard such an action as objectively evil. Problems, however, arise from the effort to derive moral propositions from scientific bases. Science speaks to facts, not devoid of theory, but the theory intends to explain the facts. The existence of man and the world requires no explanation. The guarantee of morality and human values lies in science and not in any supernatural causality. Values are geared to the enhancement of personal life and to the promotion of social well-being. Science can tell us how men act, or how societies act, or even what men regard as good or evil, but it has nothing to say about how men or societies *should* act. Science can tell me how to produce an atom bomb, but it has no way of determining the good or evil of such a bomb. With respect to ethical issues, science is blind and dumb.

The humanistic brand of naturalism views man as part of nature and as a product of evolutionary development. Evolution may reveal the direction of human development, but not necessarily the direction we ought to develop (G. F. Moore 1903). The influence of Charles Darwin weighed heavily in this arena, identifying moral progress with biological, evolutionary development. Herbert Spencer erected the darwinian suppositions into an ethical principle—as man evolves his ethical status and conduct reach higher levels. Goodness and right were judged in terms of their contribution to the preservation and prolongation of both individual and race. Moral science was evolving to a more scientific and advanced state of moral perfection. George Moore (1903) objected that in these terms "better" meant nothing but "more evolved," another version of the naturalistic fallacy. A quite different view was taken by Thomas Huxley who insisted that the survival of the fittest was in no sense an ethical principle, and that man's ethical ideals had to rest on a nonevolutionary basis: moral principles were necessary to overcome the law of the jungle and its primitive impulses and desires.

William James had a strong naturalistic bent, focusing on the meaning of ethical terms like *good, evil,* and *obligation* in pragmatic terms. He rejected any absolutist or metaphysical answer, preferring to see them as derived from feeling and desire. The morally good was whatever satisfied a need or desire—"That act must be the best act, accordingly, which makes for the best whole, in the sense of awakening the least sum of dissatisfactions" (1891, p. 205). Similarly John Dewey adopted an increasingly naturalist and pragmatic approach to ethics, postulating moral value to be that which promotes the fullest growth of the human being. Science can help us understand the potentialities of growth and discover the means to such growth, but it does not stake a claim to knowing how or why such growth is a moral value. Dewey's view is radically experiential: there are no essences, only process; there are no absolute ends, only those determined by human intelligence, and none are absolute. Morality pertains to problems arising from the practical conflicts between ends or standards of conduct. Thus, instrumental ethics stresses the habit of making prudent ethical judgments rather than concern with objective moral values. In balancing the conflicting claims of egoism and altruism, Dewey leaned toward the latter in the light of the more inclusive claims of social interest. He reacted against the derivation of duty from antecedent laws, emphasizing the role of ethics in seeking the good defined in terms of self-realization, happiness, or other ideals. He saw every moral situation as unique and calling for pragmatic solution (1920).

Dewey did not have much truck with psychoanalysis. He rejected Freud's theory of unconscious instinctual drives (1922) and any notion of an original individual consciousness. He excluded fixed standards of ethical judgment, but focused on the proximate ends of action and tried to describe how these concrete goals operated in the field of human action. They were intermediate ends that then became means to further ends. Ethical judgments could not ignore the consequences of action. He showed increasing interest in value theory, distinguishing valuation from value (1929). All values may be liked or desired, but not all desirable actions are valuable. Value-judgments function as regulators of affective and motive experiences. Psychological reports of human preferences have no more than instrumental utility in determining value-judgments, requiring further reflective interpretation. He became critical of positivist assertions that value-judgments were unverifiable (1939) and without meaning. Rather he contended that judgments regarding the suitability of certain objects for given purposes are practical generalizations substantiated by means-ends relations that could be tested by comparison of actual with intended consequences.

As we have seen, naturalistic ethics became the whipping boy for G. E. Moore's assault on the "naturalistic fallacy." Naturalism has also been criticized, especially by theistic ethicists, for the narrow conception of human knowledge, limiting the field to sense experience and to the scientific purview. Any knowledge of God or spiritual values are excluded, not only limiting the scope of human knowledge but complicating the explanation of morality. The naturalistic account can only go so far in providing a consistent rendition of moral value, before it is forced to find some other ground to substantiate the understanding of values. But, so the objection goes, this additional and ultimate value itself remains unexplained; they are either accepted blindly or not. Related to this difficulty, there is the persistent problem of explaining moral obligation. If certain naturalistic values are accepted as desirable, this does not argue to obligation.

As Richard Rorty (1991) commented, modern pragmatists tend to shy away from validation of ideas and values based on any contrast or comparison with reality. They prefer to circumvent such contrasts—inside versus outside, subject versus object, and so on—preferring to cast their inquiry in terms of the contrast between present beliefs and alternative beliefs. The choice is between two hypotheses and whichever works best, rather than between any questions about what makes one or the other true. Thus, problems related to the objectivity of values, the rationality of science, or the validity of language games are obviated—"All such theoretical questions would be replaced with practical questions about whether we ought to keep our present values, theories, and practices or try to replace them with others" (p. 41). The standard of truth, then, is both what works best and what in the long run receives unforced agreement in open dialogue with others holding other beliefs.

Naturalism has a good deal of sympathetic overlay with psychoanalysis. Psychoanalysis restricts its purview to the natural world, as does naturalism. Even more, psychoanalysis intends and acts as a science, even though some of its adherents would prefer to see it as a form of humanistic discipline (Meissner 1985b). In any case, psychoanalysis as a form of scientific knowledge lends itself to the naturalistic paradigm. But as such, we can question whether it falls heir to the limitations and shortcomings of the naturalistic approach to ethics. To an extent it does. But, at the same time, it may have something to contribute to understanding the development and functioning of the ethical agent, particularly the development and nature of conscience and moral values as psychic entities and functions, and may shed some light on the phenomena of guilt and obligation. But again, the question remains open as to the extent to which it has anything to offer regarding determination of what particular goods should be desired and what particular courses of action one ought to follow.

But I would also argue that psychoanalysis is not limited as to the scope of the objects of its inquiry. As a method of investigation, it has its own competence to explore the significance and unconscious ramifications of moral and religious beliefs and commitments. Religious behavior is motivated behavior and as such is open to psychoanalytic scrutiny and analysis (Meissner 1984c). If the naturalist has a prior commitment to rejecting any supernatural deity, psychoanalysis does not share this belief commitment; if the patient, for example, is committed to a set of religious beliefs, the analyst does not necessarily share those beliefs, nor does he disavow them. Such is not his business. Rather his task, along with the analysand, is to explore, understand, place in perspective, and formulate the unconscious, infantile, and possible conflictual underpinnings of such beliefs, and in the course of this process enable the patient to expunge infantile and conflictual derivatives and to achieve a more meaningful and adaptive religious orientation. The analytic process has no license to devalue or pass judgment on the belief system, except to the degree to which the patient's commitment to it involves pathological determinants or outcomes. Even then, the ultimate decision as to acceptance, in whole or in part, of the belief system lies with the analysand and not with the analyst. The same provisos apply to ethical principles and moral values.

The naturalist emphasis on empirical connection is compatible with the analytic view of the reality principle as framing and conditioning the pleasure principle. But inevitably moral judgments are inherently subjective and the determination of what constitutes reality often reflects the patient's psychic reality more than material reality, that is, more the individual's perception or interpretation of the real state of affairs than anything actually existing or happening.[6] The individual patient's psychic reality is determinative, but not exclusively or without context or compromise. The real must ultimately make sense, not only to the patient but to the analyst who shares the patient's journey of discovery. Especially, I would argue, ethical judgments are contextualized, in the sense that not just any evaluative stance is acceptable—and even less normative—but one that is open to consensual validation and reference. The appeal of a Rorty to subjective congruence seems to me to be a highly fallible criterion: subjective estimates are rarely, if ever, congruent; consensus may require an objective reference or standard of some kind. If ethical acts involve or impinge on others (as they are wont to do), the operative psychic reality in question belongs not merely to the moral agent but in some sense includes these others. This opens the door to consideration of complex issues of individual subjectivity and motivation that on analytic grounds are underplayed in the naturalist purview.

The naturalist effort to derive the ethical from the nonethical has its reflection in certain analytic views. The derivation of guilt feelings from childhood experience through development of the superego has this resonance. But the argument that adult guilt is synonymous with infantile derivatives is fallacious since effects resulting from prior causes cannot simply be reduced to those causes—analysis can determine the preceding causal events, but the outcome may involve more than is inherent in the causes. Then too, as we shall see later on, the guilt feelings resulting from superego action are not necessarily ethical—ethical guilt is a much more complex matter involving the practical judgment of conscience and resulting in real rather than neurotic guilt—that is, guilt as an ethical conclusion rather than guilt as a feeling state.

ANALYTIC PHILOSOPHY

The English analytic school envisioned the task of philosophy as seeking clarity of meaning by the analysis of language and language usage. Logical analysis has affinities with logical positivism with its view of scientific knowledge as the only valid form of knowledge—for one the object of analysis was scientific knowledge, for the other language. But logical analysts paid little attention to practical ethical issues involving personal moral issues, and were only moderately concerned with philosophical principles and methods of moral decision-making. Only the level of the logic and epistemology of ethics, of metaethical discourse, provided the primary locus for logical analytic reflection. The critical question was how to distinguish valid knowledge from nonsense. The test took the form of the verification principle: a sentence had meaning if and only if it was empirically confirmable. Verification thus lay in an appeal to experience, specifically to experiment, analogous to scientific method. Any proposition not meeting this criterion was meaningless. The problem was whether ethical propositions are open to such verification or not. How does one verify that stealing is right or wrong? "Right" and "wrong" are not thing-predicates open to such experimental verification.

R. M. Hare (1964), for example, who viewed ethics as the logical study of the language of morals, argued that moral language was a form of prescriptive language telling us what is right to do and what not. Starting with the imperative sentence, he distinguished simple from general imperatives, and from there progressed to analysis of value-judgments as a subform of prescriptive sentences. These sentences use terms like *ought, right,* or *good,* some pertaining to moral matters, others not. While this form of analysis allows considerable room for description and classification of linguistic usage of moral terms, it says nothing about the origin of the sense of obligation they express. The terms and their meaning were regarded as more-or-less given.

But over time, logical analysts became increasingly concerned with ordinary language. This led to a division of camps, one still under the shadow of logical positivism accenting factual experience, the other turning to a broader interpretation of human experience, finding meaning not only in factual statements, but in value statements as well. Although he was not counted among the logical analysts, G.E. Moore exercised a profound effect on the movement. He was rooted in the commonsense facts of experience, insisting on the validity of everyday perceptual experience. His commonsense approach to ethics recognized other goods besides pleasure and relied more on experience and consequences than on formal principles (Ewing 1962). He held that there were ethical facts open to our experience, and on this basis launched his attack on the "naturalistic fallacy." Against the positivistic background, he argued that goodness was not a fact to be empirically verified, so that on positivistic grounds verification was impossible unless the term was reduced to something else, for instance, utility or pleasure. But ethical facts were a different kind of fact, Ludwig Wittgenstein to the contrary notwithstanding. Ludwig Wittgenstein's postulate that all meaningful statements must be factually verifiable seemed to disqualify ethical statements. But Moore argued that goodness was as much a fact as any natural quality: it is given in experience just like any natural, yet indefinable, term, like *yellow.* Yellow can be related to certain wavelengths of light that are not in themselves yellow and do not define it; so good can be related to utility or pleasure or other qualities that are not the good and do not define it. If you try to define it in terms of anything else, you change its meaning. He concluded that in the ethical sense "good" was a simple, indefinable quality that had to be known directly in itself. As Moore (1903) put it, " 'Good,' then, if we mean by it that quality which we assert to belong to a thing, when we say that the thing is good, is incapable of any definition, in the most important sense of that word. The most important sense of 'definition' is that in which a definition states what are the parts which invariably compose a certain whole; and in this sense 'good' has no definition because it is simple and has no parts" (p. 9).[7]

Thus the basis of Moore's ethics was intuitive, especially as to the nature of the good, but in pragmatic terms Moore slipped into a brand of utilitarianism all his own. On the level of ethical discourse, determining what actions we should do was simply a matter of deciding what would produce the most good. Duty called us to perform that act most conducive to producing the good. The only valid criterion, however, lay in investigation of the consequences of the act. He stated unequivocally that rightness or wrongness of an action *"always* depends on its *actual* consequences" (1912, p. 83, italics in original), but this required weighing all the varieties of goodness in the consequences against whatever evil they possessed. Thus he had to face the basic conundrum of all utilitarianism, How can we ever know the full complement of good or evil that might flow from any given moral act?

Following Moore, A.J. Ayer, restricting ethical inquiry to analysis of ethical terms, came to regard moral statements as simply meaningless since they described no state of affairs. Or as Hare (1964) put it, "The substance of Ayer's theory is that moral judgements do not ordinarily function in the same way as the class of indicative sentences marked out by his verification-criterion" (p. 9). This position was consistent with the positivist claim that there was no distinction between "You murdered that man" and "It was wrong of you to murder that man." The addition of "It was wrong" added no meaning to the simple statement, but rather expressed only a feeling of disapproval. The feeling as such had no meaning. Thus value statements affirm nothing more than a wish—ethical statements appear to say something, but in fact say nothing. If I say some action is morally good, I am saying nothing more than that I like it; if morally bad, that I dislike it. Ethics is nothing more than a catalog of likes and dislikes. Thus, the connection between imperative and obligation, seemingly assumed by Kant, remains to be demonstrated.

More recent contributors, like Stephen Toulmin and Stuart Hampshire, are more interested in describing moral thought and action than in finding justification for it. They distinguish between good and bad reasons in morals, but, despite the appeal to reason, they provide no ultimate criteria for determining good and evil. When they offer "good reasons," the question as to why these reasons are good is not addressed. Toulmin argued for a form of evaluative inference leading from factual reasons to ethical conclusions. Yet statements of fact carry no imperative connotation and so cannot contain any prescriptive validity (Hare 1964). Hampshire (1959) connected speculative and practical reason in the decision-making of the moral agent, but saw no basis for deciding whether one moral standard is better than another. One difficulty is that most analytic philosophers regard questions regarding the basis of morality as irrelevant to ethical reflection. They remain satisfied with a descriptive ethics that explains how people make moral decisions, and explores reasons motivating such decisions, but offers little basis for determining which set of decisions is right.

Surprising as it may seem, psychoanalysis has little in common with logical analysis. Most of the thinking in logical analysis falls under the rubric of metaethics, focusing on the meaning of ethical terms like *good* or *ought*. Wallwork (1991) opined that analysis had little or nothing to contribute to such reflections. But I prefer not to rush to that conclusion. If it does not fall to psychoanalysis to determine the meaning of such terms, it may yet have a role in suggesting some of the psychic grounds that may have to be taken into account to reach an adequate understanding of these meanings for the moral agent.

Freud was none too sympathetic with intuitionist claims, as in Moore's *Principia Ethica* (1903), to knowledge of the good since they failed to provide adequate justification for ethical standards. Freud seemed as little inclined to accept moral propositions as self-evident as he was to accept them on the basis of divine ordination (Wallwork 1991). The appeal to intuition and self-evidence ran counter to Freud's reliance on reason. Wallwork refers to

> psychoanalysis's emphasis on trying to find out why we do what we do and on taking responsibility for the reasons that inform our actions. In Freud's words, what is actually "revealed" to whoever claims to have received moral insight from on high is only "primitive, instinctual impulses and attitudes, . . . valuable for an embryology of the soul when correctly interpreted, but worthless for orientation in the alien, external world" (Letter to Rolland in Freud 1975, p. 393). (p. 231)

In addition, Freud had expressed his distrust of intuition, whether moral or religious, on other occasions (Freud 1927a, 1930, 1939).

Even on the simple level of attribution of meaning, psychoanalysts look beyond mere commonsense or everyday experience. It is in fact in realms of mentation beyond the commonsensical and commonly experiential that psychoanalysis stakes its claim. Despite claims of the hermeneutical wing of psychoanalysis, the database of analysis in both clinical and theoretical terms includes a good deal more than verbal productions and exchanges between analyst and analysand (Meissner 1989, 1991b, 1996b). Rather analysis encompasses the full range of human behaviors, cognitive, conative, affective, and motoric. In this sense, the data relevant to ethical decision making and judgment, to operations of conscience and value systems, are appropriate objects for psychoanalytic investigation and understanding. But the scientific status of analytic knowledge may leave it vulnerable to the same criticisms of science generally—that it does not allow for making ethical judgments. I would prefer to leave that question open for further consideration later. But to a certain degree, the ethical relevance of psychoanalytic understanding is contingent on the extent to which it involves an explicitly ethical component in its thinking.

EXISTENTIAL ETHICS

The existential emphasis on "existence" versus "essence" drew attention away from concerns about understanding human nature as a given, and instead saw man as entering the world devoid of a nature or essence. Each human person starts from nothing, but has the capacity to freely make something of himself. That something is his essence so that existence precedes essence, and what that essence comes to be results from the exercise of human freedom. In this sense, preoccupation with the individual existent has been the hallmark of existentialist thought—as, for example, Søren Kierkegaard's emphasis on the moral life of the individual. His was not a speculative moral philosophy, but a more-or-less secularized inquiry into the individual's path to religious salvation. Concern with individual morality was cast in concrete and specific terms, rather than in abstract principles. Rather than treatises on morality, existentialists preferred to produce novels and plays displaying their thinking in concrete terms. The works of Jean-Paul Sartre, Albert Camus, Simone Beauvoir, and others abound in moral situations and contexts that speak to their ethical views quite directly, but not in philosophical language.

Thus, man is faced with the challenge of creating his own morality and adapting it to the changing conditions of life. Values are created by man and for man. In this sense, existentialism fades into humanism—all standards, norms, and laws are man-made. But the principle runs into difficulty in relation to its existential suppositions. If each human individual creates his own morality, his own norms and standards, how can there be general rules or laws, and what meaning or application would they have? Sartre's critics, for example, accused him of complete relativism and absolute individualism. If God is dead, as Fyodor Dostoyevsky put it, everything is permitted, and there is no law. Sartre answered that freedom is a law unto itself and only through it can one arrive at a truly moral law. Choice is a choosing for or against others, just as their choosing is for or against me. For Sartre there was no human nature or essence of man, only the radical contingency of the *pour-soi* constituting man's freedom. Historical conditions and contexts may vary, but the fundamental human situation remains—I am necessarily in the world; I am among other fellow men; I must work to sustain myself; I must die—these are the unchanging components of human existence and the invariant conditions for the exercise of human freedom. Thus the normative conditions for human life are not random or capricious, but must be worked out in the dialectic between human freedom and the fundamental and universal conditions of life.

On these terms, ethical theory can have little to say about objective conditions for morality in any traditional sense. There is no law in the sense of antecedent prescriptions regarding right and wrong. Awareness of the human condition gives us some sense of what to expect, but no suggestion of what must be done or what is objectively right or wrong. Man can only seek to act freely in the concrete situation. This maxim to act freely becomes almost a new form of sartrean categorical imperative. Nothing is right or wrong in itself exclusive of individual free choice. Right and wrong pertain to the relation between human freedom and human action; no human action, taken in isolation, is either right or wrong. In objective terms, everything is relative. Only in subjective terms of human freedom can we speak of morality, of good or bad. Each human life is a "project," whose goodness or evil is not determined by the actions it involves, but by whether the individual makes his choices freely or not. For Sartre, the primary virtue is authenticity in making free decisions, and the primary vice bad faith, by which man negates his freedom and undermines his potential to be fully human.

Psychoanalysis has many resonances with existentialist thought (Weisman 1965). Freedom is not only one of the inherent goals and values of the analytic process, but as I have argued at some length elsewhere (Meissner 1992a, 1996b), forms a necessary constituent of the analytic process, particularly in reference to the therapeutic alliance. But this degree of centrality does not elevate freedom and free self-determination to the transcendent status of existentialism. Much of the work of analysis aims at enabling the patient to achieve a greater and more effective level of unencumbered freedom and the capacity not only to know his own desires and inclinations, but to pursue them freely and without neurotic baggage to impede his exercise of free choice. But such freedom is not an absolute; it must be integrated with other reasonable, realistic, adaptive, and social concerns. In other words, freedom is not the "be all and end all" of psychoanalytic creativity, but is a capacity of the self to find its creative and constructive realization in and through integration with a host of other realistic and dynamic concerns and interests. In this perspective, then, if moral goals are to be set, or if moral decisions to be made, they are not made on the basis of a criterion rooted solely in freedom or in the maximization of the capacity to choose freely; they are the product of a complex integration of multiple factors and considerations leading in the direction of a choice of a course of action deemed ethically right or a choice to avoid a course thought to be ethically bad. In addition, it should be clear that nowhere in the psychoanalytic lexicon is there any claim that such choices are inherently normative, let alone that that choice that emerges from greater freedom has any greater claim to moral validity.

AXIOLOGICAL ETHICS

Axiology studies values in the broader terms posited by R. B. Perry (1926): "Value in the generic sense attaches promiscuously to all objects of all interest" (p. 28). Generally, idealistic value theorists rely on intuition, looking not to any objective quality of good or bad in an action, but to something like an essence of the good. They also appeal to a sense of morally good action as somehow self-perfective or self-realizing. Perry provided a generic definition of value as a starting point for other naturalist ethicists—value was "any object of any interest," so that moral good took the form of fulfillment of any organization of interests. He proposed four criteria of value: correctness, intensity, preference, and inclusiveness—the first determined what a value was, the rest the degree of value. His moral imperative became "Cultivate that kind of will that is qualified to bring harmony through its universal adoption" (p. 682). The objection that at times people desire evil things is countered by the claim that wrongdoing is not due to desire for evil but to sacrificing a greater good to a lesser one (Ewing 1962). More recently, Stephen Pepper's social adjustment theory, in surveying empirical ethical theories, led to the conclusion that they are all limited to a point of view—individual value systems to hedonistic pleasure and self-realization, theories of social value to reduction of social tension and cultural conformity, and biological values to evolutionary progress through natural selection. His own theory held that when there was no special problem in social adjustment, then ordinary naturalistic norms are adequate; but when conflict arises, decisions may depend on the degree of social pressure.

The psychoanalytic interaction with the axiological perspective would have to be—as far as I can see—somewhat mixed. While analysts would stake a claim for the role of pleasure-pain as determinative of ethical choices, the titration of these affective measures would also fall within the compass of the reality principle and thus would not be calculated (consciously or unconsciously) solely in terms of a schema of such values, however intuitively grasped. The framing and basing of any value-system in reality would have to enter the picture as an important basis for assessment and decision. However, the qualification must immediately be added, as with the utilitarian calculus, that within psychoanalysis pleasure and pain do not operate as affective states, but as regulatory principles (Meissner

1995b). Caution is thus required in comparing these terms in ethical theories and in psychoanalysis. Moreover, to the extent that reliance for evaluation and decision falls on the affective side of human experience, analysts are too aware of the pitfalls in matters pertaining to emotional life and to the immense potential for distortion, whether transferentially derived or not, and self-deception, to endorse that emphasis too readily. As an analyst, I would maintain this stance even in the face of the usual analytic respect for, and openness to, affective experience, which may and should be constantly acknowledged and monitored, but not taken as normative.

However, it should also be said that the theory of values within psychoanalysis is far from satisfactory articulation. At this writing, it is probably safest to take a wait-and-see attitude, since there lies open an extensive field for analytic reconsideration and rethinking of issues related to understanding values and value-systems in relation to the analytic experience before any effort can be made to extend such perspectives to ethical concerns. I will return to this issue later as a topic open to further exploration.

POSTMODERN CRITIQUE

Contemporary moral discourse has been scored for its lack of coherence and moral consistency. The traditional philosophical claim to moral authority rested on articulation of the particular with the universal—the relation of a particular action with general moral principles by which we judge the action as just or not (Doty 1995). The aristotelian turn to the empirical to discover moral principles previously housed in platonic universals set the course of subsequent moral inquiry. The fundamental option of regarding man as a piece of nature, a hobbesian form of matter-in-motion, or as possessing an autonomous range of specifically human capacities for reason, choice, and cultural experience, pervades the psychoanalytic reflection on the moral dimensions of human behavior and even the analytic conception of human nature. Freud's early physiological-energic speculations remain in tension with his later more clinically based views of the mind and its powers (see chapter 1).

The modernist ambition to establish universal principles of moral decision and ethical behavior foundered on multiple and conflicting views regarding the validity of such all-encompassing moral schemata. The modernist trust in reason as a guide to consistent moral principles has faded in the face of postmodern critiques, leading to the conclusion that fundamental moral principles do not exist and that moral rules are relative to social, cultural, and historical contexts. The postmodern mentality is essentially historicist, emphasizing plurality of approaches to the making of meaning in the world and to the relativity of standards and principles governing human action and behavior. For Martin Heidegger, for example, the search for truth was an uncovering of the meaning of being and bringing it into the light of understanding that is linguistic, historical, and social. Man dwells in this semantic space, in which we make sense of ourselves and the world we encounter around us by means of the resources of language. The result is not one, but many worlds and many meanings.

Freud seems to have found a place in postmodern thought, at least as a potential model for personal ethical thought (Smith and Kerrigan 1986). Rorty (1979) drew a distinction "between men as objects of explanation and men as moral agents, concerned to justify their beliefs and their actions" (p. 256), but saw no need for these perspectives to seek further synthesis. Justification for knowledge claims or beliefs and the explanation of their origins are separate matters—explanation of how someone came to hold a certain belief does not justify the belief. It is not clear that analysts have consistently observed these boundaries. Freud's views on matters such as sublimation, ego interests, even moral concerns, are tinged with ethical implication—as Philip Rieff (1959) and others have made clear. The line between explanation and justification seems thin and readily crossed. His reflections on war and death (Freud 1915c), for example, are meditations on egoistic and altruistic transformations without much appeal to metapsychological considerations. As Smith and Kerrigan (1986) note:

> On the model of Freud's account of love and hate—phenomena that refuse "to be fitted into our scheme of the instincts" (Freud, 1915a, p. 133) and are not "relations of *instincts* to their objects, but . . . relations of the *total ego* to objects" (p. 137)—one could say that these remarks on ego interest, morality, sublimation, and health refer to behavior, attributes, and relations of the whole person. There is no reliable concept of the whole person or the self in psychoanalytic metapsychology, despite the efforts of [Heinz] Hartmann, [Heinz] Kohut, and others, and for that reason metapsychology cannot be a language of moral deliberation or moral judgment, both of which address the entire person. When Freud writes of love, work, and other sublimatory processes, he writes not so much as a psychoanalyst wielding an authoritative technical vocabulary, but as a person. (p. xiii, italics in original)

This principle embraces the direction of thinking advanced by Donald Winnicott and developed by Eric H. Erikson; it is also the basic orientation followed in the present study. The position of the self in formulating a psychoanalytic ethic is central. As Smith and Kerrigan (1986) further conclude, "the level of discourse pertaining to the whole person provides the best way of bringing to light the Freudian ethic—the ethic in Freud and his discourse, and the ethic bequeathed by him to subsequent vocabularies of moral deliberation" (p. xiii).

CHAPTER THREE

Psychic Determinism and
Motivational Principles

FREUD AND DETERMINISM

Ethical decision-making requires a degree of autonomy and the capacity for free decision and choice in the ethical agent. We are immediately confronted, therefore, with the problem of determinism in psychic actions and the extent to which choice and autonomy can exist under conditions of psychic determinism.[1] We can envision a split in this respect between the theoretical Freud and the clinical Freud. The theory, to which he had committed himself and on which he staked his scientific reputation, demanded that everything the patient did or said had to be determined, that is, in some sense caused. But at the same time, clinical experience made it evident that unless the patient achieved some degree of autonomy, some level of self-determination, and free self-mastery in the interest of overcoming neurotic dispositions and conflicts, the prospects for therapeutic change were dim at best. With what mind-set, then, was Freud to engage his patient? Should it be Freud the scientist, or Freud the humanist-clinician?

True to his scientific weltanschauung, Freud declared his uncompromising faith in scientific determinism—he referred to the "strict determination of mental events" (1923c, p. 238), "the illusion of Free Will" (1919b, p. 236), and remarked that "psychoanalysts are marked by a particularly strict belief in the determination of mental life" (1910a, p. 38); and again, "you nourish a deeply rooted faith in undetermined psychical events and in free will, but that this is quite unscientific and must yield to the demand of a determinism whose rule extends over mental life" (1916–1917, p. 106).

These formulas sound decisive and unequivocal, but there are fringes of uncertainty. Did Freud always adhere to his avowed scientific principles? It seems not. As with equality ("some are more equal than others"), there

53

is determinism, but some determinisms are more deterministic than others. The form of "hard" or complete determinism of physical science may not allow room for any degree of freedom or responsibility, but the same cannot be said of "softer" forms of determinism allowing space for freedom of choice necessary for moral action. The problem in interpreting the freudian texts is whether Freud at any point is speaking the language of hard scientific determinism or something else. Where hard determinism prevails, it undermines the basis for ethical judgment and action; many interpreters read Freud in exactly this sense. However, a claim can be made (Wallwork 1991) that "Freud never makes as clear a commitment to determinism in the hard sense that rules out there being any responsibility as most secondary interpreters seem to think" (p. 52). Nor is it difficult to understand the reasons for this qualification, since clinical praxis would become meaningless and irrelevant without such capacities. Freud's discussions of determination have to be placed alongside his insistence that, among the goals of therapeutic psychoanalysis, were growth and increase of the patient's freedom, autonomy and initiative, particularly freedom to decide between conflicting motives and courses of action (1912a, 1921a, 1923a).

Freud struggled to resolve the contradiction—a kinder term would be *tension*—between hard and soft determinism. Hard determinism, even cast in the extreme terms of physical causality, seemed mandatory for his ideas to gain scientific credibility;[2] but at the same time the nature of the phenomena and the complex conditions of motivation and choice he encountered clinically made application of such rigid determinism problematic. Freud settled for an ambiguous compromise, retaining hard determinism for theoretical formulations in his metapsychology, particularly in regard to drives and drive forces, and allowing for softer determinism in his clinical discussions.[3]

Resolution of this unsatisfactory ambiguity of questions related to choice and motivation require reconsideration of the meaning of determinism in the theory of motivation and the capacity for free choice.[4] I have argued (Meissner 1995a,b,c; 1999a,b; Rizzuto, Meissner, and Buie, in process) that these considerations and the understanding of motivation and intentionality in general are inconsistent with a theory of drives and drive-determinants, and that the metapsychological underpinnings of analytic theory need to be readdressed and recast in more consistent and humanly meaningful terms. My theoretical effort to resolve these difficulties separates psychic causality and motivation,[5] locating the source of causal efficacy and action in the self-system, specifically in the self-as-agent (Meissner 1993), and retaining the motivational components as separate and distinct considerations unrelated to drive energies or forces. This separation of agency and motivation is a radical departure from the classic theory, in which both are attributed to the same source, the drives.

PSYCHIC DETERMINISM

Psychic determinism remained primary in Freud's thinking as undergirding his reliance on the method of free association. According to the principle of determination, nothing could enter the mind haphazardly, so that whatever came into consciousness by way of free association had to be determined. A basic question is whether psychic determinism should be interpreted in terms of causes in the mental apparatus (as were drives in the classic theory), or as reasons or meanings having more to do with motivation. The idea that human actions involve intentions is ancient—Socrates held that one always acts according to what he thinks best—voluntary actions were determined by a known good intended as such. Freud himself commented that psychoanalysts had a particularly strong belief in the determination of mental life, meaning that there was nothing trivial, nothing arbitrary or haphazard, and that psychoanalysts expected in every case to be able to find sufficient motives for behavior. But the tension persisted in Freud's thinking between the view of man as an object moved by natural forces (causes as in other sciences) versus man as motivated by meanings and reasons (Holt 1972). As Freud envisioned it, the drives were causal forces acting as sources of the causal energy driving the mental apparatus. Even though his clinical experience drew him closer to the latter view, he could not altogether abandon the former. Abandoning such a fundamental energic view would have meant, in his mind's eye, creating a model of the psychic apparatus without causal effectiveness or executive capacity. At the same time, finding meaning in otherwise meaningless symptoms and behaviors was paradoxically one of Freud's definitive contributions.[6]

Causes and reasons. We are confronted with the issue of whether and to what extent determining factors involve causes or meanings or both. For some the distinction is radical—science deals with causes, humanities with reasons (Home, 1966; Schafer, 1976). Jacob Arlow (1959), for example, at one point wrote: "Essentially psychic determinism implies the application to the phenomena of mental life of the same criteria for causality and relatedness that apply to the phenomena of nature in other sciences" (p. 205). Accordingly, metapsychology was regarded as a natural science, the realm of causes and not reasons; motives and meanings would have no place in such a theory. Thus, Michael Sherwood (1969) distinguished between goal-directed actions and physically determined movements—actions were related to reasons, and movements to causes. But the human organism experiences both actions and movements in various degrees of integration. Reasons have more to do with purposes, causes with mechanisms. Thus reasons and causes both have influence in determining the outcome of a given behavior. But clearly stating a reason is not the same as stating a cause anymore than a chess rule moves the pieces on the board (Oldenquist 1967). To the contrary, some movements occur without any reasons—the classic knee-jerk. But furthermore, there cannot be either action or movement without an energic source of power (Meissner, 1995a).[7]

The distinction is framed by the view that says that, if I cite my reasons for a given intended act, I am not on that account listing the causes of my action. Nor, if I state the reasons for my anger, am I giving a causal account. But many would regard explanations by reasons as causal. Possible sources of confusion might include the following: (1) Ordinary usage often uses "cause" and "because" to express reasons involving motives or meaning; the term *cause* in this usage may express metaphorically the urgent or compelling nature of the reason. Clearly, in this case, the use of "because" carries no weight as indicating causal connections: it may even be used to connect the premise and conclusion of a logical argument, where the relation is not causal at all. (2) Both terms are appealed to as explanations, even though they may point to radically different forms of explanation. (3) The regularities between motives and reasons on one hand and actions on the other hand may lead some to presume such a connection as causal. David Hume's view of causality as based on regularity of antecedents and consequences would endorse such a view. However, even if we regard reasons as causes of intentional acts, we cannot conclude that such an explanation is causal. A further argument points out that it remains possible to perform an action, to have reasons for doing it, and *not* have done it for those reasons (Donnellan 1967). The act could not have occurred without causes, but if the reasons were held to be the causes, the act would occur without causality. Also causes and reasons differ in their relation to effects—causes always precede effects, reasons need not: even if the reason is never actually produced it need only be producible (Oldenquist 1967)—its temporal connection, prior or post, is irrelevant.

Reasons and motives. It certainly seems as though any appeal to reasons as explaining an action rests on a quite different basis than an appeal to causes. If I assign reasons for my action, I do not find it necessary to support them with empirical evidence, as I might in an appeal to causes, and there is nothing in the explanation that would suggest that anyone else would act in a similar way if they had similar reasons.

I would argue the case for causality as follows. Let us take for an example the case of a deliberate murder using a handgun. The causal sequence would run something like this: an intention forms to injure, even kill, the victim; this murderous intent is motivated by powerful and emotionally intense reasons—hatred, revenge, jealousy, and so on; the intent is put into execution by an act of will resulting in moving my hand to pick up the gun, aim it at the victim, and pull the trigger; the behavioral sequence involves a series of psychic actions leading to physical behaviors—intentional and purely psychic activity produces a series of physical motoric acts; the rest of the causal sequence is purely mechanical—the trigger releases the hammer, the hammer strikes the shell, exploding the powder and propelling the bullet on its trajectory toward the victim; entrance of the bullet into vital organs creates tissue damage resulting in death. The process is powered by energies at all points—at some points purely psychic energy, at other points purely physical. The psychic processes differ from the physical by reason of complex feedback effects in the former and none in the later, and by reasons and motivations in the former and none in the latter. Causal efficacy in this sequence of connected actions is due to energic dynamics; the effects are determined, but while physical effects are causally determined (propulsion of the bullet is a direct effect of explosion of the powder), the psychic effects are motivated, that is, determined (have purpose and meaning) through reasons and motives, but not caused by such motives but by the agency of the self-as-agent. Thus psychic and physical causality are of quite different orders of intelligibility.[8]

But the principle of determination plays a somewhat different role in different causal settings. Psychic causality is not linear—Freud himself introduced the notion of overdetermination or multiple determination, implying that a particular psychic event or set of events could be explained in terms of more than one set of determining factors. Our putative murderer in the example may have had more than one reason for wanting to kill the victim—hatred, envy, revenge, and so on. We can also conjecture that internal and conflictual struggles may have taken place, stirred by powerful affects, between the enraged wish to kill and the inhibitory restraints of conscience and morality. Psychic determination in these terms would be difficult to reconcile with stricter notions of physical determination and cause-effect relations. Furthermore, the problem of determination in psychoanalysis becomes more complex by reason of the fact that its subject matter does not simply have to do with physical or behavioral events, but involves human actions and intentions carrying meaning and purpose. The question then arises whether psychic determinism has more to do with meanings and relations of meanings than with causal connections (Rosenblatt and Thickstun 1977a,b).

Freud's translation of the clinical data, having to do with affective experience, meanings, and motives, into terms of psychic energy served a dual function: it allowed him to plug his thinking into current scientific concepts, simultaneously providing his psychological science with a presumption of underlying causal determinism. In other words, if human experience could be translated into terms of the transformation of psychic energies, then causal influences involved in such energic transformations could likewise be regarded as causal determinants of such experience. Obviously, such a formulation obscures the inherent differences separating energic concepts in the realm of objective processes from meanings and motives in the realm of subjective human experience.

Certainly, views of determinism have changed, not only in scientific thinking generally but particularly in psychoanalysis. For Freud, at least in his early approach to psychological problems, determinism was absolute and particular in the sense that every mental event, no matter how trivial, had to be causally determined. Today, many analysts would not apply the principle in this same mechanical sense, and many would raise serious doubts whether mental structure can be adequately viewed in the rigidly deterministic manner Freud originally suggested at all.

Determinism in psychoanalysis can be conceived more broadly and flexibly. In his original formulations, for example, Freud would have explained every instance of the psychopathology of everyday life, every forgetting, every slip of the tongue, as something that could be interpreted like a dream, and its relation to a specific unconscious wish then established. The wish and its related motive were seen as determining the particular act of forgetting. Currently, however, analysts would accept that one might not be able to explain each individual act in terms of its immediate determination. For example, we might have to recognize that in early development a general tendency might be established, let us say, to losing things, which might have become part of the individual's character structure—as Anna Freud (1967) suggested. The central issue then would be the general trait, the tendency to lose things, rather than seeking out the immediate determinants of every specific loss. Determinism pertains to the level of character formation and development rather than to each individual action. Moreover, it would take into account the history, developmental and otherwise, of the personality and the internal conditions contributing to the behavior outcome, and not merely the immediate causal context.

MULTIPLE DETERMINATION AND MULTIPLE FUNCTION

Psychic determinism was further compromised by the principle of multiple determination of psychic events. Freud himself introduced the notion of multiple determination (overdetermination), meaning that a particular psychic event could be explained in terms of more than one set of determining factors.[9] In this sense, he envisioned a sort of "layering" of determinations in the patient's psychic life. The patient's behavior could be understood not only in terms of determining events and motives in his present life, but also in terms of determining events and motives of the past. Thus, psychic formations, particularly those expressing unconscious determinants, could result from multiple influences, rather than from only one. Furthermore, such psychic events were related to a multiplicity of unconscious elements that could be organized in different meaningful contexts, each having its own coherent and specifiable meaning.

Overdetermination is seen most clearly in the study of dreams and hysterical symptoms. Analysis of dream content suggests that each element of the dream, as well as the dream as a whole, are overdetermined. A number of different latent trains of thought may be combined into one manifest dream content that lends itself to a variety of interpretations. Such determining sequences of meaning need not be mutually independent, but may intersect at one or more points, as suggested by the patient's associations. The dream, or symptom in the case of hysteria, reflects a compromise out of the interaction of such determining significances, which may in themselves be relatively diverse. In this sense, the classical paradigm for hysteria reflects convergence of more than one opposing current of wishes, each arising from a different motivational system, but finding relative fulfillment by converging in a single symptomatic expression.

The principle of multiple determination lends itself readily to determination in terms of meaning and motive, as just delineated, but less readily to causal determination as understood in linear cause-effect models. If overdetermination is to be consistent with the determinist perspective in psychoanalysis, it must be formulated in terms of motives and meanings rather than in causal sequences. The issues of psychic causality and multiple determinism can be integrated into a more complex perspective involving multiple and complex forms of causality (read determination) that intersect in varying forms and proportions in the genesis of any psychic activity or behavior (Wallace 1985). The perspective of multicausality (multidetermination) lends itself to an understanding of behavior as the resultant of multiple and variant influences, each of which exercises a determining effect, but no one of which can be regarded as the sole causal agent. On these terms, psychic determinism translates into meanings and motives; psychic causality pertains to the causality peculiar to psychic actions, for example, the action of the will in initiating actions whether mental or physical.

Psychic causality in the murder described above can involve multiple variants of meaning and motive—what Freud meant by "overdetermination"—but it also results from the intersection of multiple causal influences including genetics, characterological determinants, developmental experiences, personal history, drive endowment, moral commitments and prohibitions, motor capacities, and eye-hand coordination. Pulling the trigger is the final common path for these multiple causalities and determinants. Each of the multiple causalities has its own form of influence and causal effect that intersects with others to produce a common outcome. Multiple determination, however, in the psychoanalytic sense, works orthogonally to these causal inputs—it is a matter of condensation of psychic meanings and motives providing the motivational structure of the action in question.

Along with overdetermination, another complexly determined psychoanalytic principle is that of multiple functioning. While multiple determination looks to causal origins or determining sequences of meaning, multiple functioning looks to results or purposes—any psychic activity or action may have more than one purpose as part of its intention. As Robert Waelder (1936a) originally formulated it, the principle stated that no solution of a problem is possible that does not at the same time in some way or other represent an attempted solution of other problems simultaneously. By implication, any psychic event or human action is not directed simply to one outcome or to attaining a single purpose or goal, but may, in fact, serve multiple purposes and be governed by varying and diverse intentions. This principle too runs counter to concepts of linear causality and is better cast in terms of meanings and motives.

MOTIVATIONAL CONSIDERATIONS

Refocusing issues related to the determination of psychic action and recasting the distinction of causality and motivation draw us on to further considerations of the basis of motivation and to the role of motivational systems in determining psychic action. Motivation concerns the setting of stimulus conditions and dispositional states that elicit a response from the self and result in either action or lack of action as the case may be. I am focusing specifically on the modalities and conditions on which motivational factors operate and play their part in the economy of psychic action. The discussion focuses on motivational factors in terms of wishes, wish-fulfillment, and desire.

Wish and Wish-fulfillment

Wishes are forms of mental expression of motivational states, whether conscious or unconscious. Wishes played a central role in Freud's early formulations, especially in the *Studies on Hysteria* (Breuer and Freud 1893–1895), in *The Interpretation of Dreams* (Freud 1900), and in the early case discussions (Freud 1905a), where *wish* was treated as the primary motivational term.[10] Wish became the primary mover of the mental apparatus, in accord with the pleasure principle, rather than will. Wish-fulfillment was the primary dynamic behind the formation of dreams, and was thought to contribute to symptom and fantasy formation as well. In this early model, the mental image associated with satisfaction referred back to a previous excitation of a need that had earlier found satisfaction, so that when the need arose again it sought association with the memory image left by that earlier satisfaction and thus evoked the actual experience of satisfaction. Recovery of the perception connected with earlier satisfaction constituted wish-fulfillment, and the impulse to achieve such satisfaction was the wish itself.

The organization of wishes, however, involved a model of internal motivational forces extending beyond Freud's early reflex arc model. Despite his reliance on simple energic models, wishes held a central position in Freud's clinical thinking—as Robert Holt (1976) commented: "[wish] is a cognitive-affective concept, framed in terms of meanings and potentially pleasant or unpleasant outcomes of possible courses of action" (p. 179). The memory trace of pleasurable satisfaction, associated with lessening of tension from instinctual demands, was required for formation of a wish. The wish thus required activation, not only of a memory of satisfaction, but of all the stimuli and conditions of the situation of satisfaction.[11] Allan Rosenblatt and James Thickstun (1977a) reformulated the notion of wish as "the experiential correlate of an activated motivational system, including the conscious experience of the internal image or concept of the set-goal and the accompanying appraisal processes reflecting the degree of mismatch between the internal standard and reality" (p. 555).[12] The wish is, then, by definition, always incomplete, unsatisfied, and frustrated—an emptiness yearning to be filled; if and when it achieves satisfaction, it is no longer a wish. They add that the wish as such may remain unconscious, similar to unconscious affects, but it is still potentially experiential.

The operation of the pleasure principle can be seen optimally in regulation of the need to re-create such contexts of satisfaction or at least their memory traces in the service of the formation of wishes. Conceived in terms of drive theory, emergence of the wish marked an important transition from the mere physiology of needs to the more psychological realization of instinctual or other drive derivatives operating as mental representations of somatic stimuli impinging on the mental apparatus—a point made succinctly by Max Schur (1966): "the emergence of the 'wish' marks the beginning of the functioning of what we call psychic structure. I have also stressed the difference between the physiological concept 'need' and the psychological concept 'wish'" (p. 68). It also marks the transition from mental functioning after the manner of a reflex apparatus to that of a more developed model of internal motivational states. In this view, the unpleasure principle regulates avoidance of stimuli that create a disturbance of internal equilibrium. It is thus concerned with excessive or discordant external stimulation and is developmentally the more primitive principle. The pleasure principle, on the other hand, was conceived as regulating the need to recreate the situation giving rise to the previous experience of satisfaction by way of a diminution of drive tensions.

Corresponding to the psychological shift implied in the notion of wish, it carries with it the implication of purpose and direction to a goal. Holt (1976) stated cogently: "With the concept of wish, we can assert, in answer to the behaviorists and other mechanistically inclined theorists, that behavior *is* purposive, that fears, longings, plans, fantasies, and other mental processes are not epiphenomena, but must be central to any adequate psychology of human behavior, and that the person is often not conscious of what his purposes are" (p. 180, italics in original). From the beginning, Freud's notions of defense, repression, and conflict were impregnated with meaning and purpose. Purposes remained clinically related to dynamic considerations of conflicting motives and aims; the economic-energic considerations were theoretical attempts to explain these qualitative differences by quantitative means (Klein, 1976a,b).

Wishes and needs. Wishes as such are distinct from needs that give rise to the motivational state involved in the wish. Needs are in the first instance derived from internal states of tension, whether physiological or psychological. Hunger as a need state is related to a condition of physiological tension caused by lack of food. The need for achievement, shaped within a certain developmental and social context, relates to a state of internal tension of a different sort, less physiological than psychological. The wish, however, arises as a motivational state aimed at satisfying the need. Even in Freud's early model, then, wishes were impregnated with meaning, an understanding that extended the motivational reach of the wish well beyond its energic claims. While the classic view tended to see wishes as amalgams of (drive) force and meaning, the present view would prefer to cast the wish in terms of motivational meaning and to ascribe the "force" to agency of the self, that is, the person, rather than to independently acting forces. To whatever extent, however, that fantasy can serve the requirements of wish-fulfillment, some needs are hardly satisfied adequately in fantasy—certainly hunger and achievement are far from adequately satisfied except in real terms.

Satisfaction of the wish in dreams, symptoms, and fantasies all carry this impression of compromise in realizing fulfillment, but for wishes whose adequate fulfillment requires some accomplishment in reality, these processes are half-measures. It is one thing to dream about getting the top grade in a final examination, another to actually do so. Wishful thinking may carry some of the burden of wish-fulfillment, but it is fulfillment falling short of accomplishment. The notion of wish-fulfillment emphasizes the dynamics of the wish and its fantasied satisfaction, whether conscious or unconscious; reality is kept aside, as in dreams (Laplanche and Pontalis 1973). This reasoning was implicit in Freud's insistence on the complementarity of the pleasure and reality principles.[13] Besides the memory trace of pleasurable satisfaction, required for formation of a wish, the wish involves activation of the complex of stimuli and related contextual conditions of the situation of satisfaction. The wish as such may remain unconscious, but still potentially experiential. The need to recathect these complex elements makes it clear that the wish is reflecting dynamics operating beyond the range of the principles of constancy and avoidance of unpleasure as conceived by Freud. The pleasure principle comes into play in regulation of the need to re-create such contexts of satisfaction or at least their memory traces in the formation of wishes.

Desire. *Desire* has a broader connotation as a motivational term, and has acquired a more central place in analytic thinking through the contributions of Jacques Lacan for whom it served as the primary motivational term. As such it is distinct from need and demand, and occupies a place intermediate between them. Need aims at a specific object in which it finds satisfaction, while demand addresses itself to others from whom satisfaction is sought. As Jean Laplanche and Jean-Baptiste Pontalis (1973) put it: "Desire appears in the rift which separates need and demand; it cannot be reduced to need since, by definition, it is not a relation to a real object independent of the subject but a relation to phantasy; nor can it be reduced to demand, in that it seeks to impose itself without taking the language or the unconscious of the other into account, and insists upon absolute recognition from him" (p. 483). I would want to qualify this view of desire as not related to real objects; my sense is that restricting desire to fantasy or mental contents creates a closed solipsistic system and ignores the inherent intentionality of desire. Like other motivational terms, such as *wish* or *purpose,* they cannot be confined within the scope of the pleasure principle without admitting the role of the reality principle and the associated relevance of the real as the object of intentionality (McIntosh 1993).

The operative freudian term to express the dynamics of desire is *wish* as discussed above, but usually concretized in reference to single acts or specific objectives. The French translate the German term *Wünsch* as *désir*, setting the stage for Lacan's usage, making desire a more general and largely subjective dimension of the human subject. For Lacan, desire is not restricted to seeking satisfaction of a wish or need. In the gap between need and demand, there is a "wanting-to-be" transcending satisfaction of particular needs and demands. Any demand is addressed to another, but, whatever the specific object of the demand, what is really sought from the other is his love, the deepest and most persistent desire of the human subject. "Desire, then, is a want-to-be in the subject that is unsatisfiable either through gratification of his needs or acquiescence to his demands" (Muller and Richardson 1982, p. 281). The transition from this approach to desire to the lapidary lacanian formula, "Desire is the desire of the Other" is ready enough, but carries with it some weighty assumptions. Between desire-as-insatiable and desire as desire-of-the-Other lies the supposition that desire as well as demand are transmitted in the symbolic order and that the other in question is not only the Other whom I can address in speech but the other within the self, that is, desire is the desire of the unconscious.

But in searching for the derivation of this fundamental desire, Lacan (1992) extends the argument to its most infantile sources. A convoluted argument unravels through a series of complex considerations of *das Ding* (the Thing), the reality paradoxically beyond knowing in the kantian sense, but that is nonetheless synonymous with the good as the object of desire and guide for moral action. At the root of desire, the place of *das Ding* is occupied by the mother of infantile experience, embedded in the complex psychology of mother-child interaction and developmental experience, expressed inadequately in categories of dependence, satisfaction, and frustration. Thus, "Freud designates the prohibition of incest as the underlying principle of the primordial law, the law of which all other cultural developments are no more than the consequences and ramifications. And at the same time he identifies incest as the fundamental desire" (p. 67). In short, for Lacan there was no sovereign good, only *das Ding*, the mother, the object of incest, a forbidden good, but there is no other. At the same time, the Thing, the primordial real, may encompass a principle of evil, so that the ultimate object of desire is as much evil as good, not unlike the kleinian vision of the primal mother.[14]

This fundamental desire entered consciousness and moral action through sublimation that lends itself to the formation of conscience and values. In the realm of conscience, that is, the superego, the residues of desire and love are mingled paradoxically with hate and destructiveness. But since the fundamental object lies beyond the pleasure principle, erotic life instincts do not suffice as organizing principles of psychic development. We encounter then the demands of reality, translated into social demands; the gap between the fundamental desire and the attraction to objects (substitutes for *das Ding*) is moderated by sublimation—"thus, the most general formula that I can give you of sublimation is the following: it raises an object . . . to the dignity of the Thing" (Lacan 1992, p. 112). The Thing itself is always veiled; it can only be circled or bypassed, never reached. The object is always derivative, always refound, even though we never knew it was lost and know it only as represented by something else. Only in this way does the object and the signifier come together. All created derivatives of the Thing belong to sublimation, while the Thing itself can only be represented by emptiness. All forms of religion are devoted to avoiding this emptiness.

Without venturing further into the opacities of the lacanian metaphysics of language, this view of rudimentary motivational dispositions posits desire more as a constant inherently unfulfillable state of need. Whatever the implication and meaningfulness of this concept of desire, it seems to depart substantially from the original freudian notion, and brings into focus more profoundly existential concerns having greater relevance to philosophical understanding of man's nature than a more restrictive psychoanalytic account. The extent to which identifiable psychoanalytically relevant desires remain linked to such a primitive and fundamental desire remains an open question. The lacanian view of the infantile root of desire provides almost a mirror image to the kleinian view of primal destructiveness in the paranoid-schizoid position. It strikes me as just as questionable to locate the root of all desire in the primal desire for the unreachable incestuous object as to derive all aggression and sadism from the primal destructiveness of the death instinct.

From the perspective of clinical experience, it seems more satisfying to view desires pertinent to analytic concerns as assuming various forms and functions within differentiating contexts. If desire is to serve as a motivating principle, it must be highly diversified and heterogeneous. We must decide whether it is a single, unitary, primary, originating principle, or whether it consists of multiple, multifaceted, and highly diversified forms that may effectively stand on their own. In the former instance, the argument would require demonstration of the connecting links between the primal desire, however conceived, and particular specific contextual desires. Within a lacanian framework, we would have to demonstrate the connection between, for example, the desire to pass an examination or to consume a plump red apple and the primal desire to possess the mother. If the symbolic connection between apples and breasts might facilitate this task, we would still have to substantiate the claim that such a meaningful connection was in fact operative. The theoretical symbolic equation does not demonstrate the fact. The desire (wish) of the student to pass the examination may be more meaningfully related to complex ambitions and wishes to master certain material, accomplish certain goals, gain some form of recognition, achieve a level of accomplishment and earning capacity, and so on. Motivational concerns, in other words, may be more relevant to particular goals and purposes related to the exercise of cognitive capacities than to a primordial state of infantile desire. Even eating the apple may have more to do with the wish to satiate hunger pangs or even to enjoy the taste and flavor of a delicious fruit.[15] As an explanatory account of this piece of behavior no more is required; the effort to extend the analysis to infantile derivatives may accomplish little more than strain credibility. This touches on David Rapaport's (1960) complaint that the appeal to instinctual motivations had overreached itself.

I would argue instead that every constituent subsystem, capacity, functional process, and structural component of the psychological apparatus can be connected to goals and purposes specific to its nature and capacity. Setting goals and directing effort to achieving such objectives is actualized through organization of motivational states. The intellective capacity of the human mind, for example, has goals and purposes suited to its nature. Learning, development of communicative skills, mastery of complex tasks, development of linguistic competence, development of economically valuable and work related skills, development and expression of talents, development of meaningful relationships, seeking and finding love and intimacy, and so on, constitute goals and purposes appropriate to the intellective aspect of the mind. The list could be expanded, but my point is that these relatively specific objectives have validity and motivational impact on their own without appeal to any infantile or primal motivational state. The potential linkages to other levels and contexts of motivation remain open to exploration: it may turn out that some part of the student's motivation to study intensively and do well on the examination is related to wishes to please his mother and to gain her recognition and acceptance. This additional component would point our attention to other dimensions of complex motivational states as aspects of the overdetermination of behavior—readily recognizable in terms of oedipal dynamics—but the added dimension does not replace or invalidate the former intentionality. The analytic perspective thrives on the potential for the analytic process to unearth hidden, usually unconscious, components of motivation, but we should not lose sight of the fact that such unconscious motives are codeterminants of behavior and, however useful or important for clinical understanding, they are not the sole motivational components, and often not the most important. The range of variation in motivational considerations is wide and complex.

Desire vs. drive. This consideration puts the meaning of "desire" and its congener "wish" in a somewhat different light. Instead of arising from a source providing a push *a tergo* as in classical drive theory, motivational states, in functional adults, arise from the setting of goals, the implementation of purposes, the translations of hopes and ambitions into effective action, and so on. Motivational determinants lie in the contexts and circumstances within which the organism operates. The athlete gifted with certain locomotor and coordinative talents may ambition becoming a star in the NBA and earning millions of dollars in the process. This goal motivates him to train, practice, and develop his skills to the maximum. Fundamental to his motivational state is his desire to achieve not only certain immediate objectives (learning to shoot a jump shot) but long-term goals. The desire for wealth and status may carry its own validity; it may also be overdetermined by other related wishes—to prove he can achieve a greater status and earning power than his father, for example. Both motivational components can be understood and explained on their own terms without appeal to infantile or instinctual motivations. The circumstances and contexts for both contributing motivations may be sufficient to understand their effects. The appeal of power and wealth in a consumer society in which affluence is highly valued, especially for a poor boy whose family could barely eke out a minimal existence, has a high valence.

Even the obviously oedipal competition with the father can be recast in terms of developmental needs for self-assertion, self-validation, and parental recognition and acceptance. The circumstances of parental relationship and involvement can stimulate fundamental desires for love and acceptance without appealing to a libidinal drive; and by the same token issues of competence, independence, and competition can be rendered intelligible without appeal to an aggressive drive. Needs for love, acceptance, and recognition are endemic to the human condition, but the eliciting of such needs and their engagement in a motivational state need not be determined by a drive pushing from the rear, but can be activated and elicited just as meaningfully by the conditions and context of relationships and mutual involvement with significant others. In other words, the same dynamic issues and concerns addressed by the classic theory in terms of drive-derivatives can be addressed in motivational terms related to goals and purposes without any linkage to drive considerations (Rizzuto et al., in process). Action directed toward achieving such goals and purposes does not require any drive force for their accomplishment, but only activation of the capacities of the self-as-agent (Meissner 1993).

Given the primitive state of infantile dependence, the conjunction of survival needs of the infantile organism with nurturant and ministering functions of the maternal object can give rise to forms of attachment, anaclitic dependence, and mutual cuing and responsiveness characterizing the infantile mother-child symbiosis. Stimulus conditions for this complex interaction are not only hunger or elimination needs, but more fundamental needs for response, mutuality, empathic resonance and attunement, qualities that transcend the merely physiological and that have a prepotent impact on the course of psychological development. Here again, the pleasure-unpleasure principle holds sway, but not necessarily as the expression of a libidinal drive (Meissner 1995b). Along the same line, Michael Basch (1979) commented:

> Affective reaction provides inherent basic controls for adaptation by placing a qualitative value on percepts thereby providing the motivation for goal seeking behavior. The interaction and union of ever more complex sensorimotor schemata guided by the affective tone of past experience, results in a network of error correcting feedback cycles which are perfectly adequate for the infant's needs and, most important from the psychoanalytic point of view, explain how it is possible to permanently embody a record of an infant's affective/behavioral transactions before recall or reflection is a possibility. (p. 16)

Sexual desire and sexual drive. Because sexual needs and desires assume such central import for psychoanalytic understanding, the distinction between sexual drive and sexual desire requires clarification. Sexuality is part and parcel of the human organism, both physically and psychically. This includes sexual needs and desires as inherent qualities of sexual existence. The desire for sexual expression results from possession of sexual capacities involving men and women in object relations, family relations, life commitments, and in a host of other meaningful involvements that are contextualized by social and cultural conventions. Sexuality is not simply a matter of operating one's genitals, but involves the full range of complexity of human relational potential. Sexuality, then, involves issues of self-expression, self-fulfillment, achievement of meaningful human relationships, and a variety of social involvements and interactions. Sexuality is thus expressive of profound and meaningful human needs and values on a variety of levels that extend well beyond genital satisfaction. Genitality connotes much more than genital proficiency. Consequently, adult love relations involve a good deal more, and cannot be reduced to the vicissitudes of libido: sex is a matter of need basic to the human condition, but love is a matter of desire extending beyond sex to the level of human relationship and satisfaction of needs for love and affection transcending the biological and physiological.

Consequently, consideration of issues related to sexuality cannot be confined to questions of drive integration or competence. But expression and contextualization of sexual desire differs from individual to individual. The anaclitic model proposed by Freud (1905c) takes the infant sucking at the mother's breast as the original model for sexual satisfaction. However, the infant's need-state creates a motivational state marked by desire for the mother's breast and satisfaction of the hunger need accordingly. Later sexual attraction in this view is a recapitulation, in which "the finding of an object is in fact a refinding" (p. 222). An analogous argument can be made for narcissistic object-choice. But there is nothing in all this that speaks to the existence of a sexual drive. Needs and desires, yes! drive, no! In this revised perspective, nothing of the complexity and variety of sexual experience is omitted, but none of it requires or suffers any softening of explanatory power by looking to motivational factors rather than to drive-derivatives.

However, the quality of the sexual need-state varies considerably from individual to individual, and stimulus conditions and contexts providing fulfillment or satisfaction vary accordingly. If, for one individual, a sexual need is of such intensity and is experienced so peremptorily that he must seek immediate gratification, he might masturbate; or he might go out on the prowl to engage in a one-night stand; or depending on the motivational terms and regulatory capacities built into his self-system (or lack thereof), he might commit rape. For someone else, ordinary forms of sexual experience may not satisfy the need and may carry a burden of meanings and associations (largely unconscious) impeding normal sexual satisfaction, causing him to seek it in other forms—in perversion or same-sex objects. Yet another individual would find such forms of gratification repulsive and totally unsatisfying, and direct his efforts to seeking a meaningful and loving heterosexual object relationship that would offer the possibility for a caring, mutual relationship, mutual gratification, commitment, fidelity, and an enduring relationship. The quality of the motivational conditions would differ radically among them.

Drive vs. Capacity

These considerations give rise to a chicken-and-egg dilemma that plagued freudian metapsychology, Which comes first, drive or wish? In Freud's approach, motive force takes precedence over motive (purposive) aim. But, even within that theory, it is also possible for aims to precede and actualize drive components. Do sensual aims, for example, result from pressure of the sexual drive on the mental apparatus, or might we think of drive more as a capacity activated by appropriate and specific stimulus conditions—so that stimulus and reactive wish create the conditions of activation of behavior? Drives in such a schema would not be sources of constant striving and pressure on the mental apparatus as conceived in Freud's model, but potential capacities for action put in operation only under certain stimulating conditions and contexts. With regard to this division between the primacy of drives versus motives, Allan Rosenblatt and James Thickstun (1970) observed, "This division implies a distinction between energy 'using' the organism and the organism 'using' the energy, which may be related to the contrasting views of the organism as instinct-dominated and relatively passive versus a more active organism directed by an ego with relatively autonomous functions" (p. 268).[16] The former option forecloses on any autonomy or independence of volitional or self-determining processes; the latter leaves that possibility open. This organism in the latter view directs the action and is not driven by it.[17]

The latter schema would shift the accent to stimulus qualities and contexts requiring cognitive evaluation and assessment, and on the inherent meaning of the stimulus complex—all of which are basically cognitive and informational (Klein 1967; Rosenblatt and Thickstun 1977a)—rather than on drive energics. The drives would no longer function as forces driving the psychic apparatus from below or behind, but rather as capacities of the self that can be elicited and triggered into action and direction by appropriate stimulating conditions in relation to motivational states, thus providing the necessary conditions for effective functioning. Libido and aggression would thus take the form of specific motivational determinants or potentials capable of being drawn into activity by specific stimulus conditions; the conditions for such capacity activation extend beyond activation of specific psychic functions to involve potentially any psychic structure. The energy of these capacities and their functions is understood as potential for action, responsive to specific forms of motivation, libidinal or aggressive (Compton 1983; Knapp 1966; Meissner 1995a). Libidinal capacities would operate only in contexts of libidinal arousal and interest; aggression only in circumstances calling for overcoming of an obstacle (Buie et al. 1983; Meissner 1991a; Meissner et al. 1987; Rizzuto et al. 1993, Rizzuto et al., in process). Other models may prove to be more homologous with current understanding of central nervous system functioning. The crucial component, then, would be qualitative meaning of the stimulus rather than merely the quantity of energy release or tension reduction (Klein 1967). These formulations are entirely consistent with Magda Arnold's (1960) emphasis on "appraisal" or Silvan Tomkins' (1962, 1970) view of motivational feedback.

Thinking in these terms tends to drive a wedge between the concepts of drive and wish, so that we no longer need to think of drives as the only source of unconscious wishes. Wishes may operate on other grounds—

undoing or avoiding narcissistic injury, or wishful fantasies driven by anxiety, shame, or guilt. This also opens the door to wishes based on other than libidinal or aggressive motivations—curiosity, incentive motivation, effectance, and competence (White 1963). White has argued, anticipating some of the more recent developmental findings (Stern 1985), that the infant's engagement in the environment is clearest when instinctual motives are quiescent, so that such ego motives may be regarded as independent of the instinctual.[18]

The tension in Freud's thinking reflects problems inherent in his failure to deal with issues related to subjectivity and agency (Meissner 1993), and his resort to neurophysiological mechanisms to explain psychic action. This point has also been addressed by Moran (1993): "The definitions of wish and will provide clear evidence of the lack of an assumed human subject who has at times to come to terms with will versus counter-will in day-to-day life—that is, a subject who wills and wishes, not a neurophysiological apparatus" (p. 35). By the same token, this argument also draws the line of differentiation between motives as causal and as noncausal quite definitively.

CHAPTER FOUR

Volition and Will

THE PROBLEM

Our conclusions regarding psychic determinism, its relation to issues of causality, and the universality of the principle of determinism in psychic acts, led to questions regarding motivational variants. Certain motives correspond to the level of man's intellective[1] capacity and function. Matters of intellective motivation and appetition, along with functions of deciding or choosing, have traditionally been ascribed to the "will." What meaning, then, might "will" have in psychoanalytic terms and what functions does it serve in the psychic economy? What relation does it have to the sources and patterns of motivation we have been discussing? I will argue that the will is that function of ego (therefore of self) accounting for the decision process and translation of the final judgment of practical reason and choice into action. In other words, once the mind has reached a determination of what it believes to be right or wrong, it falls to the will, in virtue of its executive capacity, to put the intention into action.

The will has not enjoyed a very significant place in the analytic lexicon, although it does pop up here and there. The lack of systematic development of the concept requires that we explore it in sufficient depth to justify its central place as a functional dimension of the ethical agent.[2] And, of course, we are not interested in such questions as a matter of abstract philosophical reflection, but our interest remains focused in psychoanalytic terms. If the term *will* carries any meaning, if it can be attributed meaningful psychic functions, they must be formulated in terms of relevance to psychoanalytic concerns and issues and in terms conveying psychoanalytically relevant meaning.[3]

73

THE WILL IN PSYCHOANALYSIS

Will in Freud

In the framework of nineteenth-century concepts regarding human nature, it was assumed that the mind no less than the body was a natural living phenomenon. Freud charted the psychological development of the mind from phase to phase of its emerging complexity like any natural object, say a plant or sea urchin. Consequently, the implications of the past in the present and the fundamental unifying thread of desire were inevitable features of his thinking. The conviction prevailed that the mind possessed inherent natural desire-like forces comparable to those in the physical realm.

Such forces were loosely associated with "will." Will can be conceived either as an impulsive urge to act or as a kind of striving, but in either case this can lead to a view of will as a form of psychic force exerted both *on* (impulse) and *by* (striving) the individual, the latter deriving from the former. But the will in either sense was a self-affirming capacity reflecting the individual personality with all of its distinctive beliefs, desires, hopes, and values (O'Shaughnessy 1980). In Freud's formulation, the transition from desire to act was initiated by a kind of impulse that seemed at least analogous to a force: it seemed quantitatively variable, produced an effect, and led directly to the willed act without any representational mediation. The translation of these features to a model based on forces in the mind was easy to make, as Freud did. But both cause and effect here are psychic events, and the cause is not a separate agency acting on a separate mind or will—it is not the will that feels impelled to act, but the person; it is not the mind that acts but the person in virtue of his mental capacity for agency (Meissner 1993).[4]

The term *will* appears in Freud's writings, but only incidentally and never with any theoretical articulation. A core dimension of his theory was that there were not only life-enhancing psychic forces, but equally profound and natural destructive and self-destructive forces in the mind, culminating in the death instinct of 1920. The existence of contradictory forces in the mind—what Arthur Schopenhauer called the "variance of will with itself"—disrupted the smooth harmonization of nineteenth-century romanticism and idealism and accounted for a radical refocusing of the concept of will. Despite his early referral to a "counterwill" in the genesis of hysterical symptoms, Freud generally regarded unconscious derivatives as "involuntary"—as in the repressed thoughts responsible for obsessional symptoms (1909c).

However, the normal mature adult had the capacity for reasonable and realistic decision-making and for acceptance of moral responsibility—

capacities we would usually attribute to "will." One important goal of therapy, as he saw it, was to enable the patient to become aware of unconscious and conscious reasons for his actions, so that analysis "does not set out to make pathological reactions impossible, but to give the patient's ego *freedom* to decide one way or the other" (Freud 1923a, p. 50, italics in original). But Freud was not especially interested in the dynamics of consciousness, including issues related to the will and freedom; he regarded these as the business of philosophers, whereas exploration of the unknown frontier of the unconscious was the task of analysis. Thus, while the concept of the will was by no means alien to Freud's thought, it served as a recurrent idea in his conceptual lexicon, albeit without a systematized place among analytic concepts. He referred quite specifically to "conscious willpower" (1905b, p. 266) governing conscious processes as opposed to mental compulsions deriving from the unconscious. We would have to conclude that Freud more-or-less assumed a concept of will, taken as the capacity for choosing among possible alternatives, which loosely fell within the province of the conscious ego, but never found it necessary to probe further into its mysteries.

Postfreudian Views

That did not prevent his successors from trying their hand at elucidating the will and its functions. Flugel (1945) emphasized the distinction between instinctual forces and their derivatives and capacities for instinctual restraint and control of appetite encapsulated in concepts of conscience and will. He saw the will act as the highest achievement of moral life, but also as subject to ambivalent conflicts; the necessity for deliberation made it unsuited to more immediate action demands of everyday life. More routinized dispositions, such as habits or "determining tendencies," were more often called into play. But the capacity for deliberation and moral choice enabled man to live a moral life in accord with moral values. Will was essentially the capacity for moral decision-making, echoing Freud's fragmentary views.

Among analysts who recognized will as a legitimate function, reliance on earlier versions of psychic determinism dictated exclusion of a notion of the will as self-determining, certainly on any absolute terms. For Erich Fromm, moral character was shaped early in life by influences over which the individual had little control—genetics, early environmental influences, parental interactions, and so on. Consequently, any theory of will as absolutely autonomous, having control over actions regardless of determining external conditions, would be inadmissible. The alternative was not fatalism, since reason enables man to understand these determining forces, adapt to them, and chose among available alternatives a path leading to greater productivity. Fromm (1947) thus rejected both any extreme version of free will and hard determinism. Freedom lay in knowing the real possibilities offering potential for choice and distinguishing them from unreal options. Such choice is both intellectual and emotional, and must often run the gauntlet of opposing or conflicting desires and wishes. This can challenge the strength of the will, but ultimately that choice is real and also responsible—the moral challenge is to answer for one's choices and to pay whatever price is entailed in making them. And in turn, lack of such spontaneity is a defect that may be socially or culturally sustained, as in the example of Calvinism, but even so remains an obstacle to achieving fuller realization of individual potential and maturity.

Rollo May (1969) staked a strong claim for the connection between will and the capacity to love—both described movement of the person into the world, to engage, embrace, relate, affect, and be affected—the opposite of schizoid withdrawal or apathy. As May saw it, Freud's assault on Victorian "willpower," displacing conscious willing by unconscious drives and wishes, had the unfortunate effect of undermining the role of will and decision, and with them the sense of individual responsibility. He pointed to a critical problem regarding the role of will in a psychoanalytic perspective: "Neither the ego nor the body nor the unconscious can be 'autonomous,' but can only exist as parts of a totality. And it is in this totality that will and freedom must have their base. I am convinced that the compartmentalization of the personality into ego, superego, and id is an important part of the reason why the problem of will has remained insoluble within the orthodox psychoanalytic tradition" (p. 199).

May (1969) tried to carve an independent path between the extremes of *willpower* on one hand and *free will* on the other, both misleading terms in that they seemed to withdraw exercise of the will from effective motivation and causality. He offered a definition of will as "*the capacity to organize one's self* so that movement in a certain direction or toward a certain goal may take place" (p. 218, italics in original). He contrasted this with wish as "*the imaginative playing with the possibility* of some act or state occurring" (p. 218, italics in original). Despite their contrasting characteristics—conscious versus unconscious, possibility of choice versus none, self-determination (control) versus other-determination, and so on—they were, far from being incompatible, more like polarities lending mutual support and reinforcement to each other. Wish offered color, imagination, fantasy, possibility, richness and playfulness to will; will gave direction and maturity to wish; will, with one eye on reality, protected and guided wish, keeping it from running needless risk. In May's terms, "If you have only 'will' and no 'wish,' you have the dried-up, Victorian, neopuritan man. If you have only 'wish' and no 'will,' you have the driven, unfree, infantile person who, as an adult-remaining-an-infant, may become the robot man" (p. 218).[5]

WISH VS. WILL

Recasting the metapsychology of action and motivation in terms of the self-as-agent (Meissner 1993) envisions the self as the relatively autonomous source of agency acting in relation to motivational influences shaping the course, direction, meaning, and purpose of psychic acts. In Freud's early model of motivation, the wish, as expressive of drive-determined forces, played the dominant role as the only force capable of setting the mental apparatus in motion. This model, with its insistence on hard determinism, created tension with the concept of the will, as the capacity to spontaneously initiate action in the line of presumably self-directive behavior. In his earliest account of hysteria, Freud regarded symptoms as beyond the scope of conscious control yet postulated a form of "counterwill" as part of his explanation.[6] The question had to do with whether the will was self-determining and therefore free, in the sense of choosing between alternative nonnecessary alternatives, or whether the choosing itself was determined and in what sense. To the extent that wishes found expression unconsciously in symptoms or consciously as conflictual, they could act as a form of counterwill.

We can hear echoes of William James's (1890) account of wishing and willing. He contrasted wish and will—the wish is an expression of sheer desire without any intention or hope of fulfillment, a mere velleity. If the desire is without promise of fulfillment, we go no further than the wish itself. But the will adds the prospect of fulfillment. James made his own distinction as to forms of willing—the first is simple and straightforward; we decide to do something that is neither complex nor conflictual, or at least minimally so—I decide to stop writing and get a cup of coffee. Other decision processes are more complex and require further operations of concentration, well-ordered motives, and weighing of alternatives, and finally a decision is made and a choice leading to action. The process sounds simple enough, but complications can arise from many sources, for instance, from affects it may arouse or from related conflicts. In contrast to a healthy will, there can be an unhealthy will, an "obstructed will" as James called it. The necessary attention is subverted by distractions, interference of other thought processes, or even fatigue, or in more extreme forms apathy or even abulia.

But wish and will are not necessarily set in opposition—rather we might well argue that if there is no wish there is no will. If my wish is non-conflictual and ego-syntonic, there is no reason for me not to accept that degree of satisfaction and fulfillment. If the wish, however, is conflictual and ego-dystonic, that is a different matter. There was a tendency to view action of the will as somehow undetermined, as though choosing were somehow removed from, or independent of, any motivation. Rather choosing itself is motivated and thus determined. The role of the will as expressing the inherent relatively autonomous capacity of the agent to determine its own course of action implies only that the wish, conflictual or not, syntonic or not, does not cause the self-determining action or choice, but does motivate it. The choice of the autonomous will is made in the context of stimulus conditions and contexts, in the light of reasons for or against, and is directed toward purposive intentions and objectives—in other words within the full context of motivational considerations. This is what constitutes the essence of the concept of freedom of the will.

WILL AND THERAPY

Despite the singing of such voices *extra choram,* the will has found little place in psychoanalytic therapy. One noteworthy exception, of course, is Otto Rank's brand of time-limited rebirth-oriented therapy based on the dialectic between dependence and separation. In Rank's view, movement from dependence to separation (individuation) involved self-assertion requiring an act of will. Rank was critical of Freud's neglect of the will and of Alfred Adler's will-to-power, but Rank's (1936) own view of will remained obscure. Adler had broken with Freud over the issue of making libido the source of all potential for action in psychic life, and opted for a modified nietzschean motif, the "will-to-power," as a dynamic source of human creative potential. Rank insisted on assertion of a "positive will" as essential to successful therapy, probably equivalent to making an effort, desiring and striving for control of impulses, and commitment to certain goals or ideals. Will for Rank was essentially the capacity to control and regulate drives and a source of motivational power to seek growth, maturity, and the integration of personality. Unfortunately, this approach tended to bypass painstaking exploration of the patient's inner world and the often extensive search for inner meaning and development of insight in favor of an intensified relation to the therapist that brought issues of union versus separation to a head. This rankian act of will seems to have been an exercise of willpower (negative will assertion) by which the patient declared his or her independence of the therapist in order to take a more adult and mature stance vis-à-vis the world.

Rank's views were sufficiently divergent from mainline analytic thinking to prevent any significant integration, but similar themes found their echo in analytic circles nonetheless. Wheelis's (1956) summarizing article is a case in point. His dissatisfaction stemmed from the frustration of cases in which interpretation and insight seemed to run out of gas and a push was required, from patient or analyst, in order to bring about any change, especially in character. But such volitional interventions were criticized as unanalytic, reflecting the analyst's inability to analyze more skillfully. But, he asked, Is there a place for such volitions in analysis, and, if so, what are they?

An analytically meaningful sense of "will" must steer a path between extreme versions of willpower on one hand and free will on the other. One cannot will one's way out of neurotic misery.[7] But, as Wheelis (1956) observed cryptically, "Knowledgeable moderns put their backs to the couch, and in so doing may fail occasionally to put their shoulders to the wheel. As will has been devalued, so has courage; for courage can exist only in the service of will, and can hardly be valued higher than that which it serves. In our understanding of human nature, we have gained determinism, lost determination" (p. 289). In this sense, will is a capacity or strength, after the fashion of "ego strengths," so that a strong will comes to mean not just the strength of desires, but the capacity to engender, sustain, and implement such desires for realistic purposes and objectives, whether personal or social.[8]

But, Wheelis (1956) argued, character change sought in analysis called for an act of will—"experienced as effort, determination, tenacity, or perseverance—reinforcing the motivation toward the indicated action" (p. 291). This may sound like a parroting of Rank's insistence on will for therapeutic change, but Wheelis viewed will as a capacity to move beyond mere intentionality to effective resolution of conflict and goal-achievement. Will was thus a product of conflict and drive-motivated—equivalent to the ego sanctioning and reinforcing a drive vector. Under ordinary circumstances, then, insight can be mutative, but when conflict is sustained and despite ample opportunity and capacity there is no movement, the therapeutic balance may shift to the will as the relevant factor. Optimally insight and will work together—action of the will is guided by valid insight. By the same token, will guided by misleading or fallacious understanding, can go astray. But when understanding achieved an insight making possible formulation of a goal resulting in reconciliation of conflicting needs, the way was opened to consideration of available means and their adoption as intermediate ends. Valid insight carried with it the understanding that "never can a compromise goal promise full gratification of opposing needs; something of each must be renounced. This renunciation, quite apart from the inertia with which character resists change, adds another force which opposes the compromise goal. Will, which is the ego-reinforcement of the vector drive, may be just enough to swing the balance" (p. 295).

Psychoanalysts have tended to view the effective exercise of will as the privilege only of the healthy, denied to neurotics because of their immersion in conflict—as Wheelis (1956) put it, "the experience of considering major alternatives, of choosing with a sense of inner freedom, of applying one's will to the selected course of action, and of translating the aspiration into reality is not possible for the neurotic because his energies are bound up in conflict" (p. 297). The only recourse was through analytically generated insight, but this assessment essentially overvalued insight at the expense of the will. This not only contributed to a false picture of the neurotic will, but did not take into account that will might play a role in the patient's capacity to achieve insight—he might even choose analysis as a suitable means to accomplishing this goal.

By the same token, the will can be put to serve neurotic needs, and may function in analysis to reinforce repression or reaction formation, even to impede development of a transference neurosis or therapeutic alliance. And there is the possibility that development of insight may in some cases interfere with and forestall will action and impede execution of insight in real terms. Given that both terms can serve the interests of resistance and avoidance of change, and that both patient and analyst can easily collude in such a misalliance, the possibility remains open that they can both also serve the purposes of the analytic process. As Wheelis (1956) put it:

> But will, as such, is not opposed to analysis. There can be no quarrel between insight and effort. They may be distinguished from each other, and in any specific situation one or the other may be more relevant. But there can be no question of which is the more important. Insight without action is impotent; action without insight is chaotic. Together they form a whole; separately they are nothing. They belong together as do thinking and doing, means and ends. When a patient disparages insight and wishes to rely on "will power" he is making an untenable separation; when an analyst elevates insight and disparages will he mirrors the same error. (p. 301)

In effect, the concept of *will* is not entirely foreign to analytic usage, but the meanings attached to the term and integration of the concept into a meaningful analytic theoretical framework remain rudimentary, if not unclear. The predominant view seems to regard will as a capacity of the ego to translate desire or wish into action. Another view sees will as the capacity to love (May 1969). How these views are related, and in what terms they can be brought into conjunction are questions requiring further elaboration.

WILL IN THE LIGHT OF PHILOSOPHY

When we open the philosophy books, we find several meanings for the term *will*, the major categories being will as intellectual preference, as rational appetite, as synonymous with free choice, as dynamic power, and as affection or love (Bourke 1964).[9] Briefly, as intellective preference willing involves a judgment, a form of practical reason.[10] As rational appetite, the will was a capacity or desire tending toward objects seen as intellectually good and away from those seen as bad.[11] Those favoring will as dynamic power place volition in the line of efficient causality: for David Hume will was synonymous with effort, and with development of associationism spontaneity (the sense of having the power to control bodily movements) became primary, making will a kind of executive capacity rather than a knowing or feeling one. The view of will as affection made the capacity to love a special function of will, often portraying it in terms of affects associated metaphorically with the "heart."[12] We might question the extent to which these perspectives hold validity for a psychoanalytic concept of will.

Will as intellective preference. The view of will as a form of intellective choosing, that is, selecting one possible object or alternative course of action in preference to others, has ancient and honorable origins. The socratic view thought that knowing the good was automatically translated into choosing and acting accordingly. For Plato, acts of willing were attributed to the rational part of the psyche, and distinct from acts of appetite or desire deriving from lower parts of the psyche, not from reason. Aristotle argued that the act of choosing required a practical cognitive judgment. In the thirteenth and fourteenth centuries, some Christian thinkers would claim the will to be an active power not influenced by any other natural cause, while others adopted a more intellectualist position that the will was basically passive and under the influence of intellect by which possible options were decided.

Among modern philosophers, Thomas Hobbes thought of will as the last act terminating the process of deliberation, thus a form of thinking. John Locke referred repeatedly to willed choice as "preference," regarding will as simply the power of the mind to make choices. Benedict Spinoza equated willing with intellectual preference, a form of intellectual judgment making willing and judging synonymous. Immanuel Kant, in turn, equated rational will with practical reason, that is, acting according to reason, principles, laws, and as such central in the categorical imperative. Kant's effort to retain the will as the principle of moral action was purchased at the expense of expanding will to include many of the functions appetitive theorists would have assigned to the intellect. Finally, with the emergence of American pragmatism, cognition and volition seemed to coalesce. Most pragmatists see little difference between a preferential judgment and a volitional decision to pursue a certain course of action. Rather than willing becoming a cognitive function, knowing has become a volitional activity closely connecting willing with intelligent decision. The theme runs through William James, Josiah Royce, and John Dewey.

Would psychoanalysis find the view of willing as intellectual preference palatable? The answer, as far as I can see, may have to be ambiguous. The role and scope of determining factors plays a role here. When all is said and done, at the end of the chain of determining events, is there room for that which is possible and nonnecessary as the object of choice? What options can there be in a world of necessity? If causal factors like constitution, heredity, history, and unconscious determinants play their respective roles, can such possibilities really be valid options? Even after the deliberative events—acknowledgment of options and consequences, deliberation over alternatives, and finally choice—we might conclude that, given these antecedent conditions, the choice could not have been otherwise. Does choice become an illusion? But even so, if there is a sense of genuine possibility (open to more than one alternative), and we choose to see it as an illusion (as many do!), we would have to regard it as an illusion that is "necessary for the adaptive, socialized, and moral behavior of many or most individuals" (Wallace 1986a, p. 944).

I would relate this issue to the problem of insight and action in analysis. The older view of intellective insight as determinative and mutative in the analytic process might lean toward the intellective side, but even that view was never totally intellectualist in emphasis. There was always much discussion of other contributing factors besides the cognitive that accounted for the impact of authentic insight. There was enough evidence from clinical experience to substantiate the claim that insight could be mutative, but only within limits. Insight did not occur in a vacuum, but evolved out of a complex process involving the quality of relationship between analysand and analyst. Early theorists appealed to vicissitudes of transference, particularly positive transference by which it was thought the analysand became receptive to the analyst's interpretations and was thus drawn to the threshold of insight and change. The classic statement of James Strachey (1934) articulated this approach with special emphasis on the role of superego dynamics in the transference as providing the conditions and driving force behind mutative interpretation effecting change and therapeutic results.[13]

But these were emotional factors, not intellectual. Accordingly, little was said about volitional factors—it was thought that volition had been subsumed, or assumed, in the combination of affective and intellective elements composing insight and therapeutic change. Even in the most current revisions of the dynamics of therapeutic interaction, emphasis falls less on interpretation and more on the interaction between analyst and analysand, including transference-countertransference interactions and enactments on one hand, aspects of the real relationship and its transactions on another, and dimensions of the therapeutic alliance on still another (Meissner 1996b). Among these approaches, therapeutic alliance comes closest to incorporating volitional factors insofar as it requires a degree of community of motivation, collaboration, effort, and will on the part of both analyst and analysand, factors that operate beyond the range of transference and instinctual dynamics. At the same time, contemporary formulations of therapeutic effects tend to stake their claim less on the efficacy of interpretation and more on personal and relational components (Meissner 1991b).

Will as rational appetite. The view of will as appetitive resonates with the motivational theory specifying proportional dynamic factors for all psychic functions and levels of psychic structure (Meissner 1999a,b). The dynamic principle embraces psychic activity at all levels, rational or intellective as well as irrational and instinctual.[14] In this sense, will would connote an appetite by which the subject could desire and be drawn toward objects apprehended intellectually as good and away from objects apprehended as evil; this appetitive function of the will is a form of intellective desire. In this schema, intellect is activated by sensory experience and achieves an understanding of reality through complex processes of abstraction and reasoning. Acts of will are elicited and directed by concomitant acts of intellective cognition: the intellect does not work in the line of efficient causality causing the will to act, but rather in knowing that the object sets the stage for the will to be attracted to, desire, and seek to attain the object or to be repelled, disdain, and avoid the object. Will cannot act without some understanding of the object, but volition and cognition are different acts operating in distinct spheres of activity.

Most theorists would also draw a line between intellective appetition and sensory desires and pleasures. As an intellective appetite, will is directed to intellectual goods understood in terms of general or abstract principles (ideas rather than sensory perceptions)—for example, the sensory appetite, driven by hunger needs, might desire a juicy red apple, but intellectually at the same time the individual might be motivated by the good understood in terms of the nutritive value of the apple and the vitamins and minerals it provided. Thus sensory and intellectual motives can operate simultaneously, either congruently or in opposition. Clearly the motivational theory encompassing the theory of will as appetite is complex and leaves room for intertwining of conscious and unconscious motives. But the distinguishing note is that the will does not act simply as efficient cause of an action, but as drawn to an end presented as a good to be attained or an evil to be avoided. Not many modern thinkers talk this way, largely because the role of final causes has been obliterated in favor of efficient causality. Most modern thinkers equate agency with efficient causality producing effects.

In a sense, desire has an internal relation with action, not unlike volition and action, but in different ways. The relation of willing to action is easier to see, since in most actions the connection, at least phenomenologically, is immediate. My wanting to move my hand is mediated by a series of physiological processes, but willing and acting are psychologically synchronous. Desire, however, is effected only in virtue of another act of will translating desire into action. I can see and desire the aforesaid apple, but it requires an initiative of will to move my hand to grasp it and convey it to my mouth.[15] By the same token, desire influences the will, moving it toward acting. This influence is an attraction, an apprehension of apple-as-good-and-desirable, offering promise of satisfaction and alleviation of hunger, setting the stage for will action. Desire thus apprehends the object as an end or means, as good to be sought and attained, and thus prompts the will to act—knowledge and attraction to a good in this fashion is in the order of finality, and such finality has an intrinsic linkage with the corresponding efficiency.

Still the act of will is different from the process of determining the object of the will act. The person can will or not will, can will to act or not to act, or can consider what kind of object to will. No object can necessitate an act of will; it is always possible to refrain from willing or choosing. Thus, choice results from the combined activity of both intellect and will, under the guidance of the intellectual judgment as to what is good and what not, leading the will to make a preferential decision. Such inclinations can operate without consciousness—the desire to reach a destination can influence behavior without being the object of conscious thought, presumably operating on a preconscious level. Some elicited acts of willing, deciding, or deliberating would be simply voluntary actions, while others, for instance, wanting or intending, may be more states than actions, involving complex interactions with other cognitive capacities. Deliberation, for example, both arises from, and culminates in, acts of will—desire for an end leads by way of deliberation to desire of the means; these are states, dispositions, inclinations, and attitudes, not actions. Some further determination is required to set the act in motion (Kenny 1975). Acts of will are not unmotivated; every act of will is directed to some reason or end, that is, is motivated.

The understanding of will as rational appetite contains many sympathetic resonances with psychoanalytic perspectives. From one perspective, the analytic process can be cast in terms of the progressive uncovering and discovery of layers of motive and meaning leading to gradual clarification of desirable end-states of affective regulation and adaptive and realistic ego-functioning. Apprehension and acknowledgment of meanings and the conceptual grasp of means-ends connections and implications is one expression of possible analytic insight. In terms of the theory of rational appetite, these aspects of the analytic process would be regarded as work of the intellect gaining understanding of significances and connections in the conceptual realm. When this process of discovery and increasing understanding reaches a point where concrete alternatives and specific courses of action are in focus, analytic deliberation can move to a point at which the analysand makes effective choices and begins to translate them into patterns of action representing therapeutic change. Deciding and putting into action would be functions of the will. The process of gaining prior understanding is sustained by the complex mechanisms of the analytic work—transference, alliance, free association, analysis of defenses and resistances, and so on. In this sense, will would have to be active throughout the entire process from beginning to end. Determination of ends and means comes into play at almost every step. The patient must decide whether to pursue analysis or not, whether to engage with this analyst or not, whether to say what happens to be on his mind or not, whether to accept of reject the analyst's interventions, and on and on.

While this rendition points up the congruence between this view of will and the analytic process, there are also points of potential difference. When philosophers address the rational appetite, they have in mind something conscious, if not deliberate. Some acknowledge possible interaction between intellective and sensory appetites, so that sensory desires can be at times integrated with intellectual ones. But these are regarded as separate and conscious functions. The analytic view, however, is centered more pervasively on unconscious mental processes. Analysis adds the consideration that sensory, and even intellective, appetites may operate at an unconscious level and thus may make determining contributions to the effort of conceptual understanding. Thus clearly, overdetermination of these putative intellective acts plays an important role in functioning of this intellective appetite.

Analysis may not be able to settle the case, but it at least raises the issue—are some acts of the intellect unconscious, or does the realm of the unconscious only include sensory appetites so that unconscious influences on intellectual mentation occur only as a result of sensory appetitive processes? Or, to put it in other terms, what is the relation between sensory and intellective desires? How do they interact? What role do they play in the choice of means and ends? How do we classify something like transference desire? Is it sensory, intellective, or both? Clearly, the answers are not simple, and asking the questions makes the reflection on the place of will and its relation to cognitive factors considerably more complex. It is not clear at this juncture whether the philosophical understanding of will as intellective appetite could be transplanted—lock, stock, and barrel—into analytic theory, or whether the essential understanding of will would require some degree of qualification or modification in order to meet the demands of an analytic understanding, and on what terms. In any case, the general outlines of the appetitive view seem potentially integrable in some part with analytic perspectives.

Will as dynamic power. While the view of will as appetite emphasized final causality in will action, this view accents efficient causality. Willing in this sense is an act bringing about some effect or result, and as such resonates with notions of force or energy conceived as the capacity to do work. An act of willing in these terms, therefore, differs from simple desire: willing implies that an action is enacted; mere desire does not.[16] The work being effected can be conceived in at least two forms—either as mental or psychic activity, or as physical, corporeal, or organic activity.

By implication, all human actions would be either elicited (initiated and completed by the will) or commanded (initiated by will but completed by another potency whose activity was under direction of the will). Intellect is thus reduced to a minor role. Exponents of this view (like Hobbes) of will dispense with concepts of appetite as merely metaphoric, minimizing the role of final causality and abandoning the view of will as intellective appetite, turning it into the source of efficient action.[17]

Reasons, wants, wishes, desires, and even beliefs undoubtedly influence our choices and thus our behavior. But they do not influence behavior in the line of efficient causality. If I say I typed these words because I wanted to, this does not stipulate that my wanting caused my action in any sense other than motivational. The wanting is in this sense *not* a cause of my typing, nor does it make my action voluntary. The *willing* makes the act voluntary and serves as the source of efficiency.[18] Willing reaches beyond wanting or desire to the realm of action—it involves choice and self-determination as an exercise of self-initiated agency. I do not have to appeal to any source of agency beyond myself-as-agent, which serves as the source of its own capacity to act. Thus, if the house is burning, my belief that the house is on fire can move me to act, in the sense that it elicits a purpose that can vary according to circumstance—I may want to save my own life, in which case I choose to run out of the house; I may want to save someone else in the house, in which case I may want to run into the house; or I may not care one way or the other, in which case I may just watch or à la Nero take up my fiddle.

The distinction between choices and reasons is operative here. Choice is an act of will setting the executive capacity of will in act and in initiating action. Choice as an operative component of the causal sequence must precede action. Reasons are expressions of motivational factors. The motivational factors are determining but not as causal factors—as motives, they too, along with causes, must precede the action. But they are not necessarily expressed as such—when they are contrasted as nondatable with causes as datable (Oldenquist 1967), it is as expressed reasons that they are nondatable. In an analytic exploration of the motives underlying the patient's choice or sequence of action, what is discovered and articulated are reasons for the behavior; these reasons may have been unconscious and unknown until their analytic unveiling. But the motives they express were active and influential in determining the choices and actions the patient made in the past, even though unconscious or preconscious.

We are left with the question—does the view of will as dynamic power have a place in psychoanalysis? The answer, of course, is "Yes and No." Freud was much influenced by Arthur Schopenhauer, who viewed knowledge as a servant of the will, and Freud himself thought of consciousness as developing out of and expressing the psychic forces in the mind akin to "will" in its broad sense. In clinical terms, whatever psychic process is entailed in moving analytic understanding, including self-understanding, from a condition of potentiality to actuality would entail some form of will as dynamic power in some sense. The process requires deciding and acting. The intellective process leading to understanding presents the alternatives and their meaning; the will chooses, decides, and moves to action. Understanding may be partial, incomplete, in some degree uncertain as to meaning and outcome, but in making the decision the individual breaks through the irresolution of uncertainty and indecision, and guided by whatever understanding he has acquired in terms of conscious and unconscious meanings, he moves to act. This would approach at least one analytic paradigm of therapeutic resolution and change. The will in this instance acts as the originative efficient cause pushing the self toward further action. But here the elements of choice and decision are critical; mere effort directed to overcoming obstacles and achieving goals falls more specifically under the rubric of aggressive motivation rather than simply a function of will (Buie et al. 1983, 1996; Meissner 1991a; Meissner et al. 1987; Rizzuto et al. 1993; Rizzuto, Meissner, and Buie, in process).

Will vs. drive. However, there are problems. A view of will as a source of psychic activity runs counter to the classic theory deriving the principle of action from drives. In drive theory, we have multiple sources of agency all divorced from the sense of self as originating action. All such actions are determined in the hard sense, attributing efficiency to the drives and requiring that any other form of apparent agency be derived from them. In this sense, any experience of effort, striving, or putting into action is due not to the self or will but to some modification of drive components and energies involving drive-derivation or compromise formation. Analytic theorists have struggled with this early metapsychological perspective; ego psychologists found it necessary to postulate independent ego-energies in addition to forms of neutralization and sublimation of drive components to cover this ground.

There are alternative possibilities: my response to these issues is to see the self-as-agent as the dynamic source of all activity, whether psychic or physical (Meissner 1993). The actions of the self, however, are determined in the soft sense,[19] that is, motivated by intentions, purposes, and goals toward which activity is directed and drawn. This form of agency is channeled through component subsystems of the self, each of which carries out its respective functions as synonymous with the causality of the self-as-agent. Thus, if I scratch my nose, the action originates in the self-as-agent and is mediated through complex psychic and motoric mechanisms mediated by neural connections and muscular contractions. The finality lies elsewhere and serves as the basis of motivation—I could want to relieve an itch, or I could be signaling the man on first to steal second. But the intention is never the (efficient) cause of my action—rather it gives direction and significance to my action (final cause); but the action could never take place without an additional impetus or thrust from the will as efficient cause. The mere intention to scratch my nose will not move my arm without an act of will to translate intention into action. This form of agency could include both conscious and unconscious levels of functioning, so that unconscious processing is as much due to agency of the self as conscious activity.[20] Unconscious fantasy or affect are as much functions of the self-as-agent as my writing this paragraph. In this conjunction, commenting on the connection of will with the sense of "force," Brian O'Shaughnessy (1980) observed: "Thus, this force is applied, not to *phenomena* in the mind (for it is the man, not some phenomenon, that 'feels impelled to act'), not to *the mind* itself (for it is he, not his mind, that 'feels impelled to act')—but to he himself. After all, the man and not the mind is a substance and is in any case uniquely the bearer of the phenomenon of will" (p. li, italics in original).

In any case, we have a problem. Is the will involved in all such agency or not? Can we, in the context of drive theory, claim the will as a separate or somehow derived source of agency? If it is such, is it independent of drive energies or not? In the alternate formulation of the self-as-agent, is the will the source of all such agency or not? Again the question of conscious versus unconscious comes to haunt us. Philosophical views of will-as-cause regard it as conscious—the individual knows when he is willing and when not. On these terms, willing cannot be synonymous with agency. In the classic theory, the experience of willing is generally regarded as illusory since the actual causality lies elsewhere in an unconscious instinctual source. However, if efficiency resides in the self-as-agent, some agency is unconscious and some conscious—will can be included at least in the latter category, if not also in the former. But then will is not a source of agency independently from the agency of the self—acts of willing are actions of the self acting in the conscious or unconscious decision-making modality. In this latter view, instinctual drives and drive derivatives have no place.[21] As a legitimate psychoanalytic function, will would seem to come into play both as an ideal or goal of therapy and as essential to the process. Also, it would encompass more than mere efficiency or power to act—it would also have an appetitive function of seeking the good in addition to enacting it. The troublesome question for the moment remains open as to whether the will so conceived must be confined to conscious processing, or whether it can function as well at an unconscious level, even if we regard it as an intellective function. Here analysis would challenge the philosophical presumption that intellection is always conscious and open to the possibility of unconscious intellection, comparable to unconscious mentation, desire, fantasy, and motivation. Can the mind, in fact, grasp intellectual connections, the linkage of means and ends, on a prereflective, preconscious, even unconscious level? Correspondingly, can willing, whether conceived of as appetition or inclination to action, operate even on unconscious terms?

Will as affection or love. The will, acting as an appetite, is drawn to the intellectively known good object. Such appetency, or attraction to the good, is a form of love, so that willing is associated with love—that is, loving whatever is known as good and desirable by rational intelligence. The view of will as affection or capacity to love opens a Pandora's box for psychoanalytic consideration. The tension between views of the will as elective or executive and the view of will as appetitive comes to the fore. And at another level, the question of what is meant by "love" becomes critical. At this point, I would prefer to postpone the latter discussion since the issues of the meaning of love and its congeners is central for psychoanalysis and ethics.

The line of thinking connecting will with love stems from the understanding of love as a form of appetite, desiring, seeking to possess, and valuing the other in itself. But will, so conceived, would also involve other capacities than simply intellective appetition, even in the act of loving.[22] Appraisal of the object presumably precedes the act of will, but appraisal relevant to the will is a function of intellect. The appraisal process would focus and recognize the good toward which the will is drawn in its loving response. That response involves some process of selecting, choosing, and moving the self into action with the intention of possessing the object in a loving relationship. Thus, I would argue, the act of loving is more than a simple attraction to natural good, but involves complex intellective and volitional operations called into play, if not in all love relationships, certainly in those at a more mature and mutually satisfying level. But this makes of loving states more of an ideal than is usually found in reality. Mental processes, more often than not at a subconscious or unconscious level, involving selection, appraisal, apprehension of the good qualities of the object, and so on, are often either interfered with, or complemented by, libidinal needs and desires, by unconscious wishes and infantile and instinctual urges, which can precipitate, reinforce, or inhibit or pervert the process in the myriad ways that analytic experience has discovered.

In analytic perspective, then, love is never simply a function of will as a purely intellective appetite, but is always a function of will caught up in varying degrees of amalgamation or distortion with complex layerings and varieties of appetitive desires stemming from other segments of the self-organization. Loving in this sense is overdetermined and contains many levels and dimensions of meaning and affective reverberations, including instinctual dynamics of both libidinal and aggressive kinds (Kernberg 1976). But in considering functions of the will in this complex reaction, we should not confuse affects generated in this process with functions of the will itself in its appetitive capacity, or with other nonwill appetitive functions for that matter. We are all prone to identify love with the feeling states that are usually associated with these appetitive responses, but feelings remain a distinct and different phenomenon demanding explanation and understanding on their own terms. Acts of love attributed to the will are something quite different. Despite the tendency of many philosophical views to ascribe affective functions to the will, analytic clarity is better served by keeping the affective dimension distinct. Affective usages tend to confuse motivation with both affects and acts of will, but I would suggest that there is room for distinction between motivational factors and their associated affective states (Meissner 1995c; Rizzuto, Meissner, and Buie 2003). The former would pertain to the instigation of the activity of the will, the latter not. Similarly with the idea that affects precede and stimulate the will to action—motives serve this function, not affects.

AN ATTEMPT AT SYNTHESIS

My effort here is directed to formulating a concept of will in meaningful psychoanalytic terms. Any meaningful psychoanalytic contribution to ethical thinking requires recognition of a capacity in the human organism for decision-making, choosing among means and ends, and for movement to action. These functions are essential to ethical decision-making and ethical responsibility. Hovering over these considerations, there is the additional question of freedom of the will and the role it might play in a psychoanalytic perspective, a subject meriting separate consideration.

Functions of Will

The will is first of all an intellective capacity, that is, it functions in relation to intellective understanding concerned with those aspects of experience characterized by generality, abstractness, immateriality, and meaning. This aspect of will pertains not only to appetitive functions, but also to executive functions in relation to factors of intentionality, setting of goals and purposes, and grasping means-ends connections. Although often said to be autonomous, autonomy belongs more properly to the person, to the self, and to will only as exercising the agency of the self; will has no autonomy of its own separate from that of the self (Meissner 1986c). Pursuit of self-selected goals transcending the immediate environment in spatial and temporal terms requires use of intellective symbols and involves goals and purposes extending beyond the temporal and spatial present. Moreover, the use of symbols is different from the instrumental use of tools and takes place in an order of efficiency divergent from ordinary physical causality. The mind is thereby both cognitive and volitional in character and capacity.

But, if we accept this specification of mind and will as inherently intellective, we also realize that for the most part human experience cannot be so neatly divided into intellective and sensory spheres. As intelligent beings, our experience by-and-large reflects an interpenetration of sensory and intellective components, side-by-side and intermingling. Simple sensations do not occur without some measure of intellective processing—I do not simply see an object with a wagging tail; I also know that it is a dog, a member of a certain species with certain identifiable characteristics. My fantasies may be concrete and specific, but to the extent that I am conscious of them I am also aware that I recognize the contents much like my perceptions of external objects: I recognize their content and meaning. Thus my attraction to objects of my experience as good and as objects of my desire is an amalgam of sensory and intellective components. In analytic terms, objects of my desire can involve both instinctual (concrete sensual) and volitional (intellective) motives.

Will and desire. This understanding would suggest that will is involved in complex ways in most, if not all, situations of attraction to and/or desire of whatever presents itself as good. Insofar as analysis would contend that it is possible for these processes to take place beyond the range of conscious mental processing and awareness, analysis would diverge from most philosophical accounts of the will, since by and large the notion of will as intellective appetite presumes that intellective activity is also conscious. But analysis has discovered that a good deal—perhaps even most—of mental processing goes on at a less-than-conscious level. If so, we need also remind ourselves that analysis has also learned that the quality and organization of mental processes can differ from level to level of psychic organization. As formulated here, the will would function primarily in secondary process terms, but never as completely divorced from, or uninfluenced by, other appetitive desires coming from other more primary process levels.

By implication, then, action of the will can find itself in congruence with, or in opposition to, wishes or desires generated at other levels of the psyche. This is the kernel of truth at the core of Freud's understanding of conflict. Acts of will are, like all psychic acts, motivated, that is guided, drawn, attracted, in the order of finality and intentionality, by objects of desire or wish. The translation of wishes into action in its optimal ethical trajectory follows a process of assessment, appraisal, and integration with demands of reality as processed by practical reason, thus adapting the wish to restraints of reality in conformity with both pleasure and reality principles. The will initiates action by setting efficient processes to work aimed at attaining the goal or fulfilling the purpose. Thus the act of will is brought into congruence with realistic and reasonably modified desire.

But, we also know that wishes and desires have a way of exercising their influence in a fashion divorced from the demands of reality and can insist on fulfillment on their own terms. We regard such desires as wishful or fanciful and not real. We all know what wishful thinking looks like. Will can be drawn into this device in ways that obscure its intellective and self-regulatory functions. In such cases, will acts less in terms of its autonomous capacity than as moved by other motivational considerations and pressures. Such a will may be weak in the sense that it fails to follow the course of greatest advantage rather than least resistance. Or it can, under some degree of misunderstanding or misapprehension, take a strong stand and become willful in more absolutist terms by which determination to reach the goal overrides any considerations of real consequences or costs. We regard such acts as unreasoning, bullheaded, obstinate, foolhardy, and so on. Thus we would have to conclude that operation of the will is not absolute or independent of other motivational influences, but that it functions with varying degrees of autonomy and attunement to reason and reality.[23]

SUMMARY

To summarize, the will, conceived in analytic terms, represents a complex function involving appetitive and executive functions.[24] Appetitively it serves to incline the self toward an intellectively apprehended good, or away from, an intellectively apprehended evil; one of the most important appetitive functions is the capacity to love, that is, to be drawn to and seek connection and union with an object apprehended as good and lovable. Executively it serves an intermediary function between the apprehension and appraisal of a good and the initiation of action directed to the attaining or accomplishing of that good. These functions are intimately imbricated with intellective processes involved in apprehending, appraising, deliberating, analyzing, evaluating, and comprehending the nature and quality of the good to which the will is directed. Choosing and selecting the goal or object of potential action belongs to the will, along with the initiating volition putting the organism in action to achieve the goal or to accomplish the purpose contained in the guiding intentionality. It may be that combining these functions under the concept of will may overburden the term and cause undue confusion in its application. I would suggest retaining the term *will* to refer to executive functions as just described, and using some other expression, for example, "intellective appetite" for appetitive functions.

Both these functions can operate on a conscious or unconscious level, and involve a complex interplay of factors deriving from the functions of all three tripartite entities—ego, superego, and id—acting as component substructural constituents of the self-system. In this sense, the will is properly not a function of any one of the component structures, but is a function of the self, specifically of the self-as-agent. It is thus operative and expressive of the desires and externally directed actions of the self as it engages in relating to the real external environment and particularly in the context of interpersonal object relationships. The scope of its activity is twofold—on one level it acts and interacts with other intrapsychic structures in its function of deciding and choosing, but on another level it reflects the integrated functioning of all three tripartite structures as a function proper to the self acting upon and interacting with the outside world.

It almost goes without saying that these functions come into play in central and vital ways in the course of the analytic process. Almost every facet of the process Freud described in his maxim "Where id was, ego shall be" would seem to involve actions of the will in one or other of its guises. In addition, it seems clear that the therapeutic process has at least for some part of its aims the consolidation and growth of those capacities belonging to the proper domain of the will as conceived in these analytic terms. It remains to consider that aspect of will functioning that can be regarded as free—with what implications and under what circumstances? For this, I turn to chapter 5.

CHAPTER FIVE

Freedom of the Will

FREEDOM IN FREUD

Freud often cast aspersions on psychic freedom,[1] for the most part, in defense of the determinism of inadvertent acts, like slips of the tongue, and against arbitrariness implied in appeals to psychic freedom. Such acts, he contended, were motivated and not simply haphazard or random.[2] Freud's criticisms of the subjective sense of freedom were intended to make the point that acts of decision, conscious or unconscious, are similarly motivated and thus determined. Other texts can be read as supporting rather than denying the idea of free choice.

The tension between determinism and freedom was inherent in Freud's thought from the start, but it also went through stages of evolution.[3] His earlier views on determinism remained open to the continuing influence of his own deepening clinical experience, resulting in a series of sequential models developed at different stages of his career. In the early neurophysiological model of the *Project for a Scientific Psychology* (1895), the mechanistic orientation with its attendant hard determinism was ascendant. But even in this early period, his use of mechanistic metaphors was ambiguous, complemented by his realization of the necessity for freedom in clinical terms. In the *Studies on Hysteria* (Breuer and Freud 1893–1895), Freud pointed to deliberate and intentional acts of volition by which Miss Lucy suppressed the memory behind her hysterical symptoms declaring this an "act of moral cowardice" (p. 123).[4] Moreover, in the papers on technique, he cast a vote for the patient's freedom: "At the same time one willingly leaves untouched as much of the patient's personal freedom as is compatible with these restrictions, nor does one hinder him from carrying out unimportant intentions, even if they are foolish" (Freud 1914b, p. 153); and among the gains of analysis we find an "increase of self-control" (1912b, p. 117). Other statements suggested that the goal of therapy was to provide a degree of freedom for the patient to be able to choose, for instance, whether he wanted to continue a homosexual lifestyle or not (Freud 1920b); again, "Analysis does not set out to make pathological reactions impossible, but to give the patient's ego freedom to decide one way or the other" (1923a, p. 50); as well as many places where he indicated controlling, regulating and deliberating functions of the ego, functions which (along with Heinz Hartmann) we could regard as conscious volition acting in parallel with and in some cases independent of unconscious determination. As Freud (1901) suggested:

> According to our analyses it is not necessary to dispute the right to the feeling of conviction of having a free will. If the distinction between conscious and unconscious motivation is taken into account, our feeling of conviction informs us that conscious motivation does not extend to all our motor decisions. *De minimis non curat lex*. But what is thus left free by the one side receives its motivation from the other side, from the unconscious, and in this way determination in the psychical sphere is still carried out without any gaps. (p. 254)

But at the same time, he viewed this possibility in quite limited terms: "Very rarely does the complexity of a human character, driven hither and thither by dynamic forces, submit to a choice between simple alternatives, as our antiquated morality would have us believe" (Freud 1900, p. 621).

After 1919, the "ghost in the machine," the relatively autonomous knower and willer of the earlier formulations, received formal acknowledgment in the form of the ego. Despite its roots in the infantile past and drives, the ego was gifted with a degree of independent activity and a capacity to make free choices within limits set by drives, defenses, and the regulatory principles. Any contention that Freud was unequivocally committed to hard determinism will run afoul of the kind of statements found in *The Ego and the Id* (1923a): "Analysis does not set out to make pathological reactions impossible, but to give the patient's ego *freedom* to decide one way or the other" (p. 50, italics in original).

Efforts to reconcile Freud's paradoxical views on freedom by appeal to a thin theory of freedom, drawn from British empiricism, sought to preserve universal determinism by reducing freedom to a lack of coercion, that is, the act is free if it is not externally forced. The opposite of a free act is one that is compelled or coerced. The individual can act freely according to his own preferences, but these preferences are themselves determined. The universal determinist claims that conscious desires and preferences have their own causal history, but the person cannot act otherwise since that history is determined. Human actions are free in this usage if the agent is doing what he wishes, even when he has no real choice. But such a reduced notion of freedom falls short of the concept of freedom of choice required for moral responsibility. A free act is not merely consistent with desires and preferences, but implies that the course of action could be different in some way, that given the same circumstances the individual could choose to do otherwise—at least in the sense that other options are available.

Freud's formulations, regarding liberating the neurotic from unconsciously driven compulsions, might be read as endorsing such a thin version of freedom. The contradiction between determinism and freedom could then be resolved—the patient was free insofar he was no longer compelled by his drives and wishes. But Freud was not altogether consistent on this score and did not adhere to the view of freedom as uncoerced behavior. In later writings, he attributed a more robust sense of freedom to the ego—the power or capacity to deliberate about and choose among competing motives for action and thus direct itself to different courses of action.

His thinking about determinism (chapter 3) gradually became more appropriate to psychological understanding and increasingly distanced from the prevailing causal determinism of physical science. Freud never abandoned the principle of causal determinism, but the determinism of psychic causality had to account for the relatively mature capacity for deliberative decision-making and for self-determining choice among possible realistic alternatives. Psychic causality and laws came to mean something different than physical causality and laws. The determinism of psychoanalysis had to be *psychic determinism*, dealing ultimately with motives and reasons rather than with causes. As Ernest Wallwork (1991) put it, "Freud holds on to the paradox that freedom of choice is compatible with determinism not by narrowly restricting freedom to a contrived definition but by seeing that the emergence of the capacity for relatively free decision-making and action occurs within a context of psychological determinism" (p. 73). To keep things in focus, we are concerned only with mental or psychic actions, not with actions that may be coerced—although the question remains open as to whether there *are* any such psychic actions. The question comes down to the fact that there seem to be certain psychic actions involving choice among alternative possible objects or actions or courses of action in which the decision does not seem to be predetermined and options remain possible but not necessary, and therefore not necessarily determined.

FREE WILL AND DETERMINISM

The ambiguity in Freud's views on freedom of will is reflected in the subsequent psychoanalytic literature. The presumption of the mutual exclusivity of free will and determinism prevailed. Robert Knight (1946), while suggesting that determinism and free will were not strictly opposed, could not shake free from the freudian persuasion that causality involved real causal effects and that free will was no more than a subjective experience. He wrote:

> In the psychological and philosophical realm there is also no real alternative to psychic determinism. . . . Determinism refers to the complex of causal factors, heredity and environment, internal and external, past and present, conscious and unconscious, which combine to produce a certain resultant in a given individual. Determinism is thus a theoretical construct which fits the observed data, as demonstrated by predictions which were fulfilled, and which is essential to any psychology which claims to be scientific. The antithesis to this construct is the construct, indeterminism— pure chance, chaos. "Free will," on the other hand, is not on the same conceptual level as are these constructs. It refers to a subjective psychological experience, and to compare it to determinism is like comparing the enjoyment of flying to the law of gravity. (p. 255)

With due allowance for the overconfidence regarding prediction, Knight, not unlike Freud, really sidesteps the issue by disqualifying freedom of the will as mere experience without any consideration of volition as an act of will. Determinism and freedom are not opposed, but not for the reasons Knight proposed. Freedom does not lie in the experience but in the actual capacity and function of choosing and deciding among possible alternatives.

The reduction of freedom to subjective experience, the "sense of inner freedom," leaves it in a conceptual limbo without real impact or efficacy. It gives rise to the question whether freedom of the will is a real psychic capacity or an illusion. It seems more than paradoxical that psychoanalysis, a process directed to gaining and enhancing personal freedom, has done as much in some of its theorizing as any contemporary discipline to convince modern man that he lacks freedom, that his life is determined by forces beyond his control. No one has ever been able to choose his parents—so the argument goes—his early environment, or the complex of early influences that shaped his emerging psychic structure and personality. The past is irreversible, and much of it was unchosen, a reality that happened to him or was imposed on him. Furthermore, freedom is an illusion; we are creatures driven by unconscious forces within us and any promethean illusions or self-images are false and deceptive.[5]

There is no argument that certain motives can be so urgent and impelling, certain needs and/or desires so compelling, that action of the will is coerced and therefore not free. But whether this is *always* the case so that every experience of free choice is illusory, we may question. Not all determining motives are so compelling. I can choose to continue to write, and, if I do, my choice is determined; but I may choose to do something else— watch a football game on TV, for example—and, if I do, my choice is determined. In choosing to write, my motives are different than in choosing to watch the game. But in either case, my choice is both determined and free. The evidence of my experience of noncoerced, nonnecessitated choice is a valid piece of evidence that cannot be explained away as mere illusion. As Leo Rangell (1989) commented:

> The implication of these new, or at least for psychoanalysis unfamiliar theoretical foci, of choice, decision, and will, need to be integrated, with intellectual conviction and clarity, with the basic psychoanalytic tenet of psychic determinism. The execution of will and of directing activity on the part of the ego does not speak against causation, and exists side by side with psychic determinism, both of which are soft and relative. Man's will, built upon constitutional givens, added to and further developed by acquired life experiences, joins the chain of causation and determinism which exists in nature. Man is subject to causation and determinism, yet can change. Both fit the empirical observations, and both formulations are necessary in theory to encompass the basic tenets upon which psychoanalysis stands, that man can influence and change the deterministic forces that guide him. (pp. 193–194)

CONTROVERSY

We are forced to set the free will-determinism controversy against an uncertain background. Even universal causality rests on an uneasy basis, as more axiom than proven postulate (Wallace 1986b). Proof is especially weak or lacking in social sciences and sciences relying on hermeneutical resources; not only is the relation of hermeneutics and causality far from settled, but "it is *patterns* and *meaningful and productive continuity* that investigators are concerned to identify, demonstrate, and reconstruct; and those principles (causal or otherwise) that are used to make them intelligible reflect interpretive commitments" (p. 125, italics in original). Opposing camps each hold to their interpretive commitments. There is no decisive test to determine after the fact whether an action could have been otherwise, or whether the agent could have chosen otherwise in the moment prior to acting. Determinists insist that if the actor could have chosen otherwise he would have, and libertarians counter that he could have chosen differently if he had wished to—both interpretive assumptions that elude definitive demonstration. As Anthony Kenny (1975) noted: "No doubt there is a sense, and an important sense, in which a man who has the inclinations he wants to have is freer than one whose inclinations go against his own view of the person he wants to be. But this refinement of freedom is not necessary at the basic level of rational appetite, the level which is concerned with rationality and responsibility" (p. 27).

The distinction between final and efficient causality continues to trouble this discussion. The idea of a "cause" that does not cause effects troubles some minds. Edwin Wallace (1995) recently took up the issue in reviewing Wallwork's (1991) reading of Freud's ethical views. Wallwork introduced the distinction thus: "To speak in terms of causes is not necessarily to speak in terms of *determining causes*. A cause may be any phenomenon that affects the occurrence of an outcome, even if its existence does not require that outcome" (p. 75). Rejecting the distinction between ordinary (efficient) causes that necessitate and psychical (final) causes that merely incline, Wallace (1995) argues that causation is multifactorial, embracing a mesh of conditions each of which is necessary but insufficient to produce the effect, and that appeal to telic or motivational influences does not circumvent the ordinary concept of (efficient) causality. He writes:

> In fact, the *entire constellation* of unconscious conflicting and converging motives and mental processes ("overdetermination") necessitates (i.e., "causes") the resultant behavior, *rather than any one of its interlocking components*. It is axiomatic that altering any of its constituents would yield a different outcome, however subtly so. Nevertheless, this is not enough for Wallwork. In effect, he desires the possibility of a different result (i.e., enacted choice) from *precisely the same* set of operative causal conditions! (p. 1225, italics in original)

This way of addressing the issue may overstate the case: if Wallwork does indeed stipulate the possibility of a different outcome from the same prior conditions, his view would have to be set down as extreme and libertarian. But I'm not sure that the shoe fits. Looking at the outcome retrospectively, a different outcome would suggest that a different set of determinants or at least a different weighing of only one of the determinants might have shifted the course of decision. But this weighting cannot be anticipated or predicted antecedently.

Freedom resides in the weighing and choosing. This would seem to have been the point of Freud's distinction between a retrospective view, giving an impression of inevitable sequence, and an anticipatory view in which nothing can be predicted.[6] That degree of uncertainty, in conjunction with the causal integrity of final (motivating) causes and causal efficiency of the will as executive capacity, should be enough to guarantee the place of freedom of the will. On these terms, Wallace's *contracausal* label would not fit since both final and efficient causality are brought into play in a free act of will leading to action. But this conclusion would have to accept the fact that the person, that is, the self, is the autonomous source of its own agency. Wallace is quite correct that recognition of such self-determining causality would call for a revision of our metapsychological perspective, but I would demur his conclusion that "the whole psychoanalytic theoretical and methodological apparatus, as Freud (1916–1917, p. 104) recognized, would collapse" (Wallace 1995, p. 1225). Undoubtedly, any or all of the determining influences on the behavior in question may have been different at any instant, but the point at issue is that, should any or all of these variables have been different antecedently, the individual would have been differently motivated and chosen differently. But a posteriori the retrospective reconstruction retains its validity, as we have come to expect in everyday analytic experience. Had we accompanied the patient step-by-step through the moment-to-moment passage through these experiences, we could not determine which alternatives present to him he would have chosen since in fact they were nonnecessitated.

MEANING OF FREEDOM

Certainly the experience of choosing actions or courses of action provides a sense of freedom, and this can be accepted as part of the database on analytic terms. The question of what this means remains moot. Analytic thinking, in the wake of Freud's somewhat ambiguous and vacillating opinions, has split between those contending that universal determinism of psychic actions precludes any concept of freedom of the will and those holding the opposite opinion that psychic determinism properly understood in no way contravenes the idea of freedom.[7] My position is that freedom is one of the essential characteristics of will as delineated in chapter 4, but that the exercise of free will is itself determined, that is to say motivated (Meissner 1999a,b), and is operative only under limited and specific conditions.

But this understanding of will and freedom shares the stage with many diverse perspectives and viewpoints that have strode the boards of philosophical history. The concept of freedom itself is diverse—Mortmer Adler (1958–1961) delineated five distinct meanings of freedom in Western culture: circumstantial freedom of self-realization, acquired freedom of self-perfection, natural freedom of self-determination, political liberty, and collective freedom.[8] The first three are relevant to our inquiry, the latter two less so. There would be general agreement that an agent is not free when prevented from acting or forced to act by efficient causes outside himself, and that an agent is not free when his acting is necessitated by his own nature, that is, without choice.

Our ideas of rationality and responsibility hinge on the capacity for free choice and self-determination (Weisman 1965; Wolf 1972). Common experience supports not only free choice, but also the sense that the capacity for free choice is subject to degrees of expression and often mitigated by levels of passivity and influences from emotional factors and external constraints (Ewing 1962).[9] But freedom in these terms does not imply that the act of free choice be unmotivated, that is, there is no necessary contradiction between freedom and determinism (see below). Motives are not, as I have argued at length (Meissner 1999a,b), mechanical (efficient) causes, necessitating my actions. Autonomy, conceived either in terms of specific functions or as a property of the self (Meissner 1986c, 1996b), implies a degree of self-control, immunity from causal necessity imposed by emotions or unconscious instinctually derived motivations or external forces, and the capacity for self-determining action.[10] Motivational determinants are in the nature of final causes (aims, ends, purposes, and intentions) whose effect is to incline, draw, attract, not to necessitate, make happen, or force some behavior or action.

Free will is situated within a context determined by birth, heredity, developmental history, life experience, by who and what I am—not a hero, or a Promethean ideal, not a disembodied spirit, but a man, a human being, embedded and embodied in a physical body, a being at once conscious of itself and much of its action and experience, but also in large measure unconscious, subject to influences and motivations of which I know nothing and have little to say about, but over which I can have some degree of limited jurisdiction and responsibility. My freedom is therefore limited and impaired, and the relation to psychodynamics can be cast in terms of congruent goals and intentionalities or in terms of opposition and exclusive dichotomization. I would opt for the former alternative, since both ethician and psychoanalyst are concerned, each within their own perspective, with the human act, achieved only in and through freedom and expressive of a hierarchy of values, both personal, social and, for some, religious.

Free will is articulated within the framework of efficient causality. Just to be clear, no one would hold that all human activity involving use of the will is free. The will is free only when not forced, when it has the opportunity to choose among more than one available options. If and when I appraise an object as unreservedly good and desirable, the action of my will is no longer free, but necessitated. But, in fact, the essential conditions of such necessity are rarely realized, since the objects and involvements to which we mortals are drawn in this life are seldom unmixed goods, that is, they are mixtures of positive and negative, advantage and disadvantage, and benefit and cost. When I am confronted with a nonnecessary but attractive object, I am capable of choosing whether to pursue it or not. Under such conditions, free will would mean that there is nothing outside of me or within me forcing me to choose or choose between available alternatives. The choosing is of my own volition and therefore free.[11]

In this connection, Anthony Kenny (1975) concluded that physical determinism—in whatever modality it comes into play, including heredity, congenital factors, and whatever other biological physiological dispositional factors may be involved—does not mean that the scope of volitional control is eliminated. Even if we admit universal determinism, at least some of the processes determining my movements may be outside my control—for instance, those taking place before my birth—but it does not necessarily follow that all the processes determining my movements are outside my control. As he comments:

> But laws may be exceptionless (apply to all items of a certain kind) without being complete in the sense of determining each item of that kind: as the laws of chess are exceptionless (they apply to every move in the game) without determining every move in the game (as the rules of, e.g., beggar-my-neighbour do, so that every move can be predicted from the initial hands dealt). Philosophers more professional than Tolstoy have not escaped this confusion." (p. 160)

With respect to the problem of determinism and free will, phenomenological approaches have brought a certain congruence of perspective to psychoanalytic understanding of these processes by emphasizing the role of meaning. The determinism in question is not a determinism of third-person forces operating on or in the psyche, but rather concerns connections of meaning. Psychic determinism becomes a matter of the necessities of meaning. Thus freedom is not associated with a lack of determinism, but, paradoxically quite the opposite, that act is most fully free which is most fully determined. But the self does not impose this determination on itself in deliberate conscious awareness of the necessities imposed by the inner and outer world. In the analytic process, for example, free association can establish a chain of meaningful necessities (signifiers), but the necessity is retrospective and reconstructive. Freud (1920b) himself provided one of the best formulations of this aspect of psychoanalytic explanation:

So long as we trace the development from its final outcome back-wards, the chain of events appears continuous, and we feel we have gained an *insight* which is completely satisfactory or even exhaustive. But if we proceed the reverse way, if we start from the premises inferred from analysis and try to follow these up to the final result, then we no longer get the impression of an inevitable sequence of events which could not have been otherwise deter-mined. We notice at once that there might have been another result, and that we might have been just as well able to understand and explain the latter. The synthesis is thus not so satisfactory as the analysis; in other words, from a knowledge of the premises we could not have foretold the nature of the result. (p. 167)

In other words, what may be "freely" established at any point in the chain of events becomes in retrospect one of the necessities of meaning (Fisher 1961).

Within this perspective real freedom can coexist with necessities of meaning or motivational intentionalities. Such necessities are not totally determinative of the ongoing flow of behavior and experience. The experi-ences from which they derive are part of a personal history embracing both past experience and present reality. In transference, for example, infantile love and hate for the parent are directed to the analyst: that love-and-hate is an immediate, vital, present, and active force. Relations with others, stamped with these affective qualities, can be internalized to become more-or-less permanent structural acquisitions of the personality. The past lives on, transformed and unconscious, as a functional and dynamic aspect of present ongoing life experience. Necessities of meaning have explanatory relevance, but they are also caught up in a complex interaction of causal dynamics and psychic influences giving rise to psychic experience and behavior. Thus the determinants of action are complex, partial, and multi-ple, so that explanation is never complete and the personality must be regarded as a truly open system in which there is room for the exercise of freedom, not without determination, but as a determining element in its own right interacting with other determinants to produce a course of action. This perspective has been summed up aptly by Robert Holt (1972):

What then about free will vs. determinism? Briefly, the two con-cepts are *not* antithetical: both are necessary and the two can coexist. To maintain that the subjective experience of being able to make a deliberate choice among alternatives is a delusion on the grounds that freedom means a capricious act unrelated to any-thing else is to miss the point entirely. Truly free behavior is not acting on an unpredictable whim, but acting in *self-consistent* ways, in harmony with one's ego-values. The person who is able to exert will power against temptation and to act with a sense of autonomy is just as much a part of the lawful natural world as one who feels utterly compelled by influences beyond his control, whether these are unconscious needs or external compulsions. Freedom of the will (or, more generally, ego autonomy) is not a philosophical absolute, it is a quantitative psychological variable, which can be diminished or enhanced in ways that are lawful and predictable. (p. 14, italics in original)[12]

FREE WILL IN PSYCHOANALYSIS

To what degree does this description remain open to psychoanalytic perspectives? To my reading, there is nothing in these formulations that precludes these processes taking place on an unconscious level,[13] nor anything to exclude sensory or instinctual desires and wishes from intermingling with and determining volition. In other words, the concept of will in psychoanalytic terms is one that is reasonably and effectively integrated with unconscious and instinctual dynamics and does not operate beyond or outside the range of motivated, and in that sense determined, functionality.[14] Freedom of the will, on these terms, can serve quite adequately as in some part the *terminus ad quem* of the analytic process. At the end of a successful analysis, the patient should emerge with this capacity not only intact but capable of functioning on more rational, reasonable, realistic, and effective terms.

Our task, then, is to find a meaning of freedom that skirts the twin illusions of idealized and disincarnate freedom and leads us to an interpretation of freedom that is empirically based, consistent with conscious everyday experience, and psychoanalytically relevant. From a clinical point of view, we look for a meaning of freedom subject to degrees of autonomy, of strength or weakness, of variable patterns of self- and other-determination. That freedom is subject to all the vicissitudes and compromises of human living and to all the constraints of reality and existence. Psychoanalysis can claim a somewhat unique position in its consideration of freedom. Its efforts are directed to reaching into the inner being of man, into the inner reaches of the conscious and unconscious mind, and grappling there with the complexities of human freedom in its existential realization. It confronts the human mind as it struggles to achieve or escape its own freedom. Above all, the vantage point is therapeutic. The analyst's concern is why this concrete, existing, living human being has not been able to achieve that degree of freedom of mind and spirit that is his human heritage, and why he cannot realize it in the ongoing flow of his life experience.

The analytic perspective starts with the experience of freedom—and in this sense Robert Knight (1946) was not off the mark in focusing on freedom as experience. The question is whether we can go beyond that experience to a deeper understanding of the phenomenon of free will. Waelder (1936b) had put the question in these terms: "the problem to be investigated is the purely psychological one of freedom *from* something, for example, from affects or anxiety, or freedom *for* something, say freedom for coping with a task set before one. Anyone afflicted with an obsessional neurosis and acting under a compulsion is psychologically not free; if he is 'freed' from his compulsion, he will have acquired a measure of freedom" (p. 89, italics in original). In Waelder's sense, man was not bound by his biological or social environment, the *hic et nunc* of existence, but by virtue of his freedom man was able to abstract himself from his immediate situation in a form of transcendence, the capacity to rise above concrete limitations and circumstances.

The analytic perspective on freedom is thus generated out of experience and governed by it. While Knight's (1946) phrase "sense of inner freedom" emphasizes the experiential quality of the concept, it also limits further inquiry. Further questions as to the reality of man's freedom are left unanswered and uninvestigated. Development of structure, autonomy— especially secondary autonomy (Hartmann 1939)—and the capacity for free choice are correlative. Waelder (1936b) had attributed the capacity to transcend the conditions of human existence to the superego: "Freedom then in its most general sense is found in the existence of the superego, in that formal function of the superego in virtue of which man rises above himself and apprehends the world from without and beyond his immediate perceptions and his biological needs" (p. 92). But from the perspective of a more updated metapsychology, the capacity to transcend instinctual levels of psychic integration and achieve some degree of autonomy, both from internal influences and external environmental forces, is not due simply to superego any more than to ego, but is a property of the self-system. The optimal degree of functional autonomy and the balance of forms of secondary autonomy in both ego and superego require integral functioning of both subsystems, an integration accomplished on the level of self-organization. Freedom, then, properly belongs to neither superego nor ego, but to the person. The acceptable aspect of Waelder's statement is that an optimal degree of superego development and functioning is essential for the internalization of capacities for internal control that contribute to autonomy and freedom.

In these terms, the concept of real freedom is viable in a meaningful psychoanalytic theory. However, it does require a degree of maturity of structural subsystems, especially ego and superego, to insure some degree of autonomy from other determining components and influences impinging on and influencing the choice of course of action. An act of free choice derives from the executive function of the self-as-agent, operating specifically through the capacities of will, in both its appetitive and executive capacities, responding to a meaningful motivational context and autonomously choosing and directing action to one conclusion rather than another among available alternatives. Insofar as this model of autonomous self-determination serves as a meaningful goal of the analytic process, the process does not move the analysand from deterministic enslavement to nondeterministic freedom, but from one mode of neurotically and maladaptive self-determination to another mode that is more open, adaptive, and realistic.[15]

Other analysts have accepted the compatibility of free will and determinism. Charles Hanly (1979), while rejecting libertarian views, regards the brand of determinism allowing room for the exercise of free will as ambiguous, as if to suggest that only strict causal (hard) determinism were theoretically acceptable. Regarding Knight's (1946) position, Rollo May (1969) noted that the experience of successfully analyzed patients that their lives were freer and more self-determined than before therapy may be an illusion, but then it was an illusion induced by treatment that otherwise helped the patient gain greater realistic perception of himself and his world—a paradoxical, if not contradictory, state of affairs. Along the same vein, Marjorie Brierly (1951) observed the same paradox that, while determinism was evident in the analytic process, patients seemed to retain some capacity for choice—a paradox that pervades the daily experience of those who declare for universal determinism but live as though they were agents capable of free choice.

Free association. A fundamental issue for psychoanalysts is whether admitting the possibility of free decision-making capacity undermines the essential associative process on which analysis depends as a method of psychic exploration and discovery (Kris 1982). The assumption is that the pattern of associations is necessitated, that it is determined to be as it is without alternative possibilities. Undermining the necessity in this process, so the argument goes, compromises the causal links and introduces a degree of unintelligibility and arbitrariness. But the distinction of determination from necessitation remains in effect. The string of associations is always determined, and the intelligibility hinges on that factor. But that does not mean that the associations are at any point necessary—they can always be different. But whatever path they follow can lead to analytically relevant connections. The patient can always choose not to associate or not to divulge a string of associations occurring at the moment, thus resisting the process. But under ordinary circumstances, the patient does not choose his associations; they arise from a nonvoluntary sector of his mind, or so we envision the process. Determinism insists rightly that what comes into consciousness is not capricious or arbitrary, but has meaning and is motivated. This does not contravene the further possibility that associations are unconsciously selected and processed, but these too—even though they arise in a nonconscious part of the mind—are likewise determined and motivated. The same conditions for necessity versus nonnecessity, and determinism versus nondeterminism, obtain.

THE LIMITS OF FREEDOM

Psychoanalysis, then, as psychiatry more generally, focuses on the presence or absence, and the degree or diminution, of the sense of inner freedom. Like the will, whose vital functions are constrained and limited by a variety of operational conditions, freedom is also subject to constraints impinging on autonomous functioning of the will and limiting the scope of free choice and decision. Analytic patients are people who have suffered some degree of impairment or disorganization of intellective and/or emotional functioning. The range of such impairment is considerable, from the most extreme to the relatively minor, even minimal. At one extreme, it is not hard to determine that states of loss of consciousness are synonymous with suspension of the capacity for volitional acts and the capacity for free decision and choice. Death, the most extreme case, puts an end to life and thus all vital functions. In states of coma, the individual remains alive but conscious mental functioning is severely impaired; whether subthreshold functioning continues or whether unconscious mental processing of some kind is intact in any given case remain often mute and irresolvable questions. But deliberate volitional activity is suspended. Sleep, although it is a normal and regular experience, is marked by a loss of consciousness of significant degree. There are differences of opinion regarding dream activity, but certainly if there are phases of the sleep cycle without dreaming, the character of sleep mentation is not conscious even if there is little more we can say about it. And, of course, dreaming itself involves a modified form of consciousness.

At a less extreme level in which consciousness is preserved but altered, mental states marked by the prevalence of instinctual activity and primary process organization are also associated with the diminution of the sense of freedom. In acute schizophrenic episodes, the patient feels as though he has lost control and that his behavior is driven by forces over which he has no control, leaving his inner world and his behavior disorganized and bizarre.[16] Similar loss of a sense of control and organization can be found intermittently as a feature of chronic schizophrenic conditions. Secondary process organization is weakened and fleeting, while primary process comes to dominate patterns of psychic activity. This disorganization is accompanied by a diminished sense of mastery and by an overwhelming sense of helplessness and powerlessness in an ego inundated by unintegrated impulses and desires. The situation is much the same, sometimes with varying degrees of intensity in other psychotic conditions, psychotic bipolar affective states, or depressive psychotic pathology. In the manic phase of a bipolar disorder, the patient feels as driven and incapable of control as the schizophrenic; and in the depressive phase, the patient feels correspondingly helpless and impotent.

On another level of less severe impairment, borderline patients present a spectrum of degrees of dysfunction and vulnerability to regression (Meissner 1984a, 1988b). Anxiety tends to be chronic, diffuse, and free-floating; symptoms are multiple and complex and often include obsessions, phobias, conversions, dissociative states, hypochondriacal concerns, and paranoid trends. The syndrome reflects a developmental inadequacy of the self-as-ego lacking an evolved capacity for impulse control and whose capacities for sublimation or other realistically attuned defensive functions are impaired. Lower-order borderlines are constantly threatened by fear of loss of control and by the inner turmoil of conflicting emotional states and needs. The sense of self-possession and autonomy essential for the sense of inner freedom is significantly impaired or lacking. Higher-order patients may show these impediments to freedom only in more regressive states.

The capacity for free choice can also be significantly impaired in depressive states. This is certainly the case in psychotic depressive states in which there is a relatively complete loss of a sense of inner control and terrifying fantasies of impending destruction. But also in less acute depressive conditions patients often describe a feeling of lethargy, being weighted down, burdened, and guilty. Simple decisions or initiatives seem to require more energy than they can muster. The patients are burdened by a pervasive sense of worthlessness and inner impoverishment; they do not seem to feel out of control as much as unable to assert control, feeling weak, deprived, and empty. The sense of inner control and capacity for deliberating and deciding characteristic of freedom are absent or minimal.

In circumstances in which extreme need states—hunger or thirst, for example—or extremes of fatigue are involved, the sense of inner freedom is compromised or weakened. Similarly in states in which intense sexual desires are aroused or aggressive purposes intensified, the individual may feel impelled to action, rather than being able to calmly and deliberately choose a course of behavior.[17] Certain neurotic conditions are attended by diminished freedom—compulsions, intrusive obsessional thoughts, and phobias come to mind. But, in fact, all neurotic manifestations are derived from conflicts between desires and needs operating at an unconscious level and needs and values on the conscious level. To the extent that such conflicts are operative and ego resources focused on defensive exigencies, the sense of inner mastery and control is accordingly modified. In short, whether we think of ourselves as psychically impaired or neurotic, or whether we regard ourselves as relatively normal and are accepted as such by others, we are not as free as we might think, feel, or wish to be. We cannot always do what we want, even when we might consciously imagine that we are acting freely. Thus feeling that we are acting freely does not indicate that we are in fact free—to put it more explicitly, the sense of inner freedom is not synonymous with real freedom.

States of diminished freedom can also be artificially induced. Hypnotic and other states of increased suggestibility seem to involve a transient diminution of the sense of free will. Drug-induced states incur something similar: hallucinogenic agents often produce experiences of forced thinking or of passive modification of thoughts and feelings. LSD produces experiences of this kind, and even marijuana can induce states of less intense but still significant modification of the sense of autonomy and control. Amphetamines can result in driven thought processes and associated loss of control along with its concomitant anxieties—at times taking a more or less paranoid form. This can in some part mimic loss of control and ego-disorganization familiar in other psychotic conditions.

Organic syndromes, particularly those affecting central nervous system functioning can produce similar phenomena. Brain tumors, cerebrovascular accidents, traumas, and other organic afflictions can lead to ego-disorganization and dysfunction paralleled by an impaired or diminished sense of freedom. Temporal lobe seizures, usually affecting the limbic lobe and identified currently as complex partial seizures, are a case in point. They can be associated with impaired impulse control, amnesia, complex psychic experiences that are often illusory or hallucinatory in quality, bizarre experiences of derealization (déjà vu is not uncommon), or depersonalization, as well as forms of automatic behavior often quite complex and carried out in a kind of fugue state of dissociated awareness.

Even in normal dream experience the sense of freedom and control is also diminished (Hartmann 1966). The experience is more of the dream "happening," as though the dreamer was caught up in a process over which he had little or no direct control. Events in the dream seem to happen to the dreamer rather than directed by him. The quality of consciousness in daydreams occurring while the dreamer is awake is somewhat similar, but entail a degree of conscious control intermediate between the dream state and deliberate conscious control (Freud 1908b; Raphling 1996). We may lapse into a reverie in which thoughts and fantasies to a degree seem to run their own course, until we snap out of it and return to normal conscious control.

I have not attempted a complete catalog of such states of diminished freedom, but enough to convey an impression of the range of possibilities for limitation and impairment of will activity and thus of the exercise of freedom.[18] In all of these instances, however, there are certain points worth noting. First, these conditions represent either permanent or transient weakening of the ego. The ego, as a functional subsystem operating in virtue of the agency of the self (Meissner 1993), loses some degree of control in its defensive and executive functions, especially in its capacity to direct and regulate other psychic systems, and instead the organization of psychic systems derives from other sources of intrapsychic agency. Second, in all of these states there is a shift from a predominance of secondary process mental organization to primary process organization. Third, short of death, in none of these conditions is the capacity for freedom of choice ever completely or permanently lost. Even in comatose states, we are never certain whether at some level the patient is not aware and capable of continuing mentation. In conscious individuals, the experience of inner freedom is quite variable and can vary along a spectrum from states of more or less diminished freedom to states of relatively intact or even enhanced sense of freedom. The capacity for freedom, however diminished or compromised by pathological conditions, is never totally absent in conscious individuals. Even in the most regressed and primitive psychotic states, as Freud observed, there is always a hidden psychic corner in which the residue of the ego preserves its nonpsychotic and observant capacity—in this hidden segment of preserved ego and self the capacity for freedom is also preserved and maintained.

THE DIALOGUE

This formulation of the concept of free will opens the way to a potential dialogue between psychoanalysis and ethical and moral theory. Among traditional moralists certain aspects of the fundamental mind-set have been radically challenged by psychological, and especially psychoanalytic, perspectives and interpretations. In the best of us, there are residues of primary process psychic organization, potentialities for mental disturbance of one kind or other, of one or other degree of regressive disorganization and pathological vulnerability.[19] Mental health cannot be assumed to be the secure and unruffled possession of most ordinary and relatively normal people.

A major point of difference is the ethical focus on consciousness on one hand versus the psychoanalytic view of human action as resulting from the confluence of both conscious and unconscious influences on the other. Moral theory has tended to embrace a relatively naive psychology of mental processes and motivation for action. Stipulations of relatively clear self-consciousness, the existence of a personal moral conscience, more-or-less unconditioned freedom of the will, and a correlative sense of responsibility provided the basic premises for ethical behavior and decision. Introduction of the possibility of unconscious determination and mental processing has brought significant turbulence to these relatively tranquil waters. We have been at pains to illumine the polarities of such dichotomous thinking whereby determinism of any kind is thought to undermine and eliminate the possibility of freedom. The threat was real enough, since elimination of freedom would have undermined the very basis for the understanding of human personality, including the very possibility of responsibility and morality.

If this ambivalent dialogue is to reach any productive and meaningful conclusion, it will require greater openness of the ethical perspective to considerations of psychodynamic influence, unconscious dynamics, and potential and real compromises and limitations on the scope and exercise of free will. By the same token, it requires from the psychoanalytic participant a willingness to rethink the foundations and metapsychological construction of the mental apparatus and a greater respect for, and understanding of, conscious processes of conscience and moral decision-making as they maintain a degree of autonomous capacity in the face of, and under the continuing influence of, unconscious motivations and causal determinants.

Ethics does not derive from law, or from dictates of the superego, or from any other impulsion extrinsic to the will, but from the free and autonomous capacity to choose among alternative intellectual goods, an act that is a joint accomplishment of intellect and will. A human act, therefore, is moral only to the degree that it is free. Human acts are congruent with human desires and these can be sensory or intellective. Sensory desires are directed to some form of pleasure (the pleasure principle) and intellective desires are drawn to the good, whether the attainment or possession of that good gives rise to pleasure or not. This is another way of expressing the integration of pleasure and reality principles. In morally good acts, the person derives pleasure from the good, but only when he seeks it as good rather than as pleasure.

CHAPTER SIX

Psychodynamic Hedonism
and the Pleasure Principle

Psychoanalysts, beginning with Freud, have made a good deal of the role of pleasure in human motivation, considerations that led Freud to posit the pleasure principle as a central regulatory principle governing affects and motivation. Ethicists, under various guises, have appealed to a principle of happiness as a guiding norm for ethical decision-making and for determination of right from wrong. The question is, How are these related? What, if anything, do they have to do with each other? I propose to approach this discussion by a consideration of forms of *hedonism* and an exploration of the meanings of *pleasure*. It turns out that the meanings of these terms enjoy a rather surprising degree of variety.

ETHICAL HEDONISM

Hedonism as a principle of human action proposes that attraction to pleasurable and avoidance of unpleasurable states of mind are governing factors directing human behavior. Implications of this view can be traced in both ethical and psychological terms. For ethical hedonism, only pleasure is intrinsically desirable and only unpleasure or pain undesirable—pleasure and unpleasure usually are understood as states of mind or experience. The various forms of psychological hedonism include a common theme that human desires or actions are determined by the balance of pleasure and unpleasure, past, present or future. Ethical thinkers, for whom happiness is the only intrinsically desirable good, express a form of ethical hedonism, an egotistic hedonism, insofar as happiness is synonymous with experiencing personal pleasure (Ewing 1962). The identification of *happiness* with *pleasure* is not universally accepted, however, and there is no clear consensus even about the meaning of the terms.

113

Hedonism has been considered a branch of traditional utilitarianism, in respect to the principle of greatest happiness. The utilitarian principle of the greatest good for the greatest number was blended with the principle of greatest pleasure to define the intrinsically good. Some continued to hold the generic utilitarian principle, while rejecting hedonism (e.g., G. E. Moore, 1903),[1] while others regarded hedonism as concerned only with the nature of the intrinsically good or desirable rather than as a principle of moral action. An object or state of affairs is said to be intrinsically good or desirable if it is desirable, good, valued, and worthy, when viewed in abstract terms in itself, without any reference to consequences. The range of things that are desirable from consequences and not in themselves is not small—a surgical operation may be far from desirable in itself, but it is chosen by reason of expected or hoped for consequences. The hedonist would contend that, although many things may be desirable, they are not so in themselves, that is, intrinsically. And, of course, I can desire many things instrumentally, as means to an end, even if they are not intrinsically desirable. There are also things that are both intrinsically and instrumentally desirable—a good dinner can be pleasant and satisfying and provide valuable energy for the day's work.

Pleasure. Central to the hedonist thesis is the meaning of pleasure. "Pleasure" can bear a multiplicity of meanings and nuances. It can refer to pleasures of the flesh—wine, woman, and song—but such sensory and instinctual satisfactions are not what is intended by the *hedonist* perspective; rather the term seems to intend enjoyment of pleasure in any form. I can enjoy a demanding physical workout, or I can enjoy the effort and concentration required to write this chapter—even though both would entail relinquishing other more sensually gratifying pleasures that would hardly require the same expenditure of energy and effort nor the same degree of stress or tension. The hedonist thesis says simply that an experience or activity is pleasant if I enjoyed it, that an intrinsically desirable event always involves a state of consciousness in which the subject is enjoying himself in some manner. Work, exercise, even at times arduous and even painful experiences, can be enjoyed, whether intrinsically or instrumentally. These are as much pleasures as the pleasures of eating, drinking, and sex.

From the perspective of ethical hedonism, then, it is reasonable to say that an individual is enjoying himself, or is in a pleasant state of mind, if he likes the activity in question for itself, aside from any moral considerations or consequences, even if there might be something else he would enjoy more that he could be doing at that time. On this basis, then, the hedonist thesis comes to mean "the affirmation that a state of affairs is intrinsically desirable if and only if it is, or contains, an activity or experience which, at the time, the person likes for itself, and one state of affairs is more desirable intrinsically than another if it is, or contains, an experience or activity which, at the time, is liked better for itself" (Brandt 1967, p. 433).

Pleasure as Utilitarian. The principles of ethical hedonism, as propounded in Jeremy Bentham and John Stuart Mill, were vigorously challenged by G. E. Moore (1903).[2] Moore charged that the hedonistic principle involved the naturalistic fallacy, meaning that any attempt to define "good" in terms of anything else was mistaken—utilitarians equated good with useful, hedonists with pleasant. Utilitarians view those acts as right or good that are conducive to general happiness.[3] The argument would require a demonstration that general happiness was not simply good, but that it was *the* good, the only good. Moore pointed out the circularity—pleasure is used to define the good, so that we can readily conclude that the only good is pleasure. If I regard the statements "I think this is good" and "this pleases me" as equivalent, I cannot logically conclude that only pleasure is good. Were I to conclude that pleasure is good along with other kinds of good specifically as ends to be sought, I have left the ground of ethical hedonism; if I endorse the idea that pleasure can be a means to an end or that pleasure is a good to be desired, I may still be in the realm of psychological hedonism. As Moore put it, "Hedonists, then, hold that all other things but pleasure, whether conduct or virtue or knowledge, whether life or nature or beauty, are only good as means to pleasure or for the sake of pleasure, never for their own sakes or as ends in themselves" (p. 63).

Mill, for example, argued that "good" was synonymous with "desirable." But the meaning of "desirable" is determined only by what is actually desired. But, as Moore averred, "desirable" does not mean "able to be desired," but what ought to be desired. The test of what is good to desire cannot rest on what is actually desired—a clear case of the naturalistic fallacy. Desire usually suggests some state of mind referring to something not yet existing—the thought of drinking a glass of port gives rise to a feeling of remembered pleasure that stirs a desire: the pleasure of the anticipated wine gives rise to desire. Such past pleasure may be involved in any desire; at least the idea is not absurd. But Mill would contend that it is not the wine that is desired, but the expected pleasure—the pleasure is not actual as it would be for Moore, but only anticipated. There is some confusion between a pleasant thought and a thought of a certain pleasure—in the latter case, pleasure can be said to be the object of desire; but if only the pleasant thought is present, then the object is desired and the pleasure is neither the object nor motive of the desire. The identification of thinking of an object as desirable and thinking of it as pleasant rests on the naturalistic fallacy. The fallacy contends that good can be defined in simply natural terms of what is desired. Thus we ought to desire something simply because we do desire it—the formula is thus emptied of ethical implication.

Moore (1903) raised another question that cut closer to the psychoanalytic chase. He asked, "Can it really be said that we value pleasure, except in so far as we are conscious of it?" (p. 87). Might attainment of such pleasure, of which we might never be aware, be something to seek for its own sake? Psychoanalysis would maintain the existence of such unconscious pleasures, but the ethical issue is whether it is the pleasure that is sought or its consciousness. The issue cuts across the question of whether pleasure is conceived in experiential terms as a feeling state or as a regulatory principle. Clearly the relevance of the pleasure principle in analysis is applicable to conscious and unconscious mental processing, so that if pleasure has a place in analytic thought it cannot depend on its conscious experience. But Moore pointed out that even consciousness of pleasure cannot be the sole good for the same reasons that pleasure itself cannot be the sole good.

Moore's exegesis and critique of ethical hedonism helps to bring into clearer focus the utilitarian implications of a hedonistic doctrine and some of the logical difficulties it encompasses. As the ensuing discussion will suggest, psychoanalysis circles somewhere on the fringes of this ethical perspective—if there are elements of utilitarian and hedonistic viewpoints resonating in analytic thinking, it is not clear that the psychoanalytic perspective can be reduced to hedonistic terms, even a psychological hedonism. There is still the further question, given the role of pleasure in the dynamics of human motivation and action, as to what possible ethical implications it carries. For it is one thing to say that all psychic action is determined by a principle of pleasure-pain, but quite another to say that what is so motivated has any status as an ethical norm.

PSYCHOLOGICAL HEDONISM

Ethical hedonism has traditionally enjoyed support of psychological hedonism, but this doctrine has taken a variety of forms, each having different ethical implications. The common note is that human actions and desires are determined by actual, previous, or prospective pleasures and displeasures. The doctrine does not assume normative force, since it concerns itself only with what is actually desired rather than what might or should be desirable. One form of psychological hedonism posits that action is motivated by pleasure as a goal—that is, a person is motivated to one action or state of affairs rather than another if he thinks it will prove more pleasant or less unpleasant for himself. The thesis applies to chosen actions, and the belief need not be explicit, but may serve only as an unformulated assumption or value. It also applies to desires, insofar as the person may desire one thing in preference to others if he thinks having or attaining it will provide him greater pleasure.

The link to ethical hedonism is formed by the assumption that humans only seek pleasure for its own sake, and, therefore, pleasure is the only intrinsically desirable good. In this form, the theory runs into obvious difficulties, in that common experience indicates that individuals often put themselves at harm's risk or undertake courses of action that entail loss and suffering for the sake of principles or values, or out of a sense of duty or obligation, or even out of neurotic need. Erich Fromm (1947), for example, concluded that "pleasure cannot be a criterion of value. For there are people who enjoy submission and not freedom, who derive pleasure from hate and not from love, from exploitation and not from productive work. This phenomenon of pleasure derived from what is objectively harmful is typical of the neurotic character and has been studied extensively by psychoanalysis" (pp. 24–25).

Another variant on the theme bases motivation on pleasant thoughts or feelings. According to this view, I would chose one thing over another if the thought of the thing chosen (with its anticipated consequences) is more pleasing, or less repugnant, than the alternative. While this view may shed light on conditions for preference, it does not cover the situation in which I may not think of an action as more pleasant, or even think of it as less pleasant and more repugnant, and still decide to do it. In addition, even if this form of psychological hedonism were valid, it would not provide any support for ethical hedonism since it says nothing about the kind of goal or action that would be more-or-less attractive or repulsive. There is no support for the view that men desire only pleasure—if I assume that desiring something means finding the idea of it pleasant or attractive, it would not follow that only the idea of pleasure is itself attractive, or that only pleasure is desired (Brandt 1967).

Another variant on the theme would look to causal conditions for the individual's desires or values. This view would contend that fundamental values can be related to past enjoyments and rewards, and that these pleasures at least partially account for the individual's values. Furthermore, the individual's values can be regulated by manipulating his enjoyments. If I prefer chocolate, it is because my past experience of chocolate has been pleasant and not distasteful. Certainly past experience influences my likes and dislikes, but this falls far short of a satisfying account of personal desires and values, which result from a variety of factors, only part of which involves past experience. This view of pleasure does not deny that certain wants can be reinforced by subsequent experiences of pleasure, but it does question whether we can derive pleasure from anything except by satisfying some preexisting want. Ordinary developmental experience would suggest the opposite—the infant may relish shaking his rattle, but grasping and shaking the rattle is a new experience prior to which and for which he could have had no desire. Freud solved the problem of the infant's enjoyment of sucking the breast by postulating inborn oral instinctual drives. The last option, based on a momentary preference, shifts the emphasis from prior want to present preference. One may thus take pleasure in something never previously experienced, and the quality of the experience on the basis of which it is valued remains open to the full range of human likes of whatever kind. But again the theory does not impose any conclusion that humans desire only pleasure, since it claims no more than that, whatever the person's likes and dislikes, they may in part reflect past rewards and punishments of whatever kind. The analytic view connecting superego standards to past parental praise or reproach may serve as a case in point.

In any case, since the theories do not demonstrate that we desire only pleasure or things thought to provide pleasure, they fall short of demonstrating the validity of ethical hedonism, and thus weaken the reliance of ethical hedonism on psychological hedonism to support its claims. The fly in the ointment is that people from time to time regard other things besides pleasure as intrinsically good, or even regard some kinds of pleasure as intrinsically bad. This makes identification of "intrinsically good" with "pleasant" difficult to maintain. In order for ethical hedonism to prevail, we need to assume that at least some forms of pleasure are intrinsically good, and that comparable claims for any other possibilities are refuted. But, as critics claim, if some forms of pleasure are intrinsically bad—for instance, malicious pleasure at another's pain or suffering—or if some unpleasant experiences are intrinsically good—for example, punishment for crimes committed—this does not augur well for hedonism as an ethical principle. The critics further point out that some things beside pleasure can be regarded as intrinsically good—such as knowledge, positive character traits, virtues, good deeds especially when they involve self-denial, abnegation, or self-depletion, even life itself regardless of whether it is pleasant or not, or whether it is accompanied by other rewards or achievements.

Motivational theories have the advantage that the mere fact that an activity is enjoyable may not be a reason for doing it. I may enjoy playing the piano, but I may choose not to do it—other considerations, such as seeing a patient, may take precedence. Holding to a motivational view, moreover, does not commit us to psychological hedonism, since it maintains not just that pleasure is intrinsically desirable, but that pleasure is not the only thing that might be intrinsically desirable. In terms of the last approach, other things might take precedence over pleasure as intrinsically desirable—self-fulfillment, intellectual consistency, moral behavior, and duty, regardless of the amount of pleasure they may involve. In other words, motivation is not synonymous with pleasure in this view: many motivations may involve pleasure, but the range of human motives is not restricted to pleasure.

PLEASURE IN PSYCHOANALYSIS

Clearly, pleasure played an essential role as a motivational principle in Freud's thinking from the beginning. In his *Project for a Scientific Psychology* (1895), he postulated the pleasure principle as playing a central role in complex mental states. The idea of wish-fulfillment, so central in his view of the dream process and the unconscious (1900), was governed in large measure by the pleasure principle.

Pleasure Principle

However, the pleasure principle involved its own complexities and left in its wake a degree of uncertainty as to its fundamental meaning. Was Freud appealing to pleasure as a sensation or feeling state as his fundamental principle of mental processing?[4] Did he intend it as a conscious experience of feeling or sensation or did he mean it to apply to unconscious states of the mind? Or did it have some other less immediately apparent meaning? The question gave Freud a good deal of difficulty in clarifying his thinking, since any rewarding experience would have the effect of reinforcing behavior, and conversely any unrewarding or unpleasant experience would have the opposite effect. But Freud soon discovered that his patients were often enough drawn to acts or courses of action that were less than pleasurable, or even resulted in significant degrees of pain and discomfort. The masochistic inclination in some patients even seemed not only to draw them to unpleasant effects, but at times made it seem that they actively sought out such experiences and effects. Whether pleasure could serve as a governing principle for such diverse experiences remained a perplexing problem for Freud.

We previously discussed the pleasure principle in relation to psychic determinism (chapter 3), but our interest here is in its implications for ethical theory. We should note that this regulatory principle does not sustain a merely hedonistic doctrine, viewing human activity simply as intending or seeking only pleasure. Rather, Freud's postulate meant that psychic acts were determined by the balance of pleasure and unpleasure,[5] operating as regulatory principles governing the possibilities of action in the system, but not restrictively as conscious experiences of pleasure or pain. Rather the principle is inherently heterogeneous, its application varying depending on what system or subsystem is in question. As Ernest Wallwork (1991) noted, "Freud's highly general definition of the pleasure principle as aiming at the reduction of tension leaves room for very different operations in the specific contexts in which he discusses it—as applied to a fictive primitive psychic apparatus, the unconscious, or id, the ego, and the whole mind. Too often, what Freud says about the pleasure principle in one of these contexts is taken by the unsuspecting reader as the whole of Freud's explanation of it" (p. 111).

To the extent that the pleasure principle, taken in isolation, departs from implications of a hedonistic calculus, at least in the narrow compass of pleasurable or unpleasurable states of feeling or sensation, it tends to distance itself from any theory of psychological hedonism. But, even so, the pleasure principle does not stand on its own and does not provide an adequate account of the regulation of the mental apparatus. The mental apparatus does not operate in isolation, on the basis of internal operational conditions considered in themselves exclusive of external conditions. As Freud discovered, the pleasure principle could only be considered in relation to a complementary regulatory principle adapting it to the limitations and demands of reality, namely, the reality principle (Meissner 1995b).[6]

PSYCHODYNAMIC HEDONISM

This line of thinking leads to a view of psychoanalytic motivation as extending beyond the circle of theories based on psychological hedonism. On these terms the goal of action is expressed not in pleasure as a feeling or mental state, but in terms of competence in function and achievement of goals and purposes. Nor does the pleasure principle, of itself, suggest that my choices are guided by the experience of pleasure associated with a selected outcome. Effective functioning and the accomplishment of goals and purposes may be accompanied by satisfaction and pleasure, but these are not guiding norms but secondary complements to the primary event of goal-achievement or purpose-fulfillment. Freud (1915a) himself came close to this view in speaking of the ego's enjoyment of its own competence, a view later elaborated by Robert White (1959, 1960, 1963). The accusation that analytic regulation according to the pleasure principle means being self-absorbed and selfish, thus undermining any moral consideration, runs afoul of this contradiction.

Individual hedonism. But these considerations leave open the question whether the classic analytic view of motivation based on instinctual drives (Rapaport 1960) would not still qualify as a form of psychological hedonism, as some have claimed. Donald Abel (1989), for example, argued that, despite Freud's frequent disclaimers, psychoanalysis does contain an implicit moral philosophy, that is, a set of principles guiding one's choices and directions in life. He characterized this ethical bent as "individual hedonism."

The basic moral assumption in this view is that one should live so as to fulfill his nature—in freudian terms, living to fulfill one's human nature as psychoanalysis understands it. The aim of analysis in these terms is to help patients understand their own human nature and to live within their psychic means. Psychic health means living in consonance with one's own psychic nature rather than complying with or adopting some analytic ideal. Analysis does not seek to mold patients to any preexisting ideal, but to enable them to find what is meaningful and purposeful in their own lives. Abel argued that, in view of Freud's instinct theory and ego psychology, this assumption implied individual hedonism insofar as pleasure, and only pleasure, was regarded as intrinsically good. Therapy, on such terms, would aim at maximizing pleasure in the patient's life.

However, this proposition would have to be subject to all of these qualifications. Seeking maximal pleasure must be qualified by reality considerations. Other things being equal, seeking to fulfill uninhibited sexual instincts would be preferable to accepting inhibited fulfillment; but other things are not always equal. Complete fulfillment of uninhibited impulses may not be possible because of circumstance, social consequences, or punitive action from the superego. In such a case, prospective unpleasure may outweigh prospective pleasure; the pleasure principle thus yields to the reality principle. Nonetheless, says Abel, the basic ethical principle stands—maximal satisfaction is better than partial. Even though dictates of the pleasure principle can never gain complete satisfaction, the principle requires effort to continually seek such maximization. Thus Freud (1930): "The programme of becoming happy, which the pleasure principle imposes on us, cannot be fulfilled; yet we must not—indeed, we cannot—give up our efforts to bring it nearer to fulfillment by some means or other" (p. 83). But this rendition of the pleasure principle would seem to overlook qualitative differentiations in handling pleasure. If the unconscious seeks immediate and automatic gratification, the ego can select and defer its gratifications in the interest of long-term and realistic goals—even in terms of lifelong finality.

Freud (1916) gave the lie to this aspect of pleasure "beyond pleasure" in his discussion of the religious ascetic's self-denial in favor of the rewards of the afterlife. Even the degree of self-renunciation involved in ascetic denial is not inconsistent with the pleasure principle: "Even religion is obliged to support its demand that earthly pleasure shall be set aside by promising that it will provide instead an incomparably greater amount of superior pleasure in another world" (p. 311). As Wallwork (1991) observed:

> When Freud talks about the ego's transformation of the pleasure principle, he is obviously being drawn away from his drive-discharge theory of hedonism by his nascent ego theory. In place of a present-oriented psychic apparatus regulated solely by the immediate aim of lowering tension through discharge, there is an "I" capable of acting *teleologically* in terms of beliefs about satisfactions over the whole of a lifetime, including satisfactions experienced by substituting more refined pleasures for raw drive gratification. (p. 122, italics in original)

Insofar as the superego represents in some degree the voice of morality, it contravenes this view of individual hedonism. As an internalization of parental and cultural prohibitions and ideals, superego morality may run into conflict with individual hedonism's demands for maximizing pleasure. Cultural and social norms are not often calculated to maximize personal pleasure. Consequently, the individual hedonist would have to evaluate the pleasure or pain connected with observing or violating superego prescriptions as part of his deliberation over a course of action. If the degree of potential pleasure outweighs anticipated superego costs, the hedonist should act against superego demands—following the voice of superego morality in this sense becomes paradoxically immoral (Abel 1989).

The fact is that Freud was influenced considerably by the utilitarianism of Bentham and Mill.[7] On those terms, whatever the quality of the action, it had to be pleasurable in some sense in order to be performed. Bentham had argued that even motives of ill-will and malice could involve a kind of pleasure, for instance, at the anticipated pain of an enemy. Thus wishes, desires, interests, and actions of all kinds involved pleasure. Suicide pleases the suicide, sadism the sadist, masochism the masochist. Pleasure in this sense becomes synonymous with motivation; even the repetition compulsion with its repeated rehearsal of trauma turned out to be a subtler form of pleasure based on hidden neurotic needs. Furthermore, Freud's system included an economics of pleasure and its distribution echoing utilitarian perspectives. But, if utilitarianism offered an ideal of freedom to pursue one's own pleasure, as long as it did not interfere with the pleasure-seeking of others, Freud proposed a less optimistic rendition requiring subjection of such freedom to an "education to reality" (1927a); the restriction of pleasure proclaimed at one and the same time both freedom and its limitations. As Philip Rieff (1959) observed: "The reality principle does not completely supplant the pleasure principle, but it tries, through compromise, to exert discipline enough to meet the basic need for efficiency. There is a human reluctance to give up pleasures—especially those of the past—for barely acceptable and certain realities. . . . Far from advancing the ethical hedonism with which he is mistakenly charged, Freud in his psychology of pleasure indicates the futility of hedonism" (p. 357). Thus, Freud's psychology might be regarded as a psychological hedonism, but only in a qualified sense. Neither does it rest on any overriding requirement for achieving gratification through drive-discharge, nor does it obviate altruistic motivations.

Needless to say, the argument for individual hedonism is diametrically opposed to these considerations. The argument hinges on the primacy of the pleasure principle as an unbridled expression of moral purpose. Whether this captures the essence of Freud's intention is open to question— I rather think not. Elevation of the pleasure principle to such a dominant position seems to ignore necessary qualifications required to make it an operative aspect of the psychic economy. While its centrality is apparent, it remains one of several regulatory principles whose interests must be integrated in any meaningful account of psychic functioning. In Abel's (1989) construction, other regulatory functions are simply put into the service of the seeking of pleasure—this strikes me as an overbalanced interpretation. A further obscurity is the failure to clarify whether pleasure is understood as sensation or feeling state, or as regulatory principle. As regulatory principle, the pleasure principle has nothing to do with hedonism. Furthermore, conflict between the "morality" of maximizing pleasure and the "morality" of the superego seems artificial. The implication that the superego is always contrapleasure may not be the case: the superego can also be seen as tolerant and accepting, even encouraging, of pleasure within certain constraints and perspectives. On these terms, the push for maximal pleasure may have to yield to attaining optimal pleasure—maximal pleasure is never obtainable and the best one can look for is optimal pleasure within the frame of the reality principle and other moral constraints.[8] Heinz Hartmann (1960) at one point observed:

> One may find gratification in acting according to moral standards. Not only does every human being start by attributing goodness, in a still undifferentiated way, to objects and actions in the measure they provide satisfaction. This linkage of satisfaction with goodness does in a way persist although the pleasure conditions have changed and pleasure in moral behavior has evolved and become differentiated from that which characterizes instinctual gratifica-

tion. But we learn not to attribute greater value to what provides us with more immediate or more intense gratification. (pp. 47–48)

But even this presumes that the norm of moral choice remains pleasure, a presumption not at all assured in a psychoanalytic perspective. I would prefer to think that a wide range of motivational options are operative in determining moral decisions and choices. As variously described or interpreted, pleasure may accompany or result from such choices and actions, but gaining or realizing pleasure is not in itself the determinant of the morality of the action in question.[9] The putative opposition of a hedonistic principle versus the superego creates a schema of internally divided morality that substitutes one arm of the moral conflict for the whole picture. Morality is not so compartmentalized—the existence of moral conflicts does not argue to multiple moralities; rather the ultimate course of decision and action results from a deliberation weighing various alternatives and coming to a conclusion encompassing all relevant factors pro and con.

The hedonistic hypothesis is further weakened by considerations of masochism, particularly in its moral form. As Fromm (1947) pointed out over half a century ago:

Psychoanalysis confirms the view, held by the opponents of hedonistic ethics, that the subjective experience of satisfaction is in itself deceptive and not a valid criterion of value. The psychoanalytic insight into the nature of masochistic strivings confirms the correctness of the antihedonistic position. All masochistic desires can be described as a *craving for that which is harmful* to the total personality. In its more obvious forms, masochism is the striving for physical pain and the subsequent enjoyment of that pain. As a perversion, masochism is related to sexual excitement and satisfaction, the desire for pain being conscious. "Moral masochism" is the striving for being harmed psychically, humiliated, and dominated; usually this wish is not conscious, but it is rationalized as loyalty, love, or self-negation, or as response to the laws of nature, to fate, or to other powers transcending man. Psychoanalysis shows how deeply repressed and how well rationalized the masochistic striving can be. (pp. 182–183, italics in original)

But it can be argued that this antihedonistic strain in Freud's thinking can be read as an outright repudiation of psychological hedonism calling for radical revision of the pleasure principle—pain as well as pleasure can serve motivational aims, as seems to be the case in sadomasochism and self-destructive compulsions.

DESIRE AND MOTIVATION—THE LACANIAN ARGUMENT

In all of these considerations, it becomes increasingly clear how central the role of desire is to the analytic dynamic. Perhaps in no other analytic theorist has desire come to have such a dominant position in the motivational schema as in Jacques Lacan. He (1992) states: "It nevertheless remains true that analysis is the experience which has restored to favor in the strongest possible way the productive function of desire as such. This is so evidently the case that one can, in short, say that the genesis of the moral dimension in Freud's theoretical elaboration is located nowhere else than in desire itself" (p. 3). This perspective points to further questions regarding the interconnection between desire as a motivational component and the pleasure principle on one hand and the implications for ethical perspectives on the other.

Pleasure and reality. Lacan (1992) pointed out that the problem of the function of pleasure in the mental economy was present even in Aristotle, and persists in psychoanalysis. But ethical implications do not rest merely on pleasure as such, but on modification of the pleasure principle introduced through appeal to the reality principle: "the question of ethics is to be articulated from the point of view of the location of man in relation to the real" (p. 11). Pleasure played a central role as a guiding principle of ethics for Aristotle—happiness was no more than the bloom of pleasure; but pleasure for Aristotle was a quality of action, while in Freud's metapsychology pleasure was cast in terms of inertia and passivity. In this sense, pleasure fell short of serving as a valid ethical principle, and Freud advanced the understanding of the essential nature of morality by pointing to the role of the real. Lacan (1992) summarized his view of the ethical nature of psychoanalysis:

> The experiment consisted in adopting what I called the point of view of the Last Judgment. And I mean that by choosing as the standard of that reconsideration of ethics to which psychoanalysis leads us, the relationship between action and the desire that inhabits it. . . . The ethics of psychoanalysis has nothing to do with speculation about prescriptions for, or the regulation of, what I have called the service of goods. . . . And it is because we know better than those who went before how to recognize the nature of desire, which is at the heart of this experience, that a reconsideration of ethics is possible, that a form of ethical judgment is possible, of a kind that gives this question the force of a Last Judgment: Have you acted in conformity with the desire that is in you? (pp. 313–314)

Primordial desire. Lacan (1992) looked to Immanuel Kant to grasp the nature of the real—particularly with reference to the kantian *das Ding*, "the reality that commands and regulates" (p. 55). It is toward this that moral action directs itself and within which it seeks and finds the good. By a convoluted argument, Lacan comes to the conclusion that the ultimate *Ding*, itself unknown, is that reality that holds the primacy of place in the experience of the infant and serves subsequently as the ultimate object of desire. The fundamental law for Freud, where culture arises in opposition to mere nature, is the prohibition of incest. Lacan comments, "the whole development at the level of the mother/child interpsychology—and that is badly expressed in the so-called categories of frustration, satisfaction, and dependence—is nothing more than an immense development of the essential character of the maternal thing, of the mother, insofar as she occupies the place of that thing, of *das Ding*" (p. 67). The prohibition of incest thus becomes the primordial law, of which all other cultural developments are merely consequences and implications. But at the same time, incest remains the fundamental and primordial desire, however buried in the depths of the unconscious. He concludes: "Well now, the step taken by Freud at the level of the pleasure principle is to show us that there is no Sovereign Good— that the Sovereign Good, which is *das Ding*, which is the mother, is also the object of incest, is a forbidden good, and that there is no other good. Such is the foundation of the moral law as turned on its head by Freud" (p. 70).

But desire as such cannot emerge from the level of mere desire to that of ethical demand without connection to the reality principle related dialectically to the pleasure principle. Pleasure and libido do not measure up to the demands of life—"Neither pleasure nor the organizing, unifying, erotic instincts of life suffice in any way to make of the living organism, of the necessities and needs of life, the center of psychic development" (Lacan 1992, p. 104). It is only through diffusion and domestication of the primordial Thing by displacement into real signifiers that we can locate the good and the relevance to the real that becomes ethically relevant. Thus finding of an object is equivalently a refinding of the object, such that the Thing is always represented by something else and remains itself unknown. The pleasure principle serves only to draw the subject from signifier to signifier in order to maintain the lowest level of tension required to regulate the functioning of the psychic apparatus.

Jouissance. The complexity of the lacanian perspective on pleasure reaches an omega point in his discussions of *jouissance*, which I take to indicate that ultimate and primary pleasure buried in the unconscious and surrounded by repressive barriers and connected with the ultimate and fundamental desire of the maternal object. As such it is inaccessible, but at the same time as it exercises motivational power it also raises the specter of the forbidden and the exemplar of the ultimate transgression. The theme will return, especially in the discussion of conscience (chapter 11); at this juncture it conveys the sense in which Lacan raises doubts about any linkage of pleasure and ethical good. The dynamic of desire in this sense points beyond the good, which acts as the first barrier to the "unspeakable field of radical desire," to another level of barrier in the aesthetic, which points further in the direction of a "field of destruction." Lacan (1992) decries hedonism because of its insistence on connecting pleasure with the good and failing to go beyond to the ultimate meaning of pleasure and the perils of *jouissance*. The good is thus a barrier to desire—"The sphere of the good erects a strong wall across the path of our desire. It is, in fact, at every moment and always, the first barrier that we have to deal with" (p. 230).

Problem of reduction. Lacan's discussion of pleasure leads us into the heart of the freudian problematic of motivational dynamics. Setting aside the interpretive uncertainties of whether, when Lacan says "Freud," we should read "Lacan," there are two dimensions of his argument that provoke reflection. The first is radically reductive and the second points inexorably to further issues regarding moral questions concerned with the meaning of good and evil, and right and wrong. First, Lacan proposes that the primordial desire is incestuous desire of the mother, and that all subsequent desires are fragmented displacements of this fundamental urge. Can we accept this as a fundamental truth about human nature unveiled by psychoanalysis? I would go slow at this point.

Lacan's assertions may have a degree of validity in the order of abstract inference and plausibility, not unlike Freud's postulate of primary narcissism. The argument has yet to be settled whether primary narcissism ever exists as such, or whether it should be regarded as a theoretical postulate providing coherence and theoretical plausibility to a more clinically relevant theory of narcissism. If I choose to address primary narcissism as a theoretical postulate, I must also recognize that any empirical validation of the concept may have to go begging. However, the idea may still have its usefulness. Is there any evidence for Lacan's primal desire? Certainly, clinical experience attests residues of unconscious desire for the incestuous object at the level of oedipal dynamics—the scenario is familiar often enough in patients suffering from a variety of clinical pathogenic states—impotence comes to mind as a classic example. Also it seems reasonable to assume that the mother is the first object of infantile (preoedipal) desire. Can we infer that the primordial desire and attachment is reflected in all subsequent desires and attachments?

Here we seem to be on slippery ground. We would be hard-pressed to show that even oedipal investments are necessarily derivative from the primordial. But it may still be so. The connection may be found in certain patients, but I have never been able to discover it and I do not know whether others have. I would prefer to withhold judgment unless evidence were available to support the hypothesis. Nor does Lacan offer any evidence to support his claim; he relies solely on the force of his argument. At the same time, it carries with it a certain reductive assumption that may do violence to other forms of motivational explanation closer to clinical validation. It may not be necessary to connect every pleasure to the primordial in order to understand and explain its motivational structure.

Pleasure and desire. The second dimension of Lacan's discussion of pleasure leads to another speculation on the relevance of pleasure to morality. His argument leads beyond mere pleasure to an uncertain and perilous realm loosely delineated by *jouissance*. In the pursuit of pleasure, one crosses a boundary from which, once crossed, there is no return. For Lacan, this is the critical difference separating Freud and psychoanalysis from philosophical hedonisms. If desire(s) is(are) a refraction of the ultimate pleasure, desire also acts as a barrier to *jouissance*—"For desire is a defense, a prohibition against going beyond a certain limit in *jouissance*" (1977, p. 322). The transformation of *jouissance* into desire posits a limit, filtering, fractionating *jouissance*, creating a gap, an ineluctable lack that is the permanent deficit of desire. Access to man's ultimate pleasure can only be achieved at great cost—the pound of flesh. However one sublimates his desire, there is a price to be paid. In the surrender to desire lies the root of guilt.

I take Lacan to be suggesting something profoundly true of human nature: that the search for the good in the service of the satisfaction of desire is a perilous enterprise in that the good is always ambiguous, even ambivalent, and carries within it a betrayal of desire and disappointment of the hope it entails. Lacan, to my knowledge, does not use the example, but the eating of the apple in the Garden of Eden would seem to provide a telling instance—the pleasure of the apple as fruit and as offering the promise of becoming like gods betrays the desire and opens the way to abandonment, loss, and evil.

Thus Lacan's interpretation of the freudian dynamic of desire sets us on the path to a pervasive tragic image of man. The purification of desire found in catharsis cannot be accomplished without crossing those limits beyond which lie pity and fear—the realm of aristotelian tragedy. We get a sense of the extent to which the lacanian vision is determined by the primordial extremes of human existence. His image of man is a tragic vision bound in Promethean servitude to the extremes of existence, to its origins and end—and the forces and fates operative at the beginning determine the fateful resolution at the end. But, whatever merits the argument may have on philosophical grounds, we may well question whether it does not draw us beyond not only the pleasure principle, but beyond the range of meaningful analytic and even ethical discourse. Lacan's vision of the pleasure principle is cast in the shadow of Freud's *Beyond the Pleasure Principle* (1920a), and even as Freud's mythic speculations regarding Eros and Thanatos may have transcended the limits of analytic theory, the shadow they cast on the lacanian speculations may entail the same costs and cautions.

CHAPTER SEVEN

Narcissism and Egoism

Probably no concept in the analytic lexicon carries as heavy a weight of ethical implication as narcissism. There is little in the realm of ethical action that is not tinged, if not deeply permeated, with narcissistic dynamics and implications. To think for a moment of the polarity of egoism versus altruism, for example, both sides of that dichotomy are riddled with narcissistic implication. This is more obvious in the case of the narcissistic self-enhancement and self-centeredness associated with egoism, but narcissism is also imbricated in the web of altruistic devotion to the welfare and well-being of love objects—love of the other and being loved by another is self-enhancing, and forms of altruistic sacrifice or surrender are tinged with narcissistic gratifications related to the ego ideal. The asceticism of the saint, in this sense, is narcissistic insofar as it involves fulfillment of an ideal of religious self-denial and devotion.[1]

These issues are pervasive in the analytic consulting room as well. Much of the patient's neurotic difficulties—some patients more than others, but to some extent all patients—are caught up in the patient's need to balance narcissistic needs with the demands of reality, not only the reality of the world he lives in, but more especially the reality of those who he loves or hates and who form the intimate fabric of his life. I am arguing that the patient, who proclaims and defends his narcissistic needs and entitlements regardless of consequences for himself or others, is caught up in a struggle that has ethical implications. Actions dictated by such needs and demands have effects both for the actor himself and for those whom they might affect. In some measure, he does good or evil to himself or to others. Neither the analyst nor the analytic process take any direct interest in the patient's doing good or evil, but they do concern themselves with helping the patient come to a realization of these consequences and facilitating that development within him that enables him to become a relatively autonomous, free ethical decision-making agent, capable of making mature, prudential, and responsible choices and decisions regarding the courses of action that have meaning, purpose, and adaptive advantage in his life.

One patient particularly comes to mind.[2] He was a young man in his early twenties, who at the time of his analysis had graduated from medical school and was still in residency training. His neurotic burden centered around his narcissistic entitlement. His prevailing attitude was that he was entitled to recognition, acknowledgment, an easy life, and generous loving attention and consideration from anyone with whom he had any involvement. Life, love, and work should be easy, nondemanding, and convenient. Any demand, any infringement on his time, and any requirement for extra energy or work, were responded to as if insufferable outrages that were met with resentment, righteous protests of unfairness, and violations of his sense of privilege. If a patient spiked a fever requiring extra lab work, or if a patient were to be admitted shortly before his time to leave the hospital, if his girlfriend asked him for a favor, and later after they married if she insisted that he help with the household tasks, and even later that he help in taking care of the baby—all were occasions for outraged protets and bitter resentment. He protested angrily that they were *her* dishes, *her* garbage, *her* baby, and not his.

The narcissistic quality in all of this was unmistakable, but what about the ethical dimension? I would argue that, at minimum, there are two aspects of this pattern of behavior that speak to ethical issues. On the object-related side, he treats unfairly and does wrong to those with whom he has to deal and toward whom he is in some fashion obligated and for whose well-being he is responsible. He owes his patients careful, caring, solicitous, thoroughgoing, and responsible attention. His attitude is more likely to short-circuit these qualities and to undermine not only the quality of his work but the quality of his personal involvement with his patients. If he blames them for his problems, these feelings will inevitably corrode his interaction with them. And the situation would be no different with his wife—how long would she tolerate his pejorative, uncooperative, and thoroughly selfish attitude? The other side of the ethical equation is injury and disadvantage he causes to himself. His entitled, demanding, and self-centered interaction with others does not earn him any gratitude or credit from them. Rather he creates a milieu around him that promises opposition, an unwillingness to help, support, or make things easy for him. In intrapsychic terms, moreover, he creates and carries with him an impoverished self-image and a faltering self-esteem that requires constant reinforcement, leaving him no sense of inner integrity or self-value. I see these as ethical issues, in which his pathology leads him not to do good to himself and others, but to do himself and them wrong, if not harm.

Clearly, the predominance of ethical deviations related to narcissism center on its pathological forms. By the same token, constructive aspects of narcissism are related to values and ideals and to other positive contributions to ethical character. We are left, then, with the question—what are we talking about when we call behavior or persons "narcissistic"?

THE CONCEPT OF NARCISSISM

Freud began to think about narcissism first in relation to homosexuality (1910b),[3] in which the subject takes someone like himself as love object, and in his discussion of the Schreber case (1911) as contributing to the genesis of paranoia. The implications were not altogether negative. In *Totem and Taboo* (1913b), he related it to the libidinal complement of the egotism in self-preservation. But the first systematic crystallization came in "On narcissism" (1914a). Among the protean manifestations of narcissism, Freud focused on psychotic withdrawal and megalomania (the "narcissistic neuroses"), omnipotence of thoughts characteristic of children and primitives, withdrawal of libido in illness, sleep and dreaming, hypochondria, and in narcissistic as opposed to anaclitic object-choice.[4] These all displayed recentering of libidinal investment in the self rather than in outside objects.

Freud argued that this recentering in the self was due to withdrawal of libidinal cathexis from objects and reinvesting it in the self. He drew an analogy to the amoeba, putting forth and withdrawing its pseudopods. The model envisioned a quantity of libido as distributed either externally or internally, and, in closed system fashion, the more of one the less of the other. The more, for example, one became libidinally invested in outside objects, the more depleted was the quantity of libido invested in the self and vice versa. Thus libido can be sent out from the central reservoir to be attached to objects and then withdrawn again to be focused on the self or ego; thus object-libido can be converted to ego-libido and back again.[5]

Narcissistic object-choice. But one can also relate to others according to a narcissistic model. Choice of an object and love for that object could involve narcissistic elements so that love of the other was equivalent to love of oneself in that other. Freud (1914a) described this mode as loving in the other either what the subject himself is in the present, or was in the past, or would wish to be or become in the future, or finally as loving something once part of oneself, for instance, children, students, and protégés. The question of whether relationship with another was narcissistic or not hinged on the motives brought into play in the relationship. Freud tended not to draw a strong distinction between narcissistic and anaclitic object choice, but rather assumed that object choice, for the most part, involved elements of both (Eisnitz 1974). On these terms, love for another may involve self-love in one way or another, but self-love plays a minor role in normal and mutually loving relations.[6]

PATHOLOGICAL NARCISSISM

Manifestations of pathological narcissism are protean. They include infantile and neurotic wishes to remain the special, protected, weak, and defective child; hidden convictions that one is special and privileged so that love, extra consideration, and deference should be paid to him regardless of the cost to others; grandiose delusions that one could be a powerful and invincible godlike figure; embattled and hostile confrontations with the world in which patients see themselves as constantly watched, surveyed, and as objects of the evil intentions of others; intense clinging to a position of infantile dependence, in the continually frustrated demand and expectation of gaining the love and caring affection one feels is one's due; and continual rage at parents for not having given one what one always expected and continues to expect from them.

Often, the narcissistic core in these cases is well concealed and well guarded. It often takes long periods of intense therapeutic effort to work one's way through the layers of defense and self-justification to the narcissism at the heart of the matter, and for protection of which all the rest is stoutly maintained and preserved. This narcissistic core is expressed in a basic conviction that life should not have been as it was or is, that the world should treat the subject with greater consideration and kindness. Along with this basic sentiment, there is a sense of outrage, of resentment, of bitter disillusionment, and of frustration. These patients are all victims of the inexhaustible tyranny of narcissism, with its unending and uncompromising demands and expectations. Theirs is a narcissism traumatized and brutalized, and deprived and dishonored. The pathology is an elaborate attempt to redress and redeem this sense of loss and deprivation. Myths and legends tell this tale again and again: Oedipus' narcissistic need to know led to tragic consequences. Adam and Eve fell victim to the desire for omniscience and for the knowledge of good and evil that would make them like gods—to their and our regret. Faust was willing to sell his soul to the devil for the sake of omniscience and omnipotent power over nature. And if these themes are played at a high and discordant volume in frank psychopathology, they are also rehearsed in muted tones and minor keys in the lives and relationships of everyone.[7]

DEVELOPMENTAL ASPECTS

We should not allow ourselves, on this account, to be deceived into thinking that concerns over narcissism are limited simply to pathological manifestations. Rather, they form a fundamental human concern from the cradle to the grave. From earliest childhood to the last gasp of dying breath, human beings are caught up in the preservation of a sense of self-esteem that remains highly vulnerable and fragile. Whatever threatens our status in life, whatever throws into question our accomplishments and attainments, whatever defeats us or limits us, or prevents us from attaining objects of our desires, all these and more are forthright assaults on our narcissism. They bring our self-esteem into question and make us feel vulnerable, defeated, and humiliated. We must struggle to find ways to protect ourselves, to sustain a threatened sense of selfhood within us, to preserve and support in whatever way possible the diminished sense of self-esteem accompanying such attacks.

From birth the child is dependent on his relationship with significant others for building and maintaining of his sense of self. The child's ontological security rests on a fundamental commitment to others, along with a commitment of others to him. Whatever the subsequent developmental history of such relationships, we nonetheless cling to them as to a tap root of our existence. As Gregory Rochlin (1973) commented: "To lose them would mean to give up our demands for imperishable relationships, and to acknowledge the transience of all things and therefore of ourselves. It would signify, too, a willingness to forego denials of vulnerability and thereby relinquish our religious beliefs, renounce our expectation of altering reality, and thus in consequence abandon wishes for fulfillment" (p. 3).

The force opposing any such relinquishment is narcissism. Any separation from the things or objects we value is poorly tolerated. Loss of a loved object inflicts a deprivation upon our narcissism placing self-esteem in jeopardy (Freud 1917). Patients with personality disorders are highly susceptible to fear of loss of objects and of love, or of the symbolic losses involved in castration anxiety. But in the narcissistic disorders, fear of loss of the object takes first place (Kohut 1971). A narcissistic investment of self in objects sets the stage for susceptibility to loss. The result is a narcissistic disequilibrium disrupting the sense of self-cohesiveness and self-esteem so dependent on the presence, approval, or other narcissistic gratification from the object. Diminution of self-esteem is a major parameter and signpost of narcissistic injury.

According to Heinz Kohut's (1971) schema, disturbance of the original narcissistic equilibrium, produced by unavoidable defects in maternal care, leads to replacing the original narcissism with a grandiose and exhibitionistic self-image, the grandiose self, or alternatively, by attributing narcissistic perfection to an omnipotent object, the idealized parent imago. These narcissistic configurations serve to preserve part of the original narcissistic perfection. Optimally, the exhibitionism and grandiosity of the grandiose self can be gradually contained and integrated into a more mature personality structures and thereby supply the basis for an emerging sense of healthy self-esteem. The idealized parent imago can be similarly internalized and integrated by way of introjection in the form of the ego ideal or idealized aspect of superego. Under the burden of narcissistic disappointment, however, the archaic narcissistic self tends to retain its grandiosity, and the idealized imago remains unaltered and unintegrated.

But the claims of narcissism on us cannot be restricted to a more-or-less pathological concept of fixated and infantile narcissism. Rather, the claims of narcissism are universal, and its demands for satisfaction inescapable. As Rochlin (1973) observed: "Neither the beloved child nor the fabled heroes of legend, any more than a people chosen by God, are spared outrageous trials. The flaw and the virtue in all is in the peril to self-esteem. Its defense may bring the highest honors and justify the lowest violence. But its loss risks our extinction" (p. 216). Alice Miller (1979) described the grandiose person as being in desperate need of admiration: whatever he undertakes must be accomplished brilliantly; he stands in admiration of his own admirable qualities, particularly when they are supported by success and achievement. But if one or other of these supports to his fragile narcissism should fail, he is plunged into catastrophic depression. The need for admiration in such a personality is insatiable and consuming: it is his curse, his tragic flaw, and the mark of the tyranny of his narcissism that demands total admiration and leaves no room for admiration for any others. Credit, acknowledgment, or praise given to another is the same as though it had been taken away from him, and gives rise to intense envy. Caught within this overpowering need, he can even be envious of healthier people around him, who do not have such a need for admiration and do not have to exert themselves constantly to impress others and to gain their acknowledgment. The grandiose person can thus never really be free, not only because he is excessively dependent on others for admiration and acknowledgment, but because his own precarious narcissistic equilibrium depends on qualities, capacities, and achievements, which are inherently vulnerable and can at any point in time fail. In such personalities, depression looms whenever grandiosity is undermined as the result of sickness, injury, or simply aging. As narcissistic supplies and continual reinforcement of the sense of self-importance and specialness are eroded, depression looms as a desperate alternative.

Grandiose fantasies, along with depression, are primary aspects of pathological narcissism. The persistence of grandiose fantasies were described by Annie Reich (1960) as forms of primitive ego ideals related to primitive internalizations. The degree of pathology depends on the capacity of the ego to function adequately on a realistic level and on the availability of, or capacity for, sublimation in the service of partially realizing or transposing fantasy ambitions into realistic attainments. Often, the grandiose fantasy is overvalued due to the intensity of inner needs, and the distinction between wish and reality becomes obscure. Such unsublimated and relatively grandiose fantasies easily shift into feelings of utter dejection, worthlessness, or to hypochondriacal anxieties. Often, the narcissistic affliction takes the form of extreme and violent oscillations of self-esteem: periods of elation and self-infatuation are followed almost cyclically by feelings of total dejection and worthlessness. The infantile value system knows only absolute perfection and attainment or complete destruction and worthlessness. The shift can be precipitated by the most insignificant disappointment or experience of failure. In the logic of such extremes, there are no degrees or shadings. The situation is all-or-nothing, black-or-white, all good or all bad, or omnipotent or impotent. Any shortcoming or failure to attain absolute perfection is translated into terms of absolute failure.

At all levels of narcissistic pathology, we find degrees of intermingling of both narcissistic vulnerability and grandiosity—these qualities are inherently linked and never found in isolation. Frequently, one or more dimensions may be found as explicit or conscious manifestation of the narcissistic aspects of a given personality, but even in such cases the correlative aspect of narcissistic pathology can also be found on further clinical investigation. Thus, the phallic or exploitative narcissistic character who displays his vanity and grandiosity in a variety of more-or-less public ways can be found to carry a concealed core of narcissistic vulnerability and feelings of inferiority, shame, weakness and susceptibility. Similarly, the clinging, dependent, needy, and demanding type of more primitive narcissistic or depressive character will be found to carry a concealed core of grandiosity. This core underlies the infantile expectations and extreme sense of entitlement allowing them to feel that they have a right to demand concern, care, and attention from others, often to the point of considerable self-sacrifice and disadvantage or detriment to those others. This same grandiosity also expresses itself in the sulking, pouting, whining, and demanding quality of efforts to gain narcissistic supplies.

There is often an implicit supposition that others owe it to the subject to make up for deprivations and deficits the subject feels he has suffered at the hands of depriving others and for which he feels expiation is owed him. The obligation falls upon others, therefore, to make up this deficit and to exercise themselves to undo the wrongs done to the subject rather than the subject taking upon himself responsibility for dealing with his own difficulties. This goes along with a general blaming tendency in such individuals to lay responsibility for their difficulties at someone else's door—frequently parents or other caretakers, but not infrequently other family members, friends, employers, coworkers, and so forth. In its more extreme form, this tendency may become paranoid (Meissner 1978a).

One of the most significant disappointments a child suffers comes with termination of the oedipal period. His expectations come to naught, and the experience of failure of his oedipal wishes serves as a template for subsequent losses and disappointments. As Rochlin (1973) pointed out, there is no reason to suppose that when such longings or wishes are thwarted that the result is ever resignation or abandonment of frustrated wishes. The disappointment of the oedipal situation is accompanied by a serious loss of self-esteem, but this situation also provides the stimulus for recovery of lost narcissism. The child is thrust into a latency period of development, in which the heroes of myths and fairy tales serve as a means of retrieving some sense of power and high-minded worthiness. Similarly, the child's immersing himself in the rigors of learning and attainment of skills, both mental and physical, serves to channel his energies toward restitution of the narcissistic injury he has suffered. The persistent infantile wish to attain the impossible thus reveals a lack of ability to face both inner and outer reality. The injury to self-esteem is often compensated by narcissistic self-inflation and grandiosity. Such deprivations are narcissistic injuries, and in the early years of childhood, when the sense of self-esteem is delicately forming, they are experienced as a loss of self-esteem.

As the growing child comes to know reality, his narcissism is inevitably and profoundly effected. He is forced on countless fronts to accept limitations, to give in to the insistence and convictions of others. The child must learn that his capacities are limited, that his existence is finite, that choice and determination are fraught with anxiety and uncertainty. Through all of his painful learning experience, there runs the thread of the child's continuing sense of helplessness and weakness. Children manage to transcend the real world and its limitations by the force of imagination, active and vivid fantasy, a belief in magical power and omnipotence, and a capacity for imitation and assimilation to the powerful figures around them. Identification with the aggressor is a striking example. It is through such devices that the child gradually turns from the precarious weakness of passivity and victimhood to the relative activity and striving for mastery that is essential for psychic growth.

Narcissism is incapable of self-sustaining action. By its nature it is uncompromising and continually requires fresh gratification. Nor is it self-limiting: it has no inherent stability, but has a quality of insatiability. Pathological narcissism can allow no allies; it can tolerate only enemies. The narcissistic image must be endlessly restored. The struggle with reality convinces the child, undoubtedly quite correctly, that but for reality he would not be deprived and would have what he wished. The very nature of his wishes precludes their realization, and it is this that is at the basis of his deprivation.

Not the least of the narcissistic assaults that all men must subject themselves to is the threat of death. The struggle between the realization and acceptance of the fact of death and the wish to repudiate and overcome it is lifelong. Facing the remorselessness and inevitability of death leaves us with a sense of helplessness and ultimate vulnerability. Primitive man turned to magic, and more contemporary man turns to religious beliefs that find their most profound motivation in restitutive attempts to overcome this fundamental narcissistic assault. Man can also turn to less realistic and more pathological forms of restitution as well—particularly fantasies of omnipotence and invulnerability, or to investments in the treasures of this world—power, wealth, sexual indulgence, and so on to salvage his imperiled narcissism.

HEALTHY NARCISSISM

Analysts tend to emphasize narcissistic aberrations, rather than seeing it as diffused into all aspects of human activity and life. Paul Federn (1952) distinguished healthy from pathological narcissism. First of all, healthy narcissism does not interfere with or replace libido directed to objects. Where narcissism begins to interfere with investment in real objects or with the capacity for investment in objects, the result is pathological. In normal narcissism, the level of satisfaction resulting from narcissistic self-investment is moderate, not excessive. Furthermore, satisfaction from conscious and unconscious fantasies depends in part on the capacity to achieve real accomplishments and/or libidinal attachments in relation to real objects. Real satisfaction predominates, whereas in pathological narcissism satisfaction of narcissistic fantasies is primary. In addition, fantasy material of normal narcissism is more reality-oriented, less infantile, and much less a vehicle for perverse infantile sexual desires. Such narcissism is, therefore, by its very nature more adaptive and mature, more supportive of normal psychic development and adult psychological functioning. Even Freud, who tended to emphasize the narcissistic component in love relations, could recognize the role of ideals, including themes of brotherly love and moral responsibility, ideas calling for constructive narcissistic variation. Even redirection of object libido onto the ego was not necessarily pathological, but could be put to the use of creative and artistic endeavors, as he suggested in his discussion of Leonardo da Vinci (1910b)—a process later described by Ernst Kris (1952) as "regression in the service of the ego."

Ego-ideal. These developments were adumbrated in Freud's notion of the ego-ideal. In his view, narcissism was an expression of libidinal drives directed to the self. On these terms, the infant cannot love another until he develops a capacity to differentiate self from object. Differentiation of self from the external world brings with it the possibility of directing libido either to external objects or to the self as an object. In his paper "On Narcissism," Freud (1914a) explained repression by appealing to the ego ideal:

> Repression . . . proceeds from the ego; we might say with greater precision that it proceeds from the self-respect of the ego. The same impressions, experiences, impulses and desires that one man indulges or at least works over consciously will be rejected with the utmost indignation by another, or even stifled before they enter consciousness. The difference between the two, which contains the conditioning factor of repression, can easily be expressed in terms which enable it to be explained by the libido theory. We can say that the one man has set up an ideal in himself by which he measures his actual ego, while the other has no such ideal. For the ego the formation of an ideal would be the conditioning factor of repression." (pp. 93–94)

The ego-ideal was heir to the original infantile self-love. The success of the struggle for identity depends in part on satisfactory transfer of this original narcissism into a self-sufficient ego and its ideal (Murray 1964). The residues of infantile narcissism were thereby distilled into the ideal, which comes to possess every perfection of value (Milrod 1990; Steingart 1969).

The ego-ideal thus becomes a repository for secondary narcissism and the inheritor of primary narcissism. Freud (1914a) explained:

> This ideal ego is now the target of the self-love which was enjoyed in childhood by the actual ego. The subject's narcissism makes its appearance displaced on to this new ideal ego, which, like the infantile ego, finds itself possessed of every perfection that is of value. . . . He is not willing to forgo the narcissistic perfection of his childhood; and when, as he grows up, he is disturbed by the admonitions of others and by the awakening of his own critical judgment, so that he can no longer retain that perfection, he seeks

to recover it in the new form of an ego ideal. What he projects before him as his ideal is the substitute for the lost narcissism of his childhood in which he was his own ideal. (p. 94)

This formulation was one of Freud's fundamental contributions to understanding the development and functioning of the human personality. He later (1933a) would distinguish it more clearly from superego and reformulate their relation (Steingart 1969). The importance of this transformation cannot be overestimated. John Murray (1964) commented: "This transformation and socialization of narcissism would then consist in directing it toward an aim other than the egoistic pregenital one, in deflecting its expression and satisfaction to the area of idealistic, personal, and social values, and in striving to create realistically a world appropriate and suitable for such a highly regarded ego to live in" (p. 501). The mature ego-ideal is a significant factor in maintaining psychic integrity and mature balance between the expression of libidinal motives and legitimate restraints fundamental to the sense of identity. The ego-ideal serves as a kind of internalized standard by which the ego measures itself and that sets the norms of personal perfection toward which the ego constantly strives. Freud called it a "precipitate of the old idea of the parents," the powerful and omniscient beings of the child's early experience, and it undoubtedly reflects the child's admiring attitude toward them—Heinz Kohut's (1971) "idealized parental imago." The implications of the deployment of narcissistic libido in the organization of many aspects of mature psychic structure is not settled even today. But it seems clear that from the very beginning the notion of the ego-ideal was impregnated with ethical implications.

The ideal arises by way of identification, redirecting the child's object-directed love for the parents again to himself and focusing it in the internalized ideal he sets up in his own ego. Through this identification with loved and admired objects, the child assimilates ideals and values. While derived originally from parental imagos, there is an accretion of other identifications and idealized elements that enlarge and modify the ego-ideal as it evolves (Chasseguet-Smirgel 1975). The ego-ideal embraces new images of self-regard and competence as development proceeds—some from internalizations from later objects, teachers, coaches, heroes of adventure and romance, sports and movie stars, even attractive and admired peers. The illusion of perfection is progressively challenged and confronted, but can find support and confirmation in parental approval and endorsement of the child's enlarging capacities. Praise and approval for learning to dress oneself, for example, provides a degree of narcissistic confirmation and enhances the child's self-evaluation and sense of competent self (Benjamin 1988).

It is clear, on these terms, that the ego requires a fund of narcissism both for normal development and for normal functioning (Grunberger 1971). Narcissism embraces a spectrum of psychic states serving as normal complements of mature functioning. Narcissism is the libidinal component of comfort, gratification, self-regard, self-confidence, peace of soul, inner tranquillity, self-respect, balance, in addition to those specified by Kohut (1966) as mature transformations of narcissism—creativity, empathy, the capacity to contemplate one's own impermanence and death, sense of humor, and wisdom. Enjoyment of simple pleasures, whether in the satisfaction of basic needs like hunger, a good pipe, good music, gratifying sexual relations, or whatever, carries a component of narcissistic gratification. Over and above its pathological expressions, narcissism must be considered as a natural resource rooted in basic inclinations that can be diverted to serve and support man's best interests.

Further vicissitudes of narcissism in the course of development are complex and often quite perplexing. On one hand, we have to reckon with the relation between narcissism and the ego-ideal; on the other, there is the complex relationship between ego-ideal and superego. Some would argue that they involve separate sets of functions (Lampl deGroot 1962; Novey 1955; Piers and Singer 1953; Reich 1953), others that they serve an integrated function. I will have more to say on these subjects when we return to the question of values. On these terms, narcissism has an indispensable role to play in healthy and adaptive functioning. The maintenance of self-esteem requires a sufficient degree of narcissistic self-investment to enable one, particularly when confronted with limitations, disappointments, and failures, to preserve a degree of self-respect and optimistic self-feeling that allows for absorbing and integrating losses and failures, narcissistic assaults and injuries, mourning the losses and disappointments involved, and focusing one's resources in an effort to reconstitute and redirect oneself to recuperative and restorative adaptations. This dynamic has been carefully described and analyzed in terms of the loss-complex involving processes of loss-and-restitution (Rochlin 1965) and along similar lines in the mourning-liberation process (Pollock 1989).

It also remains a fact of experience that healthy narcissism is one of the major requisites for the capacity to love. Only in the measure that one has a constructive sense of self-worth and self-regard can one allow room for the valuing another that is implicit in the love relation. Love is also a mutual relational experience, so that even as one loves one is loved. The experience of being loved and valued by the other is self-enhancing, a major form of narcissistic gratification. Just as object loss, rejection, or devaluation is a form of narcissistic injury, so their opposites have the effect of narcissistic self-enhancement and gratification. Despite his closed model of libido, Freud was not slow to recognize that inability to love could undermine self-esteem and that love for another could enhance self-esteem (Pulver 1970). He observed, "part of self regard . . . proceeds from gratification of object-libido" (Freud 1914a, p. 58), and again, "the realization of impotence, of one's own inability to love, in consequence of mental or physical disorder, has an exceedingly lowering effect upon self regard" (1914a, p. 98).

NARCISSISM AS MOTIVE

We should not ignore the fact that these observations give the lie to Freud's basic model of narcissism—the amoeboid model of libidinal extension and retraction. However ingenuous, Freud's model, relies on a closed-system concept of libidinal distribution, according to which a set quantity of libidinal energy is variously distributed internally or externally. The libidinal model of narcissism comes up short of accounting for basic facts of self-esteem regulation and for the capacity for loving relations. Our explanations of motivation must look elsewhere than to a theory of drives. With respect to narcissism, appeal to libidinal drive-derivatives gives way to a consideration of motives involved in whatever form of narcissistic investment is in question, for instance, a need to preserve self-esteem or self-respect. Appeal to narcissistic motives is a different kettle of fish than appeal to a narcissistic drive.

I would insist that the freudian perspective enjoys a high degree of validity with respect to its observations and descriptions; it is the explanatory theory behind the observations that is suspect. In the view of narcissism as motive rather than as drive, the entire lexicon of analytic terms retains its descriptive validity—I would argue that terms descriptive of narcissism and its vicissitudes remain intact and analytically valid. Even the term *narcissism* itself has descriptive merit, given that we can understand by it a certain constellation of behaviors and attitudes having to do with self-valuation and importance. The term, however, makes no commitment to a theory, libidinal or otherwise, and need not. The same qualification would apply to the rest of the catalog of terms related to the description of affective and motivational dynamics—libidinal, sadistic, masochistic, oral, anal, phallic, incestuous, object libido, and so on. Obviously, divorcing these dynamic considerations from drive theory calls for a theoretical alternative. The alternative I have proposed is to view the self as the source of agency and dynamic action in the person (Meissner 1986c, 1993), thus explaining the "how" of behavior, and to appeal to principles of motivation (Meissner 1999a,b) to explain the "why." What are the implications for this conceptual shift for narcissism?

Descriptively narcissism is essentially a matter of affective attunement and responsiveness to the self, reflecting complex derivatives of developmental experience, the record of accomplishment and failure over a lifetime, and the quality of relations and interactions with others. We all have affective reactions to everything we experience—I would wager that we humans do nothing, carry out no piece of behavior, do nothing without a measure of affectivity accompanying our action. This is a by-product of being human and being an embodied entity (Meissner 1997, 1998a,b,c). Our actions, of whatever description, are bodily actions and as such carry a component of affective resonance. This is no less the case in our actions of self-regard and self-attunement than any other. We can readily recognize pathological states of narcissism in conditions of inadequate or diminished self-investment on one hand and in excessive self-enhancement and regard on the other. The middle ground is the territory claimed by relatively healthy and constructive narcissism, in which an adequate degree of self-esteem and self-regard is preserved along with acknowledgment and acceptance of limitations and failures.

ETHICAL IMPLICATIONS

Freud's views on narcissism and the pleasure principle have often been charged with underwriting unbridled egoism (Gregory 1975). But Freud never went so far as to deny the importance of love for others in the traditional sense (1921a) or the role of moral principles; he was concerned more with impediments to loving and unrealistic views of morality. He protested (1916–1917):

> It is not our intention to dispute the noble endeavours of human nature, nor have we ever done anything to detract from their value. . . . We lay a stronger emphasis on what is evil in men only because other people disavow it and thereby make the human mind, not better, but incomprehensible. If now we give up this one-sided ethical valuation, we shall undoubtedly find a more correct formula for the relation between good and evil in human nature. (pp. 146–147)

Freud's personal commitment to ethical principles like justice and consideration for others, and his aspiration that analysis would help patients become better human beings are clear (Hartmann 1960; Wallwork 1991). But this only leaves us with the further question as to what the implications of these renderings of narcissism might be for ethical understanding and decision making.

Narcissistic motivation can be reasonably said to be ubiquitous in the sense that there is little that we humans do or desire that is not in some sense connected with our own self-interest, self-regard, or needs for narcissistic support and equilibrium. Despite this pervasiveness, which prevails on an unconscious level and only exceptionally finds expression on a conscious level, narcissistic concerns are only one dimension of the motivational influences that converge on the concrete decision-making process determining ethical action. Self-esteem is a good example, since we obtain it largely in interpersonal situations or in endeavors thought to be valued by others. In this respect, self-esteem, whatever narcissistic investment it connotes, is a function of adequate self-cohesion, self-integration, structural integrity, and the capacity to function competently, effectively, and to measure up to the expectations and standards of significant others and society at large. Such processes are overdetermined so that an underlying current of narcissistic self-interest does not in any way preclude or contradict other motives that may operate entirely independently from narcissistic derivatives. At the same time, the role played by narcissistic derivatives may be highly diverse depending on the form narcissism takes in a given individual at a given moment and in given circumstances of decision and action. Whether as developmental variant, mode of relating, quality of object choice, or form of self-investment, narcissistic determinants can enter into the process in many guises and with varying influences.

Psychoanalysts would maintain that residues of early narcissistic motivation remain embedded in the adult personality, however modified and transformed in the course of developmental experience. Under certain stimulus conditions and circumstances, or in the course of regressive pressures and strains, these narcissistic elements can be reactivated and play a determining role. As Freud (1915c) put it, "The earlier mental state may not have manifested itself for years, but none the less it is so far present that it may at any time again become the mode of expression of the forces in the mind, and indeed the only one, as though all later developments had been annulled or undone" (p. 285). But there is also good reason for the claim that narcissistic determinants play some role, however minor and muted, in almost all behavior. Self-interest, the need for acceptance and approval from others, the need for adequate self-esteem, accord with personal values and ideals, and the maintenance of basic narcissistic equilibrium are pervasive in our experience and play some part in everything we do. There is no attempt at reductionism here, since these narcissistic currents are mingled with other motivational determinants and transformed in various ways to bring about a course of action or pattern of behavior.

It seems safe to say that healthy narcissism has a role in determining ethically constructive action, and correspondingly that pathological forms of narcissism have a potential for contributing to unethical action. Aspects of pathological narcissism contributing to ethical pathology are given little attention generally: in the diagnosis of narcissistic personality in the *Diagnostic and Statistical Manual* (DSM-III or IV), for example: we find little more than "entitlement" and "interpersonal exploitiveness." But it is difficult to envision any form of unethical behavior that would not, in some guise, involve pathological narcissistic determinants. There are some crimes that we might not ordinarily think of as narcissistic—murder, for example, may express hatred or rage, but such affective states may well involve some underlying or hidden narcissistic injury or threat for which arousal of destructive and hostile impulses is intended to compensate (Rochlin 1973). Along similar lines, lying, cheating, stealing, taking unfair advantage of others, or manipulating or exploiting others for one's own ends and purposes to their disadvantage or undoing, all lie open to narcissistic motivations.[8] The combination of a pathological grandiose self and stunted superego development produces ethical impoverishment and a need to achieve narcissistic compensation at any cost. Intense envy and devaluation of others, ignoring or faking of reality in the service of self-interest or self-promotion, unscrupulous exploitation, entitlement and egocentricity, corruptibility of values (something is not just good but good for me regardless of what it does to others), and self-justification and rationalization of whatever means are required to serve the ends of self-aggrandizement and self-enhancement, are all hallmarks of narcissistic pathology gone unethical. Recognition of such narcissistic ethical deviations may offer another avenue to the diagnosis of pathological narcissism (Svrakic 1986).

Clearly pathological narcissism runs counter to the direction and intent of ethical principles. Not only are egotism and selfishness repudiated by sound ethics, but much ethical argument and discussion has gone into efforts to dispose of them. Ethical systems rooted in religious origins decry and attack egotism and self-centeredness. Religious traditions, Protestant, Jewish, and Catholic, inveigh against pride and self-love, emphasizing the unworthiness and humility proper to a sinful and rebellious creature. Self-love was assumed to be synonymous with selfishness. But the psychoanalytic understanding of narcissism is more inclined to view selfishness as reflecting a lack of self-love; rather than being identical, they are opposites—selfishness is the mark of narcissistic deficiency or depletion. To the extent that this form of narcissistic self-investment pervades the inner world, an individual becomes relatively incapable of love. Erich Fromm (1947) described this narcissistic insufficiency:

> The *selfish* person is interested only in himself, wants everything for himself, feels no pleasure in giving, but only in taking. The world outside is looked at only from the standpoint of what he

can get out of it; he lacks interest in the needs of others, and respect for their dignity and integrity. He can see nothing but himself; he judges everyone and everything from its usefulness to him; he is basically unable to love. (p. 135, italics in original)[9]

Like many other aspects of narcissism, self-interest can have a positive or negative spin. Fromm (1947), following Benedict Spinoza, distinguished a subjectivist and an objectivist view of self-interest. The objectivist form was virtuous in seeking the good of the self, striving for one's own profit and preserving one's own existence—a healthy and constructive spin. The subjectivist variant, however, had a more pathogenic connotation. Self-deception regarding one's needs and interests is easy to come by. Self-interest has come to mean a more subjective assessment of what might feel to be one's needs or interests rather than an evaluation determined by an objective account of human nature and its needs. In this perspective, reality yields to psychic reality; the reality principle gives ground to the demands of pleasure shaped in narcissistic terms. The narcissistic wish predominates to the exclusion of other considerations—and we know that narcissism unconstrained is inexorably driven to an extreme since it has nothing within itself that would call for restraint or limit. Of itself, it knows only all-or-nothing.

Correspondingly, I would argue that healthy narcissism plays a role in most ethically good action. Not only does ethical behavior contribute to self-esteem and self-respect insofar as such behavior is congruent with standards of the ego-ideal, but ethical behavior has additional self-gratifying rewards in the acknowledgment of virtuous actions and the good that is often done to others by ethically good behavior. The narcissistic satisfaction associated with telling the truth, for example, under conditions that may result in some disadvantage to oneself, may well outweigh potential negative consequences of truth-telling. Virtue, as the saying goes, has its own reward. In the context of both intrinsic and extrinsic reinforcement, ethically proper action has potential for enhancing self-esteem, even as it serves to modulate narcissistic needs and to attune them with realistic and adaptive ends. The ethical dynamic thus operates to both express and contribute to substantiating healthy narcissistic self-integration.

The converse applies to pathological narcissism and unethical behavior. Unethical action both violates internal self-confirming standards and runs the risk of external disapproval and devaluation. But, in addition, it does not modulate inherently disproportionate or poorly equilibrated narcissistic needs. Such pathological needs, far from achieving satisfaction or appeasement, are only further intensified and become even more unbalanced and demanding of satisfaction. There is an analytic truism at the bottom line—pathological narcissism is abetted by unethical behavior, just as healthy narcissism is abetted by ethical behavior. Extension of this line of thinking leads inexorably to the conclusion that clinically disordered or deficient narcissism is never alleviated or modified by unethical decisions or actions. In fact, unethical behavior would seem to have the opposite effect, confirming and reinforcing pathological narcissism. To the extent that a patient seeks unethical outlets for narcissistic satisfaction, his narcissism remains pathogenic and unresolved. And conversely, to the extent that a patient's decisions and behaviors begin to take a more ethically attuned and acceptable form, pathological narcissism is undermined. Ethically right action, then, is guided by an integrated balance of narcissistic self-interest and other-directed concern and regard.

THE PROBLEM OF EGOISM

Egoistic stereotype. Freud's discussions of self-interest, self-preservation, and motivations to do good to others, especially when it might involve a degree of self-deprivation or self-sacrifice, tended to emphasize the narcissistic and even masochistic aspects of such inclinations. To read Freud with only one eye open to this aspect of his thinking is to settle for only half the story. But, unfortunately, Freud's rhetoric has led to subsequent misconstrual of his meaning. Both Erich Fromm (1955) and Philip Rieff (1959) have cast Freud's view of love in egotistic and antisocial terms, yet also, in somewhat paradoxical terms, in Freud's endorsement of the ideals of brotherly love, reduction of suffering, self-determination, and responsibility.

But if we take into consideration the pleasure principle, first as a regulatory principle (Meissner 1995b), and second as applied in divergent contexts, for instance, to the whole mental apparatus, to primary process, and in conjunction with the reality principle in regulating ego and other functions along with the dynamics of narcissism, the resulting version of psychological hedonism becomes entirely compatible with seeking potentially nonegoistic goals and the good of others. Even G. E. Moore (1903) had noted:

> Egoism, as a form of Hedonism, is the doctrine which holds that we ought each of us to pursue our own greatest happiness as our ultimate end. The doctrine will, of course, admit that sometimes the best means to this end will be to give pleasure to others; we shall, for instance, by so doing, procure for ourselves the pleasures of sympathy, of freedom from interference, and of self-esteem; and these pleasures, which we may procure by sometimes aiming directly at the happiness of other persons, may be greater than any we could otherwise get. (p. 96)

And as Ernest Wallwork (1991) added: "Thus, it is consistent with psychological hedonism for people to desire the good of others and to obtain satisfaction from benevolent conduct, even when it is at considerable cost to themselves" (p. 109). This echoes earlier views propounded by Fromm (1956) to the effect that if one is only able to love others without loving himself he cannot really love at all, and that selfishness and self-love, far from being synonymous, are diametric opposites: "It is true that selfish persons are incapable of loving others, but they are not capable of loving themselves either" (p. 61).

Egoistic self-love. The claims of narcissism are likewise readily taken to mean that we are always motivated to give primacy to our own personal needs and desires, especially self-aggrandizement. More altruistic and socially oriented behaviors have been explained as forms of aim-inhibition or reaction formation, suggesting that they are for the most part thin veils for underlying selfishness and egotism. This is essentially the view proposed by Rieff (1959) who interpreted Freud to mean that all human relations are simply devious expressions of self-love. But Freud was not the first to enunciate such themes. Thomas Hobbes earlier and later John Locke had translated the desire for the good into terms of self-preservation and self-interest, and following not far behind Jean-Jacques Rousseau made self-love the source of all desire. But these claims of self-interest do not involve any necessary contradiction or exclusion. Aristotle's advocacy of self-interest related to happiness was linked to the pursuit of moral values. Aquinas's view of the primacy of the injunction to self-preservation did not exclude obligations to others. Even the utilitarian insistence on the motivational role of pleasure and the absence of pain did not contravene self-abnegation or renunciation for the sake of others or for the increase of general happiness.

Efforts to impose any such contradictions on Freud would seem to be artificial at best. Freud had also argued that the inability to love can be a source of diminished self-esteem and that loving another could enhance self-regard. He observed, "A strong egoism is a protection against falling ill, but in the last resort we must begin to love in order not to fall ill" (1914a, p. 85). Rieff's interpretation failed to take into account the difference between pathological narcissism and healthy narcissism and their respectively differentiated roles in moral action,[10] even though Freud himself was explicit about the dangers of judging the normal by standards of the pathological (1921a, p. 138). We can regard doing good to others in this light, such as a parent's benevolent self-sacrifice for a child or a lover for the beloved, as in some degree narcissistically motivated. Freud (1915c) drew a hard-and-fast line between those who act morally only for egoistic reasons, for selfish purposes, and those who act morally on the basis of "instinctual inclinations"—but these inclinations had to be those already subjected to the transformation of development and demands of social and cultural adaptation (p. 284). Roy Schafer (1992) has more recently laid the ax to the root of the burlesque caricature of analysis as creating moral monsters that would be "maddeningly and tediously selfish"; he asks: "Is this the business that analysts are in? Is it the analyst's mission to help people to be selfish? Is the attainment of unconflicted selfishness a criterion for successful terminating analysis? It seems rather that that mission could bespeak only poverty of spirit on both sides of the couch" (p. 3).

Beyond the borders of analysis, however, this caricature may be in danger of becoming more-or-less normative in contemporary society in the form of values asserting the primacy of individual needs and desires over those of others and of society as a whole (Lasch 1979). The narcissistic need for self-enhancement can lead to a perversion of autonomy expressed as "doing one's own thing" (Guttman 1983). This is a thinly disguised form of selfishness, often masking inner feelings of emptiness, inadequacy, a sense of inferiority, and lack of self-fulfillment. By the same token, the opposite extreme of self-sacrifice can take a masochistic expression in which self-value is salvaged by sacrificing oneself to fulfill the needs of others—akin to the altruistic surrender described by Anna Freud (1937) in which the narcissistic component is often well disguised as an aspect of the ego-ideal.

The ethical problem, and ultimately the therapeutic issue as well, is for the egoist, especially insofar as he is embedded in his narcissism, to come to a realization that his own happiness and advantage is better served by a more altruistic orientation and concern than by his egoistic commitments. As the moralist P. B. Rice (1947) wrote: "If a man is an egoist to begin with, I see no way of weaning him from his egoism except by showing him that a larger egoism would involve self-transcendence: that to save his ego he must first lose it" (p. 65). This was the ethical mountain the patient I just described had to climb.

CHAPTER EIGHT

Object Love and Altruism

The object relations viewpoint speaks directly to ethical dimensions insofar as relationships with others and particularly the capacity to invest in others and to engage in loving and caring involvements with significant others, are core ethical concerns. The tension between narcissistic self-investment and care and concern for others remains a persistent aspect of interpersonal relationships with important ethical implications.

FREUD AND OBJECTS

The object relations viewpoint brought an added dimension to Freud's view of libido and libidinal relations. Psychoanalytic theories increasingly focused on early disturbances in object relationships as instrumental for development of later psychopathology, particularly on the role of early affective disturbances in the relationship between the child and significant caretakers, especially the mother. Freud's early views tended to minimize the role of the object, opening him to criticisms that his view of psychosexual development took place in a "social vacuum," without taking into account the developmental influence of the adults with whom the child was involved. But the criticism does not seem to be altogether warranted. From his earliest writings on sexual development, Freud incorporated the notion of object relationships as related to the sexual instinct. He considered drive discharge and object attachment as closely interwoven. Even from the very beginning, the child's sexual instinct was "anaclitic," meaning that attachment to the feeding and mothering figure was based on physiological dependence.

In any event, throughout his descriptions of libidinal development, Freud constantly referred to the significance of the child's relationships with crucial figures in his environment. Specifically, he postulated that the choice

151

of a love object in adult life, the love relationship itself, and relationships with others in a variety of spheres of interest and activity would depend largely on the nature and quality of the child's relationships with the parents, particularly the mother, during the earliest years of life. The object relations viewpoint further developed and revised these ideas. The emphasis in their work fell on early vicissitudes of mother-child interaction and developmental processes by which relations with others evolved in the direction of mature adult relatedness.

LIBIDO VS. LOVE

Within the framework of the distinction between sensory and intellective appetites, I would take "love" to mean desire for, attraction to, and union with the other beyond merely sensual or libidinal dimensions—not divorced from them, but different and not reducible to merely sensory terms. The term *love* is much abused and overloaded with many meanings—all the way from the crude animality of sexual lust to the highest connotations of sublime charity and the love of God. Love between humans, unless based on nothing more than sexual interest, involves apprehension of the object in terms transcending the limited perspectives of sexual gratification and speaks to more enduring and meaningful levels of relationship, mutual caring, and valuing of the other for his or her own sake. Love in this sense values the other more than the self and desires the good of, and for the other more than of, and for the self. This appetitive dynamic exceeds the limits of self-interest and concrete sensual satisfactions. If we can accept the participation of such intellective elements in human love relationships—and I would argue that the successful mutuality of mature and enduring love relationships demands and reflects this dimension—then there is room for the corresponding intellective-appetitive capacity in our view of human nature and in our understanding of human love.

Freud was not unaware of this differentiation and layering in the meaning of love. He wrote (1921a):

> Libido is an expression taken from the theory of the emotions . . . of those instincts which have to do with all that may be comprised under the word "love." The nucleus of what we mean by love naturally consists (and this is what is commonly called love, and what the poets sing of) in sexual love with sexual union as its aim. But we do not separate from this—what in any case has a share in the name "love"—on the one hand, self-love, and on the other, love for parents and children, friendship and love for humanity in

general, and also devotion to concrete objects and to abstract ideas. (p. 90)

Although concepts of libidinal object attachment and object constancy are essential components for engagement in significant object relationships in adult life, the capacity for mature loving relations also involves elements of more mature object relatedness transcending merely libidinal implications. Rollo May (1953), for example, defined adult love as "delight in the presence of the other person and an affirming of his value and development as much as one's own" (p. 206). Such love presupposes self-awareness, a capacity for empathy, a degree of healthy and appropriate narcissism, and freedom—love not freely given is not love.[1]

Consequently, it would seem useful, both theoretically and clinically, to distinguish between a libidinal object and a love object. The libidinal object is related to libidinal forms of sensual desire, possessing qualities that may satisfy various sensual or sexual needs and their associated libidinal desires, resulting in satisfaction (pleasure) or dissatisfaction (unpleasure). In contrast, the love object implies an added dimension by which the object is valued for itself, over and above its need-satisfying functions, and in consequence transcends levels of libidinal desire and need and their satisfaction. This consideration applies with equal force to genital desires and motives as well as to specifically pregenital and need-satisfying kinds of relationships. Thus, the concept of a mutually satisfying, reciprocally rewarding love relationship extends beyond the limits of libidinal attachment, even at the genital level. Love, as such, is directed not to a partial aspects of the object, for instance, as serving one's needs, or as offering the prospect of sexual gratification, or as enhancing one's status and esteem, but to the person himself, as valued and desired in and of himself, for what and who he is in and of himself.

Furthermore, advance to more mature levels of loving also connotes a shift from passive satisfaction to active loving. When we speak of the need for love, the common assumption is that this refers to being loved, whereas the primary questions and the inherent difficulties in love relations have more to do with active and responsible loving (Fromm 1956, p. 1). Although such a mature love relationship must be responsive to a wide variety of human needs in both partners, including libidinal needs and desires, the regard and valuation of the love object are neither limited to, nor wholly determined by, those needs and their satisfaction. One can thus conceive of meaningful love relationships in which such needs are in some degree frustrated or denied, just as one can conceive of libidinal relationships that do not reach a level of love relationships. The libidinal object is not synonymous with the love object.

PHILOSOPHICAL NOTES ON LOVE

Psychoanalysis has had little to say about love as described above. We can turn here to the philosophical tradition for help. Love is certainly a complex subject, but the primary question we are posing here is whether the fullness of its meaning can be reduced to libidinal derivatives. Even Freud (1915a) had to admit that "the case of love . . . refuses to be fitted into our scheme of instincts" (p. 133), and "we become aware that the attitudes of love and hate cannot be made use of for the relation of instincts to their objects" (p. 137). Ernest Wallwork (1991) noted, "But when he attempts to describe the origins and growth of love and affection, Freud clearly slips out of drive theory and concentrates on describing the dynamics of the subjective experience of the individual's real and imaginary relations with other people as central factors in the development of personality" (p. 171). This faltering of the drive theory opened the way to the development of object relations theory. The developmental progression from infantile dependence to the adult capacity for libidinal investment and loving relations brings us to the threshold of a more searching consideration of the love experience.

Forms of Love

The classic forms of love, drawn from platonic and aristotelian roots, handed down by the tradition are three: *agape, eros,* and *philia.* To simplify the distinctions for purposes of this discussion, *agape* is love of the other totally and simply for his sake. Most interpreters regard *agape* as volitional rather than merely affective—as C. H. Dodd (1951) noted, *agape* "is not primarily an emotion or an affection; it is primarily an active determination of the will.[2] That is why it can be commanded, as feelings cannot" (p. 42). And again, Rudolph Bultmann (1958): "Love does not mean an emotion . . . but a definite attitude of the will. . . . Only if love is thought of as an emotion is it meaningless to command love: the command of love shows that love is understood as an attitude of the will" (p. 117). One promises to love in marriage, but one cannot promise how one will feel in the future (Fletcher 1967). Loving one's neighbor in this sense is neither liking nor feeling any affection for him; it is wishing and doing him good. As Martin Buber (1958) put it: "Feelings accompany the metaphysical and metapsychical fact of love, but they do not constitute it. . . . Love is responsibility of an *I* for a *Thou*" (pp. 14–15, italics in original).[3] Joseph Fletcher (1967) added, "*Agape,* as distinguished from *philia* and *eros,* is the "love" of the commandment. And it is an attitude, a will-disposition, a matter of the conative—not the emotive . . . the result is that we are to love the unlikable. Only in this way can we make sure we grasp the meaning of "Love your enemies" (p. 49).[4] The theme is echoed by Erich Fromm (1947): "Genuine love is an expression of productiveness and implies care, respect, responsibility, and knowledge. It is not an 'affect' in the sense of being affected by somebody, but an active striving for the growth and happiness of the loved person, rooted in one's own capacity to love" (p. 134).

Eros in contrast is love of the other, not simply for his sake, but for one's own sake, that is, what one seeks in the relation is what is good for oneself rather than for the object. The romantic phenomenon of falling in love is often connected with this sort of implicit bargain—the object is valued for its social value and for whatever enhancement accrues to the subject by reason of the relation. Erotic love is then by its nature exclusive rather than universal—the love of the other in these terms does not extrapolate to others, except on narrow narcissistic terms: if my love for my spouse is erotically based, that love may extend to our children, but they are not loved in themselves but for the way in which they bring me narcissistic enhancement. If and when they no longer do so, they may no longer be loved.[5]

Philia, the love of friendship, seems to occupy a relatively middle ground in which love for another is based on a mutual relation between the one who loves and the one loved. If the love of *philia* is for the sake of the object, it is also for the sake of oneself. Both subject and object have something to get out of the relation, especially since in the context of mutuality both persons are both subject and object of the relationship. In this discussion, I shall emphasize the love of friendship since it is the form of love most closely congruent with the psychoanalytic object love, given the complexity of love relations and the universal ambivalence of human relationships. Since *agape* seems to run afoul of ambivalence and *eros* seems more closely aligned with narcissism, *philia* may be the only form of traditional love that can stand up to the analytic critique.

The locus classicus for study of the love of friendship is Aristotle's *Nichomachean Ethics* (1941). In his view, friendship was a fundamental virtue, necessary for human life, since without friends life was not worth living. It is part and parcel of all meaningful and constructive human relations. What then is friendship? The love of friendship means that we wish that good for our friends that is good for them and for their sakes; but in friendship this is reciprocal and mutual. As Aristotle put it, "To be friends, then, they must be mutually recognized as bearing goodwill and wishing well to each other" (Book 8, chapter 2). The best form of friendship is between those who are themselves good and wish well to each other well for the sake of the friend, and not for their own sake. But such friendships are rare and take a great deal of time to develop. When friendships are based on utility and pleasure alone, they can be regarded as friends only by analogy in the sense that they each get something out of the relationship. Such friendships endure as long as the friends treat each other well and do each other good and thus continue to give pleasure to each other.

Thus, love involves affect, but friendship is more a matter of character, in that mutual love involves choice and choice reflects character. Aristotle commented: "And in loving a friend men love what is good for themselves; for the good man in becoming a friend becomes a good to his friend. Each, then, both loves what is good for himself, and makes an equal return in goodwill and in pleasantness; for friendship is said to be equality, and both of these are found most in the friendship of the good" (Book 8, chapter 5). *Philia* results in uniting hearts and minds, and can render irrelevant whatever discrepancies exist between partners. Relations based on pleasure often come to resemble friendship, especially when both participants derive pleasure either from each other or from common interests.

Another kind of friendship involves some degree of inequality—examples are father to son, elder to younger, man to wife, and ruler to subject. Each of these relations involve love but in different forms. The exchange may not be equal, but when each party renders to the other what is his due, then a sort of secondary equality arises similar to friendship. But when there is too great a disparity between the parties, in virtue, vice, wealth, or anything else, they are not and do not expect to be friends—the greater the disparity, the less possible friendship. Yet even those who are unequal can become friends where they can establish some basis for equality—especially with respect to virtue. But often a basis of equality can be found in utility—as between contraries: poor and rich, ignorant and learned, beautiful and ugly, and lover and beloved. Thus "what a man actually lacks he aims at, and one gives something else in return" (Book 8, chapter 8).

The love of friendship is shared for the sake of the mutual relationship; the relationship itself is cherished in addition to the person who shares it with me. *Philia*, then, implies a common life that friends share together that enhances both of them. This notion falls into conjunction with Eric H. Erikson's (1964) formulation of the Golden Rule: "Truly worthwhile acts enhance a mutuality between the doer and the other—a mutuality which strengthens the doer even as it strengthens the other" (p. 233). This is the love that serves as the basis for a sense of community and allows for collaboration in the pursuit of common goals. Erikson (1964) intended his reformulation of the Golden Rule as an ethical principle: "Truly worthwhile acts enhance a mutuality between the doer and the other—a mutuality which strengthens the doer even as it strengthens the other" (p. 233). The principle extends Freud's theory of genitality, in which the strivings of sexuality and love lead to mutual activation of the potency and potentialities of each partner.

By implication, *philia* means sharing life experiences by persons who freely interact and communicate with each other in a commitment that is progressively self-involving (Vacek 1994). Such a relationship is mutually transforming. Friendship connotes mutual affective involvement, whether positively or negatively. My friend is not another me, but through our friendship we share in the same joys and sorrows: his joy is not mine but I share in it for the sake of the relation, and so with his sorrows. The mutual involvement of *philia* also includes certain responsibilities. Moral solidarity with others requires an enduring relation in which the participants share a mutual history and a concern for mutual well-being. We become responsible in part for that history, accepting our individual responsibility, but at the same time sharing in the responsibility of others and of the group.[6] Our decisions are no longer matters of merely personal interest or gain, but take due account of the effects on the other or others in addition to oneself. The good of the other is understood as including the full development and fulfillment of the beloved.

Each of the three classic loves can be thought of as having a corrective aspect (Vacek 1994). The selfless love of *agape* corrects for disordered self-love or pride or exclusivity; *eros* may help to compensate for diminished self-esteem, self-hatred, or depression. The common belief that the more one loves oneself for his own sake the less he can love others for their sakes is simply false. Self-love need not turn into selfishness, but may overflow in the wish to do greater good for others. Psychoanalysts would have little difficulty translating these propositions into terms of healthy and pathological narcissism. Freud's use of a closed energic model, exemplified in the amoeba image, misled him in this respect, since it would imply that the more narcissistic cathexis was directed to the external object, the less was left for investment in the self and vice versa. This way of putting it may apply in some cases of pathological narcissism, but not to healthy narcissism insofar as love of self serves as a basis for love of others. In fact, the lack or deficit of healthy narcissism is predictably a basis for the failure of the capacity for love and love relations.

But among human disorders, some of the most poignant are relational: a fundamental problem of human life is loneliness and isolation. This condition uniquely calls for that form of love that unites one with his fellowmen, namely, *philia*. The love of *eros* or *agape* do not overcome this sense of loneliness, a point central to Aristotle's approach to the understanding of friendship. It was the missing element that prompted God to give Adam a companion to share the Garden of Eden (Gen. 2: 18–24). The human life that cannot be shared in some fundamental sense is not human life at all, but reflects a basic disturbance that cries out for correction.

PSYCHOANALYTIC PERSPECTIVES ON *PHILIA*

Can the psychoanalytic perspective shed any meaningful light on these philosophical concerns? Leo Rangell's (1963a) substantive discussion of friendship remains one of the few contributions on the subject. He began with Freud's (1921a, 1930) view of friendship as a form of aim-inhibited libidinal attachment. This drew him into a discussion of homosexual and heterosexual friendships and their instinctual vicissitudes. He took note of destructive trends in human friendships, especially when bonds of friendship are transgressed or deteriorate into hostility or hatred. In this vein, friends become targets for instinctual discharge and for mastery of mutually experienced trauma. Particularly telling is the commerce of projection-and-introjection arising between friends, and at times serving developmentally, as among adolescents, to refine and clarify self-images and emerging identity (Meissner 1978a; Rangell 1963a). There is also evidence to suggest that development of good adolescent and preadolescent friendships can contribute to development of more altruistic attitudes in both sexes (Mannarino 1976, 1979).

The use of instinctual drives as a basis for the analysis of friendship necessitates deriving friendship in sexual terms, forcing analytic understanding of friendship to seek explanation reductively in libidinal terms. Conceived in such terms, friendship begins to run afoul of the implications involved in the notion of love. As Freud (1921a) had noted, although love referred primarily to sexual love and sexual union, it also applied to not only self-love but to other forms of parental, filial, and humanitarian love including friendship. As is evident in the preceding discussion of *philia*, the basis of friendship is mutual love, nowhere delimited in sexual or in merely instinctual terms.

Freud (1905c) himself described two components of love, sensuality and affection. He viewed sensuality as egoistic and possessive—the sensual desire to have and possess the object—and affection or tenderness as the nonpossessive, nonsensual aspect that binds people together in mutual and reciprocal love relations (p. 200); but even so he insisted on deriving the latter, more mature emotional expression from the infantile residues of the former as aim-inhibited libido. The infant experiences sensuality from the beginning, but affection develops only gradually as he comes to differentiate self from objects and experiences the transition from infantile narcissism to object love, usually first evident in the anal stage when gratitude and affection to parents first emerges, abetted by the affectionate matrix the child experiences in interactions with parents and with other caregivers (Freud 1912c, p. 181). This affectionate current continues to develop through latency, reinforced and stabilized by resolution of oedipal involvements and relative repression of sexuality, reaching a new level of complexity at puberty. Freud argued that sensual and affectionate currents must coalesce to insure adequate progression through adolescent development to the capacity for mature love relations (1912c). This acknowledgment of a nonsensual current of affection for the other does not amount to an endorsement of *agape,* since in his view both sensuality and affection were intertwined in one or other degree in all forms of human relationship and in all stages of development.

Fromm (1956) was one of the early contributors to this line of thinking, parting company with Freud by envisioning love as more than instinctual inclination and involving more than drive discharge of sexual tension. Rather than yielding primacy to relief of tension, he emphasized the need for sexual union. For Freud the aim of sexual desire was relief of sexual tension, a view that has a degree of validity as long as sex is viewed as comparable to hunger or thirst as a biological need-state. But satisfaction requires union with another and bridging the male-female sexual polarity. Sex can be a component of an object relation, but the essential consideration is that mature love is conceived less in terms of mere reduction of tension and instinctual discharge in favor of interpersonal relatedness and attachment. Perversions of this fundamental capacity and need for relatedness can take the form of sexual exploitiveness or sadism, distortions of masculinity, or masochism or possessiveness in women. Fromm's further delineation of this attitude as "brotherly love" aligns it with *philia* as the basic form of loving of one's fellow man: "The most fundamental kind of love, which underlies all types of love, is *brotherly love.* By this I mean the sense of responsibility, care, respect, knowledge of any other human being, the wish to further his life. This is the kind of love the Bible speaks of when it says: love thy neighbor as thyself. Brotherly love is love for all human beings; it is characterized by its very lack of exclusiveness" (p. 47, italics in original).[7]

Rangell (1963a) described friendship as a libidinal and instinctual derivative. He described the effects of loving as sporadic and short-lived, in contrast to the effects of friendship as more attenuated and durable. The question is whether such attenuation is better conceived in terms of drive regulation and modification than expressive of other relational capacities that are noninstinctual. There is no reason to think that friendship may not involve some measure of homosexual or heterosexual attraction, but not necessarily so. So, then, is the love of friendship even reductively the same as libidinal attraction? I would argue that the love of friendship is qualitatively different and separate from libidinal considerations, so that reductive explanations based on appeal to psychosexual drive-derivatives are inadequate and misleading. However, this does not mean that friendship, like all

psychic phenomena and relational involvements, cannot be multideter-
mined—the love of friendship can be partially determined by, intermingled
with, and influenced by, libidinal needs and motivations in some degree.
The conceptual issue is that friendship cannot be *reduced* to such drive
influences. Even in Freud's rendering, the sensual current in friendship is
present and active, even if repressed and unconscious; it is subordinate to,
and put in the service of, more conscious currents of nonsensual affection
and regard for the other. The point here is that the sensual current Freud
addressed and insisted on preserving in all human love relations is descriptively valid and constitutes a vital aspect of human capacities for love and
affection, but it does not exhaust the intelligibility of the human capacity
for loving relations, nor does it require the existence of sexual drives. Sensuality and libidinal attraction are psychic facts, but libidinal and sexual
drives are hypotheses that may not be required in order to understand these
phenomena (Meissner 1993, 1995a,b,c).

If we suspend the drive idea, what is left? I would argue that we are left
with a fundamental human capacity or potentiality and need for loving
relationships. In my view, the idea of a basic capacity and need for love captures the aspects of need and desire without the excess conceptual baggage
of drive concepts. We are not driven by some internal force seeking tension-
discharge in order to relate to other humans in loving relationships; rather
our capacity for loving involvement with the other is elicited, drawn forth,
and stimulated by appropriate contexts of object-related circumstance,
which, in conjunction with internal conditions of receptivity and need, acti-
vate inherent capacities for affect-related motivational states of desire and
for effective action directed to pertinent goal-satisfaction. To ascribe motivational force to the need for human relatedness does not call for postulating a drive to explain it. Actually, the direction of sexual interest and choice
is qualitatively distinct from the needs and desires involved in friendship.
The best marriages survive to the extent that sexually attracted partners are
able to establish a mutually satisfying friendship in addition to, or sometimes even in place of, their sexual relation. The distinction between falling
and being or staying in love comes into play. The emotional state of falling
in love is less a matter of will than affective gratification that does not carry
the weight of permanence and endurance. This was the dominant model of
love in Freud's view, based in sensual need and desire, bordering on the
pathological, and wedded to transferential derivatives; rational and mature
love, encompassing but at the same time transcending instinctual considerations, had little place in his thinking.

However, the satisfactions derived from intimacy and sexual gratification are in themselves time-limited and evanescent, and can all too readily
give way to boredom, dissatisfaction, even antagonism, if the need and urge

are not complemented by that form and degree of love derived from the action of the will, ultimately expressible or transformable into some modification of *philia*. I would surmise that this principle applies whether the relation is sexually homo- or heterosexual. The capacity for friendship calls on other resources and capacities than are required for sexual involvement and satisfaction. The track record of relations based only on sex and lacking the development of friendship is far from satisfactory. In Aristotle's account of friendship, the qualities he described add something quite different to the notion of friendship than would be compatible with a strictly libidinal framework. The emphasis on mutuality, endurance, and friendship as a virtue suggests qualities more directly related to aspects of character than to impersonal libidinal drives.

Rangell (1963a) hinted at a spectrum of ego states to describe levels and forms of friendship. But analysis in terms of ego states does not seem to encompass the essentially object relational aspects of friendship, since the ego's sphere of operation is essentially intrapsychic rather than interpersonal. The analysis of friendship would, then, fall under the consideration of the self-as-relational; I would argue that the self is the proper contextual theoretical term for expressing both object-relatedness and involvement, along with separateness and individuality (Meissner 2000f,g, Meissner, in press). We can distinguish the form of union characteristic of love from that found in symbiotic union. As Fromm (1956) specified:

> In contrast to symbiotic union, mature *love is union under the condition of preserving one's integrity,* one's individuality. *Love is an active power in man;* a power which breaks through the walls which separate man from his fellow men, which unites him with others; love makes him overcome the sense of isolation and separateness, yet it permits him to be himself, to retain his integrity. In love the paradox occurs that two beings become one and yet remain two. (pp. 20–21, italics in original)

This relational component and the unique compounding with the individuality was well captured by Dennis Brissett and Ramon Oldenburg (1982):

> The distinctiveness of a friend is established by the distinctiveness of the friendship. . . . Any given individual, however, does not necessarily know his friends better, or more fully, than do other people; he simply knows them differently . . . each different friendship involves the development of a different sense of individuality. . . . Friendship establishes the uniqueness of an individual through his recognition and appreciation of a unique other. (p. 331)

OBJECT LOVE AND ALTRUISM

The dynamics of narcissism (chapter 7) and considerations of object relations and object love have specific ethical implications for the tension
between egoistic versus altruistic interests and commitments. Derek Wright
(1971) defined an action as altruistic "when its outcome is primarily beneficial to someone else, and when its performance is dictated by the desire to
help another person" (p. 127). But altruism, it turns out, is by no means a
simple notion.

Genetics of altruism. The analytic debate over altruism takes place
against a backdrop of discussion regarding the roots of altruism and its role
in human affairs: one perspective is biological and evolutionary. Donald
Campbell (1975) argued that the genetics of altruism suggested that altruistic traits had a selective value for group preservation—under certain conditions self-sacrificial behavior redounds to the benefit of the whole group,
including members of the group lacking altruistic character.[8] The balance of
individual needs and desires over against social restraints and requirements
is always in question. In Freud's social milieu, the balance was tipped in the
direction of individual repression in favor of social interest. The evolutionary dynamic over the long haul would lean toward a more-or-less stable
compromise in which the modal adult would be optimally inhibited or compromised in areas where social and individual interests were in conflict.
Around this optimal point, the frequencies of altruistic (unselfish) and egoistic adaptation would distribute—close to the median the mixture and
variations of selfish and nonselfish behavior are moderate and include the
vast majority of individuals; at the ends of the distribution cluster cases of
egoistic or altruist extremes, accounting for a much smaller percentage of
cases.

Martin Hoffman (1981) in turn argued that darwinian variants (group
selection, kin selection, reciprocal altruism, and inclusive fitness) pointed to
acquisition of both egoistic and altruistic traits. Anthropological evidence
suggested that early humans lived in small nomadic groups necessitating
cooperative social interaction. Natural selection favored behaviors supporting the group: individuals may act to advance the interest of the group
rather than the individual, and evolutionary change was mediated by differential extinction of groups rather than individuals. Kin selection may
operate more parsimoniously in terms of inclusive fitness, according to
which individual genetic fitness is reflected not just in the survival and
reproduction of the individual and his offspring, but also in enhanced fitness of other relatives sharing the same genes. This allows for actions detri-
mental to the individual but beneficial to others. Hoffman also appealed to

reciprocal altruism (Trivers, 1971) whereby action to save or rescue another, even if unrelated, both benefits the group and redounds to the benefit of the individual since it tends to elicit reciprocal acts of helping or saving. Ultimately survival is served best by a balance of altruism and egoism—egoism without the constraints of altruism is as maladaptive as altruism without egoistic restraints.

Altruistic traits. Interpretations reducing altruistic behavior to egoistic motives—common in analysis—are no more than ad hoc hypotheses lacking adequate evidence. Egoistic motives may influence helping behavior at times, but the burden of evidence suggests that it is not often the case. Arousing needs for approval does not relate to increased incidence of helping behavior. But it also seems that helping another in distress has positive reinforcing qualities in itself, suggesting that what happens to others may at times be as motivationally significant for humans as what happens to themselves. Hoffman (1981) concluded, "Although by no means conclusive, the evidence adduced here that altruism may be universal and that it may have motivational properties resembling those of egoism and yet be unrelated to egoistic motive arousal, together with the evolutionary argument presented earlier, suggests the plausibility of considering altruism as part of human nature" (p. 127). This conclusion seems entirely consistent with the findings of analysis, and finds support in the universal human capacity for empathy—the empathic response to the distress of another can serve as a powerful motivator for helping behavior (Wright 1971).

From an analytic perspective, altruism is found in both normal and pathological forms. Beth Seelig and Lisa Rosof (2001), arguing in favor of a concept of normal altruism, propose a spectrum of forms of altruism including protoaltruism, generative altruism, conflicted altruism, pseudoaltruism, and finally psychotic altruism. Protoaltruism is instinctual, biologically derived, and finds its modal expression in maternal and paternal nurturing and protectiveness. Generative altruism is based on nonconflictual pleasure in contributing to the success or welfare of another. When altruism becomes caught up in conflict, as in conflicted altruism, the satisfaction of another is still enjoyed but as a proxy. Pseudoaltruism takes this process a further step, acting as a defense against sadomasochistic motives and no satisfaction is taken in the success of the proxy. And finally, psychotic altruism is characterized by bizarre forms of delusional caretaking behavior and self-denial found in psychotic individuals.

Anna Freud (1937) described "altruistic surrender" by which an individual, unable to achieve direct gratification of instinctual wishes, could do so vicariously through a proxy. She later (Sandler and Freud 1985) concluded that this was the basis of all altruistic behavior, so that the view of altruism as conflictual and compromise has prevailed among analysts. Seelig and Rosof (2001) see altruistic surrender as combining features of both conflicted altruism and pseudoaltruism. But other analysts have argued for a less conflictual and defensive altruism (Simons 1987; Vaillant 1977). Moreover, altruism must be considered in its cultural context. In Japan, altruism is regarded as a feminine ideal, particularly in relation to maternal nurturance (Kitayama 1991), and has similar connotations as the concept of *amae* (Doi 1989).

Even beyond the borders of Japan, available evidence seems to suggest that a proclivity for considering the needs of others and altruistic leanings are more predominant in females than in males. Moral standards endorsed by females tend to be more humanistic and resonant with concern for others in contrast to typical male emphases on egoistic trends and the motivational pull to achievement (Hoffman 1975). Such findings seem to anticipate later ideas pertaining to the greater titration of interpersonal and relational concerns among women (Gilligan 1977, 1982).[9] However, as Dennis Krebs (1970) noted, support for this view in research studies was not consistent.

Altruism has also been the object of extensive psychological study, not only in relation to early socialization and personality development, but as raising questions of the extent to which psychological theories (including psychoanalysis) account for altruistic aspects of human behavior. Most such research examines antecedents of seemingly altruistic behavior, assuming that motivation is congruent, an aspect that has special relevance for ethical considerations. In more specifically analytic terms, Joseph Lichtenberg (1989), citing the work of Carolyn Zahn-Waxler and Marian Radke-Yarrow (1982), noted that development of innate altruistic tendencies is facilitated by positive and self-enhancing responses from others reinforcing the child's sense of being able to effectively influence those around him. Lawrence Kohlberg (1964), following Jean Piaget (1932), has shown that the intention behind the act outweighs consequences in determining ethical behavior. In his schema (Kohlberg 1964, 1969), altruism emerges increasingly as an aspect of moral development.

Studies on behavioral aspects of altruism connect it with guilt, resulting in either expiative or reparative consequences (Krebs 1970). Harm to another elicits guilt, which in some subjects leads to altruistic responses in an expiative or self-punitive mode, but in a preponderance of studies takes a more reparative course. In addition, private transgressions are less likely to lead to reparative altruism than public transgressions, suggesting that the shame motif may play a role in determining the quality of altruistic outcome. As Krebs (1970) summarized:

Many studies have supported the notion that public transgression, whether intentional or unintentional, whether immoral or only situationally unfortunate, leads to reparative altruism. Reparative altruism seem to alleviate a negative state associated with lowered self-esteem. When amends cannot be made to the victim, reparative responses are generalized to others; in fact, in some situations reparative responses are made only if they can be directed toward a third party. (p. 267)

There is some support for situational factors, such as attractiveness of the recipient of altruistic action, as related to altruistic tendencies. Altruism seemingly arose not only from personal characteristics of either benefactors or recipients, but from the interaction between such characteristics. A given recipient may be attractive to some benefactors and not to others, while benefactors are differentially attracted by some characteristics and not others. The most persistent characteristic of recipients was the perceived need for aid—the need for aid in a dependent other was almost universal in eliciting altruistic behavior. At the same time, other studies suggest that the connection of altruism with attractiveness is weak, and under certain conditions the relation of helping to attractiveness may be negative. Also halo effects were difficult to filter out—the high correlation of altruism with sociability, for example, may mean only that people tend to see others as altruistic because they are friendly and little else. In general, no conclusions could be drawn about personality traits in benefactors, while for recipients the major factor was legitimacy of need. Situational dependency and need can usually elicit an altruistic response, but if dependency is perceived as illegitimate the effect may be just the opposite.

There is some indication that altruism increases with age, and that it is more frequently directed to friends than to strangers, and least of all toward antagonists. Along the same line, people are prone to deal altruistically with those close to them rather than those who are not. This holds true for friends, lovers, family members, and toward members of affiliate ingroups. In-group sacrifice is fairly common in the face of external threat to the group (Volkan 1988); this is a noteworthy dimension of the formation and development of religious groups and affiliations (Meissner 1978b, 1984b, 1988a, 2000a). Both friendship and in-group affiliation involve degrees of similarity, corresponding to the general finding that the more similar benefactor and recipient, the more likely that an altruistic response will be elicited. This direction, however, can be counterbalanced by other factors, for instance, attractiveness or prestige (Krebs 1970). There is much room for uncertainty in reviewing such findings, especially since the motivational substructure for such behavior remains elusive.

Nor is it certain that altruism is always a better moral alternative than egoism. Kindness, helping others in need, and not hurting others, whether physically or emotionally, are generally regarded as ethical behavior. Kindness usually gets higher moral marks than cruelty, but helping or not, sharing or not, may be more complex and depend on various factors. Judgments leading to an altruistic choice depend on the genuineness and urgency of the other's need; comparison to the level of the agent's need; the status of relationship; closeness; dependence or responsibility obtaining between the agent and the other; the characteristics of the one in need (arrogance, maliciousness, deservedness, and attractiveness); and even the conflict between the altruistic alternative and other moral obligations (obedience to legitimate authority, social demands, and other responsibilities).[10] These can all serve as excuses for selfishness, but may also have moral relevance and can influence the evaluation of the putative altruistic action. As Augusto Blasi (1980) noted: "The morality of altruism cannot be decided apriori and objectively; the same concrete, physical pattern of action may be given different labels depending on whether it corresponds to or it conflicts with more general criteria of morality. Thus generosity can become recklessness, helping can become irresponsibility, and compassion cruelty" (p. 26).

THE LOVE COMMANDMENT

The tensions between narcissistic self-love and altruistic concern for others come into focus in relation to the so-called love commandment or Golden Rule. This commandment is of interest because it draws together many of the divergent and conflictual aspects of analytic thinking about narcissism and love and their relevance for ethical reflection. This is the great commandment of the law, placed by the evangelists on the lips of Christ but derived from Old Testament sources. In Matthew's Gospel we read: "You shall love the Lord your God with all your heart, and with all your soul, and with all your mind. This is the great and first commandment. And a second is like it, You shall love your neighbor as yourself. On these two commandments depend all the law and the prophets" (Mt 22: 37–40).[11] In Luke's rendition, one of the more legally minded listeners asks who is one's neighbor, and the answer is given in the parable of the Good Samaritan (Luke 10: 29–37). Thus, the neighbor whom one is to love as oneself is not just one's family or friends but anyone—indeed everyone. The love in question has usually been interpreted as the Christian version of *agape*. The johannine commandment is confirmatory: "This I command you, to love one another" (Jn 15: 17).[12] If the tradition preferred to see the love in question as *agape*, interpretations of the term are by no means univocal or consensual.[13]

Freud's Objections

Freud made his objections to the love commandment clear enough. He declared *agape,* that form of Christian love calling for uncompromising and selfless love for all, friend and foe alike, to be psychologically impossible and ethically perverse. But the Christian interpretation has taken various forms. In one sense, *agape* is consistent with the core of morality of the mosaic or natural law, calling for charity for others, as long as it does not cost oneself too much—not inconsistently with Freud's stance. Another view stresses purity of heart as expressed in the Sermon on the Mount— what counts is not simply the deed but the disposition of heart and purity of intention, the demand for unadulterated love for the other, and the intent to do him good without any contamination of self-interest or advantage. A third position would call for greater charity than a merely secular morality, but not necessarily purity of intention. This diversity of interpretation has led some to conclude that any consensus as to what the love commandment means and requires is well-nigh impossible (Wallwork 1991). Nonetheless Freud zeroed in on the second view calling for purity of intention.[14] His objections rested on the impossibility of observance, difficulties in loving strangers, that it encouraged false illusions and paradoxical effects, led to various forms of destructiveness, and induced guilt unnecessarily.

Impossibility. Freud's attack on unnecessary or impossible moral strictures did not lead him to deny the need for civilized morality. He was staking a claim for adjusting moral precepts to the psychological capacity and functioning discovered in psychoanalytic research and clinical experience. He regarded the unadulterated outpouring of love for others as seemingly recommended by Christian moralists as unrealistic and even psychically deleterious. He knew that intimate relations often imposed obligations and demands that called for self-sacrifice (1921a, 1930), but the limitations imposed by both narcissism and aggression narrowed the scope within which universal love could be extended. Since narcissism is involved in every object choice, this limits the objects to whom object-love can be realistically extended. Freud was at odds in this respect with the kantian prescription to love out of duty or right reason; rather he staked a claim for affection or psychic connection as the basis of love. In this sense, love was not infinitely adaptable and not everyone was equally lovable. When it came to strangers, narcissistic limits meant that the same degree of love extended to intimates and friends is not available, and similarly the power of love to constrain counterdestructiveness was also lacking. In some degree, this aspect of Freud's argument runs orthogonally to the common understanding of the love commandment as calling for an act of will and not of affect (see below).

But, of course, a critical question still remains in this regard whether object love or our intentions to do good to and for others are ever purely that without an attendant compounding with narcissistic motivations. As Wallwork (1991) noted, "The real question raised by the psychoanalytic theory of narcissism is whether our purportedly moral intentions are what they seem to be or mere facades hiding deeper, self-interested purposes of the self. In other words, what must be determined is whether we are *psychologically* capable of genuinely intending the good of others for their own sake" (p. 139, italics in original). This was the nub of Freud's objections to the love commandment. But even if our avowedly moral intentions and actions are divorced from any conscious self-interest or self-regard, there is nothing to gainsay that such motivations may not be involved and even play a significant role in determining the behavior. By the same token genuine and sincere intentions to do good to others for their own sake on the conscious level may, and indeed for the most part do, involve self-related and even self-enhancing motivations on the unconscious level. The ideal of moral goodness and devotion to the welfare of others is one of the most laudable aspects of religious motivation, but it can at the same time contribute to narcissistic self-enhancement in terms of the ego-ideal. Moreover the narcissistic dynamic tends to fix the range of the extent of love to those who are in some respect like oneself, and often these limits are set in terms of group membership or group exclusion (see below).

Love of strangers. Freud (1930) further objected that, if one extends one's love and affection to a stranger, he thereby does an injustice to those who are more deserving of our love and have a special claim on it. Freud was not noted for his optimistic view of human nature, nor did he think highly of his fellowmen. As far as he was concerned, humanity in general deserved no better love than it gave. He was wary of the stranger whom he saw as the conveyor of hostility: "Men are not gentle creatures who want to be loved; . . . they are, on the contrary, creatures among whose instinctual endowments is to be reckoned a powerful share of aggressiveness" (p. 111). This innate tendency to aggression, however, was buffered by libidinal attachments, so that those we love and who love us are less likely to direct this destructive potential against us. Attachment involves a degree of investment in others that ties them to us making them and their fates important to us personally and vice versa.

But the stranger is subject to no such restraint and will waste no opportunity to harm or take advantage. The best one can expect from strangers is indifference or callous disregard. After all, one of the messages of the pericope of the Good Samaritan was that any number of strangers passed the unfortunate victim by without lifting a hand to help him. The action of the good Samaritan was the exception rather than the rule. The bottom line for Freud (1930) was that we owe the stranger no more than he deserves. "If he [the stranger]," he wrote, "behaves differently, if he shows me consideration and forbearance as a stranger, I am ready to treat him in the same way" (p. 110). With Freud you got as good as you gave. But even the story of the Good Samaritan says nothing about affectively loving or even liking the object of his charity—the story is about doing good, not feeling good.

False illusions. The love commandment, Freud (1930) contended, did a disservice to its adherents in failing to adequately prepare the young to meet and deal with destructiveness awaiting them in dealings with their fellowmen. He commented:

> In sending the young out into life with such a false psychological orientation, education is behaving as though one were to equip people starting on a Polar expedition with summer clothing and maps of the Italian Lakes. . . . The strictness of those demands would not do so much harm if education were to say: "This is how men ought to be, in order to be happy and to make others happy; but you have to reckon on their not being like that." Instead of this the young are made to believe that everyone else fulfills those ethical demands—that is, that everyone else is virtuous. (p. 134)

One might encounter goodwill in a stranger, but it is a mistake and psychologically harmful to assume that such is always, or even usually, the case.

Paradoxical effects. A demand for universal love has the paradoxical effect of intensifying hostility, particularly to members of other groups than the one of which I am a member. For Freud, along with many of his fellowmen, concern for others ended at the borders of one's own reference group. The "neighbor" was anyone belonging to the ingroup; anyone else was a stranger. The dynamics of in-group cohesiveness and belonging require both identification with group ideals, values, ideologies, and other cultural and social structures, but also separation, rejection, and devaluation of outside groups. This narcissistic dynamic (the "narcissism of minor differences" [1930, p. 114]) sets group against group and employs hostile and destructive reinforcements to defend and preserve these narcissistic investments (Meissner 1978a; Volkan 1988). Freud noted cynically, "It is always possible to bind together a considerable number of people in love, so long as there are other people left over to receive the manifestations of their aggressiveness" (1930, p. 114).

The psychological dynamic that projects error, hostility, and forms of destructiveness and evil onto the out-group and its members, can lead to a form of moral righteousness and intolerance that legitimates hostility and destructive counteraction against the outgroup. This has been a forceful dynamic throughout the history of religion (Meissner 1995d, 2000a), religious persecution, and religious wars. As Erik H. Erikson (1964), speaking of the moral commitments of young adulthood, remarked ruefully:

> It adds to the moralist's righteousness, and to the ideologist's fanatic repudiation of all otherness, the *territorial defensiveness* of one who has appropriated and staked out his earthly claim and who seeks eternal security in the super-identity of organizations. Thus, what the Golden Rule at its highest has attempted to make all-inclusive, tribes and nations, castes and classes, moralities and ideologies have consistently made exclusive again—proudly, superstitiously, and viciously denying the status of reciprocal ethics to those "outside." (p. 226, italics in original)

These dynamics of the paranoid process (Meissner 1978a) in inter-group conflicts aside, the same patterns of dynamic interaction can find proportional expression even within groups—whether in the political arena or even in the formation and evolution of new religious movements (Meissner 2000a). The challenge to the love commandment comes in situations in which love for one set of neighbors is linked with destructive attacks against others—love of the oppressed becomes tied to hatred and violence to the oppressors. The love commandment might be salvaged by the distinction between loving and liking—one can rebel against and destroy the oppressor and still love him: we can hate the sin but love the sinner. But then we would have to think long and hard as to what the love commandment really means.

Destructiveness. There is a sense in which the Judeo-Christian tradition and psychoanalysis find common ground in the realization of something awry at the root of human subjectivity. Theologians speak of original sin and concupiscence as primal roots of something evil in human nature. Analysts prefer to speak of perversion, pathology, and even the demonic (May 1969). We are forced to confront the basic ethical dilemma—is human nature fundamentally good or evil? What is it in the psychic economy that determines the course of action toward the good and loving, or toward the hateful, destructive, and sadistic. The classic analytic model appeals to man's basic destructiveness on instinctual terms. I would prefer to place the burden of explanation elsewhere, insofar as we need not think of aggression as inherently destructive. Rather aggression is open to constructive aims and purposes and can act as an important contributing factor to meaningful adaptation and development (Buie et al. 1983, 1996; Meissner 1991a, 1999a,b, Meissner et al. 1987; Rizzuto et al. 1993). Aggression on these terms is the complement to action facilitating effectiveness and accomplishment of goals by the overcoming of obstacles.

The roots of evil, however, must be sought in motivation in which the good sought entails evil or harm to others. Pathological narcissism undoubtedly plays a hand in many cases, especially when evil done to another or even his destruction is viewed as somehow connected with benefit to the self. This is clearly the case in revenge, or in narcissistic rage, and undoubtedly plays a part in all expressions of psychopathic or sociopathic enactment. Whatever is done for the benefit of oneself is not evil unless it infringes on the good or right of another, and even there it does not become reprehensible unless the demand or deprivation imposed on the other exceeds a certain reasonable limit. Balancing of goods appropriate to self and other calls for equity between healthy narcissism and benevolent object love. Erring in either direction—whether in terms of excessive self-love and entitlement, or in terms of excessive benevolence toward objects to the injury and deprivation of the self (masochism)—leads us toward the ethically deleterious. And it makes little difference in terms of the quality of evil whether the violence against another is individual and personal, as, for example, murder because of personal insult or narcissistic injury, or whether the violence and destruction is massive and widespread because of ideological convictions or paranoid delusions, as in the Nazi phenomenon and the Holocaust, or in Stalin's purges and genocide against the kulaks, or in Chairman Mao Tse-tung's cultural revolution, or in the suicidal mass destructiveness of terrorists. To paraphrase the bard—the quantity of evil is not strained! Indeed, if the numbers and scope can vary widely, the dynamic factors and motivational underpinning remains much the same—pathological narcissism injured or threatened can lead to destructive outcomes.

Guilt. Freud regarded the love commandment as not only not doing much good, but as a source of great unhappiness. Moral constraints are necessary for any human life worthy of the name, but the excessive demand in the love commandment increased the level of guilt and diminished self-regard. Despite its impossibility or difficulty, it presumes a human capacity to meet its demands—"the harder it is to obey the precept the more meritorious it is to do so" (1930, p. 143). But the psychic cost is paid in terms of superego severity, in the form of guilt and debilitating neurotic symptoms. And, of course, the greater the degree of commitment and striving to fulfill these demands, the greater the degree of superego severity. Freud

(1930) warned, "For the more virtuous a man is, the more severe and distrustful is its [the superego's] behavior, so that ultimately it is precisely those people who have carried saintliness furthest who reproach themselves with the worst sinfulness" (pp. 125–126).

LOVE AS AN IDEAL

Freud's discussion of the love commandment sketched the rudiments of an ethic consistent with both psychoanalytic perspectives and the moral potentialities of human nature.[15] If Freud's objections challenged the love commandment as a practical norm for ethical behavior, it retains its validity as an ideal, and ideals have their place and purpose, as he was well aware (1930). His supposed repudiation of the love commandment, then, is more a reinterpretation in more modest, realistic, and psychoanalytically acceptable terms.

Freud himself was not inclined to dispatch the ideal of universal love; he had written to Romain Rolland in 1926, "I myself have always advocated the love of mankind not out of sentimentality or idealism but for sober, economic reasons: because in the face of our instinctual drives and the world as it is I was compelled to consider this love as indispensable for the preservation of the human species as, say, technology."[16] He could even admit that "In the development of mankind as a whole, just as in individuals, love alone acts as the civilizing factor in the sense that it brings a change from egoism to altruism" (1921a, p. 103).[17] He returned to the same theme once again in his reflections on war (1933b): "If willingness to engage in war is an effect of the destructive instinct, the most obvious plan will be to bring Eros, its antagonist, into play against it. Anything that encourages the growth of emotional ties between men must operate against war. . . . There is no need for psychoanalysis to be ashamed to speak of love in this connection, for religion itself uses the same words: "Thou shalt love thy neighbour as thyself" (p. 212). Apparently Freud's cynicism was not without its measure of idealism too. But he never strayed far from his realistic roots—he added immediately, "This, however, is more easily said than done."[18] Despite its idealized tone, this reads to my eye, as a secularized version of the love commandment.

Fromm (1956) also argued along a similar line that "satisfaction in individual love cannot be attained without the capacity to love one's neighbor, without true humility, courage, faith, and discipline" (p. xix); and again,

> If it is a virtue to love my neighbor as a human being, it must be
> a virtue—and not a vice—to love myself, since I am a human being

too. . . . The idea expressed in the Biblical "Love thy neighbor as thyself!" implies that respect for one's own integrity and uniqueness, love for and understanding of one's own self, cannot be separated from respect and love and understanding for another individual. The love for my own self is inseparably connected with the love for any other being. (pp. 58–59)

And Søren Kierkegaard (Bretall 1946): "If anyone, therefore, will not learn from Christianity to love *himself* in the right way, then neither can he love his neighbor. . . . To love one's self in the right way and to love one's neighbor are absolutely analogous concepts, are at bottom one and the same. . . . Hence the law is: 'You shall love yourself as you love your neighbor when you love him as yourself'" (p. 289, italics in original).

Even Jacues Lacan (1992) could vouch for the fact "that the subject's experience of satisfaction is entirely dependent on the other . . . the *Nebenmensch*" (p. 39). But in the lacanian world, subject and object are less differentiated than intermingled: "It is through the intermediary of the *Nebenmensch* as speaking subject that everything that has to do with the thought processes is able to take shape in the subjectivity of the subject" (p. 39). And, "If at the summit of the ethical imperative something ends up being articulated in a way that is as strange or even scandalous for some people as 'Thou shalt love thy neighbor as thyself,' this is because it is the law of the relation of the subject to himself that he make himself his own neighbor, as far as his relationship to his desire is concerned" (p. 76). To which Stanley Leavy (1996b) comments, "The centrality of the other in Lacan's theories bespeaks a necessary ethical context, not least because the other, the *Nebenmensch*, cannot be radically differentiated from the self as subject" (p. 1278).

But at the same time, Lacan, following Freud's lead, balks at the love commandment insofar as *agapic* love of one's neighbor contradicts achievement of the ultimate goal of human desire, one's own *jouissance*. One would have to add that, within this perspective, *philia* would also fall short of the goal of *jouissance* since good of the self is radically qualified by compromise with good of the other. To the contrary, realization that self-love and other-love are not necessarily contradictory would seem to reflect an enhancement of healthy narcissism and self-regard that makes benevolent interest in others possible. It was this realization that led Fromm (1947) to conclude "that my own self, in principle, must be as much an object of my love as another person. *The affirmation of one's own life, happiness, growth, freedom, is rooted in one's capacity to love,* i.e., in care, respect, responsibility, and knowledge" (p. 135, italics in original). This is less a quid pro quo trade-off—I'll scratch your back if you scratch mine—or even a by-product of mutual and reciprocal love in which loving receives its reward in being loved, than an outpouring or overflow of benevolent good-will and the wish to do good to and for the other. In this perspective, we can entertain the possibility of at least some approximation to the ideal of *agape*. As Fromm (1956) had concluded, the Golden Rule was less a state-ment of fairness or an ethics of exchange than of brotherly love. The love of the love commandment involves charity—a far remove from mere fair-ness or justice.

CONCLUSIONS

These reflections lead to certain ethically relevant conclusions:

1. The psychoanalytic understanding of interpersonal object relation-ships, of the relations between and among persons, does not contradict the classical libido theory so much as it strains it well beyond its inherent capac-ity. Object love in its fullness and fulfilling potential expands beyond the limits of libidinal attraction and satisfaction to include the rich complexi-ties of human interpersonal involvement and relationship. Love relation-ships derive from, and express basic human needs for, attachment, connection, mutual recognition and acceptance, belonging, giving and receiving love and understanding, and union that reach far beyond the explanatory potential of libidinal drives or merely sexual-sensual desires.

2. The concept of love is itself complex and applies analogously to mul-tiple levels and forms of affectionate connection between people and other kinds of relational objects. Love and mutual affection between individuals is one form of such loving expression, but love can find expression in other modalities—for example, love of country, devotion to a cause, love of humanity, or love of God.

3. A critical distinction among the forms of love has to do with love as sensual (including sexual) affect and/or appetite, and love as intellective appetite. As intellective appetite, love is a form of desiring and seeking union and fulfillment with the beloved object. If the analytic perspective captured an essential aspect of the dynamic of love in concluding that intel-lective forms of loving are always in some sense associated with, in some degree derivative from, and inevitably intermingled with sensual and infan-tile components, it becomes misleading when it introduces the further assumption that higher forms of intellective loving are reducible to, or totally explainable in terms of, such infantile or sensual derivation. Freud himself seems to have been unable to resolve the inherent tensions created by seeking to understand forms of intellective love by appeal to the closed system dynamics of libido theory.

4. The freudian contretemps with the Christian love commandment strikes a corrective note by rejecting any attempt to divorce consideration of this command from an understanding of basic human dynamics. Freud qualified the love commandment by appeal to the basic ambivalence inherent in all human loving and by a perception of the object of love as only incompletely lovable, that is, that by and large others are potentially objects of both love and hate. Essential to this perspective, is that the loved object is in some sense a mirror of the self, and that the balance of the lovable and hatable seen in the object is a reflection of the lovable and hatable in myself. Given these qualifications, the injunction to love the neighbor as oneself makes perfectly good analytic sense. The formula is completed by considerations of the contribution of healthy and pathological narcissism— healthy narcissism tends toward love of self in conjunction with love of others, pathological narcissism toward either love of self at the cost of love of others or toward hate of self and others.

5. The intermingling and balance between narcissism and object love determines the forms and combinations of egoism and altruism in the integration of human value systems and orientations. In the analytic purview, egoism and altruism are not inherently contradictory or oppositional, but the disposition and orientation of any individual are determined by the balance and patterning of these dynamic and developmental derivatives. Pathological narcissism and impaired or inhibited object love inclines toward egoism; healthy narcissism and more mature forms of object love incline toward a capacity for altruistic orientation and behavior.

6. The understanding of love in classic terms that comes closest to the ambiguities of analytic understanding discussed above is provided by the concept of *philia*. Other classic forms of love are either impervious to analytic perspectives and qualifications—*agape* leaves little room for ambivalence and the universal conflicts between narcissism and object love—or are excessively drawn to the narcissistic pole with corresponding undervaluing or minimizing of the demands of object love—as in the case of *eros*. We are left with *philia* as the modality of love most open to the ambiguities and complexities of analytic understanding.

CHAPTER NINE

Ethical Decision-Making and Self-Deception

Given the executive role of the will in generating and directing psychic and bodily action, the decision-making process, by which the subject determines upon and directs himself to a specific course of action, becomes central to any assessment of ethical reflection and calls for psychoanalytic conceptualization.[1] While that process is probably best conceived as a function of the ego, acting as the substructure of the self dealing with assessment of reality and related functions of perception and judgment, this activity obviously does not take place in a vacuum, but is integrated with processes involving contributions from other psychic entities (superego and id, especially superego) reflecting the agency of the self-as-agent (Meissner 1993).

The present chapter extends the previous argument on will and freedom, but the focus on decision-making and responsibility conveys a further sense of its consequences and implications. I will take Leo Rangell's (1963b, 1969a,b,c,d, 1971, 1974, 1981, 1986, 1987, 1989) theory of the decision process as a function of ego-activity as point of departure for my reconstruction. He (1969a) argued that contemporary decision theorists emphasized the present stimulus situation as determining the decision process, leaving open the role of past experience and unconscious factors for analytic exploration.

THE DECISION PROCESS

In practical reason leading to decision and choice[2] of a course of action, the logical process reaches conclusions regarding not only what to do but what I should do. As Anthony Kenny (1975) noted: "In practical reasoning as in theoretical we pass from premises to conclusion. The premises, perhaps, set out our desires or our duties; they set out also the facts of the case and the possibilities open; the conclusions are actions or plans of action. But what are the rules by which we pass from premises to conclusion? What are the criteria for validity in practical inference?" (p. 70). Augusto Blasi (1980) further noted: "When moral action is considered to be necessarily mediated by moral judgment, the relations between judgment and action become problematic. How should these relations be conceptualized? How can the connections between the cognitive and the executive functions be explained? Equally important, how can the lack or the breakdown of functional relations be understood? These are the questions that a complete theory of moral functioning should address" (p. 4). Cognitive functions can include not only moral information about culturally endorsed norms of behavior and moral attitudes and values, but specific forms of moral reasoning and judgment leading to a conclusions justified by moral criteria. In his review of research in this area, Blasi commented:

> In principle, the study of the consistency between moral thinking and moral behavior should include not one but at least two sets of relations: those between specific hypothetical choices and actions and those between hypothetical choices and general structures of moral reasoning. Without information concerning the latter, the moral reasoning of the action for the individual remains unknown; without information relevant to the former, moral means would not offer an adequate basis for the study of the action-cognition consistency. . . . At present, however, it is not known how general structures of moral reasoning and general attitudes interact in the production of behavior. (p. 10)

Rangell addressed this problem analytically in terms of the decision process. The process starts with a state of intrapsychic equilibrium being disturbed by a precipitating stimulus, either external or internal.[3] Internal sources may be somatic or psychic, and if psychic can originate from any of the psychic structures (id, ego, or superego). Whatever the source, an instinctual "temptation" is aroused and confronts the ego under the critical assessment of the superego or other external judgmental sources. This tentative sample-impulse is passed in review by superego and other evaluative and judging functions of the ego, assessing the nature of the impulse and its acceptability (1969a,d). Based on this intersystemic evaluation, the self-as-ego allows a small controlled arousal of instinctual response, while testing the balance of gratification or superego criticism, which is immediate, automatic, and proportional to the minimal pleasure or displeasure encountered. This evaluation is effected by screening present partial gratification in the light of past experience, especially prior gratifying or traumatic memories potentially related to the projected motive. Rangell (1969c,d) called this the "minor preliminary phase" to distinguish it from actual psychic conflict to follow. The signal thus received conveys a sense of danger in a preliminary form of signal anxiety, or of safety, allowing the self-as-ego to assess the degree of risk or lack of it (1971).

At the core of this intrapsychic process, the ego tests every intended instinctual motive or incoming perception or unconscious fantasy before admitting it to consciousness or executing the action (Rangell 1981). If the risk is minimal or none, the ego can act to satisfy the instinctually based motive and gain a degree of gratification. If the danger is appreciable, whether from the superego or external consequences, or from the motives themselves, a full-fledged anxiety signal is elicited and the ego is alerted to an intrapsychic conflict necessitating defensive reaction. This assessment is determined in part by past memories, traumatic experiences, fantasies, and other conscious and unconscious derivatives.[4] The conflict is marked by a "decision-dilemma" taking the form of an intrapsychic conflict in the ego itself—"Possessed now of an awareness of cause and expected effect, of impulse and anticipated punishment, the ego is confronted with an internal, intrasystemic decision-dilemma as to what to do next, which path to choose, how to find a way out" (1969c, p. 66).[5]

The question, then, is how to resolve this dilemma. If the threat is minimal, the contravening forces not too strong, and the ego's resources equal to the task, mastery is possible; but even under the most favorable circumstances, a certain degree of defense will be mobilized contributing to an intersystemic conflict between ego and instinct or superego. This is the second phase of the conflict, superseding the first decision phase, and may continue even after a decision has been made until final stability is achieved. Where instinctual desires and demands are not so easily resolved or satisfied, the process may give way to symptom formation, eliciting anxiety or other dysphoric affect. The process may lead to further elaborations either of resolution or of continuing or intensified symptom formation. Weighing alternatives, my ego searches for a satisfactory plan of action, that is, which will best serve my purposes and gratify my desires once put into effect (Kenny 1975). We are more-or-less in command of desires and purposes as matters of internal regulation, but our control of extrinsic factors pertinent to the gaining of certain ends is less certain. Certain plans and circumstances are incompatible with our desires. Moreover we cannot guarantee that any given plan will actually prove satisfactory either to ourselves or to others.

The process reflects the influence of past experience and the interplay of multiple influences, conscious and unconscious. However reflective or conjectural or intuitive the conclusion may be, the more reasoned and reasonable the process the more reliable is the outcome liable to be. The process may reflect long-standing ethical attitudes and values or ideals, but the uncertain balancing of pluses and minuses, good and bad, advantages and disadvantages, may follow a more-or-less probabilistic path to the ultimate decision.[6] The outcome may not be susceptible of proof or decisively and conclusively correct, but it is sufficient that it be reasonable and realistic. Too often our decisions are not as reasonable as we might like to think, but at the same time they may be more reasoned that we know.

PRACTICAL REASONING

The logic of practical reason is concerned with guaranteeing satisfaction of wants; however, the logic leading to the necessary conditions of satisfaction can never ensure achievement of what is desired. As Kenny (1975) noted, "Having carried out a piece of practical reasoning to necessary conditions, and put the conclusion into action, the reasoner cannot then rest secure in the confidence that what he has done will bring about the state of affairs he wants" (p. 89). More may be required and, as in satisfying a negative prohibition, can be an unending process. Motivations, then, as related to desire and seeking satisfaction, determine the necessary conditions for acting, but achieving the sufficient conditions for action calls for causal efficacy of the will.[7]

Practical reason also differs from speculative reason by virtue of the truth value of its conclusions. In speculative logic, the conclusion is presumed to be "true," therefore not "false." But a proposal for a course of action may be both good and bad at the same time; an argument showing the conclusion to be good does not necessarily contradict another argument showing it to be bad—it may only show that the conclusion has both good and bad aspects. The evaluation of goodness or badness of a choice rests on the degree to which it fulfills desires, goals, principles, values, and so on, which lie behind it.[8] As A. C. Ewing (1962) suggested, some degree of subjectively determined intuition may be necessary in ethical judgments, since the balance of good-and-evil consequences cannot be calculated—at best after reviewing the relevant facts we take one set of alternatives as better than others. Thus practical reason does not necessitate its conclusions, so that this contingency can serve as the fundamental ground of freedom of the will.

DYNAMIC CONSIDERATIONS

Motivational stimuli. Rangell's account centers on regulation of instinctual pressures, but my argument renders these pressures as motivational influences not expressly dependent on instinctual drives. What then sets the decision process in motion? Any motivational stimulus may initiate the process, in the form of a wish, desire, purpose, ambition, or hope. Such instinctually derived or other desires, especially when they are experienced with some degree of impulsive force or fly in the face of otherwise reasoned conclusions, may be regarded as irrational, or at least nonrational. Thus any motivational stimulus can set the decision process in motion, but they are not limited to such "instinctual" derivatives and may arise on other grounds entirely. Such desires may, in contrast, be both rational and realistic.

As Rangell indicated, the motive may arise in conjunction with some external stimulus or context, or may arise autonomously internally. The desire, however, is not necessarily instinctual, but may aim at an objective that is realistic and reasonable, say to learn to read Middle English—the desire to enhance my learning is not necessarily instinctual, but responds to an aspect of my native endowment that seeks fulfillment and actualization in this manner. The ego acts in virtue of its self-originated capacities to assess, compare, and judge. I may consider the options as means available to gain my end, but I may be able to achieve my goal or not—an available course in Middle English may be too expensive or may interfere with other obligations. The outcome criteria are not necessarily cast in terms of instinctual dangers, but may allow for weighing alternatives and their advantages and disadvantages. The balance of factors and consequences may not be readily resolvable, so that the ego remains in decisional conflict and encounters difficulty in making the choice. But even though the possibility of error or a lack of supportive consensus may deprive us of certainty, there are some things that are clearly right or wrong, and, as Ewing (1962) observed, "On the other hand, it is even more important to insist that we must not think that what strikes us as good or right is necessarily always really so, though it is our duty to act on it as long as it really after careful consideration strikes us as so" (p. 122).

Role of superego. Rangell properly brings the superego into the picture, but in a limited fashion pertaining restrictively to evaluation of instinctual risk and/or assessment of acceptability. Other aspects of the superego may play a more decisive role, however, including the ego ideal and pertinent value systems. The degree to which the projected course of action is syntonic with the ego ideal can play a significant role in the genesis of correlative affects, specifically shame and guilt. The signal function is not restricted to anxiety, as Rangell readily acknowledged, specifically adding guilt, doubt, hate, and later shame to the list of signal affects (1969b, 1981, 1987). By the same token, gratification and a sense of security can also serve a similar signal function.

Variations. The circumstances of the decision-making can also vary widely. In some cases the decision is simple and readily made; in others complex and difficult. Some decisions have little or no ethical import—the options are neither good nor bad, but indifferent. Other decisions are ladened with ethical implication and consequence—for some of these the alternatives are clear-cut and the choice can be decisive, but for others the options are not clear, complex, and overburdened with good and bad consequences on both sides that do not allow for decisive resolution. In fact, many, perhaps even most, ethical dilemmas are of this sort. Finite and imperfect men with their limited understanding and complex and often conflicted motivations can never fully foresee the consequences of their choices and certainly can never be objective about the complexities of motives, means, and ends involved in the decision process.

Conscious vs. unconscious. An additional consideration is the question of the degree to which the decision process can take place on a preconscious or unconscious level. Rangell (1986) made an important contribution in his insistence that these functions could take place on an unconscious level. He postulated that secondary process mentation could take place on the unconscious level along with the usual primary process. In these terms, the cognitive, affective, and volitional functions, familiar in common conscious experience, can also operate unconsciously and can thus play their appropriate and proportional role in ethical decision-making and reflection (1987).[9] It would not be unreasonable to assume that the more the process followed secondary process organization, the more likely is it to be preconscious; the more primary process, the more derivatively unconscious. As Rangell (1986) aphorized, "Just as a man 'knows' more than he knows he knows, i.e., from memories and thoughts not permitted into consciousness, so does he decide more than he allows himself to know he decided" (p. 18).

Conflicts of choice. This perspective on decision-making also broadens the range of ego-functioning and extends the concept of conflict to include conflicts of choice. The traditional notion of conflict centered on the oppositional tension between instinctual demands and defensive and regulative functions of ego and superego. However the conflict of choices involves incompatibility or antagonism between courses of action each of which has advantages and disadvantages that must be weighed and evaluated to reach a conclusion accepting one alternative and rejecting the other (Rangell 1969a,c, 1989).[10] This is congruent with Heinz Hartmann's (1950) description of intrasystemic conflicts, here conflict within the ego. The decision process translates an intersystemic conflict into an intrasystemic one within the self-as-ego, thus opening the process to the option of choice between alternatives, rather than the more restrictive options of impulse-gratification or repression-defense.

William James called attention to a decision we all confront from time to time—whether to get up in the morning or not. The attractions of a warm and comfortable bed persuade us to stay right where we are; but the necessities and obligations of the day ahead call us to respond to the call of reveille and to brace ourselves for the morning air. If the prospects of the day attract us, the decision is easily made and without much delay. If the burdens of conflict prevail, we may delay and procrastinate. It is not uncommon for depressed patients to prefer the consolations of a warm bed to the frustrations and disillusionments of the looming day. As James viewed the simplified process, we get up almost without thinking—as if there were no decision. But in the light of the present argument, there would undoubtedly have been a decision process involved, albeit minimal, or even unconscious. Whatever the *lapse of consciousness* in James's terms, the gap would be filled by an unconscious process. The psychoanalytic perspective adds to this picture the dynamisms of unconscious motivation and intentionality. Intentionality becomes central insofar as it determines the degree of ego involvement and the likelihood that the judgment will lead to action or not. Motivational factors can be cognitive or noncognitive and can act to facilitate or inhibit moral action.

DECISION AS EGO-FUNCTION

Addition of a decision-making function to the ego repertoire (Rangell 1969a,d) and the capacity for unconscious operation gives the decision process a wide-ranging application in both normal and pathological behavior (1989). Ego-functions usually include cognitive capacities of judgment, discrimination, reflection, and perception; but what about after the point of judgment? The added consideration of the ego's function in moving from judgment to action is not considered as an aspect of the decision process. Rangell (1986) commented:

> While the conceptual advances enumerated above all culminate naturally in the next necessary step, for the ego to proceed to execute what it is there for, to direct the course and activities of the total organism in its navigation through the surround of its life, furtherance of this understanding has for the most part faltered, or turned back, or has at least been delayed at the threshold of the ego's unconscious decision-making functions. (p. 8)

The process is common to both normal and pathological decision-making and may or may not lead to pathological outcomes (Rangell 1969b). This decision-making function operates preliminarily to decide upon any defensive or other adaptive or maladaptive action (Rangell 1969d). The outcome of the decision process may be positive or negative or indifferent, but the moment of decision-dilemma allows the individual both the opportunity and necessity of utilizing its resources for self-direction and self-determination. While the linkage of the mechanism with degrees of signal affect, anxiety or other, has immediate application to the genesis of neurotic symptoms, the intensity of the decision conflict is not proportional to the intensity of affect (Rangell 1969c,d). Severe degrees of anxiety may accompany effective decision-making, or relatively minor degrees can result in a paralysis of decision (Rangell 1971). Even with a minimal affective component, the decision process may be forced to struggle with uncertain and irresolvable alternatives. But by the same token, the ego may be driven by the strength of associated affects to seek pathological outlets that neither resolve nor alleviate the tension—the conflict of evenly balanced and unresolved options is often seen in obsessive-compulsive disorders, just as the disaffection from the decision process and destructive consequences may follow from impulsive acting out (Rangell 1969d). But, in essence, the integrity and functionality of this decision-making process is reflective of the ego's achieved autonomy and functions in determining "ego efficiency and ego strength and in characterizing an individual in his course through life's problems" (Rangell 1969a, p. 602).

DECISION AND ACTION

As Rangell (1969c, 1971) noted, delineation of the decision process opens the way to a more comprehensive theory of action—an initiative previous undertaken by Hartmann (1947).[11] The action perspective picks up the threads of the discussion on the place of the will in the action process, specifically the executive function of will as the initiating source of human action.[12] "Human action" here has a specific meaning, namely, action that involves decision or choice.[13] Both intellect and will are involved in the decision process, but it is up to the will to initiate the process leading to action—regardless of what form the action takes.

From decision to action. The practical reasoning of the decision process leads only to an intellectual conclusion or judgment as to what action is best or should be undertaken; a further step is required to put the conclusion into action. This capacity resides in the will. And, as Kenny

(1975) noted, there is a certain flexibility or indeterminacy between the practical conclusion and the final action: "The link between a reason and an action is loose in three different ways: first, the same reasons, occurring as premises in a piece of practical reasoning, may legitimate different conclusions; secondly, different actions may each accord with the conclusion; thirdly, the conclusion may not be acted on at all—and that without the appearance of any interfering or preventing factor, as in the case of weakness of the will" (p.101). Such "weakness," or *akrasia* as it is called, results in a failure to do or not do what one has decided he ought or ought not to do. The failure to live up to moral or ethical convictions is common enough, but it comes particularly into play in analysis with regard to implementing the insights gained in the course of analytic work and bringing about meaningful change in accord with such insights.

This line of thinking seems to rehabilitate to a degree the concept of strength of will as one of the potential ego-strengths of the healthy personality. A strong will allows one to prevent minor or short-term desires from interfering with execution of long-term or more important volitions, either by avoiding or substituting for them in ways that leave the path to dominant goals and ambitions open and available.[14] In this sense, strength of will is not an ethical quality, but a necessary, if not sufficient, requirement for the good life. However, it remains indifferent to the pursuit of good or evil ends and can be put to the uses of vices or neutral character traits as well as virtues. Looked at as an ego-strength, will can effectively translate ethical decisions into action, whether for good or ill. But such strength does not carry a license to act independently of, or contrary to, the prevailing motivations involved in the decision. This is the fallacy of an extreme libertarian view that proclaims unmotivated and absolute freedom of the will and countervails any role for determinism. Such a view finds no place in psychoanalysis, nor I should think in ethics either.

Unconscious choice and action. The hypothesis of unconscious decision-making processes and acts of choice means that many mental processes leading to action can be produced without any inkling of awareness. Consequently, if the will is the initiating source of actions arising from decision, some of these actions may originate unconsciously and may not carry the stamp of reflection or deliberation on any conscious terms. Rangell (1969a) maintained that the internal scanning of the decision process was a constant feature of mental life:

> The . . . process of internal scanning goes on at all times, is characteristic of the human psychic apparatus and follows the ingress of impinging stimuli. It varies, however, from a token activity with

negative results in states of relative quiescence, as in times of soli-
tude or reflection or even in sleep, to states of acute emergency
and psychic demand at times of crises, internally or externally
induced. But from all indications there is a constant baseline vigilance maintained by this intrapsychic sequence which preserves
the stimulus barrier and gives it its qualitative selectivity characteristic for the particular individual. (p. 601)

In many instances, the patient does not know the content of his own
intentions, buried as they might be in his unconscious—circumstances in
which the listening analyst may be better situated to guess what those
hidden intentions might be. Both may agree that the patient's action is
intentional in one sense, but they may also disagree that it is intentional
under another. Here the analyst may be right and the patient wrong (or vice
versa), but if we countenance unconscious intentionality we should also
allow for its relation to or translatability into conscious terms. Freud's
(1901, 1916-1917) example of the professor who began his lecture by
saying, "I am not '*geneigt* [inclined]' (instead of '*geeignet* [qualified]') to
describe the services of my most esteemed predecessor" (1901, p. 69), suggests that the slip reveals the true intention. But the good professor may
have been well aware of his attitude toward his illustrious predecessor, but
did not "intend" to express it in his lecture.

But the patient may deny intentionality of any kind. Under conditions
of conflict, patients may resolve the tension by producing symptoms—
impotence is the classic instance of resolving a conflict between sexual
desire and the incest taboo. Having a symptom or illness is not usually
regarded as intentional, but unconscious intentionality is hard to escape in
these cases. The patient should be the best judge of his own intentions, as
long as we include his behavior as expressing these intentions. But we
cannot conclude that his judgment is best in the sense that what he says
about them precludes or outweighs what he does as evidence for them. The
space for self-deception is ample in this regard as is evident in every analytic
inquiry. Unconscious intentionality presumes a process of practical reasoning, either preconscious or unconscious.

SELF-DECEPTION

Among the welter of desires, ambitions, deliberation of options, means and
ends, the flow and counterflow of motivations and the decisions and choices
in the decision process, there seems to be ample room for self-deception. Roy
Schafer (1976) described the self-deception inherent in psychic defense:

One does not know that one knows something, wishes something, considers something emotionally, or is doing or has done some other action; one keeps oneself from discovering *what* one does not know, etc.; thus deceiving oneself once; and one keeps oneself from discovering *that* and *how* one is deceiving oneself in this way ("unconscious defense"), thus deceiving oneself a second time or in a second respect. (p. 234, italics in original)

Self and self-deception. How the self can deceive itself poses something of a philosophical conundrum. Amélie Rorty (1988b) centers the argument around the view of the self. If the self is a complex unity of integrated sub-systems, acting as a sort of rational "panoptic scanner" of its processes (A. O. Rorty 1988a,b)—a view better suited to rational self-evaluation and correction than to self-deception—the self as a whole does not deceive itself, so that self-deception becomes incoherent. But if the self is identified with an organization of relatively autonomous subsystems, for which integration is an achievement rather than a starting-point—a view better suited to com-partmentalized functioning of relatively independent psychological processes[15]—self-deception takes the form of one subsystem deceiving the rest. This led White (1988) to suggest a "homuncular model" splitting the self into multiple and mutually deceiving subsystems.

Furthermore, if affects are no more than nonintentional sensations derived from blocked drives, then self-deception would turn out to be merely verbal denial inconsistent with the rest of behavior. But if affects are connected to ideational content and are motivated, as are all psychic actions, self-deception would have to involve misdescription or misidentification of the object of affect (A. O. Rorty 1988b; Tov-Ruach 1988). Pathological mourning, for example, can involve such self-deception to the extent that the grieving subject does not acknowledge the object of the intolerable affects unleashed by the loss of the object, namely the lost object. Rather the mourning process is subverted and the disowned affects directed against the self in the form of depressive self-depletion. The affective reaction is not merely a matter of energic discharge, but is motivated and possessed of intentionality. To this extent the mourning becomes self-deceptive insofar as the real motives of the self remain obscure. One might argue that without this deception and obscuring of motives the defense against loss would not work. This can well serve as a model for the self-deceptive aspects of any or all defenses.

At best self-deception is paradoxical. It seems hardly possible to lie to oneself. Unintentional self-contradiction or deciding to follow a course of action leading to an outcome deviant from conscious belief are possible, but neither qualify as self-deception. Nor do contradictory or changing beliefs.

But one cannot consciously believe what he knows to be false, nor can one be simultaneously aware and not aware of a given belief. One can be aware of some beliefs and unaware of others. The picture of an all-scanning and integrating self with all-embracing knowledge and awareness is clearly a psychological fiction. Self-deception in such a system is not possible. But if the self is an aggregate of loosely organized autonomous subsystems, along the lines of an homuncular model, self-deception seems more possible. But splitting the self up into multiple selves, however congruent with postmodern trends envisioning the existence of multiple selves (S. A. Mitchell 1993), brings even more difficult problems in its wake. Rorty (1988a,b) argues that both renditions of the self-system are necessary to account for the data of self-deception. The survival picture of the self is better oriented to adaptive strategies than functioning as responsible and rational agents. The loosening of integrative connections and the failure of intersystemic communication causes the organism to fall back on the specialized functioning of relatively autonomous subsystems responding to specific stimulus conditions.

Rorty (1988a) offers a more detailed account of the fully autonomous self. Characteristics include simple unity dominated by rationality, complete transparence or accessibility of internal states to a central scanner, an orientation to truth or at least minimizing error, and reflexivity allowing the criteria of rationality to be open to critical evaluation. But this idealized fiction has been weakened by multiple factors—the self is less a central scanner than a hierarchical system of component subsystems that may function in a conflict-free mode or under the influence of conflict and has the capacity for more localized conflict resolution, or in the face of failure of these mechanisms can resort to less organized survival mechanisms; transparency is compromised by indirect access to some states whose existence can only be inferred (unconscious) or operate under conditions in which automatic accessibility is impeded; truth-orientation is compromised by error, misperception, misunderstanding, and lack of knowledge; and reflexivity is weakened or dissipated by contrary motives and defenses.

Both strategies of self-functioning may be necessary for adaptation and survival. Critical rationality and self-regulatory integration would not have been enough; adaptive strategies of the less integrated survival pattern are also required. In a bundle of relatively autonomous systems, not all parts of the mind are equally accessible at all times. The further postulate is that the loosening of integrative bonds and the lack of intersystemic communication can serve useful ends. In complex and differentiating environments, adaptation is better served in some contexts by an integrated central monitoring capacity; but relatively autonomous and independently triggered subsystems may serve better in contexts calling for plasticity and substitutability of functions. Central rationality can be undermined by illness or fatigue, in which case automatic and specific habit patterns can play a vital and adaptive role.

Both of these portraits of the self are in my view caricatures—the self is neither an all-encompassing, all-seeing, centrally integrated, and all-evaluating system, nor is it a loose tangle of autonomously operating fragments of unintegrated functions or functional homunculi. My preference (Meissner 1986c, 1993, 1996a, 1999d,e, 2000f,g,h) is to view the self, as synonymous with the human person (2000e), structured as a supraordinate organization of psychic and physical functions whose capacity for agency can be distributed in some degree to component substructures including, but not limited to, id, ego, and superego (2000h). These components are theoretical constructs whose autonomy is relative and whose agency is derivative; that is "ego" is nothing but self acting in an ego-mode (Meissner 2000h). On these terms, certain functional processes require the integrated capacity of an overriding structural organization in order to account for such integrative capacities (Meissner 1986c). These component structures can also operate in conflict both intersystemically and intrasystemically, so that the organization of the self-system is at best heterogeneous. There is no contradiction in a single self-system experiencing different and conflictual affective states or in holding simultaneously incoherent beliefs. But add to this that all of these component elements can function on a conscious or unconscious level (Meissner 1993, 2000g).

This schema of self-organization leaves ample room for self-deception. If one belief is espoused consciously while a contrary belief is held unconsciously, this would seem to satisfy as self-deception. If two contrasting beliefs are held consciously, as may often be the case in ethical dilemmas—one might believe in the sanctity of life, yet be convinced of a woman's right to abort an unwanted fetus—this is less self-deception than an irresolvable conflict. Either choice has its problems and consequences. Rorty (1988b) argued to the adaptive uses of self-deception, and from an analytic perspective the conclusion comes to roost in considering the defenses. Defense mechanisms are generally self-limiting and involve a universal component of self-deception, but from another perspective they also serve an adaptive function in preserving self-coherence or in selectively avoiding or adapting to otherwise intolerable or overwhelming anxiety, guilt, shame, or depression.

Unconscious factors. It remains a puzzle how a person can simultaneously hold contradictory beliefs or otherwise deceive himself. It remains impossible to consciously hold contradictory beliefs simultaneously (Mclaughlin 1988).[16] A rational person can pursue a process of reasoning that leads to a conclusion opposite to a previous belief, but the result is a change of mind, not self-deception. Or in certain concrete circumstances an independent line of thinking can result in self-contradiction insofar as previous convictions are left out of consideration. But deliberate self-deception seems impossible. This leaves open the possibility of unconsciously derived self-deception that can provide a rich soil for psychoanalytic reflection.[17] But there would be general agreement that a person cannot consciously believe what he also knows to be false. Psychoanalysis and philosophy might part company, however, over the idea that one can be simultaneously aware and not aware of one's beliefs—psychoanalysts would tend to say "Yea," many philosophers "Nay." This latter appraisal would require an autonomous, rational, and fully conscious entity—for such an entity self-deception becomes incoherent. Psychoanalysts would prefer a more loosely organized integration of relatively autonomous subsystems for whom more effective and complete integration is an ideal rather than a fact (Rorty 1988a,b). There is a middle ground in which self-deception is possible and even to be expected, and does not impale itself on the horns of a theoretical dilemma between absolute autonomy and self-consciousness and fragmentation of the self.

Another potential basis for self-deception lies in an appeal to wishful thinking (Johnston 1988). The wishful thought can take the form of a motivated belief, that is, a belief based on a wish or desire that either runs counter to available evidence or ignores or minimizes it.[18] The phenomenon is familiar in stereotypical or paranoid thinking (Meissner 1978a, 1986d). Internal need, anxiety, wish, or desire becomes imperative and overrides the truth- and reality-oriented aspects of the self-system. Self-deception has to do with maintaining a belief or evaluation of reality counter to some other contemporaneous realistic appraisal—psychic reality outweighs actual reality. But again, there is little room for both appraisals to share the stage of consciousness simultaneously—one must be pushed into the background and withdraw from the arena of conflict. Clinically, the tension between contradictory beliefs can pervade the patient's consciousness resulting in a degree of anxiety that may find resolution in a delusional thought pattern. Adopting and committing to the delusional alternative, however, implies abandoning the realistic option.

Paradox of repression. If we return for a moment to the decision process, part of the mechanism involves a signal of an impulse or desire alerting the ego and setting the process in motion. This possibility, related to repression and to the escape from repression, became a target for Jean Paul Sartre's (1965) onslaught. If an anxiety signal—so the objection goes—prompts the ego acting as censor to block access to consciousness, the ego must in some sense be aware of the affect in order to repress it and to keep it unconscious. The effect seems contradictory in that the ego is both aware and unaware of the desire or impulse. The argument rests on a concept of the repressing agent as totally conscious and self-conscious, not unlike Rorty's (1988a,b) integrated pantopticon-scanner.[19] This "paradox of repression" (Johnston 1988) may be resolvable if we could regard repression as subintentional, as if to say an unconscious process operating without conscious reasons is removed from the realm of intentionality. Wood (1988) sums up this argument:

> In self-deception my unconscious mind is aware of the falsity of what my conscious mind believes, and it hides this falsity from my conscious mind. Freud, for example, holds that certain mental processes are kept out of our conscious mind by unconscious mechanisms of "repression." Sartre, however, rejects this solution to the problem he raises, along with the whole concept of unconscious mental processes. Because of this, he is committed to accounting for self-deception as an entirely *conscious* process. (p. 208, italics in orginal)

Again, we encounter the issue of unconscious mentation. An essential aspect of the decision process is that the complex series of functions involving the appraisal of unconscious desire or impulse and the implicit judgment process leading to the decision-dilemma can be unconscious or preconscious. Analysis would hold out for the essential motivation of all of these functions, whether conscious or unconscious. If the reasons connected with specific functions are not explicit and conscious at the point of acting, they can become so under appropriate conditions of lifting of repression and availability to consciousness—as is often the case in the analytic setting. The motivational substructure is nonetheless operative in the act, even though it is only retrospectively and potentially available for scrutiny. Thus, *contra* Sartre, the knowing and unknowing are different orders of business—the knowing and associated repressing are unconscious acts, the unknowing is the state of mind consequent to repression. They might be said to be contrary rather than contradictory, so that the term *paradox* is not inappropriate (Johnston 1988). On these terms, the process is adequately described as self-deceptive.

Hidden motives. The tension between psychoanalytic and philosophical perspectives on self-deception have been explored by Erwin (1988). Psychoanalysis appeals to motives of which the subject is unaware—whether truly unconscious or only preconscious. The philanthropist, who donates generously to charity for the best of consciously altruistic motives, may also be motivated by hidden egoistic motives having to do with narcissistic needs related to the ego ideal and superego generated unconscious guilt for infantile greed and envy. The analyst would count him as self-deceived, but the philosopher might not, since one set of motives remain completely unconscious. In the analytic perspective, unconscious knowledge is still knowledge. Erwin questions why this should make a difference, suggesting that it may not. If someone tells a falsehood for unconscious reasons, he differs from the deliberate liar by reason of the fact that he did not intend consciously to deceive anyone, even himself; but he is self-deceived nonetheless. The self-deception is not deliberate, but still motivated.

Erwin further stipulates that the analytic view does not exhaust the range of self-deceptive phenomena and does not provide a conceptual analysis of it. He argues that there are cases of self-deception that do not involve unconscious motives—his man Jones may distort or deny the evidence that his girlfriend has been unfaithful or that he has terminal disease simply because he wishes it wasn't so. The analyst would have a hard time accepting these attitudes as unmotivated. But there may still be questions whether these are examples of self-deception or not, or if so what kind. They may speak to contradictory and conflictual states of mind, but in the example both are known and believed. It is not clear what the deception might be, unless it is simply the desire not to face the reality and believe otherwise. The process may be conscious, but this does not remove it from the analytic purview since the choice is an ego-function and is motivated. Furthermore, even if the conscious motives seem obvious and adequate enough, there may also be other levels of motivation that remain hidden and unconscious for which analysis might seek further understanding.

Responsibility. Erwin raises the further question of whether the person thus unconsciously deceived is morally responsible for his self-deception. Some would argue on philosophical terms that he is responsible for the self-deception and for the behavior it leads to. Erwin concludes that in the psychoanalytic case there may be no such responsibility, and this may serve as the differentiating note separating psychoanalytic from philosophical accounts. But the analytic account does not dispense with responsibility so easily. If the subject is not deliberately lying and thereby deceiving someone else, his self-deception is motivated and ultimately he must take responsibility for those motives and the intentionality inherent in them. His responsibility does not rest in the deceptive act as such, but in the prior unconscious sequence that led up to it. A correlative principle, it seems to me, is that the ethical responsibility is proportional to the content of the action—the responsibility for one's own wishes and desires, even though they be unconscious, is a far different matter than responsibility for conveying misleading or deceptive information to another. The measure of responsibility for the latter would depend on the degree to which the subject could have or should have been aware of the former and thus acted otherwise.

Disparity can occur between general beliefs or values regarding what is ethically good and right and the commitment to guide actions accordingly, leading the agent to fail to enact what he judges to be good and right. But one can also be conflicted about general principles, believing one thing consciously, but unconsciously espousing a different and opposing value. Acting in terms of the unacknowledged principle involves a measure of self-deception insofar as it runs counter to the conscious belief. My perception of particular circumstances can be distorted in multiple ways by error, ignorance, misperception, misinformation, prejudice, and so on. I can commit myself to racial equality in principle, yet judge and act prejudicially according to presumed and unexamined stereotypes in subtle, even unconscious, ways in the real order. We can also come to conclusions contrary to our own better judgment—under the influence of powerful or persuasive others, or under circumstances in which the consequences of following our own beliefs outweigh another course of expediency or accommodation. Emotional reactions can also impede acting according to preferred judgment: classic examples are the lover who desires and values sexual involvement but retreats from a conscious fear of infection, or the husband who values and regards as his duty to cohabit with his much loved wife, but avoids intercourse or becomes impotent from unconscious castration anxiety. Concepts of resistance and repression are variants on the theme—they entail a degree of self-deception and self-distortion, the inherent need to escape some truths about oneself.

The dilemma of self-knowledge—the classic *Gnothi se'auton* ("know thyself")—is that good faith is always contaminated with bad faith (Sartre 1965), and that the only path to achieving a semblance of good faith is to know and acknowledge bad faith. As Rollo May (1969) commented: "The moral problem is not simply a matter of believing in one's convictions and action on them, for people's convictions can be as dominating and destructive, if not more so, than mere pragmatic positions. The moral problem is the relentless endeavor *to find one's own convictions and at the same time to admit that there will always be in them an element of self-aggrandizement and distortion*" (p. 158, italics in original). Self-knowledge can be tolerated only in limited doses. As Avery Weisman (1965) observed:

> Confidence in one's own resources and recognition that the ego ideal is a personal possession are far different from an overweening conviction of control or—what amounts to the same thing—

from feeling an obligation to be in control of some limitless destiny. They are also quite different from being possessed by an image of responsibility that finds fulfillment only in a grandiose, transmundane phantasy of power, prestige, riches, or timeless survival. To believe in such unlikely dreams is not true responsibility. It is cruel self-deception, no better than whistling in a graveyard. *In short, to be responsible, man must believe in his own death.* (p. 185, italics in original)

Then again, there can also be disparity between a person's evaluation, commitment, and interpretation and his intention and decision to act concretely otherwise. This divergence of intention can result from drawing an incorrect conclusion from a practical syllogism or from drawing a conclusion without adequately comparing ends. When considerations are incompatible or contradictory, the options are either continuing irresolution or commitment to a line of practical reasoning based on setting priorities and arbitrary choice; but the final choice may be irrelevant or only loosely connected with the reasoning even if consistent with premises. Or a final decision can be dissociated from the practical syllogism, resulting in a seemingly voluntarily irrational choice. From an analytic perspective, such inconsistencies would be taken as reflecting unconscious decision processes responsive to alternate forms of motivation rather than as simply irrational or sporadic. The disparity arising between decision process and action, reaching a decision to do one thing and then actually doing another, can be taken as manifesting disguised and unacknowledged conflicts, whether the alternative is regarded as rational or irrational.

Excessive self-interest can serve as the basis for a self-deceptive appraisal of means and ends, under the misapprehension that the course of action chosen will best answer to personal desires and objectives. This may arise often enough in the analytic setting when the patient decides to terminate treatment prematurely in the interest of saving money or other immediate advantage. The decision may be rationalized by a variety of conscious motives, leaving the unconscious conflictual motives unaddressed—fears associated with a sense of vulnerability, of attachment leading to the inevitability of loss, and so on. The patient may recognize the harm he does to himself, but the motive of avoiding what seems to him a greater evil prevails. Thus self-deception is more-or-less built into the fabric of the decision process, whether it takes the form of rational judgment or irrational action. At times imprudent or seemingly irrational choices can serve adaptive ends.

CHAPTER TEN

Responsibility

THE NOTION OF RESPONSIBILITY

Freud's recognition that the neurotic had little or no control over unconscious wishes and defenses implied that the patient bore no moral or ethical responsibility for results of these unconscious determinants. He also recognized that development of the human person normally leads to an adult who is not inexorably driven by compelling forces of the unconscious, but is capable of a degree of self-control and moral responsibility. Freud (1909c) absolved his patient, the Rat Man, of any responsibility for his vindictive and cowardly character traits:

> I pointed out to him that he ought logically to consider himself in no way responsible for any of these traits in his character; for all these reprehensible impulses originated from his infancy, and were only derivatives of his infantile character surviving in his unconscious; and he must know that moral responsibility could not be applied to children. It was only by a process of development, I added, that a man, with his moral responsibility, grew up out of the sum of his infantile predispositions. (p. 185)

But, of course, if these traits persist in the mature man, they are no longer merely infantile, but only derivatively so. The Rat Man might not hold himself responsible for infantile traits, but he could be so charged for their contemporary manifestations, especially in any influence they might have on his decisions and ethically relevant actions. As Ernest Wallwork (1991) put it, "The reasonably healthy person can make use of realistic knowledge to come to a decision and exercise some degree of control in his or her own house—even if the relatively free ego can be understood from another point of view in terms of its multitudinous historical roots, current inputs, and given structures" (p. 64).

This relatively mature and autonomous ego with its capacities for effective choice and self-determination is the basis for a sense of responsibility. Thomas Szasz (1963) distinguished three modes of responsibility—descriptive, prescriptive, and ascriptive. In the descriptive mode, responsibility connotes a connection of cause-and-effect and implies nothing ethical, for instance, the sun is responsible for this shadow. In the prescriptive mode, however, responsibility conveys a more-or-less negative note and an implied note of command to change an undesirable situation or to prevent its recurrence. For example, cigarette smoking is responsible for the incidence of lung cancer, implying that smokers should put an end to this habit. The ascriptive mode takes a further step toward the ethical by ascribing an ethical dimension to an action or other causal connection. Szasz's example was the statement "John killed James." The first question is whether he did it or not; if the answer is affirmative, the question becomes "Is he guilty or innocent?" The law undertakes to evaluate the facts and circumstances of the case in order to determine responsibility, that is, guilt or innocence.

Responsibility is often associated with guilt. If the act is correctly attributed to John, then he is descriptively responsible, but not if the accusation is false. Thus, Szasz argued, any charge of responsibility is open to four possibilities: (1) the charge is true descriptively and ascriptively—John did it and is guilty as charged; (2) the charge is descriptively true but ascriptively false—John did it but it was an accident; (3) the charge is descriptively false and ascriptively true—he didn't do it but was framed or convicted even though innocent; and (4) the charge is both descriptively and ascriptively false—he didn't do it and the jury verdict was not guilty. In the insanity defense, the accused is determined to be descriptively responsible but ascriptively nonresponsible by reason of mental or emotional disability.[1]

THE SENSE OF RESPONSIBILITY

Positing internal regulation, choice, and self-determination as aspects of normal functioning of the self leads inevitably to questions of autonomy and responsibility. Ultimately personal agency and autonomy is the root of ethical responsibility. As Amélie Rorty (1988b) observed, "Upon the concept of personal identity hang the social functions of allocating responsibility for socially necessary tasks. However personal identity is defined, it will demarcate the unit of agency: the analysis of the nature of persons will be used to justify the distribution of rights and duties" (p. 56). In addition, we experience a sense of responsibility for actions we have decided on and chosen, just as we correspondingly hold others responsible for their choices and actions. As Leo Rangell (1971) put it, "The privilege of autonomous choice brings with it the responsibility for making it" (p. 440). And again (Rangell 1986):

> The introduction of the question of responsibility . . . moves on to an issue of the widest ramifications in human behavior. A number of applied aspects come into consideration, such as, from the standpoint of the psychoanalyst, the role of responsibility in the therapeutic process, and from the broader perspective, its place in a spectrum from the social relationships of ordinary life to the crucial and ambiguous position of responsibility in the psychosociolegal area. (p. 19)[2]

This perspective on the core significance of responsibility is echoed in Dietrich Bonhoeffer's comment that moral actions depend not so much on thought as on readiness for responsibility and Karl Menninger's (1973) wishful "If the concept of personal responsibility and answerability for ourselves and for others were to return to common acceptance, hope would return to the world with it" (p. 219).[3]

Responsibility and the sense of reality are interconnected and interdependent: what reality is to the world responsibility is to the self. And the range of our responsible action is limited by the structure of the world around us and within us. The perspective of psychoanalysis in this regard is somewhat unique in that it speaks to man's responsibility toward the real, particularly the reality of values and relationships. Avery Weisman (1965) pointed out this linkage that "can be traced by following the parallel threads of reality sense and responsibility through the transformations that each undergoes. . . . The abiding principle is that reality is primarily a human experience and that man creates his own conditions for what is true, what is effective, and, finally, what is responsible" (p. 15).

The paradox of responsibility is man's inability to predict or determine the outcome of his actions. Arraigned against the forces of fate and nature, the capacities of desire and will undergirding our sense of responsibility seem slender reeds on which to lean. Regardless people espouse their sense of responsibility and count it as real—suggesting that they are more possessed by responsibility than possessing it. The sense of reality proclaims the reality of the world around me, but responsibility speaks to the reality within me, that I am real and that no other is like me. Part of that reality is the array of unconscious processes and motives beyond reach of my awareness. I become aware of my capacity to respond to the world and to cause the world to respond to me. Responsibility embraces a sense of being alive and having a power of mastery and control, not of my world but of myself (May 1953).

Along with this sense of power and capacity, reality imposes limits within which that power can achieve its ends—the reality within as well as without. This sense of myself as responsible and capable often clashes with the world that it challenges. The effect is conflict, and defeat turns my responsibility into frustrated impotence and faltering identity: "When man is in the extreme form of conflict, he can neither protest nor consent. There is no appeal from a world that thrusts him this way and that, reducing him to a brute obligation to follow laws that govern masses and principles that guide tropisms" (Weisman 1965, p. 165). Critical decisions must often be made in the face of conflict that may result in indecision. Chronic indecision is a characterological disorder of responsibility. Patients who bring this disability to analysis often try to engage the analyst in making decisions for them, eroding his responsibility and freedom along with their own, as well as drawing the analytic interaction into the realm of reality and away from the therapeutic alliance (Meissner 1996b, 2000c). The resulting misalliance reenacts the ways in which the patient's autonomy has been violated in the past and as such reflects specific transference dynamics. The sense of reality imposes constraints on the sense of power and mastery we are capable of—in this lies the difference between realistic ethical responsibility and narcissistic grandiosity.

This set of circumstances was exemplified in one young woman who came to analysis because of difficulties she was having in her marriage centering around issues of responsibility. The problems arose from her husband's chronic lack of responsibility; her own conflicts over who was responsible for what; and her guilt-ridden preoccupations regarding how much responsibility she should assume, not only in this but in other situations, for instance, work and friendships. The basic flaw, underlying most of her difficulties, was her own lack of authentic autonomy that would have enabled her to take a more objective stance and be able to utilize her capacities to objectively assess the real situation, come to some reasonable and prudential judgment of practical reason, and then put her conclusions to the test. We were finally able to trace her inability to maintain a reasonably autonomous stance to the underlying current of narcissism that dictated that she should be the most important person in any relationship or situation in which she found herself. Her husband's profound entitlement and his unwillingness to work for a living, along with his chronic drug addiction, proved to be a powerful challenge to her own sense of narcissistic privilege and set the stage for her reaction of narcissistic rage. The therapeutic challenge was for her to discover the infantile roots of her frustrated and fixated narcissism, and to begin to disown it in the interest of facing the reality of her own limitations and the disappointing and disillusioning aspects of the reality of her life. The rudiments of growing autonomy in this process had to coalesce into a sufficient sense of realized autonomy to allow her to see things, in and outside of herself, in more realistic terms and to begin to take responsibility for her role in them. This sense of, and capacity for, responsible action had to replace her sense of entitled and victimized privilege as well as substitute more effective and responsible action for her frustrated and enraged wishful thinking and unfulfillable illusions.

SUBJECTIVE AND OBJECTIVE RESPONSIBILITY

Only when we feel empowered, capable of producing effects in the world around us, can we also feel subjectively responsible. We might be able to distinguish between objective and subjective responsibility. When he feels acted on as an object, as in the case of compulsion, he can also feel objectively responsible. Weisman (1965) attributed this to associations with mind versus body and to contrasting views of man as existential versus categorical. The narcissistic roots of grandiosity reach beyond the sense of mastery to the illusion of omnipotent control, as in this patient. The sense of reality, along with reality testing, bears witness to the fact that our powers are valid only within a narrowly restricted range of application and severely limited in the kinds of effective change they can achieve. Reality both allows us to appreciate the scope of our creative potential, and insists on the limited perspectives of that potential.

Subjective responsibility, fed by unresolved strains of pathological narcissism, can lead to the often extreme deviations in the sense of responsibility found in the conscious illusions of psychotics, fanatics, and various romantics, as well as in the secret and silent fantasies of countless others. As Weisman (1965) commented: "The significant ingredient distinguishing subjective responsibility from mere self-seeking power, quite apart from what does and does not violate laws or customs, is that responsible man seeks a standard of excellence, called the *ego ideal*" (p. 169, italics in original). From a psychoanalytic perspective, there is little incompatibility between subjective and objective responsibility, despite the conflicts so frequently evident in our patients. But, generally speaking, when analysts address responsibility they are usually thinking of subjective responsibility. This, of course, diverges from the concerns of courtrooms and legal philosophy, where the focus is on objective responsibility, conformity, or deviance from social norms and standards, and the evaluation of culpability. The psychoanalytic encounter embraces both forms of responsibility, acknowledging both the categorical objective aspects of autonomy and the subjective existential factors. The effort to establish personal autonomy enhances the capacity for subjective responsibility along with the supposition that autonomy implies that the capacity to judge oneself outstrips any judgment of others.

Decision and responsibility are paired in the sense that making a decision leads to action, for the effects and consequences of which the agent is responsible. The responsibility falls to the agent as source of the action, but the further issue arises as to the degree to which the agent accepts and feels a sense of responsibility. According to Weisman (1965), subjective responsibility

> accords primacy to man as the initiator of acts instead of man as an object acted upon. It recognizes the reality of choice, freedom, consciousness, motivation, and the capacity to control the consequences of purposeful action. These realities are a man's private property, and he cannot barter, share, or surrender them. Subjective responsibility corresponds closely with the sense of reality for what we are and what we do. Existentialists call this *authenticity*; psychoanalysts call it *identity*. (pp. 167–168, italics in original)

The decision process is responsive to motivational factors—the needs, wishes, and desires of appetitive experience—and is guided by the balance of motivational influences on the decision in question. The intentionality of the process is thus motivationally embedded, but the gain of motivational satisfaction must be balanced against the effects and consequences of the action and the associated demand for responsible acceptance. To the eye of an external observer, the decision-making agent carries the weight of responsibility for the action and its effects, but this does not necessarily connote that the subject experiences or accepts that responsibility—one can be objectively responsible and subjectively not. Furthermore, the context of decision-making is typically, if not exclusively, one of interactions and relationships with significant others, so that the calculation of potential effects of anticipated action on others, both in short- and long-term perspective, are relevant aspects of the decision dilemma.

Objective responsibility is a matter of the responsibility man encounters as an object rather than as a subject, that is, as an object responding to the impersonal influences impinging on him. These may take the form of internal processes, more-or-less physiologically derived, that impinge upon his subjectivity, or from outside the body, usually in the form of social conventions or sanctions. There is a range of socially acceptable behavior and rules that we are normally expected to observe. When the conduct is deviant or the rules broken, we blame the deviant, but we consider him primarily as an object and generally disregard his subjectivity. Objective responsibility is concerned with culpability and irresponsibility, the stuff of social judgment and legal accountability.

FORMS AND DEGREES OF RESPONSIBILITY

But it is not always easy to discern what responsibility implies. In some sense it connotes the ability and willingness to face and accept reality, not to seek escape from its obligations and demands by avoidance or defense, to forego childish wishes and attitudes, and to be willing to meet obligations and duties maturely. The opposite would be irresponsibility, which we regard as synonymous with infantility, carelessness, and unreliability. Also, responsibility can take a variety of forms—here we are particularly focusing on ethical responsibility. According to the demands of reality and good physical hygiene, I am responsible for brushing my teeth and the failure to do so has identifiable consequences, but brushing or not brushing have no ethical implications—neither brushing nor not brushing are ethically good or bad. They are hygienically good or bad, not ethically. I may experience regret for not brushing when I have to endure the torments of the dentist's drill, but not necessarily guilt. I may experience a degree of neurotic guilt induced by my rebellion against parental injunctions to brush twice daily, but the guilt would then be about rebellion and not about brushing.

Ethical responsibility is connected with the capacity for guilt based on transgression of some ethical or moral principle or value. Ethical responsibility, therefore, and conscience are tied together—a subject we shall return to in due course. By the same token, ethical responsibility is linked with freedom of the will as an aspect of the decision process. To the extent that decision is not free, responsibility is mitigated or annulled. There has to be a link between myself and the chosen action that allows me to claim it as my act. The link is an act of will that is not identical with responsibility but underlies it, enabling me to claim the act and responsibility for it (O'Shaughnessy 1980). We can also discern degrees of responsibility corresponding to levels of intentionality—from unintended accidents, to degrees of carelessness, through deliberate recklessness, to a fully intentional and purposeful act (Gutkin 1973).

DETERMINISM VS. CHOICE

Part of the debate over responsibility stems from conflicting views of determinists and libertarians. Both agree on the fact of responsibility, but not on its meaning. The indeterminist view attributes responsibility to the capacity for free choice such that the subject could always have chosen differently and followed a different course of action. He is to be praised or blamed, or rewarded or punished on this ground. The determinist, however, looks not to a free, self-determining will, but to a complex of intersecting and mediating causes, of which the personal agent is only the last in the series (Wallace 1986a,b). The question refers back to our previous discussion of determinism, and need not be rehashed here, except to note that the determinist logic undermines ethical responsibility insofar as the agent caused himself to act as he does or did. The distinction between motives and causes (i.e., final vs. efficient causality) is critical. The ethical agent and the judgment of decision are determined (motivated) but not caused by anything outside of the agent. If an agent could not have acted otherwise—presumably because of the compelling weight of motives and circumstances—the choice was not free, or only minimally so. If the agent is truly free, he can always choose otherwise, even against the current of circumstance and consequence, but that choice is itself also determined. Ethical responsibility can only have meaning where and to the extent that it is connected with a free choice.[4]

But, as Rollo May (1969) had argued, following Heinz Hartmann and David Rapaport, assigning autonomy and choice to the ego has the anomalous result of making only one part of the total personality autonomous and capable of free choice, while the rest remained determined and unfree: "Neither the ego nor the body nor the unconscious can be 'autonomous,' but can only exist as parts of a totality. And it is in this totality that will and freedom must have their base. I am convinced that the compartmentalization of the personality into ego, superego, and id is an important part of the reason why the problem of will has remained insoluble within the orthodox psychoanalytic tradition" (p. 199). But responsibility cannot be assigned to the ego or even to the superego, but only to the self, since only the self qualifies as the ethical agent. The ego, then, is autonomous, but its autonomy is that of the self acting autonomously in its ego-modality.[5] Furthermore, the problem of will, as with decision and choice, is that the decision-making process does not take place in vacuo, but in conjunction with the integrated functions of superego and id also acting as subsystems of the self (Meissner 1993, 2000h,i,j).

H. Richard Niebuhr (1963) had delineated four components of ethical responsibility: the first involved responsiveness to one's fellow men, and in the religious sphere to God—an updated version of the love commandment, affirming that "we are characterized by awareness and that this awareness is more or less that of an intelligence which identifies, compares, analyzes, and relates events so that they come to us not as brute actions, but as understood and as having meaning" (p. 61). The second concerned the ethical demand inherent in the decision process; the third that our decision and response looks to the effects of our decision on others and their reaction to it; and finally that ethical decision is rendered in the context of social belonging and solidarity. Will and decision are processes, not unlike desire and love, which connect us with and relate us to other human beings, involving us in attachments, belongings, giving and getting, influencing, and responding that create the human fabric of life.

From one point of view, love is one of the most poignant areas in which will plays a vital role: loving means selecting, choosing, and committing oneself to one and rejecting others—and in a monogamous Judeo-Christian culture the choosing and committing are intended to be lifelong and exclusive. But from another perspective, love is a function of will as an appetitive capacity, as discussed previously (chapter 4). Thus, in both loving and willing, in both its appetitive and executive capacities, the will and the decision process engage us in interpersonal linkages, commitments, and responsibilities that compose the quality of our lives.[6] As May (1969) put it, the agent is "responsive to and responsible for the significant other-persons who are important to one's self in the realizing of the long-term goals" (p. 267). He then added: "This sounds like an ethical statement and *is*. For ethics have their psychological base in the capacities of the human being to transcend the concrete situation of the immediate self-oriented desire and to live in the dimensions of past and future, and in terms of the welfare of the persons and groups upon which his own fulfillment intimately depends" (p. 268, italics in original).

CONSCIOUS VS. UNCONSCIOUS RESPONSIBILITY

The reigning assumption among analysts is that responsibility only comes into question as decisional processes approach the border of awareness and conscious control. As Edwin Wallace (1995) opines, "*If* one possesses the capacity for sufficiently consensual reality testing and rational operations, the ability to consider the likely consequences of present choices in the light of prior experience, a reasonable degree of appropriate self-restraint, and a sufficiently intact internalized system of sociocultural values, *then* one may be deemed a morally responsible agent" (p. 1226, italics in original). This would seem to echo the prevailing view among philosophers; as Richard Taylor (1967) put it: "Philosophers almost entirely agree that if a man's behavior is entirely the effect of a neurosis or inner compulsion over which he has no control and of which he usually has no knowledge, then in a significant sense he is not morally responsible, and in any case he is certainly not free" (p. 369).

However, some philosophers would want to extend the domain of the unconscious, and by implication the compromise of responsibility, over all human behavior. John Hospers (1950), for example, arguing from the basis of hard determinism, concluded that all desires, volitions, and deliberations were products of unconscious forces, defenses and compromises, and therefore neither free nor responsible.[7] As previously discussed, however, determinism and freedom are not contradictory, but by the same token any compromise of inner freedom or awareness can limit the degree of responsibility. The further issue of taking responsibility for unconscious desires and impulses, as it emerges in the analytic process for example, remains open to discussion (Fingarette 1955; Madden 1957).

Freud's discovery of the unconscious served to undermine the concept of willpower prevailing at the time—a view of will as conscious, absolutely free, and undetermined. Psychoanalysis revealed vast areas of human experience and behavior to be otherwise determined by anxieties, urges, fears, and other unconscious influences. Ascribing the source of agency to drives, as in the classical theory, tended to displace the will in its executive role, and created a revolutionary image of man, revealing the connotations of the prevailing concepts of will as riddled with rationalization and self-deceit (May 1969). As Allen Wheelis (1956) observed:

> Among the sophisticated the use of the term "will power" has become perhaps the most unambiguous badge of naïveté. It has become unfashionable to try, by one's unaided efforts, to force one's way out of a condition of neurotic misery; for the stronger the will the more likely it is to be labeled a "counterphobic maneuver." The unconscious is heir to the prestige of will. As one's fate formerly was determined by will, now it is determined by the repressed mental life. (pp. 288–289)

Willpower, then, became a last resort of rationalism and served as a culturally endorsed line of defense against impulses, urges, unruly desires, and emotional dyscontrol, so characteristic of the combined rigidities and concealed license of the Victorian age. This development, reflecting Freud's deterministic inclinations, tended to draw questions of responsibility into doubt along with the undermining of decision and will. Will equivalently was squished between the strength of instinct on one side and superego authority on the other.

This aspect of psychoanalytic thinking found enthusiastic reception among twentieth-century inclinations to see man as the victim of forces beyond his control and therefore escaping the burden of responsibility. One effect may be a form of moral lassitude that led Leslie Farber (1966) to complain of ours as an "age of disordered will." But choice and responsibility are not so easily dispatched. As May (1969) commented regarding the relaxation of sexual mores:

> If there is to be anything but anarchy, it rests now on the individual person to choose the values of sexual experience or at least the reasons for participating. But this new freedom occurs just at the time when the values which normally serve as a basis for choice (or rebellion, which also implies a structure) are most in chaos, when there is confusion approaching bankruptcy in outward guidance for sex by society, family, and church. The gift of freedom, yes; but the burden placed on the individual is tremendous indeed. (p. 187)

THE UNCONSCIOUS AND SUBJECTIVE RESPONSIBILITY

But when and how does responsibility enter the picture? Desires, wishes, impulses, urges, and even affects can arise on an unconscious level and instigate the initial stirrings of the decision process. Do they involve any responsibility? For the most part analysts would say "No"—only when the process reaches the level of awareness and conscious decision would the subject be held responsible for them, and even then not so much for thoughts and feelings as for the ensuing action and its consequences. The patient suffering from writer's cramp is suffering from an unconscious conflict—one part wishes to write; another forbids it. The decision process is stalled, choice is circumvented, and the conflict expressed in the symptom—or the choice of symptom replaces the conflictual choice between writing and not. But a dissenting voice comes from Rangell (1971):

> Although active ego decision-making . . . takes place in the unconscious as well as in the conscious and preconscious, analysts have generally tended to assume that responsibility begins to apply only as such activity approaches the border of conscious control. If the "free" of "free will" is limited to conscious freedom, however, the "will" is now seen to have a wider base and to exist in the deepest unconscious elements of ego and drive activity, as much as in their conscious derivatives and additions. Is action which is under conscious control, although there is also a world of unconscious motivation, to be considered fully responsible—and action which is unconsciously planned and premeditated but which, because of its impact, has been separated from external awareness to be con-

sidered free of responsibility? Clearly, simplistic criteria in this area of transition and ambiguity have become anachronistic. (p. 441)

This view put the emphasis on subjective responsibility. Wishes and feelings are neither good nor bad in themselves, but the actions they give rise to can be so judged. I don't know how many times I have had to point out to my patients that in some basic sense they cannot take direct responsibility for the impulses, wishes, feelings, and so on that crowd in on us from the depths of our inner lives, but we still have to accept responsibility for having the feelings or desires, and more particularly for what we do about them. If I have been deeply injured by another and am flooded with intense feelings of murderous rage against him, I am not called to judgment until I pick up a weapon and use it to do him harm. Otherwise, as the poet put it, who would 'scape whipping? Also picking up a weapon and using it to harm another translates the action into the realm of objective responsibility where it can be judged by objective norms of social and legal propriety.

Analysis of the decision process focuses more-or-less exclusively on subjective responsibility—the process as a function of the moral agent, the self acting as ethical decision maker. But there is also the question of objective responsibility. The objective consideration adds the question of whether certain actions are good-bad or right-wrong on any basis beyond the subjective determination of the ethical agent. Many actions are ethically indifferent, neither good nor bad—table manners, preference for beer or wine, or coffee or tea, and so on. But other actions are caught up in the social fabric in such a way as to imply obligations, duties, or rights and values of others, even of the whole society. We owe it to others to pay our debts; we owe it to our families to provide for them. These rights, duties, and values are the stuff of ethical obligation that extend beyond mere convention or social nicety.

Distinction between ethically indifferent and ethically relevant actions rests on the hypothetical nature of the former as opposed to the latter. Nonethical norms call for observation or observance only on condition—if I want to belong to a circle of sophisticated people, I had better observe rules of etiquette; or if I don't want to get a ticket, I had better observe the speed limit; and if I want to graduate from college, I had better study enough to pass the exams and obtain the necessary credits. Whatever necessity or obligation arises in such cases is entirely contingent on acceptance of the conditional. But in the realm of ethical obligation, the hypothesis is not applicable. My obligation to pay my debt does not depend on any choice or decision I might make—I can refuse to pay the debt, but then I am in violation of an ethical norm. One could argue that there can be an operative hypothesis even here—let's say that I want to be accepted as a bona fide member of the society to which I belong, and therefore I had better observe the social demand that I pay my debts; but such a subjective standard does not take into account my neighbor's rights that persist regardless of my decision.

Such objective moral standards are independent of any ethical decision made by individuals. Living in society demands sharing certain ethical values and accepting duties and obligations of a social order, including respect for the rights of fellow citizens. I am obliged to respect his rights, just as I have a right to comparable respect from him. These framing considerations form a context of meaning and reflection that enters decisively into the decision process effecting ethically relevant actions. But at the same time, our grasp of the objective is never complete, always filtered through the psychic reality of our inner lives, the mingling of subjective and objective, seeing the world and our place in it through lenses without which we cannot see at all. My point here is that the decision process cannot function effectively in a solipsistic subjective cocoon; it must remain open to objective structures, terms, conditions, and foreseeable consequences of action, particularly action that engages with the external world and produces effects in it.

Responsibility in analysis. In analysis the patient is called on to explore his inner life and to take responsibility and ownership for what he finds there. Only to the extent that such possession is effected does analytic potential for internal change and growth come into play (Paul 1964). The patient is ultimately responsible for unearthing his innermost and most infantile desires and impulses, identifying them and their sources, understanding the meanings and purposes they carry in his mental life, grasping the reasons why they persist, and finally renouncing or modifying them in the interest of greater adaptation and maturity, or integrating them in more effective and productive ways. For this the patient must accept responsibility, since only he and not the analyst can do so.[8] As Erich Fromm (1947) commented, "We are therefore not helpless victims of circumstance; we are, indeed, able to change and to influence forces inside and outside ourselves and to control, at least to some extent, the conditions which play upon us" (p. 234).

Rangell (1981, 1989) also minces no words over the place of responsibility in the analytic situation—if the process is to succeed, the patient must take responsibility for his part in the process, for developing insight, and for translating insight into effective and meaningful change. Mature responsibility, then, is both a necessary component of the process and an achievement at which the process aims as part of the patient's progression toward increasing maturity and adaptive functioning. Clearly patients vary over a considerable range in their capacity for taking such responsibility, and in many patients avoidance of such responsibility can constitute a major resistance to the analytic process.

But if there is avoidance of responsibility, there can also be inappropriate hyperresponsibility of a hyperactive superego. As Edward Joseph (1987) commented: "Whether we like it or not, the nature of the world is such that we are held responsible for what we say and do. Equally important is that we usually hold ourselves responsible for what we say and do, judging ourselves partly by the standards others apply to us, but often judging ourselves by standards that are more strict and rigorous than others use" (pp. 14-15). And as Weisman (1965) added, "Psychoanalysis recognizes that to feel responsibility for everything is no less a deception than to feel responsibility for nothing" (p. 176).

Analysis has occasionally seemed to succumb to the illusion of being able to achieve complete knowledge of another's motivation, a fiction that rides on a conviction of hard determinism and runs diametrically counter to the capacity for autonomous choice and responsibility. This categorical reduction tends to eliminate subjective responsibility and leaves the patient in the anomalous dilemma of either complete culpability for all of his actions or complete exemption. But analyst and analysand meet on an existential plane, on which neither can be excused from his or her appropriate subjective responsibility. If the analyst in any manner should seek to absolve the analysand from facing and accepting his proper responsibility, he violates his own responsibility and creates a form of misalliance that undermines the therapeutic alliance (Meissner 1996b). Confrontation with one's own subjective responsibility brings with it its own measure of discomfort and anxiety, a source of both considerable resistance to the analytic process and of efforts to subvert the alliance. Once the patient's transference expectations and illusions have been worked through, he is forced back on his own inherent responsibility and must take account of his own healing process. Nor is the analyst exempt from this process and existential mutuality. Any sense of neutrality that connotes uninvolvement or complete objectivity is impossible; the best we can hope for is some form of "enlightened impartiality" (Weisman 1965, p. 173).[9]

UNCONSCIOUS DECIDING

Insofar as the decision-making process may also take place on unconscious or preconscious levels, do the same conditions and qualifications, discussed in the analysis of "free will," apply equally well beyond the range of consciousness? To what extent does the analysis of objective responsibility, seemingly consistent with an unconscious process, imply moral responsibility, even when subjective responsibility may be lacking? Analysis of the decision-making function broadens the implications of the concept of will to include elements of unconscious activity, whether of ego, superego, or unconscious motivational systems. Rangell (1971) rightly asked whether, given layers of unconscious motivation, an action under conscious control can be regarded as responsible while another action, unconsciously considered, planned and chosen, is not. There are no simple answers. Shadings of gray abound that do not translate easily into practical or pragmatic terms. As we have seen, the variety of factors, including pathological conditions, which mitigate or interfere with free, mature, and responsible judgment and decision are legion.[10] Responsibility is probably best regarded as a spectrum, extending from none, through little and partial, to full responsibility—rather than the dichotomous duality prevailing in legal contexts—and allowing a spectrum of degrees of consciousness-unconsciousness (Rangell 1989). The issues of degrees of responsibility and the possibility of unconscious responsibility has important implications for ethical evaluation as well.

Culpability and intentionality. There is the question as to whether and to what extent I can be held responsible for unforeseen consequences of my decisions and actions. Children tend to judge the degree of culpability by the damage done, but as they grow older intention plays a more determinative role (Gutkin 1973). We can hold a person responsible for his actions if he intended the consequences. If I slip on the rug and knock over a priceless vase, I clearly do not intend the breakage and am not ethically responsible. If I am rushing to finish washing the dishes so that I can watch my favorite TV program and I break a glass, I bear some degree of responsibility due to my rushing and carelessness. If I am driving too fast and recklessly weaving in and out of traffic and hit another car, my behavior is reckless and disregarding of ordinary rules of the road for safety; my responsibility is greater not because I intended to have an accident, but because the likelihood of an accident was measurably increased by my recklessness and I should have known that such was the case. If I lose my temper and deliberately smash a delicate crystal goblet to the floor, I not only caused the damage, I intended it; my responsibility is commensurate.

The earlier examples involve zero to minor responsibility and presumably minimal intention to do damage; in these, analysts would reserve a possible role for unconscious motivation. Society generally holds us responsible for consequences of our actions that we did not intend on the basis of recklessness, carelessness, negligence, dereliction of duty—as John Austin (1970) put it, "We may plead that we trod on [a] snail inadvertently, but not on a baby" (p. 196). There is a reasonable expectation that people behave so as to avoid undesirable consequences. There are also circumstances in which an individual takes on certain responsibilities—a doctor for patients, a father for children—and the roles we adopt in life carry certain duties and obligations with them for which we assume responsibility. If a father fails to support his family out of his own failings, negligence, foolishness, or irresponsibility, he can be held responsible for the consequences; if, however, his failure is due to corporate downsizing, or due to his employer's bankruptcy, he is not directly responsible for consequences, even though he remains responsible for support of the family.

Clearly in an intentional act I intend what I do, but I may know what the result may be without intending it directly whether as means or end. There may also be consequences that were not only not intended but not known, or conversely foreseen yet not intended (Kenny 1975). Where does my responsibility end? I would argue that I can be held fully responsible only for effects and consequences fully known and intended. To the extent that they may be incompletely known or not fully intended, responsibility would have to be qualified. The patient in analysis may neither know nor intend his resistance, but resistance it is; therapeutic progress requires that the patient not only come to acknowledge his resistance, but that he consciously lays claim to his hidden intention and its associated motivation as his own. If the patient does take conscious subjective responsibility for it and for the intents and purposes it serves, something can be done to deal with it therapeutically—otherwise not. But then again the resistance may be known but not intended—an intermediate step in which the fact of resistance has been recognized, but the patient holds back from claiming responsibility for it. Obviously the patient cannot claim responsibility, for a set of intentions that he does not recognize, that is, which remain unconscious.

Something similar may apply to side effects of an action. These may be foreseen and intended—two birds with one stone—or not. If known and intended, I am responsible for them, but they too may be known and not intended. I may know and choose the primary effect, and at the same time know but not intend the secondary—double effect, in which case I am accountable for the former and not the latter.

UNCONSCIOUS ACCOUNTABILITY

These considerations have only conscious intentions in mind, but there is the further question as to what extent I can be held responsible for unconscious or preconscious mentation and decision-making. The question is complex. At first blush, we hold no one accountable for their unconscious thoughts, affects, desires, wishes, fantasies, dreams, or whatever other unconscious mental process. Even if the agency belongs to the self (Meissner 1993), these phenomena arise in areas of self-function beyond the limits of awareness, and in the normal course of things any kind of ethical, moral, or legal responsibility requires conscious subjective involvement. Without that, the person cannot be held accountable and is absolved of any guilt or attribution of blame. Such unconscious products remain unconscious, unless they rise to the level of conscious awareness, as is often the case, not only in analysis but in everyday experience as well. Dreams, fantasies, daydreams, and feelings are some of the conscious manifestations of such processes. Even in conscious derivatives, no objective responsibility is entailed.

If there is no objective accountability, what about subjectively? We would not blame the dreamer for his murderous dream, nor would we haul him into criminal court. But the fact remains that he is the agent who dreamed the dream. Freud was quite clear about this issue—the dreamer had to take responsibility for his own dream—and in the same vein daydreams, fantasies, impulses, wishes, and affects. As he said at one point (1916–1917), "Even if a man has repressed his evil impulses into the unconscious, and would like to tell himself afterwards that he is not responsible for them, he is nevertheless bound to be aware of this responsibility as a sense of guilt whose basis is unknown to him" (p. 331). It is common analytic experience to have to say to a patient, "But it's your dream!" in the face of the patient's effort to dissociate himself from it. Or feelings are another common area of disavowal—the patient does not really hate his mother and wish she were dead. But obviously, no therapeutic benefit can accrue unless the patient recognizes and acknowledges these feelings and takes responsibility for them.

But, of course, it is one thing to take responsibility for a dream or a feeling, another to take responsibility for enacting whatever course of action is proposed in the dream or prompted by the feeling. I can dream all I want about telling that bastard off, but it becomes a different matter if, after rousing myself from sleep, I go after him, insult him, and punch him in the nose. Dreams are not real actions, nor actions dreams. I am responsible in either case, but the substance of that for which I accept responsibility is quite different. And as Freud (1900) maintained, moral responsibility hinges on the degree of consciousness of the motive for the decision and action. I cannot be held responsible for the impulse or feelings aroused, but when I become aware of them and begin to understand their meaning and motivation, I can be held responsible for them, precisely as feelings, owning and acknowledging them as my own, as well as for the choices they lead to; and I would contend, even further, for dealing with them in ways that modify their contributing influences in the direction of greater maturity and adaptive functioning.[11] Freud's (1925b) comments in his essay on the moral responsibility of the dreamer are worth attention:

> Must one assume responsibility for the content of one's dreams? . . . Obviously one must hold oneself responsible for the evil impulses of one's dreams. What else is one to do with them? Unless the content of the dream (rightly understood) is inspired by alien spirits, it is a part of my own being. If I seek to classify the impulses that are present in me according to social standards into good and bad, I must assume responsibility for both sorts; and if, in defence, I say that what is unknown, unconscious and repressed in me is not my "ego," then I shall not be basing my position upon psycho-analysis, I shall not have accepted its conclusions. (pp. 132–133)

EVALUATION OF CONSEQUENCES

Many actions have consequences for which the agent must accept some responsibility, but not necessarily ethical responsibility. Automobile accidents are a case in point—I exclude deliberate or impulsive suicidal or homicidal gestures. Accidents happen and even if the driver is in some sense responsible, his behavior may be without ethical meaning. Or an intern administers an injection to a patient in the hospital that produces harmful effects. Was the effect an unexpected side effect from unsuspected allergic sensitivity? Did he pick up the wrong bottle by mistake? Did the nurse hand him the wrong bottle by mistake? Was he negligent, careless, inattentive, or maybe so fatigued from being on his feet all day and night that he couldn't be sure of what he was doing? We tend to judge the degree of responsibility and therefore culpability according to the measure of rational control or its lack.

But control may be either direct or indirect. If I choose to do something with awareness of its moral implication—if the intern had knowingly and deliberately injected a poisonous substance out of malign motives—the control is direct, the crime is murder, and the culpability proportional. But control can be indirect, if some good or evil results from a previous decision, even though judgment and consent in the present action is missing. If the nurse was careless about which bottle she picked up or what dose she put in the syringe, she is responsible for the harm to the patient because she was careless or negligent, not because she intended to harm the patient. Or the driver who drives recklessly, too fast, and without necessary caution, does not intend to injure the pedestrian, but he is still responsible since he should have been careful when in fact he was negligent. His responsibility is both ethical and legal.

There are also actions entailing responsibility but a minimum of choice. The decision to swing at the pitch or duck a pitch thrown at one's head are instantaneous and unthinking reactions, yet they are intentional acts. The batter can certainly claim responsibility for the home run—but the decision process is more automatic and instinctual than deliberate. Yet the immediate decision whether to swing or not is preceded by a series of antecedent choices—to learn how to play baseball, to pursue it as a career, to play for this team, and become proficient as a batter. So that even if the immediate act results from a minimized or automatic decision process, it still may involve intentionality of some sort, can involve choice and a volitional act, and can imply responsibility. And in many instances the mental process functions beyond the range of awareness—perhaps on a preconscious or unconscious level—and can be reconstructed only retrospectively.

Also immoral actions do have an effect on the moral agent, largely mediated by a sense of responsibility for effects produced by the action and by the agent's subjective view of the action as immoral (Klass 1978). Breaking a moral rule or precept results in a sense of guilt, but not apparently any lessening of self-esteem—although self-esteem measures are notoriously transparent and open to face-saving manipulation. Experiments (à la Milgram 1975), in which subjects deliberately administered electric shocks to supposed victims, resulted in negative affects proportional to the degree of justification, less if given a rationale, more if not (Ring, Wallston and Corey 1970). There is also some support for the idea that those who have knowingly broken moral rules will tend to be behaviorally more self-punitive, not merely intrapsychically (Wallington 1973). Deleterious sequelae to moral transgression may be modulated by the effects of cognitive dissonance between morally deviant behavior and self-concept (ego-ideal) (Klass 1978).

The "ethics of conscience" is distinct from an "ethics of responsibility" (Hogan 1970, 1973). An ethic of conscience looks to a higher moral law to justify the rightness or wrongness of an action. An ethic of responsibility, on the contrary, takes a more utilitarian approach to determining the instrumental value of an action as promoting the general welfare or not. Individuals following an ethic of conscience tend to take a law-and-order approach, emphasizing duty to obey existing laws in the society and distrusting individualistic or intuitive views of morality. Questions have been raised as to the relative ethical maturity of these approaches, whether a combination of these approaches reflects greater maturity (Hogan 1970, 1973) or whether a ethic of responsibility is more mature (Kohlberg 1964, 1969). One could venture to say that maturity of ethical judgment may not be so closely tied to either alternative, but may lean in one direction or other depending on circumstances and the degree to which relevant values are engaged in a given context.

RESPONSIBILITY AND FREEDOM

In the psychoanalytic view of freedom and responsibility, man lives with his unconscious, not by it. He is capable of recognizing his own uniqueness and value even in the face of obligation and conformity. The sense of inner harmony and self-esteem linked with the sense of responsibility derives from a sense of trust and trustworthiness and implies an approximation of ego functions to the implicit values of the ego-ideal. Thus superego-derived values serve as a system of internal regulation stabilizing and reinforcing the ego capacity to choose freely and responsibly. Superego functions support responsible actions only insofar as they are harmoniously integrated with ego operations.[12] Without such integration they can evoke guilt, remorse, and depression, and in fact undermine the individual's capacity for free and responsible action. As Weisman (1965) said so well:

> Psychoanalysis uses the concept of responsibility to liberate the singular existential quality in man. If the notion of insight is not the reliable index of mental health that it was once thought to be, at least insight implies that subjective responsibility is feasible, and that there is still room for conscious choice. These are not alternatives, for there is no freedom without responsibility, no choice without the limitations and obligations of unconscious processes. Genuine freedom is freedom for achievement, not freedom from obligation. (p. 178)

To catch up the threads of the previous argument, the idea of a capricious or undetermined free will on one hand or the idea of rigid psychic determinism on the other—both leave little room for responsibility. Responsibility involves the power to respond, to choose, and to carry out one path of conduct rather than another. Causal necessity without choice destroys responsibility. An indeterminism that makes choice a random selection from an unlimited range of possible courses also evacuates responsibility. The reality of the person does not limit itself to an organization of processes. The unconscious belongs to the person, not the person to the unconscious. Man uses his psychic equipment; it does not use him. "There are unique dimensions of existence in which each person exists alone, not only influenced by his unconscious processes but committed to responsible activity and able to exercise a measure of control" (Weisman 1965, p. 175).

The relationship between relative autonomy and responsibility has been noted by Ernst Lewy (1961). He recognized that autonomy along with adaptability of the ego are foundations on which individual responsibility is built. Man cannot be held responsible or accountable for his actions unless those actions are attributable to him in some authentic sense. They must be his acts, directed, governed, and controlled by him in virtue of his own inner sense of direction and intention. Yet they are not completely autonomous and undetermined. They are a response born of the individual's capacity for responsiveness to a complex and shifting interplay of determining variables. The response enabling the ego to insert itself in relevant and realistic ways into this shifting framework is adaptive in that it achieves a "good fit" with the forces of reality, but it is at the same time responsible in that it is a response and not merely a reaction. It is an operation of the ego that is determined and at the same time determining; it is responding to a complex of inner and outer determinants while it asserts in the same act its autonomy and self-direction. The delicate balance was well expressed by Werner Mendel (1968):

> The healthy individual can assert his individuality and responsibility. He can choose his behavior to some extent; he can even choose the problems on which he intends to focus. Free will is limited in each of us by capacity, history, and biology. Yet when we are healthy we have the experience of choosing and we function as though we can choose. As we organize and become "ill" our choices become more limited. We are less able to take responsibility for the conduct of our lives and we become more helpless. (p. 701)

Thus the capacity for free choice and responsible self-determination are primary objectives of the therapeutic process. To call psychotherapy a treatment process is in this sense a distortion. It is a collaboration, a cooperative venture, an alliance between patient and therapist. The therapeutic relation presumes in even the sickest patient a core of responsible ego permitting him to enter into the therapeutic process. Whatever builds that core of responsibility is therapeutic, whatever diminishes and undercuts it is antitherapeutic (Meissner 1996b).

Choice vs. compulsion. We can usefully draw a line between choice and compulsion. Compulsion and defensive counterwilling (à la reaction formation) are opposed to choice and competence. They can be confused when, in the interest of maintaining a dutiful sense of responsibility, any differentiation between trivial routines and acts of will is ignored. Acts of compulsion are not responsible—they are performed not to actively cause an effect but more passively because something has happened or might happen to the subject. The subject under compulsion is more influenced than influencing, the patterns are stereotypical and predictable, and the subject himself may feel like a victim, unable to influence the flow of events, only able to stand by and watch it happen. He is trapped in a categorical cul-de-sac in which there is no choice. But choice is essential for responsible action. As Weisman (1965) put it:

> Acts of choice are, for the most part, unique, differentiated, skillful acts which cannot be predicted by an external observer—they seem to occur at random. In a sense, choice in human acts is like chance in natural events; they baffle prediction and defy categorical rules. Choice and chance are contrary to a compulsive universe where everything is ordered and evil cannot be aberrant exceptions. There is no place for choice, chance, and counter-control in such a world and, hence, no place for responsibility. (pp. 205–206)

We conclude that responsibility is ultimately incompatible with extreme views of either unrestricted free will on one hand or inexorable (hard) determinism on the other. While responsibility connotes the ability to choose, absolute and undetermined freedom violates responsibility as surely as a causal necessity that excludes choice. The former overrides the essential relation between responsibility and reality, while the latter eliminates the essential element of choice.

CHAPTER ELEVEN

Superego and Moral Development

The locus of ethical action in the classical structural theory is the superego. Freud introduced the superego particularly to explain unconscious guilt. But our understanding of moral development in general and of superego development specifically is still largely incomplete. In this and in chapter 12, I will explore the development and functioning of superego in moral reasoning and ethical decision-making. As Rollo May (1953) commented: "Man is the ethical animal: but his achievement of ethical awareness is not easy. He does not grow into ethical judgment as simply as the flower grows toward the sun. Indeed, like freedom and the other aspects of man's consciousness of self, ethical awareness is gained only at the price of inner conflict and anxiety" (p. 55).

SUPEREGO DEVELOPMENT

Man's moral nature originates in the long period of infantile dependence on adults and reflects the vicissitudes of resulting object relations and internalizations (Hartmann 1960). My discussion of superego development will look at moral development more broadly conceived, in an effort to provide a more adequate basis for understanding the role of superego in ethical reflection. It seems fair to say that resting the psychoanalytic ethical case on the shoulders of the superego places an excessive burden on this one mental substructure and tends to underemphasize more integrated aspects of superego functioning in relation to the rest of the ethical agent.[1]

The origins and functions of the superego are to a significant degree intertwined with the ego, but they reflect different developmental vicissitudes. Briefly, Freud derived it from resolution of the oedipal complex,[2] and regarded it as concerned with unconscious behavioral patterns learned in early pregenital stages of development. The structural model proved useful for conceptualizing neurotic conflict, as between ego and id, for example. The superego participates in conflict by imposing moral demands on the ego in the form of conscience or guilt feelings. Occasionally, however, superego may be allied with id against ego, as in more severely regressive reactions, when superego functions become sexualized, or respond to hostile or destructive motivations which, whether aggressive or not, take on a quality of primitive destructiveness.

Freud came to his understanding of superego origins in stages. Early hints of an internal source of self-criticism can be found in the *Project for a Scientific Psychology* (1895) and later in *The Interpretation of Dreams* (1900) in the form of the dream censor. The idea of a such a self-critical function was apparent in his view of obsessional ideas as forms of self-reproach based on unconscious infantile guilt (1896). The first appearance of a specific self-critical agency came in his exposition of narcissism (1914a) as the ego-ideal. In the course of development, the child begins to differentiate his self-experience from that of surrounding others and encounters the world of non-self-reality; this, together with gradually acquired self-criticism, combines to undermine his narcissistically invested self-image. To compensate for his lost narcissism, he forms an ego-ideal, derived at first from parental standards and later modified by further experience, training, and education. At this point, Freud suggested that the psychic apparatus might have still another structural component, a special agency whose task was to watch over the ego, to make sure it was measuring up to the ego-ideal (Furer 1972; Sandler 1960).

This agency was further clarified in the analysis of mourning and melancholia (Freud 1917) as split off from the rest of the ego as conscience. And a diseased conscience at that: "The patient represents his ego to us as worthless, incapable of any achievement and morally despicable; he reproaches himself, vilifies himself, and expects to be cast out and punished" (Freud 1917, p. 246). Freud (1921a) continued to refer to this self-critical agency as the ego-ideal, holding it responsible for the sense of guilt and for self-reproaches typical in melancholia and depression until *The Ego and the Id* (1923a), in which superego emerged as a structure in its own right. The concept included both ego-ideal and conscience and became the vehicle of morality, of other aspects of man's higher nature, and the internal representation and replacement for the child's relation to his parents and society. Operations of the superego were mainly unconscious, and could exercise a hypermoral tyranny over the ego. Driven by unconscious superego guilt, neurotics often demonstrated an unconscious need for punishment. Freud also stressed superego's connection with instinctual drives, particularly aggression (1930). When an instinct undergoes repression, he argued, its libidinal aspects may be transformed into symptoms, whereas aggressive components were transformed into guilt. The more the child controlled or repressed aggressive impulses toward others, the more severe did his superego become. The unconscious internalized fear of castration, based in the oedipal resolution, was reinforced by these aggressive derivatives (Furer 1972).

Subsequently, Freud (1926, 1932) spoke more of the connection and integration of superego and ego functions, such that at times distinction between them seemed to disappear. Along with its role as replacement for parental authority, Freud (1927a, 1930) related its development to the evolution of culture and social relationships. The cultural superego makes demands on the individual from without, much as the personal superego dictates from within. Freud saw the demands of civilization as necessarily imposing limits on individual satisfaction, but lamented the need to renounce instinctual gratifications in the interest of social conformity.

In resolution of the oedipal period, Freud argued, the little boy wishes to possess his mother; the little girl her father. Each must, however, contend with the parent of the same sex as rival. Frustration of positive oedipal wishes by this parent evokes intense hostility, expressed not only in overt antagonistic behavior but also in thoughts of getting rid of the oedipal rival or any others, like brothers or sisters, who may also compete for love of the desired parent. Quite understandably, this hostility is unacceptable to parents and eventually to the child as well. In addition, sexual explorations and masturbatory activities may elicit parental threats in the form of real or implied threats of castration; combined with the boy's observations that women and girls lack a penis, this may convince him of the possibility of castration. On these terms, he relinquishes to a degree his oedipal desires, and enters the latency period of psychosexual development.

The case for girls in this scenario is somewhat different: when they become aware that they lack a penis, they seek to redeem the loss by obtaining a penis or its substitute, a baby, from the father. Freud (1924a) pointed out that although castration anxiety brought the Oedipus complex to an end in boys, in girls it was rather a precipitating factor. The little girl, then, must renounce her oedipal strivings, first, out of fear of loss of the mother's love and, second, from disappointment over the father's failure to gratify her wish. The latency phase, however, is not so well defined in girls as it is in boys, and their persistent interest in family relations is expressed in their play; for instance, doll play. Freud (1930) stipulated further that the fear of conscience derived from earlier fears of loss of parental love. The judgment of good and bad does not come from some given internal source, but is instead the work of an extraneous influence—namely the child's dependence and the attendant dread of losing love and parental approval. The parent is both loved and feared as the object of hatred and rivalry, but it is predominantly the negative aspect that is internalized in the morality of the superego that tends to be based more on fear than love (Money-Kyrle 1952). Even so, the superego is not completely cast in negative terms—internalization of parental attitudes inevitably carries with it elements of benign approval and loving acceptance, an aspect Freud (1927b) emphasized in his discussion of humor, that Roy Schafer (1960) focused in discussing the loving and beloved superego, and that Manuel Furer (1967) described in terms of the superego as comforter.

CONTRA FREUD

The freudian theory, however, is not without its difficulties and critics. Freud was not slow to admit its problems—once established, for example, the superego can neither learn nor adapt. The appeal to identification with the same sex parent seemed narrow and simplistic. Also the question of whether superego in any way antedates the Oedipus complex remains problematic (Post 1972). Irving Bieber (1972) complained that Freud's superego was unidimensional, emphasizing the polarity between leniency and severity—like livers, one superego is pretty much like another. Nor did Freud say much about value systems or their formation. Psychoanalysts have tried to compensate for these limitations by ascribing negative features of the superego to precursors that do not persist in the adult or do so only in pathological forms, by appealing to increasing cognitive and ego capacities modulating the destructive forces in the infantile superego, and splitting off positive moral functions to a more-or-less separate entity, the ego-ideal.[3] But these efforts fall short of providing an adequate account of the development of moral capacity and continue to beg the question of what makes the individual adapt his capacities to prosocial rather than to antisocial ends (Hoffman 1970).

Others have questioned whether superego internalization can be as focused as specifically in the oedipal resolution as Freud thought. Hansi Kennedy and Clifford Yorke (1982), for example, described the process as transformation of an external policeman into an internal one—the first difficulty is that it is not clear that both exercise the same functions, and second the internal cop is only a partial representative of the external cop, "a mere cadet, who is able to discharge only limited functions, and who repeatedly needs reinforcements, orders, and support from outside" (p. 225). Early superego formations, therefore, lack the autonomy of more developed superego functioning and require continuing support from caretaking objects acting as auxiliary superegos (Holder 1982).

Samuel Ritvo and Albert Solnit (1958) pointed to the difficulty of predicting from parent-child interaction both what aspects might be selected for internalization, and what the child's resulting superego might look like (Ritvo 1972). Anna Freud (1937) also noted the lag between internalization and the child's capacity to implement these functions, to transform internalized criticism into self-criticism. Alex Holder (1982) further commented on cases in which continuing oedipal struggles seemed to coexist with a fully internalized and structured superego. Phallic-oedipal involvements were undiminished, complete with rivalry and covert death wishes to the same-sex parent and affection toward the opposite-sex parent, along with intense guilt feelings for wishes and fantasies at variance with internalized values. Anna Freud (1937) had noted that detachment from the actual parents and the presumed integration of a structural superego was far from complete at the end of the oedipal phase. The origins, evolution, and nature of superego functioning are highly complex, resulting from multiple interacting factors. Freud himself warned against simplification since identifications derived from both parents and from other sources.

But there is a further question—why is it that this resolution does not result simply in personality traits based on the parental model rather than a separate agency in the mind?[4] Freud never addressed the question; but John Deigh (1984) argued that the same reason for superego harshness vis-à-vis the ego may also explain its independence. Freud's explanation appealed first to severity of the models, who exercised their parental authority harshly, and second to turning of aggressive impulses against the ego in the form of reproaches and guilt. Neither proposition was entirely satisfactory—the first did not allow for severity of conscience when the parents were kind and lenient; the second explained increase of superego severity but not its origin, as well as presuming superego to be inherently punitive. To salvage his theory, Freud advanced a third hypothesis according to which hostility contained in the original ambivalence to the parents was internalized with introjection of parental objects and then displaced onto oneself. However, ambivalence to parents does not require oedipal involvement—ambivalence arises out of dependency for protection and nourishment on one hand and resentment and hostility for depriving and constraining in the exercise of parental authority (Flugel 1945). Such ambivalence does not require oedipal conflict.

There is tension between the two accounts—the oedipal account was based on repression of sexual drives, the ambivalent (or nietzschean [Deigh 1984])[5] account on aggression and submission to parental authority. Each account leads to different patterns of introjection—in the oedipal account, introjection contributes directly to forming the child's sexual identity, and only indirectly or coincidentally investment of superego with moral authority. But in the nietzschean account, the child introjects specifically parental authority thereby investing his superego with moral authority. As Freud explained (1930): "His aggressiveness is introjected, internalized; it is, in point of fact, sent back to where it came from—that is, it is directed toward his own ego. There it is taken over by a portion of the ego, which sets itself over against the rest of the ego as super-ego, and which now, in the form of 'conscience', is ready to put into action against the ego the same harsh aggressiveness that the ego would have liked to satisfy upon other, extraneous individuals" (p. 123). This formulation explained the child's ambivalence to his parents without reference to the Oedipus complex. As Deigh (1984) noted, "The result was a more satisfactory ontogenetic account of the origin in man of a conscience, though, to be sure, it would be an unsatisfactory account of the formation of a superego in regard to its other functions" (p. 215).

Superego in women. The contrast between masculine and feminine development of the superego led Freud (1925c) to conclude that the morality of women was inferior—a misjudgment that cast doubt on the theoretical analysis behind it:

> I cannot evade the notion (though I hesitate to give it expression) that for women the level of what is ethically normal is different from what it is in men. Their super-ego is never so inexorable, so impersonal, so independent of its emotional origins as we require it to be in men. Character-traits which critics of every epoch have brought up against women—that they show less sense of justice than men, that they are less ready to submit to the great exigencies of life, that they are more often influenced in their judgements by feelings of affection or hostility—all these would be amply accounted for by the modification in the formation of their superego. . . . (pp. 257–258)[6]

Freud's caricature of women saw the usual superego affects of guilt and shame as weaker and mixed with wishes for approval and love from parental figures. He correspondingly regarded male moral judgment as less readily swayed by emotional or subjective impressions, and more inclined to affirm and abide by abstract principles—a judgment reflecting his own and society's prejudices (Muslin 1972).

However, in fairness to Freud, as Schafer (1960, 1992) pointed out, individual variability within and between the sexes played a larger role in Freud's thinking than this stereotypical picture suggests. He was all too aware of serious moral deficiencies in many men, and commented on the limitations imposed on male superego formation by their inherent femininity, as well as the contribution of a masculine component in feminine morality. Then too, differences in the strength and balance of maternal and paternal identifications interacted with constitutional differences and bisexuality. Whatever the biological differences, the development of ethical strengths and weaknesses in a given individual was unique and subject to wide variation in both sexes.

These inherent difficulties quickly came under fire. One of the first to challenge Freud's view was Karen Horney (1924): no sooner had his *Ego and the Id* (1923a) appeared, than she challenged the concept of penis envy and its consequences for female sexuality and superego formation. Later Jacobson (1937) argued against any differentiation of male versus female superego, and subsequently (1964) directly questioned the assumption that the female superego was defective, arguing that it was simply different and not inferior. She saw the girl as developing an early maternal ego-ideal, which, in the face of preoedipal disappointment and devaluation of the mother's and her own genital, led to rejecting the mother and turning to the father as sexual love object. She concluded:

> The experience of oedipal love and disappointment, supported by the biological increase of heterosexual strivings and of sexual rivalry with the mother, again influences the development of the little girl's identifications in a feminine direction. The final outcome of her conflict depends a great deal on the father's attitudes and on the mother's personality and love. On the whole, I believe that the eventual constitution of a self-reliant ego, and of a mature ego ideal and autonomous superego in women is all the more successful the better the little girl learns to accept her femininity and thus can find her way back to maternal ego and superego identifications. (pp. 114–115)

Another breakthrough came with Harold Blum's (1976a) revision of feminine masochism. He argued that masochism was not an essential aspect of feminine sexuality, but a residue of unresolved infantile conflicts. Rather than seeking pleasure in pain, he suggested that tolerance for discomfort or deprivation in the service of an ego-ideal was more valued in women. His assessment of the feminine superego set a tone that has widely influenced subsequent thinking about feminine moral development: "The female superego includes an ego ideal with feminine ideals and values and regulates feminine interests. The maternal ego ideal consolidates overdetermined maternal attitudes, guides the formation and integration of maternal attitudes, and directs the developmental achievement of 'the ordinary devoted mother' " (p. 189).[7] Carol Gilligan (1977, 1982) extended this point of view in delineating differences between masculine and feminine superego and ego ideal formation. Guttman (1983) summarized this view:

Gilligan finds that women's entire moral attitude . . . is informed by a high valuation of connectedness, contextuality, and care and responsibility for others. If one believes that the highest moral good lies in abstract universally applicable ethical ideals, one might consider this attitude childlike, based on a wish to please others. However, women's moral values are usually more informed by a concern for real life dilemmas, which they attempt to resolve according to a higher principle of nonviolence, reconciling their own self-interest and that of others. (p. 234)[8]

SUPEREGO PRECURSORS

The classic view of superego development, centered on oedipal resolution, was soon seen to be insufficient to account for the rich complexity of superego emergence and functioning. But even in Freud's rendition, there were hints that superego formation was in process well before the phallic-oedipal stage and that resolution of oedipal involvements pertained more to superego structuralization than simple formation. While the classic account looked more to the oedipal father, increasing concern with superego precursors have drawn attention to the preoedipal mother (Ritvo 1972).

A particular problem is how external parental prohibitions become internalized. The child encounters parental restrictions and prohibitions from the beginning, but not all of these can be assumed to serve as superego precursors. Some parental interactions contribute to ego formation and some to superego. With emergence of self-object differentiation and further cognitive and motor development, the child's wishes and intents are repeatedly frustrated by reality and especially by parental interventions (Kennedy and Yorke 1982). Developmental precursors of the oedipal situation provide some of the roots of superego formation in presymbiotic and symbiotic phases in which establishing internal regulation and psychic structures prevailed over moral issues (Giovacchini 1980; Meissner 1986b).[9]

Melanie Klein had argued for the presence of guilt in the preoedipal child and concluded that rudiments of a superego were present even before the oedipal stage (Frank and Weiss 1996). In her view, the child's superego was not much different from the adult's, and did not change much in the course of development. She stressed that the child's superego severity often did not reflect qualities of the real parents, but was the product of destructive projections onto the parents. In her developmental schema, oedipal involvements occurred toward the end of the first year, following weaning, and gave rise to a primitive and unalterable superego core prior to the Oedipus complex (Furer 1972). This early paranoid-schizoid stage gives way to the depressive position, in which superego rage is redirected inward in the form of guilt and depression. Joseph Sandler (1960) pointed out some of the difficulties with the kleinian version of superego formation—the assumption of such an elaborate psychic system so near to birth, the early development of complex and sophisticated fantasies, the equivalence of memory images, unconscious fantasies, introjections, and internal objects. But Klein's views were instrumental in stimulating others to look more carefully into preoedipal superego precursors.

There were adumbrations of this trend in Freud's own thinking, especially in regard to preoedipal guilt around issues of narcissistic injury and revolt against the love object more than with instinctual restraint or control. Creation of an internal world generated highly conflictual narcissistic fantasies and gave rise to a form of guilt well before a postoedipal superego came on the scene. The mechanism of internalization was related to mourning, but the subjective experience of loss and mourning takes place repeatedly from the beginning of the mother-child relation, not just at the oedipal juncture (Heimann 1952; Ury 1997). The ego-ideal itself was a result of loss-and-mourning (Freud 1914a), as a substitute for the lost narcissism of infancy. The resulting narcissistic vulnerability can give rise to vengeful sadistic fantasies reflected in beating fantasies (Freud 1919a) and a sense of guilt—an early variant of the guilt-shame dynamic (Ury 1997). Similar considerations enter into preoedipal anal conflicts and into fantasies of sadistic and vengeful control. Freud recognized the ambivalence of the preoedipal child, but was slow to acknowledge the role of unconscious guilt. Freud (1930) finally came to the conclusion—"We ought not to speak of conscience until a super-ego is demonstrably present. As to a sense of guilt, we must admit that it is in existence before the super-ego, and therefore before conscience, too" (p. 136).

Weaning provides an early form of deprivation and prohibition, one of the child's first experiences of frustration of oral needs. The timing and manner of accomplishing this deprivation is quite variable, depending on culture and socioeconomic level, so that the impact on superego formation varies accordingly. Much depends on the manner of the actual weaning procedure and discipline in general (Sears, Macoby, and Levin 1957; Whiting 1959; Whiting and Child 1953). Similar constraints on biting tendencies, setting a parental limit on oral aggression (Breen 1986), have similar effects. Erna Furman (1992, 1994, 1996) added another perspective to weaning, arguing that the mother first experienced the child as part of her body. The narcissistic investment in the child, as part of the mother's body self,[10] persists after birth and undergoes a series of narcissistic losses at each step in the child's progressive separation and individuation from the maternal orbit. Weaning in this sense is traumatic not only for the child but for the

mother insofar as it threatens loss of her bodily related narcissistic investment. Her reaction to this threat may take the form of counterhostility and
punitive responsiveness. Furman (1996) comments:

> I have described some of the many instances when the mother
> shifts the "trauma" of weaning from herself to her baby: she
> responds to his signs of readiness for self-feeding and rejection of
> the breast by leaving him first—by going to work, going on a trip,
> going out one night in such a way that he wakes up to an unex-
> pected sitter, i.e., leaving him just enough to convey the terror of
> abandonment (Furman 1982). (p. 433)

This dynamic brings into focus the relation of early developmental experience with maternal hostility and retaliation and associations to maternal
disapproval, implicit prohibition, and incipient identification with the hostile aggressor as potential precursors to superego formation.

Even at the earliest levels of neonatal experience, the balance of gratifications and frustrations in the caretaking negotiation between mother and
child play a role in the quality of discipline and regulation involved. Variables reflecting this balance can vary cross-culturally from excessive gratification to excessive frustration and have corresponding influences on
superego development (Whiting 1959). Important aspects were the display
of affection, protection from environmental impingements and discomforts,
degree of need reduction, immediacy and consistency of need reduction,
constancy of the presence of the nurturing object, and finally absence of
pain or discomfort inflicted by the nurturing agent. Current rethinking
about superego precursors is related to revisions of oedipal dynamics and
to the development of gender identity. Recent reassessments and revisions
of developments in sexual and gender identity have shifted the emphasis
from castration themes and penis envy to a more positive conception of
female genital anatomy and a reevaluation of castration themes in both
sexes. Freud's paradigmatic schema has receded in favor of more complex
understandings affecting not only sexual development but also superego
origins. Mahler (Mahler, Pine, and Bergman 1975) had noted signs of internalized parental demands suggesting superego precursors around the rapprochement period. The basis for such internalizations had to be clearly
different from those postulated by Freud in the oedipal resolution, and
called for revision of the theory of psychosexual development, especially the
narrow linkage of superego formation to castration, and for finding a more
meaningful basis in infantile ambivalence toward the parents (Parens 1990).

A consensus has emerged attributing severe defects in superego development to factors well before oedipal involvement. Early efforts in this

direction came from August Aichhorn (1925), from Soudor Ferenczi (1925) in terms of "sphincter morality," and Annie Reich's (1954) early superego-type identifications. Reich's (1954, 1960) analysis of early narcissistic attachments and identifications with the idealized and omnipotent parents clarified contributions of these preoedipal narcissistic components to the ego-ideal and later to superego—a view that has found wide support (Muslin 1972). Likewise, fantasies of inner destructiveness related to anal-sadistic impulses and to fantasied retribution for such wishes, can provide the basis for talion fears acting as superego precursors (Brickman 1983; Jacobson 1976).

Early sadistic and destructive projections, however, do not make up a conscience, since the child reacts to them as outside himself, but the fear of punishment and parental authority they convey play a role in the later superego (Greenacre 1945). Many patients suffering from preoedipal fixations or defects have deficient superegos, often related to maternal loss or inconstancy (Breen 1986). The role of identification with the aggressor in superego development, especially focused on the mother as constraining instinctual desires, was noted originally by Anna Freud (1937) and subsequently by others (Gillman 1982; Holder 1982; Spitz 1958). Rene Spitz focused on parental physical discipline, physical restraint, the child's efforts at mastery by imitating parental actions, and identification with the aggressor as important precursors. He emphasized auditory impressions, particularly acquisition of the parental "No," and its transformation from external prohibition to internal judgment during the second year.[11] Such early rules and constraints embodied what Phyllis Greenacre (1948) called "the morality of the nursery."

Alex Holder (1982) argued that precursors were basically ego mechanisms (identifications, defenses, and idealizations) leading to oedipal resolution, but concluded that there was discontinuity between these precursors and the superego, rather than a continuous process of development as in ego development.[12] The nature of this progression was not at all clear. Even David Rapaport (1957) had pointed to obscurities in the theory of superego formation, especially the problem of how some identifications contributed to superego formation and others not, and that much of the internalizing effects seemed to antedate oedipal resolution. It seems reasonable to think that infantile states of satisfaction, a sense that things are comfortable and right, and that states of need, displeasure, discomfort, or threat leading to a sense of things being somehow wrong, may be potential antecedents of a later moral sense of rightness or wrongness, at least in affective terms—in this sense the primary incorporative internalization of the mother in the nursing encounter may set the stage for later identifications having social and moral implication (Valenstein 1972). On these terms, the sense of goodness and badness begin to impress themselves on the child's consciousness—a form of "instinctual protomorality" connecting the innate disposition for survival with a preadapted responsiveness to the mother's nurturing ministrations pointing toward later social value and morality.[13]

The child automatically translates the sense of something being wrong into feeling himself bad, especially in the eyes of the parent. As Heinz Hartmann (1960) pointed out, there is also at issue a confusion or conflation of facts and values: "But moral value judgments, too, are presented to the child in the form of statements of facts, as 'This is good' or 'This is bad,' 'You are good' or 'You are bad.' Here a moral imperative or prohibition is implied; it means, 'Thou shalt' and 'Thou shalt not.' This may well be the point at which the difficulty originates of discerning between a statement of fact, which is on principle verifiable, and a moral evaluation, which is not verifiable in the same sense" (p. 64). The clinical phenomenon of patients who, in the course of recovering childhood experiences, resort to self-blaming—the bad child-good parent configuration—as though the idea of something being bad or wrong about the parent were too threatening to the dependent and vulnerable child's mind to allow any alternative but that the badness be in the child and not in the parent, is a common analytic occurrence.[14]

Sandler (1960) approached the problem of superego precursors by appeal to a preoedipal preautonomous superego schema, reflecting desirable and idealized qualities of the parents and prompting the child to suitably adaptive object-related behavior. These schemata serve functions of representing and guiding that allow adjustment to danger, relief from distress, and the beginnings of coherent self-images (Brickman 1983). The parents introduce the reality principle to the child, but, as Winnicott (1960b) noted, they do this by first adapting well enough to the child's needs and then by graduated failures to adapt.

Once the capacity for object-relations is established, the way is open for obedience and defiance, as well as identification. As Winnicott put it, "the child must also feel real, and if defiance is omitted from the scheme and the child only obeys, or identifies, then the child sooner or later complains of lack of feeling real" (p. 472). The schema, then, would include approving and permissive aspects along with prohibiting and constraining features, but not yet structural formation allowing for introjection of parental authority or more autonomous functioning. The schema is more a preliminary plan for later superego development. Signals of impending punishment or loss of parental love have affective connotations, but not yet the affective qualities we attribute, for example, to guilt. The schema is further elaborated during the phallic phase, but never quite loses the stamp of pregenital origins—representing admired and feared aspects of the parents without internalizing these qualities in the manner of oedipal internalizations. The schema thus serves as an intermediate step on the way to superego internalization, in which the superego schema becomes structuralized, threats of parental disapproval are transformed into guilt, and the connection with the real parents is lost.

EVOLUTION OF THE SUPEREGO

What happens to the object attachments given up with resolution of the Oedipus complex? Rapaport (1957) and Sandler (1960) commented on the lack of clarity in distinguishing internalizations integrated into the ego from those destined for the superego. In advancing beyond early oral dependence, the child must abandon early symbiotic ties with parents and in the process form initial introjections; these, however, follow the anaclitic model, that is, still characterized by infantile dependence on the objects. Further resolution of the Oedipus complex and concomitant abandonment of these object ties lead to rapid acceleration of the introjection process.

Latency. After renouncing oedipal object ties, under normal conditions striving toward masculinity in the boy and femininity in the girl leads to a stronger identification with the parent of the same sex. Because of the bisexual potential of both sexes, a child may emerge from the Oedipus complex with various admixtures of masculine and feminine introjections, which have considerable influence on later character formation and object choices. This means that, in addition to Freud's concentration on paternal modeling in superego formation, conscience is also formed along maternal lines: stereotypically, if the former demands that we do our duty, the latter asks for love and forgiveness. The mixture of positive and negative oedipal involvements adds another level of complexity, the balance and weighting of which has powerful bearing on patterns of postoedipal resolution and superego formation.

There are two discriminable stages to this process—the first a fear of external authority, of losing the love of the parent and being punished, and the second in which parental authority and its attendant fear is internalized. In the first stage, the child conforms not out of a sense of guilt, but out of the fear of getting caught and its consequences. At this stage, conformity and compliance prevail, both externally and as motivations for introjection. In the second stage, the fear is the subject's own independently of external threats or coercion (Freud 1930; Wallace 1986b). Where the need for parental approval or fear of disapproval prevail, progression to a more autonomous superego is proportionally impaired; where the motivational substructure is more loving, accepting, respecting, or admiring, superego autonomy is facilitated. The more values and ideals, parental or other, remain external, the greater scope is there for ensuing psychological conflict and tension. For this reason, too, the superego derives to a great extent from introjection of the parental superegos.[15] Furthermore, parental imagoes are not simply internalized, but can reflect the child's own destructiveness or fears of retaliation for his hostility (Arlow 1982). Often enough, severity of the child's superego bears no relation to actual behavior of the parents, and has more to do with the child's need to turn his destructiveness against himself (Hartmann and Loewenstein 1962).

Superego hostility or destructiveness, then, derives from several sources: internalized destructiveness introjected from parental objects, hostility projected onto parental objects and subsequently reintrojected, threats posed by demands of external authority that the subject renounce or disown his destructiveness (related to castration threats and anxiety), and finally the hostility generated by parental prohibitions and discipline.[16] But these dynamics also have a positive payoff, in the sense that adherence to, and internalization of, parental authority provides the child with certain and secure norms in the face of uncertainty and doubt, so that assimilation of parental authoritarian attitudes serves to buffer childhood anxieties.

Finally, throughout latency and thereafter, the child (and later the adult) continues to build on these early introjections through contact with teachers, heroic figures, and admired persons, consolidating these elements progressively into meaningful identifications shaping his character, moral standards, values, aspirations, and ideals (Havighurst, Robinson, and Dorr 1946). The child moves into the latency period endowed with a superego that is, as Freud put it, "the heir to the Oedipus complex." His conflicts with the parents continue, of course, but now in some degree are internalized, between ego and superego. In other words, the standards, restrictions, commands and punishments, imposed previously by the parents from without, are internalized in the child's superego, which now judges and guides behavior from within, even in the absence of the parents. Lawrence Friedman (1956) commented on the further evolution of conscience:

> Just as the parents are forgotten as the *source* of the conscience, the parental standards are eventually modified in the final *content* of the conscience. For with growth the child's world widens and bursts the limits of the family; the approval of still other people becomes important, varying conclusions are deduced from parental principles, and individual additions are made, all of which further guarantees that Approval and Disapproval, which

uniquely determine the Good and the Bad, shall be subjectively sourceless. (p. 17, italics in original)

Values inherent in oedipal as well as in postoedipal transformations must undergo further internalization and integration before they can be experienced as one's own, part of one's developing sense of self. Doing wrong is progressively experienced, not only as disapproved but also basically incorrect, and at odds with one's own internal standards and values. The developmental gradient leans in the direction of increasing depersonalization of superego components and toward increasingly principled self-appraisal and regulation (J. H. Smith 1986). Persistence of archaic and punitive superego precursors sustains a pervasive sense of badness, wrongness in an individual's subjective sense of self that defies easy or simple eradication. This progression is matched, however, by an equally important development of the ego-ideal or ideal self. The early internalization of values and ideals is centered on parents, but gradually through distancing from the parents and involvement in the extrafamilial world of school and play, the ego-ideal is extended, modified, differentiated, and depersonalized, to become a more complex and abstract set of personal values and ideals as the child moves on into and through adolescence. Latency corresponds to the child's first adventures beyond the immediate family, to the world of school, involving separation from the parents and exposure to other authoritative adults, teachers, and others acting as parental substitutes (Greenacre 1945).

Latency moral development follows hard on superego internalization so that the child's earlier moral outlook, from about five to eight, tends to be relatively harsh and strict, often defending against sexual or aggressive impulses by regressing to earlier developmental levels or by denial, reaction formation, or identification with the aggressor. Later, from about eight to ten, moral demands are more mitigated and the child is better able to divert his interests to schoolwork and play (Bornstein 1951; Kramer and Rudolph 1980). While these lines cannot be drawn exactly or definitively, there is nonetheless a determinable progression in moral development as the child moves from childhood into the approaches to adolescence.

During latency years, more absolute notions of right and wrong, usually acquired from parents, change to a greater sense of equity and adaptation to concrete circumstances of evaluation and decision. Judgments become less absolute and authoritarian and increasingly responsive to divergent needs and orientations in peer groups. Empathy begins to play a role in moral evaluations. Conflicts and tensions in group-related orientations, reflecting ideals and values, draw the child increasingly toward selecting and integrating these divergent influences into his own emerging capacities for self-observation, self-guidance and self-criticism. A personal morality based on rote learning of specific behaviors or avoidances, on fears of disapproval or punishment, and on the morality of constraint or automatic obedience and conformity to rules without practical reasoning or moral reflection, begins to give way to greater moral realism and autonomous judgment. As the ego- or self-ideal consolidates, it becomes more central to the individual's sense of self, to integration of self-identity, and to self-esteem regulation. Deviation from, or tension with, the ideal can create a state of internal dissonance and opens the way for arousal of dysphoric moral affects, primarily guilt and shame.

Adolescence. Clearly, this initially punitive superego must be modified and "softened," to eventually allow for adult sexual object choice and self-fulfillment. This development calls for emancipation from dependent ties to parental introjects and to their residual taboos. The way can then be open to more objective assessment of reality and construction of a moral perspective and integration of personal values uniquely one's own. Otto Kernberg (1996) formulated this progression:

> One central consequence of normal ego identity integration is the facilitation of the integration of the superego, that is, the completion of the process by which the earliest layer of persecutory superego precursors; the later layer of idealized superego precursors; the still later layer of realistic superego precursors of the oedipal period; and the final processes of depersonalization, abstraction, and individualization of the superego have been integrated. (p. 54)

Along with these developments, the adolescent can begin to experience a sense of moral personality capable of accepting ethical commitments and obligations, a sense of fidelity, and a capacity for responsibility for oneself and for one's actions and their consequences.

Adolescence poses a unique developmental hurdle in this regard. Childhood models of ideals and values must undergo revision and modification in the adolescent's struggle to attain a set of coherent and appropriate values that he can claim authentically as his own (Laufer 1964). In a general sense, this seems to involve further processing of heroic, romanticized, or excessively idealized concepts to form a more composite, realistically attuned, and positively constructed ego-ideal. At the same time, the paradoxical aspects of moral engagement begin to assert themselves—the transmission and assimilation of the moral standards of a culture or subculture is counterbalanced by "the process by which persons observe, reflect on, and deal critically with the norms and standards they have been taught, to the end of constructing or reconstructing principles to which they commit themselves" (Hiltner 1980, p. 441). Relevant criteria of healthy adolescent moral development would include the capacity to invest in values other than those involved in narrow self-interest and narcissistic gratification, an interest and commitment to areas of work, art, and culture, and ideological investments (Jacobson 1964; Kernberg 1996).

The characteristic intensification of sexual, aggressive, and narcissistic motivations during this period threatens regressive revival of the abandoned incestuous ties and undermining of superego gains. Often, rebellious acting-out behavior of teenagers can be understood as the superego's failure to curb instinctual release. In contrast, the superego of the ascetic, oversubmissive, or intellectual adolescent can respond to threats posed by these heightened motives and desires with renewed defensive vigilance and intensified instinctual renunciation. The task of adolescence is to modify oedipal identifications with parents so as to enable love-object choice not motivated entirely by the need for a parent substitute or based exclusively on the need to rebel against their internalized imagoes. Thus successful development in adolescence builds a capacity for romantic idealization and falling in love (Kernberg 1996). The morality of childhood, largely absolute in character and emphasizing constraint—a superego moralism based on authority and fear—is replaced by a more relativistic morality of cooperation. On these terms, the adolescent learns to guide ethical decisions and value choices in relation to his personal commitments and to the ideals and goals he intends as his own (Pattison 1968). As Erik H. Erikson (1964) put it: "The *true* ethical sense of the young adult, finally, encompasses and goes beyond moral restraint and ideal vision, while insisting on concrete commitments to those intimate relationships and work associations by which man can hope to share a lifetime of productivity and competence" (p. 226, italics in original).

Furthermore, assimilation of parental prohibitions and demands sets the stage for future integration of ego and superego functioning. If parental demands are reasonable and realistic, conjoint functioning of ego and superego is facilitated. If, however, demands and prohibitions become the vehicle of parental immaturities and deficits, superego formation is impaired by assimilation of these immature elements, and the ground is laid for future conflict and guilt feelings. Guilt, then, arises from the disparity between activity and the value-dependent prescriptions of the superego. Where internalized norms of the superego are based on unresolved infantile conflicts, this primitive unreasonableness of the superego underlies neurotic guilt feelings.

One of the central tasks of adolescence is reappraisal and consolidation of value systems (Esman 1972). Some identifications are abandoned, some retained and amplified, and new identifications are added from nonparental objects—all marked by an increased degree of creative selection and specification congruent with the adolescent's emerging and integrating sense of identity (Erikson 1956, 1964). Consequently the adult superego cannot be taken as the heir to the Oedipus complex in any simple terms. If the oedipal crisis is a pivotal point in the formation of the superego and related values, identificatory and integrative processes continue to operate throughout adolescence and on into adulthood—as Aaron Esman (1972) observed, "If heir to anything, then, the superego as we find it in the adult, as a stable guiding system of autonomous values, must be seen as the heir to the adolescent process" (p. 99).

The task in adolescent moral development is formation of a moral code suitable for engaging in the challenges and problems of adult life. For this, ethical prescriptions and standards of childhood will not do. The transition from child to adult morality is influenced in important ways by childhood experience, family indoctrination, and increasingly by peer influences, but, as the adolescent push to autonomy and independence takes hold, the individual finds it necessary to formulate his own moral principles and standards. In the adolescent transition, the subject becomes more aware of ethical alternatives: he is less likely to see his view as the only possible one and begins to see the family moral code as only one variation on the theme; he begins to recognize that others have a right to their different views and he becomes more accepting of differences. He also tends to relate rightness or wrongness of an action to principles, for instance, stealing is bad not just because it harms someone, but because the general welfare would be threatened if stealing were permissible. Along with this comes a general concern for justice—childhood concern for fairness for oneself shifts to a greater concern for fairness to others as well. At the same time, moral judgments tend to become increasingly cognitive, reflecting development of intellectual capacities for discrimination and analysis. While it is possible to become cognitively mature and ethically immature, this would reflect pathological deviation; rather the trend is for cognitive and mental maturity to parallel development in ethical maturity and judgment. In step with the movement from concrete to abstract, the moral perspective shifts from predominantly egocentric, whether in terms of self-centeredness or rule-centeredness, to more other-centered and concept-centered orientation (Mitchell 1975a,b).

And in all of these dimensions, moral judgment becomes a source of greater conflict and tension. These conflicts are basic to many of the behavioral and moral dilemmas of the adolescent period, having generally to do with sexuality, independence, conscience, conformity, and issues related to double standards. With regard to sexuality, the adolescent is caught between biological urges and desires and socially dictated sexual taboos. In the matter of independence, the adolescent push toward disengaging from dependence on family ties creates tensions. However, this emerging independence is still exercised normally within the framework of family expectations and standards. The limits of acceptable independence are to a degree set by parents, so that the stage is set for conflict between parental boundaries and adolescent desires, between being respectful of parental wishes and authority, and being responsive to inner needs and convictions that may run counter to parental dictates.

DEVELOPMENTAL PERSPECTIVE

This overview of the analytic theory of superego formation allows us to conclude that the classic conception of superego origins retains some limited validity, but under the impact of direct observational studies of infant development, many aspects of the classic picture have been found questionable if not wanting. The role of preoedipal precursors and preautonomous superego schemata have undercut the centrality of crucial internalizations in the oedipal resolution. As Robert Emde (1992) noted:

> First, the child's superego, or conscience formation, is not an outcome of the resolved Oedipus complex. The clinical literature of child analysis and of psychoanalytically informed observation provides many examples of superego formation without the resolution of Oedipal conflicts (Sandler 1960). Moreover, there is considerable moral development before age 3 with both moral conflict and some capacity for its resolution well before age 7 (Emde et al 1988; Radke-Yarrow et al. 1983). Both moral conflict and the capacity for its resolution is manifest at an early age. (p. 352)

Not only have origins of superego components been traced to earlier developmental strata, but the continued evolution and shaping of superego capacities and functions in postoedipal development has lent a more complex coloration to superego functioning, especially in terms of the complex interaction and blending of superego functions with the ego. Rather than the phase specific rendition of the classic theory, superego formation has been spread out over the whole of the developmental process, taking its first elements from early mother-child interactions, leading through a process of gradual separation and individuation with its preoedipal variants of internalization, to the oedipal involvement and resolution, then passing on to further patterns of superego internalizations of latency and adolescence, and finally into young adult years. Nor does the developmental perspective generated in these shifts in orientation preclude further self- and identity-shaping and modifying experiences through the rest of the life cycle (Erikson 1950, 1959, 1964).

However, the story on superego development cannot be left hanging in the air. The enriched understanding and revisions of superego formation traced here only lead us to further considerations of how superego development integrates with moral development more generally. It is clear from our reflection to this point that the superego does not carry the full weight of moral reasoning, decision, and judgment.

BEYOND PSYCHOANALYSIS

Psychoanalysis has no exclusive claim to understanding moral development. Other avenues of research into the problem of moral development may either provide a degree of empirical support for analytic perspectives, or raise questions that challenge analytic perspectives and force us to reconsider or rethink some of our conclusions. Moral development involves gradual acquisition of cognitive and affective resources to make moral judgments; to pursue a course of moral reasoning; to assess and relate causes and effects, ends and means, actions and consequences; and to be capable of recognizing and accepting responsibility for decisions made and actions taken. Analysis emphasizes that this progression toward ethical maturity can never and never does divorce itself from instinctual motivations, but draws these more infantile levels of need and desire into increasingly meaningful and integrated functioning with the rest of psychic structure. Each of us carry along through life the instinctual endowments with which we arrived on the scene, along with the cargo of reflexes, memories, experiences, and habits collected on our journey through childhood.

Beyond psychoanalysis, other major approaches to study of these issues are the developmental-structural approach, based on analysis of content and values, and the social-behavioral approach, each offering a distinctive perspective on moral development. Jean Piaget (1932) exemplified the structural approach, viewing morality as systems of rules and moral development as the increasing capacity to observe them. He found the morality of the young child to be egocentric, grounded in respect of the child for his parents and other adults, forming a morality of obedience or heteronomy. This gradually evolved into a more autonomous moral viewpoint as rules were gradually internalized and as an organized schema of values developed. The child's early heteronomous morality was authoritarian and governed by adult authority, becoming in the course of cognitive development and peer interaction more autonomous, reflecting a greater appreciation of others' points of view and mutual respect. Cognitive development and peer group experience gradually transform the perception of rules from authoritarian commands to internal principles of justice and equality. The shift from external fear of punishment to an internal sense of guilt is also associated with cognitive developments and with an increasing capacity to assess situations for appropriate behavior. Development of moral competence requires a reasonably well-developed reality sense and a capacity to discriminate and test reality. Piaget noted that the shift from an egocentric to a heterocentric orientation was related to the child's increased capacity to adopt another's perspective and to see things from various points of view. In moral terms this implies recognizing that others value their own wishes and feelings, even as the child values his own wishes and feelings.

Morality as Learned

Early classic studies of deceit and self-control (Hartshorne and May 1928–1930) revealed gradients—older children were more deceptive than younger, brighter children more honest, children from upper socioeconomic levels more honest than those from lower levels, and children with unstable personality profiles more likely to be deceptive—but overall the import was that honesty was not a unitary trait, but specific to the situation since none of the children was always honest nor always deceitful (McCarthy 1971). Among learning theorists, there is consensus that morality involves conformity to cultural norms and is learned, but that this learning is a complex process involving other motivational forces (Sears, Maccob, and Levin 1957). Appeal is generally made to modeling influences and to reinforcement resulting in internalization of socially adaptive behavior.[17]

Parental influence plays a role from the beginning of life. Parents assert authority in shaping behavior of the child, responding to his needs, balancing gratifications and frustrations, approving and disapproving, encouraging and discouraging, and reacting to him with pleasure and pride or their opposites. The child is not left to find his own way, but is directed and shaped by the guidance and limiting prohibitions of parents and caretakers. Parents do this by punishing, rewarding, and setting an example, and thus acting as positive or negative reinforcers or models (Wright 1971). This aspect of parental discipline and direction is unavoidably embedded with taboos, simply as a matter of protecting the child from the potential dangers.[18]

In discussing parental influence, Martin Hoffman (1970) distinguished two forms of internalized moral structure: one stressing adherence to institutionalized social norms regardless of circumstances, the other placing greater value on human concerns and is thus more responsive to extenuating circumstances. The first reflects excessive, automatic impulse control, more under unconscious than conscious control, akin to Freud's account of superego development based on fear of punishment and repressed hostility. But this theory has only limited relevance for the second form of moral structure in that the postulated developmental sequence occurs in early childhood so that superego operates outside of conscious control and is impervious to reality conditions; moral standards are thus not connected to current object relations (i.e., standards are adhered to out of a need to keep repressed impulses out of consciousness rather than based on adaptive human considerations); and finally when and if standards are violated defenses can be brought into play to minimize awareness of the action or acceptance of responsibility for its consequences.

The integration of superego in ensuing moral development, whether as an internalized protective and moral guide or as a tormenting and constraining source of neurotic distortion, is largely a function of parental insecurities, anxieties, or healthy or unhealthy moral dispositions. One hypothesis relates moral structure to a combination of guilt, impulse tolerance, and parental discipline (Hoffman 1970). Conventional moral structure centered on adherence to institutional norms was associated with ego-alien guilt over unacceptable impulses; humanistic moral structure, in contrast, was more related to guilt based on harm done to others. Conventional individuals would be more repressed and intolerant of antimoral impulses, and their parents would have used love withdrawal as a training technique. Humanistic parents, in contrast, would use little threat of love withdrawal, and showed greater emotional range and greater situational variation in their discipline.

Commands or prohibitions can stem from parental neurotic motivations—anxiety, envy, jealousy, and ambition, not to mention narcissistic needs. Parental discipline constantly opposes the child's instinctual demands for immediate gratification. Parents may impose delay by threats and appealing to evil consequences of gratifying impulses—candy will rot your teeth, if you don't brush them they'll fall out, or if you masturbate you will go crazy (Wilder 1973). One of the most devastating effects of parental behavior on the child's moral development is when verbally endorsed moral principles are flouted, disregarded, or circumvented by parental actions (McCarthy 1971), after the fashion of development of "superego lacunae" (Johnson 1949; Johnson and Szurek 1952). Clinical experience has taught us that one of the major burdens of childhood is the extent to which parental needs, fears, hatred, sadism, frustrations, and anxious self-concerns are projected onto the child and become assimilated into the child's own sense of himself. Parental maturity, including moral maturity, provides a meaningful matrix for planting seeds of moral maturity in the child, just as parental immaturity can plant seeds of moral immaturity.

Discipline. Hoffman's (1970) study of parental discipline found that humanistic parents were able to handle the child's destructiveness firmly and with little need for threat. In the face of the child's anger, they focused more on what led up to the anger, usually something the child wanted and the parent denied him, rather than on the anger itself as more conventional parents tended to do. Hoffman speculated that although humanistic parents are no less critical of the child's anger than conventional parents, they take it less personally. In focusing on the instigating issue, they communicate disapproval, but in a way that did not threaten the relationship, thus relieving the child of unnecessary anxiety and making the experience potentially constructive. The child's learning in these situations is affected by where attention is focused—approaches based on love-withdrawal or power point to undesirable consequences on the child himself and to his relation to the parents; more inductive approaches focus more on consequences for others and reasons why the behavior is harmful and unacceptable. Hoffman (1970) concluded

> that this difference reflects a greater tendency in the humanistic group to look at behavior in its larger context—including the doer's point of view, his intentions, abilities, and limitations, and the pressures operating on him at the time—rather than judge an act in isolation. The conventional parents, on the other hand, are more likely to ignore contextual factors, to compare specific acts with external standards of good or bad behavior, and act accordingly. (p. 113)

Identification. Similar parameters were reflected in patterns of identification. Conventional and humanistic parents provided distinctly different models—the conventional use of love withdrawal and avoidance of conflict provided a model stressing impulse control, so that impulse inhibition became a prime characteristic of conventional morality; in contrast, humanistic nonpunitive responsiveness and permissiveness pointed to a more flexible model, more empathic and adaptive and reinforcing capacities for impulse tolerance and moral relativity.

Identification may play a more constructive role in humanistic moral development than conventional, although these would seem to be matters of degree and proportion. Defensive identification (identification with the aggressor) induces assimilation of aspects of power and control from parental objects, but identifications can also be based on admired or desired qualities of the parents. Hoffman (1970) noted that humanistic boys tended to identify with personal characteristics of fathers, especially the capacity for empathic concern. Hoffman's (1971) study of identification in superego development found only moderate support for its influence in moral development. His findings were partially supportive of analytic views, but his assumption that identification takes place as a unitary phenomenon is at variance with analytic understanding of the differentiation of forms of internalization in development—more mature identifications are characterized by greater selection and differentiation (Meissner 1970b, 1971, 1972, 1981; Schafer 1968). Also internalizations operate at different levels of conscious and/or unconscious processing—early defensive and developmental internalizations tend to remain unconscious and are organized in primary process terms, later more developed internalizations can be more open to conscious processing and become correspondingly more selective and adaptive (Meissner 1981).[19]

FINAL WORD

This selective overview of moral development leaves the impression that the evolution of thinking about superego development in psychoanalysis and in at least some aspects of empirical cognitive and affective developmental research have been moving toward greater proximity, so that, if their respective contributions are not yet totally integrable, they at least at this stage occupy a common ground. This obviously does not mean that there is not more to say and more to be discovered, both analytically and nonanalytically. In all interdisciplinary efforts of this sort, it is well to remember that no one approach has all the answers, but that each captures a piece of the action leaving the way open to further refinement and integration.

CHAPTER TWELVE

Superego Functions and Conscience

FRACTIONATION

For the most part, ethical functions of superego involve integration with ego capacities in various forms (Muslin 1972). Joseph Sandler (1960) referred to the gradual absorption of superego functions into the ego as "conceptual dissolution of the superego" (p. 130). These concepts point toward a more nuanced understanding of superego integration with ego- and other self-related capacities in the construction of ethical identity. As long as we regard such instances of integrative functioning as taking place among separate, differentiated, and oppositional structures, the problem of adequately explaining such integrated functions will continue to plague and perplex us. The language of partition and attributing agency related with specific functions to specific structures—superego, ego, or id—draws our thinking into misguided metaphors of reification and afflicts our theory with the fallacy of misplaced concreteness (Meissner 2000e,h,i,j). I have argued that there is only one real agency, that of the self, the human person; if we speak anthropomorphically and metaphorically, for example, of superego judging the ego, as we shall, that is only a less complicated way of saying that the self, acting in its superego modality, judges another aspect of itself, acting in its ego modality. References in the following discussion to "superego" are meant to connote the self-as-superego, a functional constituent of the self-as-agent, and not a separate agency within the self.

ROLE OF THE SUPEREGO

A good place to start is Freud's (1940) summary statement of superego functions in his last work:

The torments caused by the reproaches of conscience correspond precisely to a child's fear of loss of love, a fear the place of which has been taken by the moral agency. On the other hand, if the ego has successfully resisted a temptation to do something which would be objectionable to the super-ego, it feels raised in its self-esteem and strengthened in its pride, as though it had made some precious acquisition. In this way the super-ego continues to play the part of an external world for the ego, although it has become a portion of the internal world. Throughout later life it represents the influence of a person's childhood, of the care and education given him by his parents and of his dependence on them—a childhood which is prolonged so greatly in human beings by a family life in common. And in all this it is not only the personal qualities of these parents that is making itself felt, but also everything that had a determining effect on them themselves, the tastes and standards of the social class in which they lived and the innate dispositions and traditions of the race from which they sprang. (p. 206)

Internalization of qualities derived from parental objects forms the core of the superego, the parents who threaten, prohibit, accuse, approve, praise, and protect. These same parents also demand obedience, conformity, set standards and ideals to be lived up to, and so on.

Jacob Arlow (1982) observed on this score,

The superego is a conglomeration of many identifications derived from experiences with objects, from fantasies and imagination, and stemming from almost all levels of development, not necessarily exclusively those of the oedipal or the postoedipal period. . . . The superego is by no means a uniform, coherent, integrated, harmonious structure. It is a mass of contradictions, fraught with internal inconsistencies, or, as we say in our technical language, intrasystemic conflicts. Its functioning is neither uniform nor reliable, and it is in this respect that the idea of a superego representing the policeman of the psyche holds up best. Like the policeman in real life, the superego is hardly around when needed most. (p. 234)

This uncertainty reflects the developmental failure to achieve a capacity to tolerate and resolve ambivalence—the child must be able to accept hateful feelings and destructive wishes toward those he also loves. The task of parents is to help the child tolerate and resolve his hostile and destructive wishes and help him realize that his destructive impulses and wishes are not intolerable or evil. When this is not the case, the child tends to cling to simple and simplistic ways of thinking and feeling about his relations with others. If he loves, he can find no room for negative feelings; if he is angered, he can find no room for love. His thinking remains either-or, all-or-nothing, black-and-white. Since, in fact, there is no significant human relation without ambivalence, such thinking can work considerable havoc in interpersonal relations. Moreover, trapped within the closed system of instinctual impulse and fantasy, the superego does not distinguish between wish and deed—the wish is the deed.

Superego judgments hardly qualify as moral, but are better regarded as premoral or pseudomoral. They are not implemented uniformly or regularly, but run the gamut of omission, affectively motivated exception, corruption, deception, distraction, beguilment, and amoral disregard or denial. To characterize them as severe or benign is entirely too simple, since superego rarely operates in such global terms. Arlow (1982) objected to the idea of superego lacunae: "It is inaccurate to think of the superego as having a uniform structure, with scattered lacunae of extraordinary, incompatible functioning standing out like foreign bodies in a matrix of morality. The lacunae image is much too static a metaphor for the subtle and complex interplay between the superego and the rest of the psyche" (p. 235). A word to the wise!

In the face of superego impingements, patients utilize a variety of strategies of diversion or escape.[1] Moral failure or breaking the moral law, causes for superego condemnation, require some requital for the transgression, typically in the form of restitutive punishment, penance or reparative action to quiet the pangs of conscience and to regain inner equilibrium (Deigh 1984). The neurotic conscience seeks punishment, and needs punishment to quiet its pangs of guilt, but the devices for placating an aroused superego are multiple. Avery Weisman (1965) listed among these strategies *"confession, masochistic surrender, scapegoating, atonement, undoing, sacrifice, reaction formation,* and *excuses, apologies,* and *justification"* (p. 195, italics in original). Some patients unburden themselves of all or most of their offenses, as though abandoning themselves masochistically to punishment and suffering rather than seeking forgiveness.

A variety of defenses can come into play to alleviate the burden of guilt. Repression may relieve the subject of conscious guilt, but not unconscious guilt. The repressive barrier can prevent guilt or shame from coming to awareness, but does not prevent them from continuing to operate unconsciously. Driven by unconscious guilt, many patients court defeat at every turn, find reasons for suffering where there are none, and always seem to find the misfortunes they feel they deserve. Pleading guilty

can for some proclaim their moral superiority. Sacrifice and self-denial can
serve this purpose, as well as buffering one from the potential guilt of
future, if unnamed, offenses. Most of us mortals are at least dimly aware
of our failings and failures to live up to the standards of our ideals. Most
of us carry some minor burden of regret, remorse, call it "guilt"—seeking
ways to ease this burden by excuses, apologies, and justification is the
common lot.[2]

SUPEREGO AND MORALITY

We should note first that implementation of these functions is largely affective, concerned with guilt, shame, fear, self-esteem, and so on (Furer 1972).
Superego effects stimulate or elicit affective reactions in the ego, responding
to superego constraints and imperatives. Second, the content of these functions tends to reduplicate parental functions—demanding, punishing,
depriving, threatening, rewarding, praising, approving, and so on. In these
terms, the superego contribution to any more developed ethical sense is
quite limited. Early freudians were preoccupied with infantile derivatives
and their vicissitudes, and paid little attention to specifically ethical issues.
It was not until Heinz Hartmann's (1960) contribution that a concept of a
reality-based and adaptive moral perspective found its way into analytic
thinking.[3] Freud may have had some ideas along this line, but in his writings, he drew no distinction between superego and the moral code (Schafer
1992). As Arlow (1982) noted, "The moral code one espouses is more a
reflection of his personality than the other way around, and moral code, of
course, should not be regarded as identical with one's superego" (p. 235).
Along the same line Aaron Esman (1972) had commented:

> If the ego is thought of as the organization of adaptive and exec-
> utive functions within the mental apparatus, I see no reason to
> assign such functions as "self-criticism," "self-observation" and
> "the holding up of ideals" to the superego. All these functions are
> adaptive, clearly geared to the need to survive in and adapt to a
> specific socioenvironmental system. . . . Thus adherence to ideals
> and prohibitions is but a special case of the overall functions of
> adaptation assigned, by definition, to the ego. (p. 89)

To explain—superego is limited to assessment and valuation of instinctual derivatives, that is, the urges, impulses, wishes, desires, hopes, and
ambitions that populate our inner mental worlds. These evaluations reflect
superego origins in the internalization of parental imagoes and fall short of

ethical decision-making. When patients, for example, express guilt feelings for destructive, hateful or sadistic fantasies, wishes, or dreams, these affects come from the superego and reflect a superego-related assessment judging them to be undesirable, threatening, or reprehensible. The arena is internal and reflects the dynamics of parental approval or disapproval from which they derive. But such affects do not reflect an ethical judgment, even if they do reflect superego morality.

Superego Sadism

As representative of infantile moralism, superego functions give rise to affective reactions to certain actions of the self, resulting in guilt or shame. In specifically moral contexts, ego and superego functions may be coordinated and synchronized, but in regressive phases superego reactions can dominate the self's responses eliciting affective responses, usually in the form of unconscious, if not conscious, guilt. This pattern is usually pictured as a sadistic superego attacking a masochistically vulnerable ego, but the metaphors should not mislead us into thinking that we are dealing with anymore than interacting functions of the self.[4] Moral masochism is a regressive departure from true morality, a form of reinstinctualization of superego functioning, a regressive shift from a more impersonal morality toward a reactivated infantile fantasy of being beaten by the father to gain unconscious sexual gratification (Arlow 1982).[5]

Short of ethical decision-making, superego assessments can have palpable effects and consequences on behavior. The internal organization of self-as-superego gives rise to primitive and punitive, harshly critical, and devaluing attacks against the self. Through superego functions, infantile sadism and hostile destructiveness can be directed against the self, leading to depression, guilt, and self-devaluation. These superego dictates are then lived out in a variety of forms of self-defeating and self-destructive activity. It is as though the superego's claim of worthlessness and evil serve as a mandate, which is then acted out—a self-fulfilling prophecy of self-defeat and self-degradation, leading in the extreme to suicidal impulses and action. In seriously sick and psychotic patients, the power and destructiveness of these instinctually derived motives are often overwhelming.

Superego vs. Morality

Reflecting on these distinctions, Roy Schafer (1992) pointed to "a radical alteration of our idea of a superego, for now we are able to see that superego is not morality at all, nor can morality grow out of it alone, for super-ego is fierce, irrational, mostly unconscious vindictiveness against oneself for wishes and activities that threaten to bring one into archaically conceived, infantile danger situations" (p. 64). And we can add to this Jacques Lacan's (1992) trenchant observation:

> We have never stopped repeating that the interiorization of the Law has nothing to do with the Law. Although we still need to know why. It is possible that the superego serves as a support for the moral conscience, but everyone knows that it has nothing to do with the moral conscience as far as its most obligatory demands are concerned. What the superego demands has nothing to do with that with which we would be right in making the universal rule of our actions. (p. 310)

With a mild demur over the absolute sound of "nothing to do with" and due consideration for the implied kantian universal, the comment anticipates our present agenda.

This view of superego functioning diverges somewhat from the typical view connecting superego with morality. Arlow and Brenner (1964), for example, described superego as a "group of mental functions which have to deal with ideal aspirations and with moral commands and prohibitions" (p. 39). Charles Brenner (1982) endorsed the Heinz Hartmann and Rudolph Loewenstein (1962) rendition as "the aspect of psychic functioning that has to do with morality" (p. 123). However, any relation of superego with ideal aspirations and moral commands and prohibitions is limited to instinctual dynamics; as soon as ethical issues come into focus, superego functions necessarily become integrated with, and at times guided by, other nonsuperego capacities. Freud recognized that superego often diverged widely from more conscious moral codes and that the ego was often involved in coping with these conscious issues and with the superego (Loewenstein 1966). I will leave open for the moment whether those ethical capacities belong to ego-functions exclusively or not. But we can distinguish between superego condemnations and moral values discriminated by the ego—a distinction little discussed and less honored in psychoanalytic thinking. As representative of infantile moralizing, we would have to question whether, or to what extent, this arbitrary, absolutizing, unconscious aspect of the mind can serve as any kind of reliable guide for mature ethical judgment. The moralistic patterns we ascribe to superego functions play a more determinative role in neurotic conflicts and symptom formation. The morality of the superego would seem at best a pseudomorality.

THE BENIGN SUPEREGO

However, the superego also has a positive side related to functions comforting, protecting, and approving. Toward the end of *The Ego and the Id*, Freud (1923a) commented:

> The fear of death in melancholia only admits of one explanation: that the ego gives itself up because it feels itself hated and persecuted by the super-ego, instead of loved. To the ego, therefore living means the same as being loved—being loved by the super-ego, which here again appears as the representative of the id. The super-ego fulfils the same function of protecting and saving that was fulfilled in earlier days by the father and later by Providence or Destiny. (p. 58)

As Schafer (1960) was to note later, Freud was probably somewhat reluctant to push this more positive dimension of superego since it was difficult to reconcile with the negative image of superego as critical and feared. Freud's early formulations were strongly influenced by his clinical experience with depressive, paranoid, and obsessional disorders in which the destructiveness of the superego prevailed. But later authors (e.g., Fenichel 1945; Kramer 1958; Schafer 1960) had no difficulty recognizing a loving and protective role for superego. Schafer (1960) put it: "There is a loving and beloved aspect of the superego. It represents the loved and admired oedipal and preoedipal parents who provide love, protection, comfort, and guidance, who embody and transmit certain ideals and moral structures more or less representative of their society, and who, even in their punishing activities, provide needed expressions of parental care, contact, and love" (p. 186). In any case, Freud's (1927b) later recognition of a comforting role for superego created a theoretical tension that he could not synthesize with previous commitments.

Freud located this protective function in humor, traumatic neuroses, and religion. In humor (1927b), the superego protected the ego from potentially threatening instinctual assault by disengaging potential danger by reducing it to a matter of something to be joked about and laughed at.[6] In traumatic neuroses (Freud 1923a), positive engagement of the superego enables the ego to withstand intense stimulation or deprivation;[7] only when one feels abandoned or deserted by the superego or its substitutes (external representatives, or forces of destiny) is the blanket of security breached and trauma experienced. In the religious sphere (1927a), Freud envisioned belief in God as protective, deriving from the protective father of infancy, against the forces of fate and terrors of existence. Another side of Freud's ambivalent view of religion was based on his repressive and punitive view of superego, picturing religion as an oppressive force with its moral imperatives and restrictions of human freedom, behind which he saw the driving force of guilt (Meissner 1984c).

Love and approval of superego, replacing the loving and approving parents, is served by the ego-ideal. By internalizing the parents' ideal standards, the child seeks approval by becoming like them and conforming to these ideals. The critical aspect of superego will continue to approve and love the child insofar as he accepts, observes, and lives up to these standards. In this sense, through such superego endorsement, the ideal becomes a positive force in structuring the sense of self and identity. When the individual becomes subjectively aware of disparity between the ideal and his actual self, a dysphoric tension arises, which can be resolved by bringing the actual self-image into closer proximity to the ideal, thus reinforcing self-esteem; a less adaptive course leads to yielding to superego condemnation and depression. Further development of capacities to modulate self-esteem are integrated with ego capacities that can reassess more primitive superego judgments combining acceptance of responsibility with remorse, reparation, and forgiveness. Forgiveness has an important place among ethically related processes involving ego-and-superego integration (Breen 1986). Forgiveness is a counterbalance to guilt internally and to blame or hatred externally. Forgiving takes place within a context of values and is motivated by ethical aims. If there is internalization involved, it may favor the mother who, as Hal Breen (1986) suggests, is both frustrating and forgiving—that is, an identification with the superego of the mother whose aggression is not necessarily destructive and can be put to the uses of loving acceptance and affirmation.[8] To circumvent a misguided sexual stereotyping in this regard, I would add that the same dynamic applies to fathers as well as to mothers, since capacities for parental discipline and forgiving love do not seem to be gender specific.

SEXUAL DIFFERENTIATION

We previously touched on supposed differences in superego formation between men and women. Mixing of feminine and masculine qualities in superego functioning raises issues of gender specificity in superego functioning or in ethical decision-making more generally. Kohlberg's (1964, 1969, 1981, 1984; Kohlberg and Kramer 1969) studies of ethical judgment were severely criticized on the grounds that his subjects were exclusively male, introducing an inherent sex bias (Walker 1984). When the same tests were applied to women and girls, they seemed to lag behind men and boys in moral development and moral reasoning seemed to be generally inferior. They were found to be less influenced by moral arguments and less inclined to act on principle than their male counterparts (Gilligan 1977).[9] Such findings were clearly at odds with commonsense perceptions of feminine morality as caring and giving—as determinably more altruistic than men. The lesser degree of violence and greater degree of caring in women of all cultures was ascribed to instinctual endowment rather than to development, and their concern with relationships was sometimes regarded as a moral impediment (Gilligan 1980). Lawrence Kohlberg's methods were by and large alien to feminine preconceptions and interests. Given hypothetical dilemmas, boys would accept the premise and go on to explore hypothetical possibilities; girls rather tended to resist the premise, reacting to dichotomous choices as incomplete and not exhausting the range of possible courses of action. This seemed to suggest that women thought differently than men about moral issues.

However, Kohlberg was not alone in these persuasions—we have already seen Freud's bias in this regard. Justin Aronfreed (1961, 1968), for example, also postulated a stronger internal orientation in males that he attributed to the dominant status of masculinity in most societies and patterns of socialization directing girls to conform to social expectations and boys to more internalized self-direction. In contrast, others (Sears, Macoby, and Levin 1957) hypothesized that women developed stronger moral values insofar as they are able over time to maintain the mother as an object of identification, as contrasted with male development involving a shift in identification from mother to father. Using an interview scale similar to Kohlberg's, Eliot Turiel (1976) put these questions to the test. Both males and females progressed through higher stages of moral judgment with increasing age, and both showed the same sequential progression with some minor divergence in rates of maturation—girls ahead around ages ten to thirteen, boys ahead at sixteen. Turiel stated:

> We can conclude from all these results that no inherent differences exist between males and females in the form, rate, or potential level of moral development. The variations in rate of development observed in this study, as well as in other studies, suggest that the individual's environmental setting relates to rate of development. It appears that it is only in certain, and not all, social settings that males and females develop at different rates. (p. 206)

The theme was taken up by Carol Gilligan (1982), noting that in Piaget's study of rules in children's games, girls were less interested in making rules, while boys were more interested in codification, more pragmatic, and more tolerant of exceptions and open to innovations. She argued that moral development in women followed a normal progression in social development, but with distinctive moral conceptions diverging from Kohlberg's all-male database (Walker 1984). In Kohlberg's approach, justice was a central organizing principle, but for women personal relationships, fostering and maintaining them and exercising due interpersonal care, proved to be much more important. Longitudinal study of adolescents and their parents (Holstein 1976) found that moral judgments in women were more closely tied to feelings of empathy and compassion than their male counterparts, and were more concerned with real life than hypothetical dilemmas. The irony is that the very traits, customarily defining the goodness of women, their sensitivity and responsiveness to needs of others, are interpreted as marks of their moral deficiency or limitation. Their emotional attunement to the needs of others forestalls developing a more objective, principled morality based on justice rather than on compassion and care (Gilligan 1977, 1982). Gilligan (1977) put the dilemma for women in these terms:

> The conflict between self and other thus constitutes the central moral problem for women, posing a dilemma whose resolution requires a reconciliation between femininity and adulthood. . . . The "good woman" masks assertion in evasion, denying responsibility by claiming only to meet the needs of others, while the "bad woman" forgoes or renounces the commitments that bind her in self-deception and betrayal. It is precisely this dilemma—the conflict between compassion and autonomy, between virtue and power—which the feminine voice struggles to resolve in its effort to reclaim the self and to solve the moral problem in such a way that no one is hurt. (pp. 490–491)

Beyond caring and self-sacrifice, judgmental initiative reactivates for some women the issue of whether including her own needs and desires as encompassed by care and concern is selfish or responsible, moral or immoral. Effective resolution of this crisis of judgment leads to a better capacity to be responsible to both self and others—this resolution honors the orientation of concern and care, even self-sacrifice, without entrapment in masochistic self-surrender. This revised paradigm of feminine morality reflects back on the inadequacies of the freudian paradigm. As Schafer (1992) commented, "If, because of her different constellation of castration concerns, a girl does not develop the implacable superego that a boy does, then at least in this respect she might be better suited than a boy to develop a moral code that is enlightened, realistic, and consistently committed to some conventional form of civilized interaction among people" (p. 65).

Questions persist as to why this male-female difference exists. There is currently less inclination to view this as resulting from biological givens or differences in temperament, although such predisposing factors cannot be ruled out (Robbins 1996). Martin Hoffman (1975) speculated that identification with mothers with humanistic value systems, may contribute something, but it is not clear that such identifications are the major factor contributing to moral development. Hoffman preferred to put the emphasis for females on a combination of maternal affection and an inductive pattern of discipline (see chapter 11) and and on infrequent use of techniques of power assertion (e.g., physical force, maternal deprivation, or their threat). In fact, meta-analysis of research literature dealing with male-female differences tends to contradict prevailing stereotypes and indicate that any differences are few, difficult to identify, and where they show any male advantage are usually methodologically flawed, usually from confounding of sex with educational-occupational differences (Walker 1984).

Beyond childhood, other factors may influence sex-differences in moral behavior. As Hoffman (1975) noted, the socially induced role for females is more expressive, that is, more able to give and receive affection, more responsive to feelings and needs of others, a configuration more consistent with the greater humanistic quality of feminine morality. For their male counterparts, society imposes increasingly instrumental norms and expectations oriented more toward work achievement and success. This instrumental influence comes less from the mother and more from the father, whose value system emphasizes achievement and performance.

PERSPECTIVES ON CONSCIENCE

When we examine the role of conscience more carefully, analytic formulations will not stand up to deeper scrutiny. The classic view of conscience as a function of superego offered a restrictive view, which falls short of ethical demands. Conscience in that limited sense was a *post factum* affective reaction, reflecting a judgment that a given action was reprehensible, undesirable, and somehow inconsistent with presumed moral principles. The question was left unresolved as to how such judgments were formed, what was meant by the principles by which the mind judged, and more important how the evaluation of goodness or badness was arrived at. We humans do make distinctions between good and bad actions; we experience a sense of obligation to do what we consider good or right and avoid what we consider wrong or bad; we experience a sense of freedom in choosing one way or the other—to do the good or avoid the bad; and finally, we have a sense of responsibility for actions we choose to perform and hold others responsible for actions they choose to perform.[10] The claim is idealized, of course, and it doesn't take a psychoanalyst or a rocket scientist to tell that these criteria of ethical capacity are not always or even often effectively applied.

The understanding of conscience among ethicists has covered a range of variants. Intuitionists regarded conscience as manifesting the moral sense, our highest moral capacity, the supreme personal authority regulating self-love and benevolence. Although ideally these and other motivational influences are governed by conscience, strong emotions or impulses can upset the rule of conscience and result in actions the subject knows to be wrong or imprudent. Conscience judges right and wrong with authority, since it alone perceives good and evil as such—self-love and benevolence may be strong motives, but lack the authoritative power of conscience.[11] Obviously such a conscience was to be followed without question. Similarly, for Jean-Jacques Rousseau conscience was more than mere feeling; it was the voice of the soul that never deceives, the infallible guide for judging good and evil that is always to be obeyed.

One version takes the "moral sense" to mean the emotion of approval or disapproval for an act the moral agent has decided to perform or avoid (Russell 1910). While this is certainly a component of ethical experience, there must also be room for a judgment of approval; otherwise there would be no reasoning and deliberation. But the sense of what is right reaches beyond mere approval, since approval may prove to be misguided; judgment is objective insofar as it does not depend solely on feeling. Following the dictates of conscience as feeling may not result in an objectively right action—what one feels or even believes to be right may not really be right. Russell concluded that we needed to look beyond the moral sense, with its affective connotations, to know what is right or wrong—that conscience must involve judgment.

If we regard ethical judgment as "objective," this tends to exclude commands or wishes (not judgments at all), apparently false judgments, and judgments referring to the psychological state or disposition of the one judging, all subjective entities (Ewing 1947). If the basis of judgment remained subjective, if one person thought an action good and another thought it bad, there would be no argument capable of refuting either, so that ethical judgments could not be true or false and total relativism would prevail. The problem points to the inherent difficulty of determining how ethical judgments and judgments of conscience can be objectively right or good. Appealing to an autonomous or categorical conscience is as subjective as appealing to emotional factors. To utilitarians conscience provided the ultimate sanction obliging observance of the moral law. For John Stuart Mill, conscience was a feeling-state, based largely on sympathy or fellow-feeling. The easy passage from what people desire to what they ought to desire is a weakness of this view.

For others, conscience was, if not the voice of God, at least an awareness of transgression against the law of God. The presumption that conscience acts to apply a moral law, divinely or otherwise derived, imposes obligation—for some, to go against the judgment of conscience was not only to violate one's best judgment and values, but to go against divine authority. Short of this, conscience was regarded as the ultimate subjective norm and individual guide for moral behavior—such a conscience may at times miss the mark, but since it was the best anyone can do, the obligation persists to follow wherever it leads. The history of ethics is festooned with controversies dealing with the problem of converting a doubtful conscience into a certain one—tutiorism, probabiliorism, equiprobabilism, and probabilism. The last of these seems to have prevailed, teaching that a solidly probable reason justifies an action, even though other probable, even more probable, reasons may weigh against the action. The judgment of conscience is no more than a probable judgment, an aspect of practical reasoning that never attains certainty.

One of the persistent problems in regarding conscience as the authoritative guide for moral action is that dictates of conscience are so variable. On one hand, we owe the advancement of human civilization to the power of conscience—the prophets of the Old Testament spoke from their consciences to the evils of their time and culture, Socrates was a voice of conscience, as was Martin Luther King Jr.—the list is endless. But on the other hand, conscience has led us to the most depraved and destructive courses of action, all justified in the name of conscience—wars, racial oppression, wars of religion, the Inquisition, the Nazi Holocaust, the random taking of innocent lives by acts of terrorism, the devastation of the World Trade Center, and the murder of millions in the name of progress (the former Soviet Union under Stalin, and China under Mao Tse-tung), genocide, and on and on. All of these devices of terror, hatred, and destruction were, and are guided by, conscience—even the most sincere and principled conscience. Josiah Royce once opined, "Ethical doctrine must tell us why, if the devil's conscience approves of the devil's acts, as it may well do, the devil's conscience is nevertheless in the wrong" (cited in Fuss 1963–1964, p. 50).

Antecedent vs. consequent. Conscience can be either antecedent or consequent. Antecedent conscience[12] involves ethical reasoning and decision-making antecedent to the act—that is, the moral capacity operating to determine choice of a good or right action or avoidance of a bad or wrong action. Antecedently the judgment of conscience decides what is lawful or unlawful, what the subject ought or ought not do. This conscience does not motivate, but its deliberations are attuned to, and responsive to, various levels of motivation. It also makes decisions taking into account the value-structures that constitute moral consciousness and identity. As such, it serves as an ethical guide, pointing the way to doing the morally good or avoiding the morally evil, and thus preparing the ground for the action of the will in making the actual choice. Since the judgment of conscience is an aspect of practical reasoning, the ought-conclusion is not simply conceptual, but pragmatic. But judging and doing remain separate: the conclusion that I ought to do X does not necessitate my doing X. Only the consequent activation of the will, as primary movement in the order of execution, brings the "ought" to fulfillment. And, as we have seen previously (chapters 4 and 5), the act of volition in order to maintain ethical validity must be free, that is, not caused by the practical judgment of ought.

Consequent or executive conscience comes into play after the action has been performed, passing judgment on the rightness or wrongness, goodness or badness, of the action, and eliciting corresponding affects of approval or disapproval. A negative judgment can result in guilt—if the judgment is unconscious, the guilt will also more likely be unconscious, and if conscious conscious. Most of the decisions of conscience end in compromise, between present desires and future goals, between fractional goods reflecting contending interests, between courses of action reflective of divergent and conflicting value orientations, and so on. In my view, these operations of conscience cannot be attributed exclusively to superego or ego, but must involve integration of both. The superego contribution is especially relevant in the integration of value systems that provide the conceptual matrix for the decision process, and in the affective resonances that attend either antecedent resolutions (anticipatory guilt or shame) or consequent evaluations (consequent guilt or shame).[13]

Integration. Conscience can also undergo degrees of integration (Fenichel 1945; Fromm 1947): nonintegrated conscience, reflecting a dominance of superego attitudes, can manifest severe moral principles and strict prohibitions along with rebellious attitudes against such standards resulting in guilt, self-reproach, and ambivalence; at the next level conscience can be moralistic-repressive, characterized by rigid moral discipline toward oneself and others, along with excessive control of impulses and spontaneity— moral standards are generally accepted without much conflict, but any failure is met with punitive response; on a higher level of integration, conscience can reflect more developed ego functions manifested in strong ethical principles and values and acceptance of social standards, not out of threat of punishment but on the basis of personal motivation and choice (Benfari and Calogeras 1968). Obviously, these degrees of integration reflect corresponding degrees of superego-ego integration and levels of ethical maturity.

Authoritarian vs. humanistic. The distinction between authoritarian and humanistic conscience, closely aligned with the distinction of instinctual versus moral conscience, was embellished by Erich Fromm (1947). The difference between authoritarian and humanistic conscience was more a matter of motivation than action. The judgment of either form of conscience about a given action may be the same, but with different motives. The authoritarian responded to the internalized voice of external authorities, and was therefore the less developed and less mature variant. It was essentially based on fear of external authorities—parents, church, state, and public opinion—that are regarded consciously or unconsciously as legislators of morality whose laws and prescriptions are internalized in conscience. Fromm regarded authoritarian conscience as equivalent to Freud's superego, the common element being that its prescriptions were not based on one's own values, but on the dictates and taboos of authorities, which are accepted as norms of conscience not because they are good, but because they are rendered by authority. Disobedience is thus the cardinal sin, submission and obedience the cardinal virtues.

Humanistic conscience, however, manifests a more authentic voice of the self and personally integrated values. It embraced conative, affective, and rational aspects of the human person integrated into the basis for disciplined and principled moral decision and judgment. In Fromm's (1947) terms, "But although conscience is *knowledge*, it is more than mere knowledge in the realm of abstract thought. It has an *affective* quality, for it is the reaction of our total personality and not only the reaction of our mind" (p. 162, italics in original).[14] This is several steps removed from the instinctually driven reactions of superego—instead of an introjected agency pitted against instinctual drives and turning the force of destructive aggression against the self, moral character is envisioned more as the outcome of an adaptive capacity integrating personal needs, desires, affects, purposes, and reason. Humanistic conscience expresses my self-interest and integrity, rather than the themes of obedience, duty, or social conformity of authoritarian conscience.[15] Humanistic conscience, contrary to authoritarian, stands aside from external laws, judges them critically and objectively, and determines the extent to which their observance or nonobservance is ethically indicated. Laws themselves are not always good ethical guides—some would say that the congruence of the law with ethical principles is little more than coincidental.

CONSCIENCE AS ETHICAL GUIDE

Gilbert Ryle (1940) rightly insisted on the private nature of conscience, but subjective reasoning does not guarantee that a particular conclusion can stand on its own. My conclusion as to what I ought to do, by the very nature of the reasoning process, remains uncertain. I can seek counsel, expert advice, submitting my reflection to the greater experience and wisdom of others, peers or superiors, to seek greater reassurance that my judgment is not in error or misconceived. Regardless of external input, the ultimate judgment of conscience remains private and personal to the individual, such that the ultimate responsibility for it and for its consequences belongs to him and to no other.

Unfortunately, we cannot comfortably assume that conscience always serves as an optimal guide to ethical behavior—it can and often does speak with a contradictory voice and may reflect superego influences reflecting primitive instinctual impulses and desires, often largely unconscious. This problem arises acutely in analysis when the analysand comes to a decision regarding some ethical choice that is clearly neurotically motivated. The question remains as to when conscience can be accepted as a reliable ethical guide and when not. This can become particularly acute when personal conscience comes into conflict with group decisions or laws, when one is convinced that the judgment of conscience is ethically more correct than social dictates, laws, or customs. Despite the uncertain ethical guidance of laws and customs and the fallibility of conscience as a guide to decision and action, one must take an ethical stance in the face of multiple uncertainties. Risks are often unavoidable, especially when one sticks to his principles— ethical probity is not without its cost, and the man of principle may be called on to pay a heavy price for his probity—for following his conscience rather than the dictates of conformity. Even if the wise man takes counsel and seeks advice and judgment from others, he cannot so easily escape the burdens and risks of judgment and personal responsibility—ultimately he must accept the credit or blame for his decisions and their consequences.[16]

Subjective vs. objective. Conscience, then, is far from an infallible guide (Dineen 1971; Granrose 1970; Nowell-Smith 1954). Out of ignorance, lack of information, misunderstanding, misinformation, faulty motivation, poor reality testing, and so forth, the judgment of conscience can be faulty—what I judge or believe to be right may not be so. There may be a disparity between the subjective judgment of conscience and the objective moral situation.[17] This realization leaves us in a quandary, How can we know what is morally right or wrong? This is a problem for the delicate conscience and it has no certain resolution. At its extreme, the scrupulous patient is driven to seek certainty, but there is none. How does one resolve the dilemma? One course is to fix upon an external authority and to make that the arbitrer of moral decision. This resolution, in the light of what we know about moral development, is morally regressive, sacrifices personal autonomy, and seeks to resign personal responsibility to that external authority.

The other option is morally more mature, but requires a willingness to tolerate ambiguity and uncertainty, to take risks, and to plunge ahead into the unknown future with some degree of courage and a willingness to take what comes and to make the best of it. Life is risk, and one can never know whether a gamble will pay off or not. My favorite analogy is the card game. To begin with, you are dealt a hand and you have nothing to say about what cards are in it. When you play your hand, you do not know what the outcome will be. Every time you play a card, it is a gamble—it may succeed; it may not. But you have to take the consequences, and look to the next hand and take the next step from where you are at that moment. Life is very like that—and the process of moral decision-making is exactly like that. But if conscience, even at its best, is uncertain and fallible, it is the only guide we have. We have no choice but to play our hand as best we can, and to settle for the outcome.

The question is, What goes into playing the hand? No one can be held to an uncertain or doubtful conscience—that is the escape hatch for the scrupulous—but if I can resolve my doubts enough to allow me to make a decision and play my hand, I am responsible for the decision and for the effects of the action. From one perspective, judgments of conscience about any issue are as variable as the individuals judging—conscience is always personal and reflects the history of developmental experiences that go into conscience formation and ethical capacity. But from another perspective, the individual's subjective assessment and judgment are not the ultimate criteria. Hitler's decisions to slaughter millions of Jews and others, however convinced and subjectively validated by his personal conscience, was neither morally acceptable nor right. If we cannot rely on conscience as an ultimate or infallible guide, this does not empty conscience of all moral authority (Granrose 1970). When we have done our best, and within reasonable limits, with due rational deliberation, conscience remains our essential and ultimate guide to moral action. At its best, it represents the best we can do, so that we have no other choice if we are motivated to do what seems to be morally right. But that decision cannot escape the confines of subjectivity and we have no guarantee of the rightness or goodness of the outcome. For that we must await the verdict of time and reality.

CONSCIENCE VS. SUPEREGO

Freud regarded superego and conscience for all practical purposes equivalent. But for our purposes, I will insist on their separation and distinction—

superego assessment, concerned with infantile dictates and needs for approval and love positively or fear of loss of love and/or punishment negatively is clearly distinct from conscience, which is concerned with the judgment of ethical goodness or badness of an act or course of action.[18] Erik H. Erikson (1964) offered a parallel distinction between between ethics and morals:

> I would propose that we consider *moral rules* of conduct to be based on a fear of *threats* to be forestalled. These may be outer threats of abandonment, punishment and public exposure, or a threatening inner sense of guilt, of shame or of isolation. . . . In contrast, I would consider *ethical rules* to be based on *ideals* to be striven for with a high degree of rational assent and with a ready consent to a formulated good, a definition of perfection, and some promise of self-realization. . . . The moral and ethical sense are different in their psychological dynamics, because the moral sense develops on an earlier, more immature level. (p. 222; italics in original)

Conscience plays its role in both moral and ethical contexts—the balance tilted more toward superego dynamics in moral contexts, more toward ego functions in ethical. Conscience on these terms is an expression of the self, acting with an integrated sense of ethical identity, involving functions from all levels of the psychic apparatus; it calls upon the functions of each of the tripartite entities, drawing together ego capacities of intellect and will, superego determinants, and instinctual needs and desires, focusing them in a final common path for evaluative decision-making directed to determining the ethical quality of an action, intended or performed. Ethical authenticity, then, does not reside in the superego, even though it plays a contributory role. On its own, in terms of its own internal dynamics, superego can be regarded as playing no more than a pseudomoral role, particularly in the genesis of guilt and shame (Odier 1943; Pattison 1968; Plé 1964a). Superego contributes to both antecedent and consequent conscience—generating affective assessments of anticipated actions, or accusing and condemning the offending self for past actions. Guilt can be antecedent to any wrongdoing—that is, the subject may be feel guilty for wishes or fantasies without doing anything to merit guilt, in contrast to the judgment of conscience that finds the agent guilty only if he did what he was wishing (J. H. Smith 1986).

Fears of separation or alienation pervading superego anxieties separate it from conscience, in which the path of genuine value-determined choice may actually lead to such isolation or rejection by fellowmen or society.

Seeking approval and acceptance can serve the interests of socialization and communal conformity or submission, but it will not serve the purposes of moral decision and choice. The superego, then, is essentially conservative, preserving traditional standards transmitted from parent to child over generations. Ethical conscience, however, demands continual exposure to risk, uncertainty, probing the limits of experience, and a creative adaptedness in the ongoing evolution of personal values and meaningful life choices. Conscience, particularly in its antecedent function, requires creativity and freedom to choose and adapt. In its consequent role, conscience serves more as an evaluator and corrective guide, recalibrating the instrument for the next antecedent moment. Freud's error, in regarding conscience as synonymous with the superego, resulted in misdirecting subsequent analytic reflection on ethical issues. The failure to distinguish superego and ego-ideal from conscience has contributed to concretizing morality in terms of superego-functions to the detriment or undervaluing of relevant ego-functions in the process of moral reflection (Nass 1966; Pattison 1968).

Conscience, in its more developed and sophisticated meaning as a capacity for moral reasoning and judgment, is an autonomous capacity involving integrated functioning of intellective and volitional strengths deriving from collaborative engagement of ego and superego. Obligation is not an external demand, but an autonomous commitment to authentic self-development and meaningful integration of personal values within the social and cultural fabric of one's reference group or groups. Conscience is a form of self-capacity embracing the power of self-determination and decision. Such conscience has no privileged access to all necessary information to make an inerrant judgment and is liable to the same failings of reason and motive affecting all human understanding. On these terms moral responsibility is always a matter of free decision and choice, and is attributable to the act of will-determining action—guilt is not due to the action itself, but only to the act by which the agent determines on the course of action. Consequently, action that is objectively bad or bad in virtue of its consequences, but that the subject erroneously judged good, is not an object of guilt; on the other hand, an objectively good action that conscience judged to be bad may become a target for guilt.

And if there is to be punishment, it comes not from some external power, worldly or otherwise, but from within, self-inflicted, calculated to redress the balance of right and wrong and to reconstitute the moral sense of self. Contrition, then, in contrast to instinctual guilt, is a matter of acknowledging one's intention and action as self-depleting and negating, accepting one's fault and responsibility for its effects, and actively resolving on self-restoration and moral improvement. Common experience and the experience of the analytic couch bear witness that these different levels of conscience are more often in conflict than harmoniously integrated. Patients often feel that they have little control over their impulses and deviant desires, and even at times when they are clear as to what they ought to do, feel unable to put it into action. To the extent that instinctual desires continue to have their say, the patient feels guilty. Or, as is also often the case, the patient feels guilty and does not know why—only during analytic exploration do we begin to get a sense of what is behind the guilt. Or, if the guilt remains unconscious, we come to know it only in its effects, whether symptomatic or acted out.

MORAL JUDGMENT VS. ACTION

We can only wonder at the rarity of this level of maturity and at the multitude of contradictory, inhibiting, and confounding factors that undermine and impede the ideal of personal and ethical maturity, particularly deriving from fears, taboos, obsessions, ambivalence, anxieties, and other factors undermining and restricting the basic freedom of decision and choice. However, even when a well developed moral capacity and maturity of conscience are attained, it turns out that they are no guarantors of moral behavior. There are no definitive answers to this problem, but certain suppositions are operative. James Rest (1980), after years of research into moral behavior, suggested a useful perspective: "I think research shows that (1) moral judgment development is significantly related to behavior, but (2) moral judgment is not the only important psychological variable involved, and (3) these other variables modify, complicate, and attenuate the role of moral judgment" (p. 548). But Augusto Blasi (1980) concluded that there was "considerable support for the hypothesis that moral reasoning and moral action are statistically related" (p. 37). Other variables have to do with ego-strength—Rest (1980) spoke of "iron will, courage, and resolve" (p. 550), suggesting the role of the will as embodying ego strength. Other data, largely psychoanalytic, indicate that ethical decisions are not always conscious, but may be largely unconscious and unreflective—as we have suggested in discussing the ethical decision-making process.

Rest (1980) also listed contributing factors to moral failure: (1) low level of moral development, reflecting simplistic or inadequate views of possibilities and conditions of human cooperation; (2) moral insensitivity; (3) lack of information and ignorance regarding long-term consequences of actions taken; (4) the fact that many moral issues arise abruptly, without warning, overwhelming our conceptual capacity with bewildering complexity and leaving us confused or befuddled; (5) other values overriding our ability to act fairly, honorably, or altruistically—such values may be egoistic, self-centered, or self-concerned, or may reflect powerful ideological commitments that obstruct reasonable moral reflection; (6) deficiencies in ego strength opening the way to distraction, failure of resolve, succumbing to external pressures and demands; and (7) deficits in rational moral orientation not admitting any influence of moral ideals and values. A psychoanalytic perspective might add unconscious motives, especially those rooted in narcissism, and superego imperatives that override moral reasoning and decisions, and finally the heterogeneous organization of moral consciousness that allows contradictory ethical states of mind and conviction. One can believe that it is wrong to kill another human being, yet drop atomic bombs or blow up airplanes out of fanatic commitment to a political or religious ideology. Or one can be a champion of freedom and human rights, yet hold other human beings as slaves, buying and selling them as so much chattel, as was the case for Thomas Jefferson.

OBLIGATION AND DUTY

Ethical inquiry is not concerned merely with the "good," but with the *bonum faciendum*—the "good that is or ought to be done"—and with the *malum vitandum*—the "bad that is or ought to be avoided." The sense of obligation, of "ought," is distinctive of the judgment of conscience. Efforts to determine the meaning of "good" or "evil" come short of the element of necessity involved in the sense of obligation. What is the nature of this "ought"—is it categorical and absolute, or hypothetical or conditional? And what are its origins? The judgment of "ought" can induce a sense of subjective rightness and conviction that may be more affective than cognitive, lending itself at times to a sense of righteousness. But conscience can be mistaken and my belief about what I ought to do in error; I would end up with a paradox—I ought to do (follow my erroneous conscience) what I ought not to do (what is wrong). Then again the "ought" may pertain to an action that seems preferable but may not turn out to be the best choice—the available evidence may be limited and consequences not foreseeable (Ewing 1947; Hunter 1963).

One of the concepts conveying a sense of obligation is "duty." Common usage treats "duty" and "obligation" as more or less equivalent and analogous to the sense of legal obligation, but the "ought" implied in obligation can have various meanings.[19] Duties are usually imposed externally by the social environment, usually in terms of moral rules conveying a sense of obligation (Falk 1947–1948). Social obligation is transformed into personal obligation—the social mandate becomes "my duty" and its acceptance requires that I make the obligation personal. An adopted duty, then, is incorporated with my ego-ideal and its observance becomes critical to my self-regard. For Immanuel Kant with a good will one did one's duty for duty's sake. But there is a radical difference between an ethical perspective based on understanding of human nature and motivation and one based on appeals to first principles of imperative obligation.[20] Ethical reflection may arrive at a sense of obligation—the implicit imperative of the "ought" of the judgment of conscience; but it does not begin with such an imperative. The imperatives of practical reason, then, may take a more hypothetical than categorical form—"if I want to act ethically, then I ought to do this."

SUPEREGO AFFECTS

Superego guilt. Freud's interest in the superego centered on unconscious guilt, which he saw as the motivating force behind obsessional rituals (1907), depressive states and moral masochism, and certain character types—those wrecked by success and criminals from a sense of guilt (1916)—all forms of subjection to sadistic and punitive superego assaults. Superego guilt is instinctually based, and directed at derivatives of undesirable, disapproved, dangerous, threatening, or reprehensible impulses, wishes, thoughts, and fantasies. While primarily unconscious, it can also penetrate conscious guilt feelings in more authentically ethical contexts. Clearly Freud's discussions of unconscious guilt do not touch strictly on ethical matters, but concern themselves only with instinctual dynamics and derivatives. Ethical matters go far beyond that, however, and require further discussion of the role of superego guilt in ethical experience.

Freud viewed superego guilt as redirecting instinctual destructiveness against the ego. The more destructiveness toward outside objects was inhibited, the more was it channeled through superego inward against the self (1923a, 1924b). The dilemma thus created, of course, is that while superego is necessary for development of civilization, engagement in civilized society requires inhibition of destructive impulses. Thus social engagement increases the destructiveness of the superego even as it sets it up as the container of destructive urges and the protector of social interests—"like a garrison in a conquered city" (Freud 1930, pp. 123–124). This internalized parental authority guaranteed that conformity to cultural imperatives was reinforced internally rather than by mere external coercion. But the cost was high—"A threatened external unhappiness—loss of love and punishment on the part of the external authority—has been exchanged for a permanent internal unhappiness, for the tension of the sense of guilt. Every renunciation of instinct now becomes a dynamic source of conscience and every fresh renunciation increase's the latter's severity and intolerance" (Freud 1930, p. 128). This led to Freud's view of ethics as "a therapeutic attempt to . . . get rid of the greatest hindrance to civilization—namely the constitutional inclination of human beings to be aggressive toward one another (1930, p. 142).

Superego vs. moral guilt. In man, however, guilt is not a simple phenomenon, but has multiple levels and meanings. Guilt is usually associated with breaking a moral rule of some kind (Klass 1978; Wright 1971). Freud (1930) himself distinguished different types of guilt, "one coming from fear of the external authority, the other from fear of the internal authority" (p. 137).[21] In contrast, guilt can be experienced consciously in relation to reasoned action undertaken in the light of meaningful and purposeful motives. Such guilt has often been described as "real" or "existential" (Buber 1965).[22] But instinctually derived guilt can also be either conscious or unconscious.

Superego morality condemns and punishes any falling short of the ego-ideal; but there is no assessment, evaluation, deliberation, discrimination of intentions and values, and so on. There is only condemnation, automatic, and with eyes only for the failure. Individuals with conventional moral structures tend to be more repressed and less tolerant of immoral impulses. However, on this level of superego condemnation, the experience of guilt varies widely from individual to individual depending on the quality of the internalized parental imagoes, persecutory or beneficent or some mixture. Guilt engendered by a persecutory superego will be accompanied by impulses to defy it or its externalized substitutes. Guilt inflicted by a benign superego focuses more on the sense of "injury to, a betrayal of, or a failure to protect, the people or values that symbolize their good internal objects" (Money-Kyrle 1952, p. 231), tending to a depressive reaction (Money-Kyrle 1955). Persecutory conscience is akin to the authoritarian: its victims are concerned with obedience to an exacting superego or its representatives.[23] More humanistic consciences are more beneficent, less concerned with laws or disobedience, but tend to be more distressed by disloyalty to persons or values they identify with, feel remorse for wrongs committed,[24] and if they are less law-abiding, they tend to be more kindly, more concerned over wrongs suffered by others, and enjoy a greater degree of personal freedom, altruistic concern, and responsibility to others[25]—all qualities reflecting superego-ego integration.

This freudian "conscience" has been faulted for neglecting the possibility that, as instinctually based, it may be at odds with its social sources; Freud saw it primarily as an internalized extension of parental and social authority (Rieff 1959). The assumptions that parents, teachers, and other authorities all preach the same values is at least questionable if not false. Freud's conscience, then, leaves little room for choice—there is room only for alternative submissions. Regardless of intention, purpose, freely chosen or not, the action is a transgression and therefore wrong and sinful, worthy of punishment. The guilt is primarily and essentially a feeling, not a judgment or conclusion, due simply to the fact of violating the dictates of conscience. If the sinner seeks forgiveness, it is not because of awareness of wrongdoing and a desire for amendment, but as an effort to escape the consequences of wrongdoing and to magically restore the status quo ante.

Shame. Shame is the affective response to narcissistic deprivation or mortification. It carries a burden of sensitivity and guardedness, as though there were a vulnerable pain center that the patient needed to keep hidden and protected at all costs. Often in therapy the patient's intense and labored resistance finally yields up a relatively trivial fantasy to which the feeling of shame is attached. This terrible secret is shared with the analyst as a privileged communication, enshrined with special importance and significance within the patient's inner world. The patient's shame is often related to relatively crude narcissistic exhibitionistic urges (Kohut 1971), and his concern is inevitably associated with his fear of ridicule and humiliation.

Following Freud's suggestion that shame, along with disgust, was one of the inhibitory forces opposing expression of the sexual instinct, Sidney Levin (1967) suggested that shame can function as a signal affect preventing overexposure to narcissistic trauma. Shame controls the degree and direction of self-exposure in order to protect from needless trauma. Trauma can take the shape of ridicule, scorn, abandonment, rejection, or feelings of humiliation, inferiority, or narcissistic mortification (Rochlin 1961; Spiegel 1966), all contrary to wished-for acceptance or respect required to sustain self-esteem. The sense of shame can also be readily externalized by projection, since the implied self-exposure must involve a sense of others perceiving oneself as a failure, inadequate, inferior, or regarding him with devaluation or contempt.

The motif of shame and its connection with these attitudes is brought sharply to mind by my experience with a young woman of about thirty who came to analysis for a rather severe depression and impaired self-esteem. Her chronic and recurrent expectation was that she would be criticized for whatever she did. These feelings could readily be traced to her hypercritical mother in whose eyes this woman could do nothing right and could do nothing to demonstrate any worthwhileness. These expectations found their way into the transference and expressed themselves in her conviction that I would be critical of her, that I would tell her she was a worthless patient who did not deserve to be analyzed; her conviction was that I was sitting, waiting, and watching her—letting the analytic material build up so I could then turn on her and show her how worthless and evil she was. She even felt at times that I was reading the perverse and degenerate thoughts that came into her mind and that I could only feel contempt and disgust at what I must be seeing in her. The whole of this material was underlaid with shameful feelings.

Shame and guilt. Shame and guilt are related affects in superego development. Susan Miller (1989) argued that intersection of two developmental lines usually regarded as noninteractive, one involving shame and self-esteem regulation and the other superego conflict and guilt, may have an important influence in superego formation. Early experiences affecting self-esteem can influence the emerging superego so that primitive shame is experienced as badness and thus a matter of conscience. In some degree, then, adult guilt may not be based on unconscious fears of destructive impulses or of castrating parental authority so much as on issues of self-esteem regulation. Shame in this context is less related to repression of exhibitionistic impulses than as a source of developmental stimulus on its own.

Shame is often connected with or associated with guilt, but it is useful and important to keep these two signal affects differentiated: (1) In shame, any aspect of the self, including actions, feelings, thoughts, and wishes, is compared with an idealized self-image, reflecting how we would wish to see ourselves and have others see us. Guilt sees the same self-dimensions in relationship to a code of standards and prohibitions of what one ought to be or do or not do. The emphasis in shame falls on qualities of the self, while the emphasis of guilt falls on actions—what is done or not done. (2) Shame is more global, focusing on a wishful self-image emcompassing the whole person with its ideal characteristics measuring our self-evaluation. Guilt, in contrast, is delimited and additive rather than global, focusing on specific actions and their consequences. (3) Shame is a form of self-contempt, while guilt expresses self-hatred. This affective differentiation reflects different vicissitudes of hostile destructiveness: hatred seeks to hurt and destroy; contempt seeks to eliminate something as dirty or evil. (4) In their signal functions, shame and guilt reflect different sets of instinctual wishes. Shame counters exhibitionistic and scoptophilic wishes. Guilt counters wishes to attack, hurt, and destroy. The shame experience involves a sequence of exposure, condemnation, rejection, scorn, and hiding; the guilt experience involves a sequence of attack, retaliation by punishment, and atonement by pain. (5) The element of suddenness or surprise, particularly of discovery, plays a role in shame; not so in guilt. (6) Both affects serve protective functions: they protect the separate private self from intrusion and merger. The protection of shame operates in the field of expressive and perceptual experience (touching, looking, exhibiting, etc.), while guilt pertains to the field of motor activity and aggression (attacking, hurting, castrating, killing, etc.) (Wurmser 1978).

Shame and guilt are often connected in "guilt-shame cycles" (Piers and Singer 1953). Shame is related to the frustration of narcissistic aspirations, but depends for the most part on the perception of such failure by others. Such attitudes can be internalized, but often the experience of shame still requires external exposure. The intense experience of shame can lead to disturbance of self-related affect, transforming narcissistic investment in the self into hostile and destructive affects, usually regarded as superego hostility against the self, experienced as guilt. In such cases, the narcissistic defense can give rise to a depressive response, which can be further defended by blaming as a device for restoring narcissistic equilibrium. Both shame and guilt can be conscious or unconscious.[26] One can feel ashamed of an action, just as one can feel guilty, but the sense of shame attaches more to one's sense of self than to an act. As with guilt, one can have a sense of shame even without having acted shamefully, as a consequence of superego condemnation. But shame can extend to wishes, intentions, dispositions, appearance, origins, race, and personal qualities, most of which lie beyond the scope of guilt. Also, if one feels guilty for something, he might also, rightly or wrongly, believe that he was in some measure responsible for it; but not so shame—I may feel shame for something, but not feel responsible for it (Lamb 1983). Guilt is a matter of transgression, violation, or infraction of a rule, precept or law, but shame has a different connotation—not that a rule has been violated but that an ideal has not been lived up to (Lamb 1983; Meissner 1986d; Morrison 1989; Piers and Singer 1953; Wurmser 1978). It should be clear from our preceding discussion that both guilt and shame are affects, not judgments, and consequently are separate from ethical judgment, and only come into play in the ethical decision process by reason of the secondary intervention of the superego resonating with, or reacting to, the judgment of practical reason, that is, conscience.

CHAPTER THIRTEEN

Character and Virtue

THE PSYCHOLOGY OF CHARACTER

The analytic psychology of character evolved through early formulations in terms of libido theory, later additions in structural terms, and later still in terms of the organization of the self. "Character" came to refer to the unique integration of structural constituents reflecting more-or-less enduring qualities of the personality as a whole rather than specific psychic agencies. As Francis Baudry (1989) noted, the concept "enables us to talk in a nonreductionistic fashion about certain global issues relating to self, style, identity, and family interactions" (p. 655). In general usage, of course, "character" has more than one meaning. We recognize literary or dramatic characters; we may refer to our relatively eccentric friends as "characters." Even within psychoanalysis, different connotations are subtly included or excluded. In the hands of many analysts, the term is stripped of any moral or ethical implications—as implied in the standard definition of "character": "The enduring, patterned functioning of an individual. As perceived by others, it is the person's habitual way of thinking, feeling, and acting. Understood psychodynamically, character is the person's habitual mode of reconciling intrapsychic conflicts. Character stands beside, but may be differentiated from, other terms for global aspects of personality, such as identity, self, and ego" (Moore and Fine 1990, p. 37). This usage circumvents any ethical connotations, as when we speak of someone as a person of character, or allude to someone's good or bad character. Character in the latter sense refers more directly to characteristic ethical qualities and dispositions, virtues, vices, and values[1] that persist in the individual's patterns of thought, feeling, and action.

Superego has a role in character formation. Otto Fenichel (1954) commented: "The functions of the conscience are a very important component of the character of personality. Very characteristic for a personality are

267

(a) what he considers good and what bad; (b) whether he takes the commands of his conscience seriously or not; (c) whether he obeys his conscience or tries to rebel against it, etc." (p. 206). From a more empirical
perspective, Robert Hogan (1973) observed that, while character was a fundamental issue for Freud, moral psychology can account for neither delinquency nor altruism without appeal to moral character. Also, society
usually defines dispositions and traits of character in moral terms; in other
words, "Character is defined not by what a person does, but by his reasons
for doing it, by the recurring motives and dispositions that give stability and
coherence to his social conduct" (p. 219).[2]

PSYCHOANALYTIC CONCEPT OF CHARACTER

Psychoanalytic ego psychology included character and character traits
among properties of the ego, acting in concert with superego and ego-ideal.
Many analysts continue to attribute character to the ego, but as Baudry
(1984) sagely noted, it becomes "necessary to interpret the term ego as
referring to the individual as a whole. It would make little sense to attribute attitudes (i.e., a subjective, introspective term) to a structure" (p. 457).
Thus character is not attributed to any of these structures separately, but
more appropriately involves all of them operating synchronously. This calls
for a more encompassing frame of reference, which in my view is better
realized by the concept of the self as supraordinate structure synonymous
with the human person (Meissner 1986c, 1993, 1996a, 1999d,e, 2000e).[3]

Erich Fromm, among others, drew attention to the ethical relevance of
character. His view of conscience as humanistic implied confrontation and
struggle with issues related to love, responsibility, productivity, autonomy,
and freedom. The principal locus of ethical relevance was not action, but
character, which underlies the individual's modes of behavior and orientations to life. Character formation depended on patterns of relations to
others, the world, nature, and oneself. Fromm formulated a series of character types reflecting productive versus nonproductive patterns of dynamic
and sociocultural integration of personality—nonproductive forms
included authoritarian, receptive, exploitative, hoarding and marketing
characters (Fromm 1955).[4] Fromm (1947) saw these patterns of character
integration as forms of failed or deviant personality development largely
responsive to cultural and social determinants. In contrast, the productive
character served as his ethical ideal, free of the chains of alienation and irrational authority (Fromm 1955), and clearly meant to be evaluative and
normative (Hegeman 1994). Productive man uses powers of reason, imagination and love to enhance his or her sense of assimilation and social

involvement in such a way as to develop personal powers and capacities to the fullest. Productive reason is realistic and practical; productive love is characterized by active concern and caring for the good of the beloved, responsibility for his or her happiness and well-being, respect for his or her individuality, and knowledge and acceptance of uniquely personal qualities (Fromm 1947).

Fromm's gallery of character-types has not been immune from criticism. His formulations lack evidential support, beyond literary and philosophical opinions. Their conceptualizations were theoretical rather than clinical, more philosophical than psychological. The portrayal of the authoritarian character is more caricature than character, never found in reality as a pure type. His analysis at times seems more driven by ideology than by empirical understanding of human behavior. His ideological and liberal ethics drew him to conclude that all forms of irrational authority—tradition, superstition, convention, authoritarian monotheism, propaganda, bureaucracy, and charismatic leaders—must be done away with. But in drawing a caricature of irrational authority, Fromm provided little help in understanding the realistic functions and existential roots of legitimate and authentic authority. Stanley Leavy's (1994) trenchant critique makes the point that Fromm's humanistic and historicist position is influenced by the culture of his own time, especially that of the happy few of modern intellectual classes, and thus approaches a self-authenticating dogmatism.[5] Heinz Hartmann (1960) also took issue with Fromm, arguing that while moral systems derived from relations with adults, who were both loved and hated and figures of authority, the resulting consciences and value systems were not necessarily authoritarian, but could be nonauthoritarian and even antiauthoritarian. The individual's moral code and values result from the mingled influence of both psychodynamic and psychosocial factors and operate on both conscious and unconscious levels.

More recently Baudry (1984) added to the distinction between character and character traits—traits are observable, but character must be inferred. Traits are generally regarded as compromise formations integrating levels of (basically instinctual) motivation, defenses, superego components, and ego functions. Character traits enjoy a certain stability along with relatively stereotyped attitudes and behaviors, including defenses, generally experienced as ego-syntonic. They represent organizations of motivational states, defenses, internalizations, traumatic residuals, prohibitions, and inhibitions. Character traits cover a wide range of behavioral characteristics; Baudry (1984) commented:

> They describe generally either ways of relating to people or reacting to situations, or ways of being (attitudes). A character trait

will include or be heavily influenced by defenses, but it is more than a defense. It combines references to a person's moral system (dishonest, cheat, liar), to his instinctual makeup (impulsive), to his basic temperament (cheerful, pessimistic), to complete ego functions (humorous, perceptive, brilliant, superstitious), and finally to basic attitudes toward the world (kind, trustful) and himself (hesitant). (p. 462)

Thus, evaluation of character must include assessment of the moral code and values. Values and their associated habitual ethical dispositions in the form of virtues and vices, are essential aspects of the ethical agent. If we add qualities of temperance, fortitude, prudence, and justice to the list of character traits we enter the terrain of the classical virtues with their ethical implications (see below).

Character Pathology

Character pathology reflects more-or-less habitual deficits or deviations in patterns of ethical behavior. The narcissism of the narcissistic personality is in itself neither morally good nor evil, but may motivate his or her selfishness and greedy entitlement resulting in unjustly depriving or cheating others. The stinginess of the obsessional likewise is ethically neutral, but may lead to withdrawing altruistic assistance from someone else in desperate need. Psychopathic or sociopathic forms of character pathology lack moral dependability (Schlesinger 1992). Antisocial characters have little capacity to delay gratification, minimal moral compunction, little ability to consider consequences of their actions for themselves or others, and little or no empathy for others. But by the same token, an excess of moral dependability can also become pathological. Some heroic characters can persist in a noble commitment or enterprise long beyond the point at which it has become clear to all that the result is counterproductive or destructive—a variant of the tragic flaw. Similarly, the "puritanical character" borders on the pathological, embodying high moral and religious standards, excessive control of instinctual urges, a tendency to dogmatism and judgmental attitudes, apparent benevolence or altruism motivated more by narcissistic needs than true generosity or altruistic concern. This brand of perfectionism, moral rigidity, and self-righteousness betray an elitism cloaked in a facade of humility (Naranjo 1982).

Our assessment of character and character traits also involve subjective value-judgments—if we approve certain behavior, we may regard their subject as possessing integrity and nobility of character, but if we disapprove, the same traits may be regarded as stubborn, rigid, or ideologically fixed (McLean 1992; Schlesinger 1992).[6] Thus, from one point of view values can easily encroach on the assessment of behavior, but on the other hand we can question whether it is either advisable or possible to dissociate human behavior from values. Psychoanalytic understanding of ethical values is not necessarily reduced to assigning responsibility and blame. But by the same token, certain ethically relevant qualities can take the form of character traits generally regarded as negative, socially undesirable, or destructive to oneself or to one's social relations—qualities such as dishonesty, cowardice, imprudence, ignorance, impulsivity, intemperateness, and inconsistency—in other words, the familiar catalog of vices (see below).

Character Formation

Character formation can follow a normal or pathological path, but in either case it is the outcome of a developmental process of growth and maturation involving both natural endowments and environmental influences (Zetzel 1964). Formation of character and character traits results from the interplay of multiple factors, including innate biological predispositions in both instinctual and ego fundaments, and involving early ego defenses and environmental influences, particularly from parents. Various early identifications with significant objects leave their lasting stamp on character formation, and continue to shape self-structure and character throughout the life cycle (Erikson 1959; Lampl-de Groot 1963).

In more empirically descriptive terms, Hogan (1973) related character formation to moral knowledge, socialization (including superego development), empathy (connoting the ability to appreciate others point of view and respect for their rights), autonomy, and a capacity for moral judgment. However, he concluded that any assumption that knowledge of moral rules has any connection with willingness to observe them would seem naive. Socialization is then a matter of regarding social rules, values, and prescriptions as personally relevant; conversely, rejection or unassimilation of the same norms of society would leave one unsocialized or alienated. Internalized norms are accepted as standards of behavior and specifically as one's own, while an external frame of reference continues to view social norms as arbitrarily and externally imposed so that they are observed only out of fear of consequences of nonobservance. Hogan, contra Freud, suggested that children may come into the world with a natural social inclination to fit in, a tendency that could be fostered by parental acceptance and nurturance. But, whatever the benefits of parental love in the early years, as time goes by a degree of consistently restrictive and authoritative parental control is still required for optimal socialization.

Morally mature characters, who are able to comply with social norms and expectations effortlessly and with compassion for the frailties of others, have a high degree of both empathy and socialization (Hogan 1973). When both qualities are in short supply, delinquency is the usual result. Where empathy is low and socialization high, individuals tend to follow rules more rigidly and embrace a conventional morality. Conversely, persons high in empathy and low in socialization are more cavalier about observing conventional rules and tend to function as mildly sociopathic members of society, but well within normal limits—they may double-park, smoke marijuana, not return books, cheat a little here and chisel a little there, but nothing big time. Overly indulgent or restrictive parents probably minimize the child's opportunities for empathic relating. Translating empathy into action probably is influenced by prior experiences of receiving empathic treatment from others (most significantly parents). Hogan (1973) added to this mix "a relative absence of repression or denial—an openness to inner experience, a willingness to attend to intuitive promptings and nonverbal cues" (p. 224). Development of empathy is probably complete by late adolescence, resulting optimally in an ethic of reciprocity and a spirit of cooperation.

Hogan (1973) distinguished between an ethic of conscience and an ethic of responsibility.[7] Upbringing has a lot to do with development of these orientations—home environments encouraging a view of natural human goodness and institutional suspicion tend to promote a ethic of conscience while the opposite configuration, suspicion, or skepticism regarding motives of others and valuing of social controls, leans toward an emphasis on responsibility. These general moral orientations can only be understood in relation to total character organization and to its development. These findings underline the centrality to the process of character formation of the development of the superego, conscience, and moral values.

Character and Identity

Further evolution toward a more articulated integration of concepts of character and the self came in Erikson's (1959) formulations of identity and identity formation. The concept of identity undoubtedly retains close links with both the ego and the self, but specific relationships have yet to be defined and depend in part on determination of theoretical links between the notion of the self and components of the structural theory (Baudry 1989).[8] In Erikson's terms, identity seems to refer to a complex set of implications, including a conscious sense of individual identity or subjective self-experience, an unconscious striving for continuity of personal character, the effects of ego synthesis, and, finally, a sense of inner solidarity with the ideals, values, and identity of a social group.[9] He assigned the psychosocial achievement of identity to the adolescent period; developmental tasks of adolescence are completed when the individual is able to subordinate childhood identifications and to fashion them into a new synthesis, representing the creative achievement of an individual sense of identity and its associated life commitments.

Thus, identity expresses the sense of continuity and coherence of the organization of the self, and at the same time articulates certain aspects of the engagement of the self with its objects and social environment. Identity, then, is highly resonant with the concept of character. Differentiation between identity and character rests more on the internal or subjective frame of reference for the former and the external or observational context of the latter. The person seen as selfish by others usually does not experience himself as such; seen from the inside character traits are experienced ego-syntonically as aspects of self-image or concept.

ETHICAL ASPECTS

This argument points to the conclusion that character, as traditionally conceived psychoanalytically, enjoys ethical relevance. That statement requires some qualification, since not all character traits are necessarily moral in import, at least not directly so. Obstinacy, for example, may well be ethically neutral, that is, neither good nor bad in itself, yet have ethical import in its consequences. But also clearly, some character traits have direct ethical implications—honesty, for example, has definite ethical connotations, insofar as we regard telling the truth as ethically commendable. Inclusion of such ethical considerations draws us more deeply into the mystery of the meaning of character and character formation. In addition to elements of character structure, we must turn our attention to other aspects of ethical agency that both determine and constitute ethical character. Two important constituents deserve further exploration: the first are the virtues. I have already suggested that the virtues are open to psychoanalytic exploration along the lines laid down for character traits, that is, habitual and stable configurations characterizing the self-structure, but with the added consideration that they are specifically relevant to contexts of moral and ethical implication. The second involves operational principles guiding and directing moral decision and ethical action, namely, the value system and its constituent values and value-orientations (see chapter 14).

Virtues and Vices

The concept of "virtue" is somewhat elusive in psychoanalytic thinking, but I will argue that virtues and vices, their formation, modification, alteration, and facilitation, are legitimate subjects for psychoanalytic understanding and praxis. We can regard the analytic process as an extended effort to dismantle the patient's long-standing neurotic and maladaptive vices and to replace them with pertinent virtues—even though many analysts would be loath to cast the enterprise in such morally tinged terms. But I would contend that replacement of deleterious habits and inclinations with those that are adaptive, reasonable, and beneficial to the patient and those with whom he spends his life are acceptable and commendable goals of analysis.

By virtues and vices we mean habits of mind that orient the ethical agent toward good or bad actions. *Virtue* is not a common term in analytic jargon, but they are usually framed in nonethical terms—as character traits, ego-strengths, and dimensions of either ego- or superego-autonomy.[10] Yet the analytic literature is richly seeded with references to virtues as aspects of the ego-ideal or even as goals of the analytic process. Honesty, fairness, courage, temperance, kindness and consideration of others, a capacity for meaningful love relations, and more, are often proclaimed as objectives of analytic therapy. In analogy to character traits, virtues and vices refer to habitual dispositions and patterns of behavior constituting in some part the character of the individual. As Amélie Rorty (1988b) commented: "Virtues form a set of extremely heterogeneous traits, traits that are believed to conduce to performing central activities well and appropriately, particularly when those activities are thought difficult to perform, because doing so requires overcoming some natural obstacle" (p. 16).

Analytic Views of Virtue

Erikson (1964) called our attention to the concept of virtue, but in terms enriched by the deeper understanding provided by his basic psychoanalytic perspective. What is that "virtue," he asked, that goes out of a man when he loses strength, and what is that strength that he acquires when he achieves that spirited quality without which "his moralities become mere moralism and his ethics feeble goodness"? Virtue, he answers, is that human quality of strength that the ego develops from generation to generation. He selected eight virtues corresponding with the eight stages of the life cycle—hope, will, purpose, competence, fidelity, love, care, and wisdom. The developmental phases provide the source and rationale for these basic strengths inherent in ego maturity. And these virtues contain the source and resource of ethical identity and value that alone preserve the integrity and vitality of human life—in individual egos as well as in the sequence of generations.

To put his schedule of virtues in perspective, they are synonymous with the "strengths" that emerge from the positive resolution of psychosexual and psychosocial crises in the course of the life cycle. As such, they emerge more as attributes of the self (rather than merely the ego) and take on the qualities of character traits. These are, then, strengths we can attribute to the mature, vital and effective personality, the somewhat idealized end product of a successful developmental course stretching from the earliest strata of infantile trust to the last stages of mature integrity in the encounter with death.

Virtues as habits. When we speak of virtues we have in mind habitual dispositions involving forms of more-or-less optimal realization of potentialities of the organism. Conceived as habits, virtues maximize the potential of human capacities to be directed toward and realize ethically good actions and purposes. Thus, if a person acts in a kindly manner, we can describe his behavior as a kind act. But we would not speak of him as possessing the virtue of kindness unless he were to perform a series of such acts extending over a significant period of time. One act does not a habit make. We can think of habits or virtues only when the kind of acts characterizing the habit are performed habitually, more-or-less consistently and persistently, so that we can regard the disposition in question as characteristic of the person. The person may not act in this way all the time, but if he does not it is clearly an exception to his general and characteristic pattern of behavior. By the same token, vices are also habits, but habits that reflect dispositions to perform reprehensible, evil, immoral, or unethical actions.

Virtues do not simply make man's actions good or better; rather they make man himself good or better as man—virtues contribute to the goodness of man as man, vices contribute to the badness of man as man. If one is caught up in a conflictual struggle with sexual desires or impulses in an effort to remain continent, he is not thereby acting virtuously, but is caught in a conflict and tension between desire and defense that will remain symptomatic as long as no compromise is found and no effective habit established. Habits arise as a result of repeated actions: if on multiple occasions, the conflict is effectively resolved in favor of sexual continence, a habit is formed that we regard as a virtue, the virtue of chastity; if the resolution is habitually in favor of sexual license, we would regard the resulting vice as incontinence. The effect of the vice is to make his indulgence in sexual actions less conflicted, easier, less anxious, and more consistent. The downside is that it makes him ethically worse as a human being, contributes pejoratively to his character formation, and imperils his development into a morally good person. There may be other undesirable consequences such as venereal disease, complications in legitimate love relations, and social disapproval. But these are extrinsic consequences and not inherent to the moral status of the person himself.

On the other hand, the virtuous man can draw satisfaction from his practice of virtue. The temperate man enjoys his moderation because he knows that it is rational and satisfying to him, whereas the same degree of moderation in the use of pleasurable goods for the intemperate man would leave him dissatisfied. Acquiring any virtue may entail pain and effort, especially in the performance of more intense acts of the virtue; intemperance is easier in that excesses involve little conflict or struggle. Acquiring temperance for the drug addict is a matter of great conflict and torment in the effort to overcome a previous intemperate habit. Moreover, acquisition of virtue is never complete or total; it remains open-ended and capable of further development and growth or retrenchment. Virtues require continuing reinforcement and confirmation in act; otherwise they can regress and weaken without effective reinforcement. The same is true of vices, reflecting the structure of both as habits. Neither virtues nor vices are set in stone. As habits they require continual reinforcement—David Rapaport (1958) described "stimulus nutriment" as essential for maintaining psychic structure. These habit formations are in effect forms of psychic structure, subject to the same vicissitudes as all psychic structure. Failure to exercise a virtue in circumstances calling for it is to weaken the habit; performance of actions contrary to the virtue, that is, those attributable to the opposite vice, will diminish and weaken the virtue. Moreover, exercise of a virtue is not automatic; in each instance it requires a process of decision and choice, but to the extent that the virtue is well established those processes become easier and more facile, so that optimally they require little or no deliberate processing or the processing may take place on a preconscious or unconscious level.

The same conditions apply to vices—no matter how confirmed in the behavior corresponding to the vice, there is always the possibility that under specific motivational and stimulus conditions and contexts, the agent will not act in accordance with the vice and may even act in a way congruent with the opposite virtue. The assessment of virtue or vice remains a matter of consistency, not only in specific contexts, but over a sufficient range and variety of contexts. A patient who is temperate in sexual relations with his wife, but indulges in sexual orgies on his business trips, cannot be said to be sexually temperate. Likewise, a man who is scrupulously honest in his business dealings but cheats on his income tax cannot be said to be completely just, since he meets his obligations relevant to commutative, but not to legal justice.

Forms of virtue. Virtues, then, are habitual modifications of psychic capacities or combinations of such capacities. They do not serve as motives but modify the capacities for action of the moral agent to make that action easier, more consistent, and more adapted to positive ethical aims and goals. They do not answer to the "why" of action, but rather to the "how." Furthermore they direct actions to good ends that improve, not merely some area of the agent's functioning, but contribute to his status as an ethically good person. We can reasonably ask, then, whether classic virtues and vices can be reformulated with particular reference to their analytic implications. To what extent do they include a degree of analytic relevance and intelligibility, which would open them to further analytic exploration and understanding. I will limit my exploration to the so-called cardinal virtues—temperance, fortitude, prudence, and justice.[11]

Temperance. This virtue addresses the use of objects of desire, any desire whether sensory or intellective, in a moderate, reasonable, realistic, proportional, and prudent manner. Temperance pertains not only to external use of objects and material goods, but is also relevant to internal desires and intentionality—in both realms it seeks moderation, avoidance of excess, and balance in relation to the interests and benefit of the whole person. Deviations of desire are more often by way of excess than default: left to themselves desires tend to become voracious, even insatiable. Their integration with ethically meaningful objectives and purposes requires that they be regulated and restrained, as Freud was quick to point out.

Temperance is essentially a virtue of regulated desire. The qualities associated with the virtue, especially the guidance of reason and prudence, indicate that desire is regulated by the intellect and will as operative ego-functions. The objective of temperance is not elimination of desire—this would itself become a vice—but the implementation and satisfaction of desire on reasonable and adaptive terms, reflecting integration with the reality principle and the guidance of the ego in terms of moderation. The freudian approach to instinctual control stressed renunciation, but the path of virtue lies less in renunciation than in regulation. The moderation implicit in temperance connotes adaptation and adjustment to the demands of reality and consistency with a specific set of values, and proportional regulation of motivational components—libidinal and narcissistic in the first instance, aggressive in the second. Temperance in this respect operates in the service of integrating the pleasure and reality principles.

Fortitude. Fortitude pertains specifically to the aggressive capacity. Aggression comes to bear when the necessity arises for overcoming obstacles to achieving a desired goal. Fortitude is then the habit of mobilizing persistent and measured aggressive effort sufficient to overcome a given obstacle or obstacles. Deviation from the norm of virtue can take place through excess or deficit. The degree of effort consistent with the virtue is proportional to the degree of desirability of the object or goal and the opposition posed by the obstacle. Excessive aggressive effort would do more than overcome the obstacle, but might spill over into other destructive or damaging effects—in effect, excessive aggression can transform into destructiveness. On the deficit side, failure of effort would take the form of inhibition or giving up too easily in the face of opposition or threat.

A variant of fortitude is courage, the capacity to mobilize one's resources and efforts in the face of not merely obstacles, but difficult enterprises or dangers, and to persist in the pursuit of the goal. By courage, I choose to put myself in jeopardy for the sake of obtaining or protecting some good either for myself or others. Courage is called on when difficult obstacles are to be overcome or endured. In its capacity to mobilize aggression, it has a tendency to color the imagination with fantasies of victory or defeat, so that avenues to compromise are themselves compromised, and anything short of winning the desired goal may be regarded as loss or defeat—confrontation may be favored over collaboration or compromise. We would have to conclude that courage qualifies as a virtue only in the degree to which it is measured and guided by prudence.

Yet a degree of fortitude and courage is essential to any capacity for self-assertion; without it there would be constant capitulation to threats of anxiety and fear. Life is risk, and without the capacity to overcome fears and undergo risk one is left in a state of inhibition or near-paralysis. It can be said that the need for courage arises in the passage from any developmental stage to another involving separation and the surrender of familiar attachments and dependencies—going to school, adolescent individuation, marriage, having children, and especially death (May 1953). Tillich (1955) wrote about the "courage to be," the courage every man must have in order to exist: in May's (1953) words, "the courage to be and trust one's self despite the fact that one is finite; it means acting, loving, thinking, creating, even though one knows that he does not have the final answers, and he may well be wrong" (p. 203). Courage also has its place to a significant degree in any form of creative activity, whether to forge into unknown realms of thought or artistic expression or to break away from traditional and familiar ways of doing things to fashion new patterns of expression and imagination (Gedo 1983; Gedo and Gedo 1992). Courage is also required in its own measure for overcoming the obstacles and responding to the challenge of change in the analytic process.

Deviation by excess here becomes daring, or foolhardiness, or an extreme form of phallic narcissistic pathology resulting in counterphobic behavior and a conviction of invulnerability. Cases of counterphobic daring are not uncommon in wartime. It is in the light of this excess of courage that some moralists regard courage as dangerous. The deviation by defect, of course, is cowardice. It is important to note that these habitual dispositions in the use of aggression can be variously motivated and accompanied by various affect responses, but that neither the motivation nor the affect pertain to the significance of the virtue itself. A man may be a coward because of fear or anxiety, but his emotions are distinct from his behavior; it is the behavior that makes him a coward—a man may suffer from intense anxiety and fear, but behave bravely in the face of danger. His motives are not fear or anxiety, but whatever they are they move him to overcome his fear and act courageously anyway. There are many instances in analysis when patients have to confront fear or anxiety and to find the resources in themselves to overcome the fears and act in their own best interest. This can require fortitude and courage.

The virtue does not consist in controlling fear, but in acting appropriately despite it. Controlling the fear is more a matter of temperance. Conversely, the lack of fortitude can have long-lasting and devastating effects on self-esteem and on the ability to deal effectively and adaptively in many difficult life situations and crises. Fortitude does not ignore, brush aside, deny, minimize, or underestimate difficulties and dangers; it faces and recognizes them realistically and prudently, with sufficient awareness of the risks and potentialities, including the limits of one's own capacities to accomplish difficult tasks—all under the guidance of reason determining what is reasonable action in facing and overcoming obstacles, achieving goals, or acquiring objects of desire.

Prudence. Prudence affects the judgment of practical reason involved in the composite action of choice by the will. Deliberation leading to the final decision is guided by intellective consideration of means-end relations in conjunction with motivational considerations and reference to value standards, all ordered to directing the will to an ethically good, realistic, and reasonable decision and choice. The final practical prudential judgment of conscience is not so much concerned with the end previously determined, but with choice of means to that end. Prudence is thus the intellective habit of judging properly the good means to a good end or purpose. The habit of faulty judgments about means-to-good-ends is called "imprudence," and the habit of judging about good means to a bad end would be some form of craftiness or cunning. Judging inappropriately about poor means to a bad end is just plain bungling.

Reaching correct judgments in particular instances does not require a habit; only when such judgments are made consistently, correctly, easily, and satisfyingly do they imply an intellective habit. When we speak of "reason" in the direction and organization of virtues, we mean the judgment of practical reason in its function of guiding the will, directing it to the choice of morally good or evil means and ends. Nor does practical judgment have to be a matter of entirely subjective deliberation; the prudent man is more likely to be inclined to seek information, advice, and counsel from others who have knowledge, expertise, or experience in the matters he is trying to decide about. In any case, the final judgment of prudence belongs only to the subject, who makes the final determination as to what to do and how to do it. Moreover, when there are conflicts in value-systems involved in decision-making, as is often the case in matters ethical, it is the part of prudence to weigh their differences and to come to a reasonable decision about a course of action (A. O. Rorty 1988b).

Prudence is unique among intellective virtues, since it not only involves beneficial operation of the intellect in selecting appropriate means, but is intimately connected to choosing a good means to a good end. Further prudence cannot be misused—a habit directing one to select ethically good means to ethically good ends can only make the moral agent good. It improves not only his mind in adapting to complex demands of the real, but it makes the man himself morally good. Consequently, prudence qualifies as an authentic virtue; its deviations in the form of imprudence or craftiness are correspondingly vices.

Clearly there is no such thing as prudence acting independently; it always operates in conjunction with other virtues. Other virtues are responsible for determining the good ends to which action is directed; but it belongs to prudence to select the appropriate means. The practical judgment of prudence does not determine the object of other virtues—the moderation of temperance in the reasonable use of objects is presumed to be an ethical good. The judgment of prudence does not say, "Moderation is a good thing;" it does say, "If moderation is a good thing, this is the best way to do it." Or, with respect to justice, it does not say, "It's a good thing to pay your debts"; rather it says, "Since paying debts is good, and I should pay my debts, this is the best way here-and-now and concretely for me to do it." Not only can prudence not be exercised in isolation from other virtues, but other virtues cannot function without prudence—temperance, fortitude, and justice are tendencies to do good as determined by reason, that is, by the judgment of prudence.

In psychoanalytic terms, prudence consists in making a judgment, and therefore involves the ego. But the judgment also is made in a context of ethical relevance and selection of good means, with particular reference to values inherent in the individual's value-system reflecting integration of superego and ego components. As a kind of ethical inertial guidance system, prudence must weave its way through the complex of conflictual motives and evaluations of real contexts and circumstance to reach a specific and reality-based judgment. In the process, desire must be adapted to the conditions of reality—the pleasure principle modified by the reality principle—narcissistic excesses and deficits must be balanced in an effective equilibrium moderating narcissistic expectations and demands and regulating self-esteem, and to the extent that obstacles are to be overcome in pursuing the good means, aggression must be regulated adaptively and proportionally. The judgment of prudence thus involves multiple complex psychic systems and integrates them to effect the specific means determined in its judgment.

Prudence thus combines sound judgment with virtuous character, but it is not the combination of belief and desire, but the man himself as ethical agent who is the cause of action—behind the psychic events and their sequencing stands the man himself whose ethical character is the ultimate determinant of virtuous or nonvirtuous action (A. O. Rorty 1988b). Thus the person is accountable and responsible for his actions, but as mediated through his virtues and/or vices, that is insofar as he knows what he is doing and is capable of doing otherwise. Even in specifically cognitive terms, the practical judgment cannot be made in abstract terms, but necessarily involves concrete knowledge rooted in experience, both sensory and intellective. Its judgment takes into account the circumstances and details of motive, time, place, and person—elements that are always concrete, individual, and personal: one man's temperance may be another man's intemperance.

Justice. Justice implies complexities not found in other virtues insofar as it specifically involves the good of others in addition to myself. In temperance and fortitude, the proper disposition of the ethical agent himself is what is in question; the morality pertains to the action and the agent. But justice includes the good of others, and this goes against the natural narcissistic inclination of my desires and will. If I give another his due, I deprive myself; if I respect another's right to engage in a particular occupation, I limit my own opportunities in that regard. Even if I recognize and accept what is just, my natural inclination is to seek the good for myself rather than to share it with others. My capacity for justice, then, involves the balance of egoistic versus altruistic motives and the corresponding titration of narcissistic need that motivates my choices and actions.

In this sense justice becomes intermingled with forms of love of neighbor, in the basic sense of desiring and willing the good of that neighbor—even though justice and charity are quite distinct and separate virtues. As Fromm (1955) noted, the Golden Rule was originally cast in terms of love of neighbor, but in a system of fairness, as would be involved in justice, it comes to mean fairness in the exchange of goods, fair dealing, and not cheating. In this respect, the good of another often cannot be immediately perceived; it is an intellectually known good that can only be grasped through a reasoning process, and then only in a secondary and derivative sense. It requires a conclusion that the good of another is related to my own good, that justice for another is implicitly justice for myself. Furthermore, if I repay a particular debt, I am acting justly; but the virtue of justice is only in question when the habit is formed; that is when such regard for, and implementation of, the good of others is consistent, easy, and satisfying.

Justice is not a simple virtue, but comes in various forms. The simplest form, *commutative justice,* involves a relation of equity, but not necessarily equality, between two individuals. Justice requires mutual respect for their individual rights and avoidance of doing harm or injury to each other. If such injury or harm has occurred, justice demands restitution to restore the balance. Further obligations can arise from contractual agreements. Justice of this sort works on two fronts—it looks to the good of the other and at the same time to the good of the self. It seeks a degree of fairness to both parties, and not to the advantage or disadvantage of either one.

Justice is also *distributive,* referring to the distribution of benefits and burdens of the society at large in the community in due proportion to all members of the society. To the extent that the government assumes this responsibility, it is legal justice; to the extent that it is a principle governing the distribution of goods in general it is social justice. Legal justice involves an obligation on the part of the government to direct the proportional distribution of goods and burdens; for the governed, it involves an obligation to support a just society and observe its laws. When the society is unjust, these obligations may be either violated or no longer valid. Decisions as to the norms of distributive justice are largely matters of objective social and economic principles and policies. Questions of what norms are pertinent to the equal distributions of goods and on what basis are hotly debated and involve issues related to questions of the best form of government (democratic vs. socialist or communist) and economic principle (equal distribution to all, distribution according to merit, distribution according to need, etc.). We are concerned in a more limited sense in this discussion only with the virtue of justice as an intrapsychic, personal virtue, that is, commutative justice; and with distributive justice only in subjective terms, that is, the disposition to effect the distribution of goods according to the norms of justice, however conceived.[12]

Issues related to justice can find their way into the analytic consulting room. One extremely obsessional and highly narcissistically entitled man expressed part of his pathology in miserly stinginess and fiscal selfishness.

The issue of justice arose in relation to his wife whom he treated in niggardly fashion especially in dealing with money matters. She also worked, and he insisted that she pay all her own expenses—for instance, clothing and medical expenses, and other personal expenses. This demand also extended to household expenses—including food and general upkeep— which he forced her to pay as well. When they went out to dinner, he demanded that she pay for her own meal, or if they went to the theater or concerts that she pay her own way. Setting aside the sadomasochistic motifs in this bizarre arrangement, his treatment of her was grossly unjust. His demands related to distribution of monetary responsibilities were disadvantageous to her and basically unfair. She had every right and expectation for more equitable and reasonable treatment. His demands were violations of commutative justice. While the analyst would not be directly technically concerned with this injustice as such, the patient's vice was indicative of gross distortions in his capacity for meaningful and loving human relations, undergirded by severely defective and pathological narcissism. The injustice consequently had to be explored and analyzed.

PSYCHIC HEALTH VS. PSYCHOPATHOLOGY

Psychoanalysis does not operate in a vacuum of criteria or norms of good health and maturity. Our diagnostic efforts with all patients come to bear on the assessment of the ways and degrees to which the patient's behavior and character structure deviates from a norm, whether explicit or implicit, of normality or good psychic functioning. This is especially the case in matters of sexuality—we recognize in the Don Juan complex a disorder of sexuality, putatively based on unconscious dynamics of castration fears, oedipal determinants, and feelings of masculine inferiority or inadequacy. We have no difficulty accepting psychic impotence or frigidity as sexual disorders deviating from a healthy and adaptive norm and having unconscious neurotic determinants. Both of these examples are deviations from the norm of temperance in sexual adjustment. But as analysts we eschew ascribing moral implications to these behaviors—we see them as forms of psychopathology and no more. The distinction lies between behaviors that are materially or factually deviations from ethical norms, but are not regarded formally or theoretically as such. The ethical diagnosis rests on violation of the norm of temperance resulting in harm to the person himself or to others with whom he is involved—with implications affecting his ethical goodness. The analytic diagnosis, alternatively, rests on the deviation from a norm of health, maturity and adjustment, which also has deleterious effects for the person and for his object relations.

The resolution of this tension in viewpoints has greater relevance for discussion of the extent to which ethical understandings and perspectives enter into and influence the psychoanalytic process than in simply the conceptual intersection of analytic and ethical understanding. The analytic effort can be directed to uncovering hidden motivations, defensive reactions, developmental impediments, and residual conflicts and compromises, which either precipitate the patient toward ethically undesirable resolutions or prevent his attainment of more virtuous adaptations. It is the patient's business to determine the goals and purposes (ends) that make ethical sense for him in his life trajectory, and to decide on the means by which he will approach and attain those goods. The unique thrust of psychoanalysis in dealing with virtues and vices is toward the motivational underpinnings involved in the formation and maintenance of these habits. Traditionally, psychoanalysis has paid little attention to the benefits or encumbrances attendant on a patient's intemperate or unjust behavior. If the analyst maintains his neutrality and suspends judgment with respect to the ethical implications of the behavior, he also recognizes it as not only motivated behavior, but as deleterious in some manner or degree to the best interest of the patient. If a patient cheats on his income tax, the analytic issue is not whether the action is unjust, but what form the motivation might take leading the patient to cheat Uncle Sam—let us say some form of narcissistic entitlement. If the behavior is habitual, we may be looking at a vice, but the same motivational issues would be relevant in understanding the patient's choices and actions. Thus, making the unconscious conscious has ethical import. I would conclude that analysis does not ignore or exclude either virtues or vices, but it approaches them in an analytic rather than in an ethical format. It is in this sense that we can conclude that virtues and vices are analytically intelligible and relevant.

CHAPTER FOURTEEN

Values

We have frequently referred in the course of this discussion to values as directive principles guiding ethical choices and actions. The concept of ethical action postulates the human person as the dynamic ethical agent, who resolves the tensions of needs and desires by selecting goals and choosing means and ends in terms of internalized values and value-systems. Claude Kluckhohn and his associates (1962) saw values as standards of action in that "actors perhaps most often think about or refer to values when they are in doubt about alternative courses of conduct: when the long-run results of the possible selections of paths of behavior are not immediately obvious or scientifically demonstrable or when pressures of personal motivation are strong on one side and social sanctions or practical expediency of some other kind are strong on the other side" (p. 395). On these terms values are critical in organizing and directing behavior, in choosing courses of actions and evaluating events (Schwartz and Bilsky 1987). Implicit is the idea that the self includes evaluative and coordinative structures and functions, integrated within an autonomous self-structure, capable of defining and directing patterns of behavior and action according to chosen and integrated values.

Classical freudian superego morality is negative and lacks a positive sense of morality (Pattison 1968); but positive morality finds more sympathetic ground in the ego-ideal, particularly in regard to values and value-systems. Morality, on these terms, is less a matter of prohibitions than of values and the norms of appropriate behavior by which we govern and direct our lives. For the social sciences and especially psychology, the exercise of weberian ethical neutrality remains an ideal, subserving scientific objectivity. The ideal is no less applicable in psychoanalysis than in any other psychological science. However, it applies primarily at the investigative, research, heuristic, and theoretical levels. Psychologists may appeal to a dichotomy of fact and value as a device to preserve a neutral stance, but the same psychologists cannot avoid making choices in all their multiple roles in life, including their therapeutic role—choices that are witting or not, responsible or not, but entail unavoidable consequences. The claim of value-free science, beyond its insistence on fact over fantasy or wishful thinking, only obscures the role played by values in methodological choices and interpretive frameworks (M. B. Smith 1969). Values, willy-nilly, are integral parts of the psychoanalytic situation and process (Meissner 1983, 1996b, 2003).

MEANING OF VALUES

In this reflection, we are concerned specifically with ethical values that direct our actions toward morally or ethically good or bad ends. Values act as guides for decision and action in both individual and collective terms. Some values are final, that is, normative and obligatory, determined by rules, and ordered to a system of social standards establishing certain actions as good and others as bad or indifferent—these are specifically moral values. Other values are merely productive and responsive to assessment in terms of cost and gain, for instance, economic values.

Ethical values that are nonmoral play an important role in psychoanalysis—resolution of conflict and achievement of psychic maturity are analytic goals and ideals toward which the process aims and the patient strives; they make the patient better as a person insofar as they approximate an ideal, but failure to achieve the goal or falling short of it does not constitute a moral fault. There is no obligation to achieve the goal, but failure to do so works to the patient's disadvantage and makes him less successful as a human person. Achieving the goal is a good, but not a moral good. If not a moral value, I would still regard it as an ethical value. Both ethical and moral values are normative, but the relevant norms differ. Moral norms pertain to judgments of good or evil—the morally good act conforms to standards of moral behavior; ethical norms pertain to judgments of what is appropriate or conducive to the person's well-being and betterment as a person.

Morality focuses on whether the agent does good or evil, ethics on whether an action makes him a better person. Most value theorists define value in behavioral terms as that which is desirable, meaning that what one values one sees as desirable; but the valuing we are considering here is somehow antecedent to the desirability and, in fact, determines it. I desire something because I value it. Moreover, the decisive quality of moral values and value-judgments, moreover, is not that of a "wish," but of an "ought"—moral value means not just that I value what I desire, but I value what I ought to desire. In terms of ethical values, what I value is not simply desired, but what I desire is appropriate and suited to my betterment as a person. As A. H. Barton (1962) commented:

> The conception of values as any and all preferences tends to go with the conception of values as implicit and manifested by observable choices in behavior. The conception of values as standards which we feel are justified, to which people *should* adhere, focuses attention on verbal statements, and particularly on verbalizations which distinguish internal feelings of "ought" from those of "liking." The "sense of obligation" or "sense of value" is what distinguishes "normative values" in this sense from "mere preferences." (p. 65)

One can argue, of course, that what is valued is always desirable in some sense. But even in the case of negative values, an object may be desirable yet rejected as a result of a value-judgment; but one can reasonably argue that the value is still dealing with the desirable, even in rejecting it. "Desirable" has clearly different connotations in these respective uses. But the subject-predicate relation of value-desirable is still not adequate to define the concept of value. The logical relation would also define pleasure, love, and more. To close the definition, one must also be able to say that the desirable is ethically or morally valuable. Clearly not all desirable things or objects are valued in the ethical sense. Someone who impulsively snatches a piece of candy is acting to acquire a desirable (and, in fact, desired) object, but this action has nothing to do with values. Ethical values cannot be conceived merely in terms of pleasure. The difficulty may arise in the very process by which values are acquired. As Hartmann (1960) noted, value judgments are often presented to the child as though they were statements of fact—"this is good"; "that is bad." The moral imperative is implied, meaning "thou shalt" and "thou shalt not." Any further distinction of fact from value may thus have to wait upon greater developmental and cognitive integration.

While many authors agree that the definition of value must include the sense of obligation, it remains questionable whether the general use of "desirable" as a defining characteristic is adequate to encompass this sense. There is a qualitative gap between what is desirable and what is obligatory. If an object or action is "proper to want," it does not yet impose any obligation on the one who wants. Strictly ethical values may be proper to want, yet not obligatory. Beyond the dynamics of desire, both choice of proper goals and obligation require an intellectual judgment concerning what is right and what wrong, what is proper to want and what not. The distinction between wishing and choosing in accord with a standard is enshrined in Freud's separation of instinctual desire from ego and superego functioning.

Judgments based on the moral value-system carry connotations of obligation—the feeling of "oughtness" as the hallmark of ethical value. In this connection, ethics distinguishes between terminal or internal values and instrumental or conditional values, the former concerned with ends and the latter with means (Rokeach 1973; Schwartz and Bilsky 1987).[1] Scientific values, as in medicine or engineering, are instrumental or conditional—that is, preserving health or keeping a machine in good working order are desirable, but as means to further purposes. Ethics has a broader scope than morality since it is concerned not only with internal values pertaining to moral purposes and ends, but can also include instrumental or hypothetical values. The nonmoral senses of value, as purely instrumental or utilitarian or customary, lack this imperative emphasis (Rokeach 1973). The voice of conscience in this sense carries very distinct connotations in contrast with violations of arbitrary positive law (breaking the speed limit) or norms of etiquette. Ethical standards in analysis also lack this imperative sense of moral obligation; they have more to do with standards of maturity and self-improvement that are largely instrumental.

When the sense of imperative obligation is contravened, the stage is set for the judgment of guilt and possibly for the experience of guilt feelings. But we should also note that the prescriptions of conscience and their attendant obligation are not altogether absolute, as we saw in our previous discussion of obligation as a function of superego or ethical judgment. Similar distinctions apply to values. M. Brewster Smith (1969) summarized this perspective:

> But superego values are only one kind that involve personal requiredness, and in persons who approach more closely the commonly formulated ideals of maturity and good functioning, they fall into the background as compared with values characterized by what I am calling self-requiredness. . . . They are actively embraced by the person and thus become constituents of the self, part of what the person feels himself to be and to stand for. Characteristically their application involves more finely differentiated cognitive discrimination than is the case with superego values, and they can therefore be applied with more flexibility, appropriateness, and rationality. . . . Since they are integrated in the self rather than sealed off in an infantile form, they are open to progressive modification and elaboration. They retain the phenomenal character of objective requiredness . . . but are sustained by the indi-

vidual's active commitment to them as the values that he chooses to live by. (p. 109)

One of the more persuasive attempts to crystallize a concept of value came from Kluckhohn and his associates (1962). Their formulation comes closest to the concept of value in this study. In their view, "A value is a conception, explicit or implicit, distinctive of an individual or characteristic of a group, of the desirable which influences selection from available modes, means and ends of action" (p. 395). The moral standard determines the moral goodness or badness of the act, the ethical standard the relevance to the person as person. Values, then, are fundamentally ideas determining action commitments. They are action-oriented, coming into play in situations where the individual has to select one course of action out of a variety of real alternatives on the basis of normative concepts. They are distinct from sentiment, emotion, drives, needs, and motives—but not divorced from them. They do not always operate consciously or explicitly, but may function implicitly and unconsciously. They may be inferred from behavior but not always introspected, but as intellectively relevant they are always introspectable and verbalizable, and capable of abstraction and rationalization. It is this aspect of value that clearly distinguishes it from mere preferences, instincts, needs, attitudes, and sentiments.

ANALYTIC APPROACHES TO VALUE

Certainly, there has not been universal agreement on the relevance of values to psychoanalysis. J. Flugel (1945) took a straightforward view that values were psychic facts and as such fell within the domain of psychoanalytic investigation. Hartmann (1960) seemed to backwater from this position, regarding the realm of values and valuation as generally beyond the scope of analytic interest or inquiry. It did not take long, however, for Erik H. Erikson (1964) to come full circle and reintroduce the theme of values as vital to human concerns, a position endorsed by Ishak Ramzy (1965, 1972): ". . . to continue clinging to the untenable pretense that it is ethically and morally neutral, psychoanalysis debars itself from contributing what no other science can contribute toward a better understanding of human values" (1972, p. 224). The insistence on ethical neutrality echoed Freud's (1933a) claim that psychoanalysis had no weltanschauung beyond that of science itself; but that view would seem to ignore the role of values in science itself. It can be argued that the exploration of values constitutes a salient direction for future development of psychoanalysis (Zinberg 1972). Ramzy (1972) stated the case as follows:

Psychoanalysis is apparently the method most suited for the study
of the ontogenesis of values. Hardly can any other method of
investigation throw as much light on the elements which go into
the structure of a man's character and determine his behavior as
can the psychoanalytic method, which studies the past and the
present, the conscious and the unconscious factors of man's
morality. Neither is any other scientist—by the very assumptions
of his specialty or the degree to which his personal equations have
been corrected—equipped as the psychoanalyst is to look at man
and his value systems as an integrated psychological unit functioning in a social environment. (p. 223)

Hartmann's distinction, however, between actual valuations, as objects
of psychological or sociological investigation, and decisions as to what
ought to be valued still stands. Mental acts by which values are formed or
realized, even on Hartmann's (1960) terms, are open to psychoanalytic
exploration. He added:

[Psychoanalysis] can contribute to our understanding of why an
individual has a moral code, and why he has just this moral code,
and how he succeeds, or fails, in realizing it in his actions. We still
remain in the domain of empirical research if we study the question
of what actual impact psychoanalysis has or can have on the moral
systems of the individual in analysis, or beyond this, the moral systems of our culture. But clearly all this has nothing to do with the
logical derivation of moral norms from statements of fact. (p. 52)[2]

Despite his demur, Hartmann (1960) offered some cogent observations, commenting that when we call an action "good," we imply that it
measures up to some standard, an ideal of human behavior or moral imperative. The judgment "good" does not refer to our good feeling or approval
of the action, but to a system of moral or ethical values. And these standards are quite distinct from "standards of efficiency," referring to means-
end connections, and from aesthetic values—in other words, the value
experience in ethical or moral evaluations is specific to that category of
value and distinct from all others. Furthermore, he argued, moral values
imply directives for action and a tendency to realize such values in action.
This may be experienced as an imperative—that is, as conveying a moral
sense of obligation or duty—but it may also reflect ethical conformity to an
ego-ideal. As we have already argued in distinguishing superego and conscience functions (chapter 12), superego and both moral and ethical values
are not synonymous and under given circumstances can come into conflict

(Ottenheimer 1972). But ethical values can be presumed to involve complex integrations of both superego influences and ethical concerns in various mixes and combinations.

We can conclude that values and value-systems are essential components of personality organization and therefore of the self.[3] The further issue is whether psychoanalysis itself, as a theory of human psychology and behavior, is inherently value-impregnated. Ruth Macklin (1973) for one argued that analysis was in fact value-ladened, in that the theory of personality proposed certain ideal-types or character structures that have become normative, such that deviation from them or failure to achieve them was regarded as diagnostic—there was an underlying assumption, explicit or implicit, not only that personality structure and genesis was describable, but what kind of personality organization was desirable. As she pointed out: "These labels do not function as mere descriptions, but contain a normative component. The notion of the 'genital ideal' serves as the ideal of health and maturity in the adult person, and failure to attain the ideal in accordance with the theoretical suppositions is a mark of the individual's immaturity, neurotic illness, character disorder, or the like" (p. 144). The ideal here is ethical and not moral. And as Riccardo Steiner (1995) commented: "In fact, both the scientific and the curative norms of psychoanalysis imply the acceptance and the use of logical presidia and moral [and ethical] values which stem from a particular blending of the liberal radical tradition with the Enlightenment and Romantic traditions of Western European culture without which psychoanalysis could not have been born" (p. 441). A similar conclusion can be applied to theories of self-actualization or realization, in which the self (in some sense) develops its natural inclinations and potentialities and functions as an ideal toward which the patient strives as a goal of therapy.[4]

One can also cast the problem in a developmental perspective. Where do values become operative in personality functioning? What aspects of the psychic organization at various stages of development are pertinent for understanding the formation of values? I would suggest that the most critical developmental phase related to value-formation is adolescence. Value-formation in a sense parallels and reflects personality organization. Eliseo Vivas (1963), in fact, spoke of personality as "an integration of values" whose "growth is a growth in the values men recognize and from which they select some for espousal" (pp. 61–62). The quality of value components internalized from significant objects goes a long way in the development of moral or ethical character. As Jacobson (1964) added:

> The history of such patients reveals that the internalization of such confusing parental attitudes at an early infantile stage may result

in lasting contradictions in a person's unconscious and conscious sets of values; this not only may affect the establishment of stable personal relations with sufficient object constancy, and hence of consistent superego and ego identifications; it also predisposes the child to identity problems which may gain a dangerous momentum during adolescence and extend into the life of the adult. (p. 142)

The emergence of the adolescent onto the world stage is complicated by the changing flux of social and cultural values that present a wide and fluctuating range of possibilities among which the adolescent must pick and choose and commit him- or herself finally, through many perils and uncertainties, to one or other path to identity (Esman 1972).[5]

ETHICAL ISSUES

Efforts of some ethicians to reduce the motivational substructure of ethics to affects of love versus hostility and exploitation lends itself to a false impression of the processes by which moral and ethical decisions are in fact made. Ethical decisions are rarely, if ever, dictated by objective facts or simple incentives, but rather derive from ingrained, habitual, subjective values, and their associated motivations operating at multiple levels of awareness and implication.[6] Ethical attitudes involving a complex matrix of opinions, habits, tastes, and values are an integral part of character structure. If we gather these attitudes from many disparate sources, we inevitably make some selection, internalize them, and make them part of our own personality structure. As such they become integral and functional aspects of our inherent moral or ethical sense and serve as guiding and directive principles according to which ethical judgments and the dictates of conscience are formed and acted on.

Values can be rational and authentic, reflecting more mature ethical decision-making capacity, or irrational and inauthentic, due to dominance of more instinctual levels of motivation and cognitive processing. Only an evolved psychology of values, however, makes it possible to clarify the bases of choice so that authentic values can be recognized and realized. The authenticity of the value-system rests on a mature and integral psychological foundation that bears rational scrutiny, whereas inauthentic values, reflecting prevailing superego effects, are rooted in unconscious fear, guilt, and infantile anxieties and wishes. Distinguishing between authentic and inauthentic values is not always simple. As Hartmann (1960) observed, expressed moral values may or may not agree with the value-system of the subject himself or of society, but we can say little more beyond that they agree or disagree. But there may still be room for a distinction of authentic from inauthentic values:

> We could call moral values more authentic in this sense when, in an individual, or in a culture, they are not only represented in ideas on ethics but also are recognizable as dynamic factors in the moral aspects of a personality or a culture. There is a process of self-scrutiny with reference to what I just called the authentic quality of moral values, in regard to their authenticity in expressing the complex and more or less integrated dynamics of those factors that constitute the moral personality. (pp. 50–51)

The distinction of authentic versus inauthentic is paralleled by another distinction of expressive versus repressive values. Expressive values can be regarded as authentic insofar as they express our fundamental needs at all strata of our existence in some integral fashion. Unquestionably, the biological and instinctual dimension is vital and significant, but an authentic system of values cannot express this dimension of human existence (the id) without at the same time expressing more complex intellective and moral levels of the mental apparatus (ego and superego). Authentic values, then, imply a certain integrality that is correlative with the spontaneity and autonomy of psychic functioning.[7] But values can be repressive as well, particularly when they serve the demands of a harsh or severe superego. But repression—or better, the repressive aspect of values—is not synonymous with lack of authenticity. Insofar as the value-system contributes to instinctual renunciation, it is repressive; but it can also be authentic and serve the same ends. Cultural values can also foster repression of autonomous self-expression out of false motives of fear and taboo; in the individual the same repressive morality can distort the authenticity of the value-system by a kind of sphincter morality reflecting the inner imbalance of personality. Neurotic guilt can only stem from an inauthentic and repressive value-structures. Yet not all guilt merits punishment. Rather, mature morality calls for respect and acceptance of ourselves even as we assess our existential or real guilt. Real guilt is resolved by forgiveness and reconciliation with those offended rather than by punishment.

Sexuality. This problem becomes more or less critical in relation to human sexuality. Human sexuality is permeated with ethical and moral issues. The broader implications of sexuality are intimately involved in the integration of the mature adult personality. Furthermore, a mature and authentic value-system is correlative to a mature sense of both gender and personal identity and highly relevant to the individual's attitudes toward, and participation in, sexual activity. From the point of view of ethics, the ethical perspective contributes specific normative standards for sexual behavior. Sexual needs and motives of themselves seek gratification and expression in action, but in the human situation such urges do not operate independently of the individual's value-system and that of his or her social group. The act of sexual intercourse of itself is morally indifferent—in many conventional circumstances it is a good, and in others an evil. Implicit, if not explicit, are values of care, concern, respect for the sexual partner as a person, the integration of sexual activity with meaningful and loving object relations, the meaning of commitment and fidelity, acceptance of responsibility for consequences of sexual behavior, and much more. Or conversely, inauthentic values tend in the direction of lack of care and concern, failure of empathy, indifference to others' welfare, dominance of personal sexual satisfaction over any consideration of responsibility or responsiveness to the needs and rights of others, and so on. If the former constellation would lead toward mature love relations, the latter would result in sexual promiscuity or rape.

VALUES AND ACTION

One of the issues bedeviling ethical theory is why people may at times consciously and even thoughtfully come to a decision about a course of action and then, when push comes to shove, actually behave in some other way. The disparity, often found between verbalized ethical standards and actual behavior, has been a major concern for theories of ethical action. Psychoanalysis would look to the influence of conflict in such a situation, whether conscious or unconscious, more often the latter.[8] The individual knows or reasons consciously that he should follow a certain course of action, but his unconscious desires and motives come into play at the moment of execution and dictate another outcome. In Amélie Rorty's (1988b) analysis, conflicts can arise between basic ends, or between more-or-less voluntary habits, whether of thought, perception, inference, or even behavioral habits. Conflicting habits can at times reveal or represent conflicting motives. Old patterns and their implicit values may be buried under a defensive character structure—principles of puritanical restraint acquired from one's parents can be repudiated in favor of satisfaction and generosity, but may resurface at critical points in the form of self-denial or seemingly severe moralizing. As Rorty put it, these patterns may not be better or worse, but seem to be "often a dark horse among the range of the agent's considered preferences" (p. 242).

Values have an inherent connection not merely with the decision process, but with action—the vectorial function of values determines not only what we might want, but what we are willing to do about it (Kovel 1982). Values act as guides to the selection of what we desire and reflect our willingness to pursue the means necessary to achieve the end in question. But in this process I may not be immediately aware of the values implicit in my choice and action, or my awareness of any value or values may at that point be false. If I say that I value freedom of choice, yet act in ways that effectively diminish my freedom, my value consciousness must be false and my behavior governed by some other implicit, even unconscious, value. Analysts can recognize this phenomenon in nearly every analytic process. Along these lines, Rollo May (1953) commented that

> unless the individual himself can affirm the value, unless his own inner motives, his own ethical awareness, are made the starting place, no discussion of values will make much real difference. Ethical judgment and decision must be rooted in the individual's own power to evaluate. Only as he himself affirms, on all levels of himself, a way of acting as part of the way he sees reality and chooses to relate to it—only thus will the value have effectiveness and cogency for his own living. For this obviously is the only way he can or will take responsibility for his action. (p. 186)

VALUES AS INTEGRATIVE

Values, then, are more-or-less persistent symbolic structures within the intrapsychic economy. Their functions are involved at the level of symbolic expression and action, and require capacities for abstraction, intellection, communication, transmission, and sharing of meaning. The value-system must, therefore, implicate ego-structures. It is, moreover, normative and directive, and therefore integrative on both psychological and social levels. Values form a point of integration of subjective derivatives of the individual's inner world with the prior communally asserted and symbolically shared systems of evaluative significance that are the common heritage of the society, a group, or even a religious tradition.

This reflection brings us closer to the question of whether psychopathology always involves some dysfunction in value-systems. Value-systems that are realistically attuned, adaptive, and constructive point in the direction of healthy, adaptive, and normal capacities for work and love (*Lieben und Arbeiten*), and reflect the harmonious integration of ego, id, and superego functions. To what extent, then, can we connect disturbances of neuroses and character disorders to dysfunctional and maladaptive value-systems, involving negative, irrational, and conflicting values? To what extent do dysfunctional values contribute to neurotic symptom formation, affective disturbances, and distorted object relations? Psychoanalysis has traditionally tried to bridge this gap by appeal to the reality principle and the ego-ideal as embodying principles of an ethic of response and fulfillment. The dictates of the infantile superego are often in conflict with the prescriptions of mature conscience, often resulting in severe neurotic conflict and disturbance. The superego often displays a stubborn intractability rooted in infantile attachments and primitive fears, but these are very different from the value-orientation of mature conscience. The problem for understanding the psychology of values arises in the complexities of the processes by which psychic structures of such divided orientation can achieve integration and collaborative action.

The potential for often severe psychopathology lies behind the failure to achieve this important level of psychic integration, particularly in areas of narcissistic transformation and establishment of a firm and consistent sense of identity. As Jacobson (1964) commented:

> The majority and consistency of superego standards and ego goals, and the consistent influence of the moral system on the goals of the ego are, indeed, an indispensable prerequisite for the ego's ability to build up not only a coherent, effective defense structure but also a hierarchic organization of the different personal relations, ego identifications, ego interests, and ego functions. Since severely conflicting scales of values are inevitably reflected in dangerous discordances within the ego, superego and ego may indeed defeat each other's purposes by irreconcilable contradictions, which interfere with the development of superego and ego autonomy, with the ego's mastery of reality, its control of the id, and its adaptation to the object world. (pp. 139–140)

In a sense, then, knowing what one wants is essential to any authentic self-direction, but that wanting itself is cast in terms of the individual value-system. It is the mark of maturity to be able to select one's own values and to implement them in the interest of attaining self-chosen goals and purposes. The direction of mature values to realistic and adaptive goals and purposes is inconsistent with more primitive and instinctually derived values of an archaic superego. Their mutual modification and integration are essential to mature ethical decision and action. The conflictual view of the superego functions as separate from, and in opposition to, ego functions, as defined in relation to depressive, obsessional, and paranoid pathology, can be complemented by a more benign understanding of superego that contributes more positively to the organization and stabilization of personality structure. This more positive aspect of the superego, derived from more constructive and realistic internalizations, offers the potential for more stabilizing integrations with ego-structures.

The integration of ego and superego is enhanced by the achievement of superego autonomy. Superego autonomy implies the capacity of the superego to function relatively independently of instinctual strivings and motivations, a capacity that draws it closer to the orbit of relevant ego-functioning. The development of a relatively autonomous superego depends on the quality of internalizations, introjections, and identifications, during development. Where introjections have been based on essentially positive and constructive object relations with mature parental and other objects and do not carry within them an excessive burden of ambivalence, and where identifications have not been contaminated by defensive components carrying unresolved and pathological residues of narcissistic, aggressive, and libidinal conflicts, the potentiality for development of a relatively conflict-free and autonomous superego is enhanced (Meissner 1978a, 1981). Ernst Ticho (1972) described such a superego: "An autonomous superego is consistent, impersonal, tolerant, accepting, and guided by abstract principles. Therefore we can say that the more impersonal the individual's superego, the more of a person he will be. The autonomous superego is neither too afraid of the drives nor too strongly influenced by social anxiety. But we do not assume that the mature superego is independent of the ego" (p. 219). Hartmann and Rudolph Loewenstein (1962) pointed out that further development of the superego, rather than diminishing the developing ego's influence, tends to increase it, leading to increasing collaboration between ego and superego.

Value-formation and value-systems provide a central focus for realization and expression of superego autonomy. The achievement of superego autonomy requires modification and substantial integration of narcissistic issues related to formation of the ego-ideal. Early narcissistic and infantile aspects of the ego-ideal must be progressively modified in the direction of less extreme, more realistic, and less potentially pathological expression. The most important sector for such resolution is the individual's value-system. Jacobson (1964) postulated a developmental hierarchy of values in the child, and pointed out the importance of superego integration and the attainment of superego autonomy for establishing such value systems. She wrote:

> The maturation of the ego and of critical judgment considerably modifies our concepts of value and our actions. Leading to an

acceptance of what is realistic and reasonable, it accomplishes at least a partial victory of the reality principle, not only over the pleasure principle, but also over exaggerated "idealism" and thus over the superego. Only then do the superego functions work with more neutralized energy. In fact, the final maturation of both the ego and superego sets in only after the tempest of instinctual conflicts during adolescence has subsided. Then we observe a gradual moderation of youthful idealism and illusions, leading to the setting up of more reasonable goals and to a further development of moral judgment: of the ability to test and to evaluate the outside and inside reality correctly, reasonably, and with greater moral tolerance, and to act according to such judgment. (pp. 129–130)

The mature value system, therefore, provides an internalized regulatory and directive guidance system for the individual personality to organize and direct its activity, most particularly its ethically relevant activity. It is, along with the ego-ideal, a repository of narcissism—but a narcissism purged and modulated so as to find its place within the limits and constraints of reality and thus become a vital force in achieving more mature personality functioning and meaningful living. "Values," as M. Brewster Smith (1980) suggested, "are a major, constitutive ingredient of selfhood" (p. 340).

Notes

CHAPTER 1. FREUDIAN AND POSTFREUDIAN ETHICS

1. I will utilize some of the conclusions of Wallwork's (1991) important study of the interaction between psychoanalysis and ethics. I will make explicit page references only for direct citations.
2. The complexity of these issues is compounded by efforts to relate psychoanalytic concepts to biological assumptions regarding the relation between mind and brain. While the freudian perspective would not deny these connections and their implications, many current hermeneutical, semiotic, personalist, intersubjective, relational, or existential approaches to analytic phenomena would. See my discussion of the relation of self and body (Meissner 1997, 1998a,b,c).
3. Ricoeur (1981) later concluded that the purposefulness and intentionality of psychic life was basically incompatible with the energic paradigm, so that any consistent thematization "would require a conceptual framework different from that of its topography and economics" (p. 259).
4. Letter to Putnam, 8 July 1915; cited in Hale (1971, p. 189).
5. Letter to Pfister, 24 February 1928; in Meng and Freud (1963, p. 123).
6. Letter to Putnam, 8 July 1915; cited in Hale (1971, p. 189).
7. See also Freud (1937, pp. 228–229).
8. Letter to Putnam, 7 June 1915; cited in Hale (1971, p. 188).
9. Letter to Putnam, 4 May 1911; cited in Hale (1971, pp. 121–122).
10. Letter to Putnam, 30 March 1914; cited in Hale (1971, p. 171).
11. The view that ethics automatically involves an evaluative weltanschauung probably reflects residues of nineteenth century views of moral philosophy, embracing far more than we would regard as the proper province of ethics. Large-scale imaginative or utopian visions impervious to logic and evidence are alien to contemporary ethics. But Hart-

mann (1960) was also cautious of extending analysis beyond its natural preserve—"One should be able to say when and in what respect such 'uses' of analysis make sense and where sense becomes nonsense" (pp. 11–12).

12. This interpretation of Freud's views can be challenged. The issue hinges on the role of superego and its integration with ego with respect to ethical judgment and behavior. See chapter 12.

13. King (1986) offered a counterpoise to this reading of Freud's ethical perspective, addressing the issue of private versus public morality. If Rieff's "psychological man" keeps the claims of the larger community at arm's length, this would neglect Freud's view of man as basically social. This same issue extends into contemporary discussions of one-person versus two-person psychologies.

14. Rorty (1986) endorsed this aspect of Rieff's reading of Freud and the lack of prescriptions for public morality. But King (1986), *e contra*, argued that "Rorty confuses the dominant thrust of Freud's therapeutic and theoretical intentions, his relative indifference to social and political arrangements, with the implications of Freud's work as they have been developed by others and with the 'social foundationism' implicit in Freud's own work" (pp. 38–39).

15. Wallwork (1991) challenged this reading. Freud did not abandon happiness as that toward which man strives; characterizing him as opposed to hedonism in the sense of seeking pleasure is not accurate.

16. Rieff failed to utilize Freud's metapsychology in explaining moral responsibility and determinism (Wallwork 1991).

CHAPTER 2. PSYCHOANALYSIS AND ETHICAL SYSTEMS

1. King (1986) noted Kant's neglect of other ethical values besides duty and responsibility, for instance, courage, friendship, and the common good, themes found in Aristotle and elsewhere in ethical thought.

2. Fromm (1947) noted that this idealized status of the individual did not include valuing of self-love, since the quest for personal happiness was a natural striving without positive ethical value. The only happiness that counted was the happiness of others.

3. Tillich (1955) distinguished unconditional-categorical imperatives from conditional moralisms—the former are absolute and universal, the latter valid only conditionally and within limits. Thus the relative moralisms studied by psychologists and anthropologists do not challenge moral imperatives.

4. Although Freud respected Enlightenment rationalism, he decried excessive reliance on reason because of the irrationality of emotional life. This also made him less than sympathetic to German idealism.

5. Lacan (1992) noted the inherent tension between utilitarian and psychoanalytic ethical perspectives : "It is a fact of experience that what I want is the good of others in the image of my own" (p. 187).

6. See my discussion of aspects of psychic reality in Meissner (2000d, 2001).

7. Ewing (1962) thought Moore's efforts to prove "good" undefinable were not altogether successful.

CHAPTER 3. PSYCHIC DETERMINISM AND MOTIVATIONAL PRINCIPLES

1. Rangell (1986) noted the unacknowledged incompatibility in analysis between autonomy and determinism. He argued that the will is not always free, but that the concept of autonomy, usually accepted by analysts as free, is linked to the concept of will. Autonomy and determinism must therefore coexist, calling for mutual compromise in understanding both. If autonomy is relative, so must be determinism—both concepts limit each other relatively and reciprocally. A determinism excluding decision and choice would make therapy impossible.

2. James espoused a similar view—hard determinism meant "that no man can help being what he is and doing what he does and that moral distinctions are therefore irrational and ought never to be applied to men or anything else" (Taylor 1967, p. 368).

3. Rangell (1986) noted that Freud never viewed determinism as absolute, and never opposed the idea of nonnecessitated choosing.

4. Russell (1910) argued that determinism did not eliminate the possibility of choice; as he put it, "What determinism maintains is, that our will to choose this or that alternative is the effect of antecedents; but this does not prevent our will from being itself a cause of other effects" (p. 21).

5. In this I differ from Wallace (1986a) who made causality and motivation synonymous. I restrict the notion of cause to efficiency as in common usage. Wallace, however, takes psychic causality to include intention or purpose, making it equivalent to motivation. I prefer to keep the terms distinct.

6. For the most part, Freud maintained a rather thoroughgoing determinism. Even so, it seems unlikely that he simply translated causal determinism from physical science to his psychological science. How-

ever, the linear (laplacean) causality Freud knew no longer has much place even in physics; it has given way to probabilistic or stochastic views of causality in the wake of quantum mechanics.

7. Sherwood's (1969) extended discussion of the causes versus reasons debate detailed the dimensions of the distinction and their implications for psychological, and specifically for psychoanalytic, theory.

8. This distinction is not universally endorsed. Wallace (1995), for example, takes Wallwork's (1991) disentangling causality and determination to task as though any appeal to motives as determining were to abrogate true causality. But the objection disavows the role of final causality, insisting on efficient causality as the only valid causality in scientific logic. Pace Wallace and Wallwork, I would argue that motivational influences determine the quality, nature, and direction of the act, but do not account for the acting itself. This requires efficient causality, but any act of will is both determined *and* caused by the will as originative efficient-cause of the act. Psychic acts are both caused (thus involve the use of energy) and determined (motivated). In voluntary actions, the act of will is the first in the sequence of causes, even though its action is determined.

9. The roots of the notion of "overdetermination" can be traced to Freud's early neurological work, *On Aphasia* (1891; see Grossman 1992).

10. Holt (1976) reminded us that Freud got along very nicely for the first fifteen years without a concept of drive; *wish* was the prevailing motivational term.

11. Satisfaction is cast in terms of the pleasure principle—more in terms of goal-attainment than in sensory pleasureful experience. See Meissner (1995b).

12. Holt (1976) suggested "perceptual-evaluative mismatch" for this appraisal, taking place at conscious, preconscious, or unconscious levels. See Rubinstein (1967) on perceptual match and mismatch.

13. See the discussion of this connection in Meissner (1995b).

14. As Moran (1993) noted, Klein's assumptions regarding good and bad are equivalently assumptions regarding an innately moral being.

15. Even Freud is reputed to have acknowledged that sometimes even a cigar was just a cigar!

16. In my understanding of the self (Meissner 1986c, 1993, 2000e), the originating source of action is the self-as-agent; autonomous ego functions are one of the subsystems of functions composing the self, not a separate source of agency exclusive of the self-as-agent and as person.

17. May (1953) noted that, properly conceived, the agency of the self circumvents two errors—the first is passivism, in which determining

forces, for instance; drives, take the place of self-determinism, and the second activism, substituting activity for awareness and aliveness. Freud's passivity in relation to unconscious motivations meant that man was no longer master in his own house; but this undermining of the will had to be balanced by the avowed goal of analysis to make the unconscious conscious and to enable the self to become more autonomous and in charge of impulses, desires, and motives.

18. In this formulation such ego motives are independent of drives and drive-energies, but activation of ego functions requires energy (Meissner (1993, 1995a).

CHAPTER 4. VOLITION AND WILL

1. I use the term *intellective* rather than *intellectual* to indicate higher-order capacities of the mind, specifically the intellect, related to abstraction, comprehension of meaning, understanding means-end relationships and purposes, symbolic capacities, understanding language, and so on. "Intellectual" has overtones of the pedantic, educated, bookish, or academic that have nothing to do with my discussion.

2. Beyond these immediate concerns lies the further issue of freedom of will—if all psychic acts are determined, what does it mean for some acts of the will to be called "free"? See chapter 5.

3. Rangell (1986) reviewed some analytic discussions of will (Esman 1985; Knight 1946; Lewy 1961; Rapaport 1953; W. Schwartz 1984) and noted confusions caused by condensing "will" with "free will."

4. I note Leavy's (1996a) pertinent questioning the customary equivalence of self and self-representation: the self is source of all psychic functions, not just as a "representation" and anterior to its representations.

5. Shapiro (1970) added that infantile volition is less involved in action since cognitive (and volitional) equipment for volitional or self-directed action is relatively undeveloped. It is an interesting question at what point in development and under what conditions volition enters the picture.

6. Moran (1993) points out that in his early view of hysteria, in Anna O. and Emmy von N. particularly, discussed in the *Studies on Hysteria* (Breuer and Freud, 1895) Freud attributed pathology to perversion of the will or "counterwill." Freud (1894) even claimed that "the splitting of the content of consciousness resulted from an act of will on the part of the patient" (p. 46).

7. Analysts generally agree that willpower has at best a narrowly limited efficacy (Weisman 1965). Rangell (1986) translated it in analytic terms: "It is man's will which gives him the power to direct the path to be taken by the self, to decide, to execute, to do, to act" (p. 28). And again: "One might say that psychoanalysis increases 'will power,' an equivalent of Freud's and Fenichel's pointing to the increased operation of the rational ego" (p. 33).

8. A similar and more recent approach, emphasizing the necessity for choice and commitment to action in making therapeutic gains both possible and effective is offered by Power (2000).

9. My survey of these concepts leans heavily on Bourke (1964) and Adler (1958–1961), and I will forego trying the reader's patience by repetitious citations.

10. This view was dominant in Greek philosophy, including Aristotle, persisted in medieval thought only to reappear in Spinoza, Hobbes, and even in some ways Kant.

11. This view would distinguish between sensory appetites and rational appetite of intellect or reason. At the end of his extensive review of philosophical notions of will and willing, Bourke (1964) offered a descriptive definition of willing: "Willing is that psychic activity of man, whereby he tends toward or away from certain objectives reflectively adopted, whereby he sometimes achieves personal freedom of action, whereby he acts with some spontaneity or self-initiative, and whereby he approves or loves what he deems good and disapproves or hates what he deems not good" (p. 235).

12. This view is frequent in scriptural usage and found its way into Augustine and Christian spiritual literature, but has more to do with affectivity than willing. I will also not discuss political implications of will theory nor the kind of metaphysics of will found in German idealism, especially Schopenauer, Fichte, Schelling, and Hegel that reach far beyond the modest confines of psychoanalytic concern.

13. See my discussion of the Strachey model of mutative interpretation in Meissner (1991b).

14. My use of the term *instinctual* is meant as descriptive and does not intend either the existence of drives or the implications of drive theory as the basis for motivation or appetition. See my discussion of motivational principles in Meissner (1999a,b).

15. Aristotle saw such opposition in *akrasia* (weakness of will), reflecting conflict between the practical judgment of reason and an unreasoned instinctual desire. The effects of instinctual desire can be felt in either bypassing reason or by inhibiting the capacity of reason to come to a decision.

16. Rangell (1986) noted that adaptation called for understanding the initiation of any action.

17. We can wonder, with Arieti (1972) at what point does the baby begin to acquire a capacity to assume control of his own actions, not merely as a function of compliance—in the anal period? Before? After?

18. Rangell (1986) adopted this perspective on the will emphasizing the causal function of the will—"Autonomy and will are not without motivation, and neither is contrary to the concept of causation, but are included within it. Both take their place as sequences within the causative chain. . . ." (p. 25).

19. Actions of the self are also determined in a hard or causal sense by reason of the fact that they are actions of the self acting as causal source. The agency of the self is in this sense causal.

20. This view is consistent with current views of the mind involving levels of parallel processing.

21. See my extended exploration and discussion of these issues in Meissner (1995a,b,c, 1999a,b).

22. The expression "act of loving" does not refer to sexual lovemaking , but rather to an internal mental appraisal of the object as good and an intellective desire to obtain and possess that good. As a mental state, loving may also be accompanied by loving feelings, but feelings do not belong to the will as such.

23. Shapiro (1970) pointed out that the more autonomous any function or capacity becomes, the less predictable will it be. But predictability or lack of it has no relation to free choice. A given choice may be free and quite predictable—at least with reasonable probability.

24. Rangell (1986) summarized his concept of will: "Will is to be differentiated from the instinctual wish, the wish of early psychoanalytic theory. It is also to be distinguished and separated from a superego demand or requirement. The human will is an ego faculty, a directing capacity following and combining motivations from the three psychic systems, external reality, and the goals and intentions of the ego itself, of which will is its culmination" (p. 23).

CHAPTER 5. FREEDOM OF THE WILL

1. As in "You nourish the illusion of there being such a thing as psychical freedom, and you will not give it up" (Freud 1916–1917, p. 49); "the illusion of Free Will" (1919b, p. 236); and "Many people, as is well known, contest the assumption of complete psychical determinism by appealing to a special feeling of conviction that there is a free will.

This feeling of conviction exists; and it does not give way before a belief in determinism" (1901, p. 253).

2. As Wallace (1985) noted, Freud opposed "not the concept of conscious and reality-oriented self determination, but the idea that a mental act could be arbitrary, that it could bear no meaningful and causal relationship to the physiology, history, prior mental set, and situation of the actor" (p. 232).

3. See chapter 3.

4. This model would require eventual revision, but the point here is Freud's ambiguity about determinism.

5. It is also paradoxical that this reading of the analytic view of freedom finds significant parallels in the behaviorist determinism preached by Skinner and by other behavioristically oriented psychologists. See the discussion of these issues in Neville (1972), Comfort (1972), and Chomsky (1959).

6. The relevant text from Freud (1920b) is cited below.

7. Gaylin (1974) commented on the discomfort of analysts with the idea of freedom. All the same, the discovery of the unconscious focused analytic interest on issues of psychic determinism to the exclusion of any acknowledgment of freedom of the will, choice, or responsibility. This trend was countered by subsequent expansion of our understanding of the ego and its functions, especially its autonomy and self-determining capacity (Rangell 1971).

8. Both Bourke (1964) and Adler (1958-1961) provided definitions of freedom. Bourke proposed that "it may be described as that power or condition of an agent which enables him to act, or refuse to act, and to do so in ways which he determines, without compelling restraints from forces external to, or internal to, his own personality" (p. 79). Adler's conclusion is that "To be free is to have an ability or power to act in a certain way and for a certain result. To be free is, through the exercise of such power, to have what one does proceed from oneself rather than from another (1958–1961, I:615). Both definitions stress the lack of coercion and the role of the will in self-determination.

9. On the basis of the possibility of freedom the judicial system holds lawbreakers accountable for their actions, and hence condemns and punishes, or excuses from culpability on grounds of diminished capacity or impaired potential for free choice.

10. See the discussion of these aspects of the will in chapter 4.

11. Most philosophers, including some analysts (May 1953) have made consciousness a condition of free will, presupposing that unconscious mentation is determined whereas conscious mentation need not be. I regard this as a false dichotomy—determination and freedom are not

opposites. I am arguing, therefore, for the possibility of free will acts also on the unconscious level. There is some suggestive evidence to support this view. Libet, Wright, and Gleason (1982) and Libet et al. (1983) found a type II readiness potential, representing nonconscious neuronal activity, about 550 ms before wrist flexion, and conscious intention to flex at about 200 ms before actual flexion. Does the earlier potential reflect nonconscious voluntary initiation of the act? See the further discussion in Brakel and Snodgrass (1998)

12. Holt relates autonomy and freedom of will to the ego; I prefer to attribute it more directly to the self, of which will and ego are functional components. See Meissner (1986c, 1993, 1996a, 2000h).

13. Rangell (1971) endorses this view, arguing that aspects of the decision-making process can take place on the unconscious level as well as on the conscious.

14. Stout (1936–1937) distinguished two meanings of "determine"—one is having an influence over acts of choice or volition, the other compelling them. At a minimum, then, freedom of will must mean that the will act proceeds from the self as its source. Action influenced by motives is potentially free insofar as "the motives belong to the nature of the self and are not external forces acting upon it" (p. 539). Again, "Freedom in this sense consists in the degree to which the volition of the moment proceeds from and expresses the self as a whole" (p. 542).

15. This translates the spirit of Freud's maxim, "Where id was, there ego shall be." See Wallace (1985). Psychic determinism does not abrogate the capacity for choice; as Joseph (1987) put it: "Many philosophers believe psychoanalysts think free will is abandoned and that individuals are so programmed by earlier experiences and unconscious processes that there is never any element of choice in their activities or mental processes. In fact, the situation is often the opposite; once the choice is made, once an intention is arrived at, we are in the position of retrospectively determining how the choice was reached, but we are not in the position of prospectively predicting the choice" (p. 12). See also Bowman's (1996) comments on analysis and the ethic of autonomy.

16. Arieti (1972) noted that the catatonic, in the face of overwhelming anxiety, guilt, and fear, paralyzes every act of will, substituting automatic obedience to the will of others. Waxy flexibility is not comfortable, but the subject cannot will to change position on his own terms.

17. May (1953) had noted that rebellion has often been confused with freedom, giving a false sense of independence—this because rebellion is always against some order of expectations, laws, rules on which the sense of freedom depends. The rebel is not free if he is caught up in this continuing struggle.

18. The capacity for self-determination, as a function of will, is also subject to limitations and constraints, as is freedom of the will more generally. See O'Shaughnessy (1980).
19. I have argued elsewhere (Meissner 1978a, 1986d, 1988b) that the potential for paranoid (and I would include depressive) regressive manifestations is universal, and that given the right combination of influences, stresses, traumas, or other precipitating factors, the paranoid potential can be activated.

CHAPTER 6. PSYCHODYNAMIC HEDONISM AND THE PLEASURE PRINCIPLE

1. Moore (G. E. 1903) argued that hedonism was self-contradictory on the grounds that if personal pleasure was the only good, this applied to everyone, so that everyone's pleasure was the only good—a contradiction.
2. See also the arguments refuting hedonism offered by Bradley (1951).
3. In this sense motivation by pleasure or avoiding pain does not exclude sacrifice or renunciation to increase the measure of general happiness in the world. A comparable idea can be found in Freud.
4. The tendency to view Freud's pleasure principle as postulating a subjective experience of pleasure as the norm of action has led to a misguided view of analysis as advocating self-interest and selfishness as central to the analytic ethic (Wallwork 1991).
5. In these terms, pleasure and unpleasure are better interpreted as success or lack of success in the performance of function. See my discussion of this issue in Meissner (1995b).
6. Rieff (1959) declared: "He [Freud] is the architect of a great revolt against pleasure, not for it. He wrote no briefs for the pleasure principle. Rather he established its futility. It is toward the reality principle that Freud turns us, toward the sober business of living and with no nonsense about its goodness or ease" (p. 355). Freud himself is more ambiguous, but Rieff's point should not be lost.
7. Freud had actually translated a volume of Mill's work into German.
8. Rorty (1988b) commented: "Of course, other things being equal, the best appears to be preferable to the merely good. Nevertheless, the best can often be an enemy of the good. Even in moral contexts, the consequences of accepting the good as good enough may sometimes be preferable to the devastation and destruction that can accompany striving for the best" (p. 19).

9. This view is consonant with Fromm's (1947) emphasis on productive living rather than happiness as a goal of moral life. Similarly for Aquinas the virtuous man derives pleasure from acting virtuously, but his act is virtuous because it is motivated by charity or by doing good rather than satisfaction. See Plé (1964b).

CHAPTER 7. NARCISSISM AND EGOISM

1. The distinction between instinctual frustration or repression and instinctual renunciation is relevant here. See my exploration of the life and personality of Ignatius of Loyola, in whom the dynamics of narcissism and the ego-ideal played an immense part in his life and spirituality. See Meissner (1992b).
2. I have discussed this case in greater detail in Meissner (1985a).
3. He had actually floated the idea the previous November 1909, in discussing a paper for the Vienna Psychoanalytic Society (Gay 1988).
4. Pulver (1970) reviewed the diverse meanings of narcissism and distinguished several subtypes—a developmental stage, a form of object choice, a mode of relating, and a self-referential attitude. The implications and consequences of each subtype are different, some connoting opposition to altruistic implications, some not only compatible with but reinforcing and supportive of object love.
5. Another major contribution in this paper was Freud's concept of the ego-ideal as the replacement for disappointed and disillusioned infantile narcissism.
6. Sandler, Holder, and Meers (1963; Holder 1982) noted the shifting use of Freud's references to "ego" and "self," and distinguished between an "ideal self" and a "ego-ideal" formed later. The ideal self corresponded to the self-I-would-like-to-be, while ego-ideal corresponded to the self-I-ought-to-be.
7. See Rochlin (1973) for an extended discussion of the vicissitudes of narcissism, especially in provoking rage and aggressive destructiveness.
8. Experimentally induced low self-esteem is associated with subsequent delinquent behavior (Aronson and Mettee 1968). Self-concept in delinquents is generally less positive than in nondelinquents (Lively, Dihitz, and Reckless 1962). Other studies have suggested that altruistic behavior is related positively to self-esteem (London and Bower 1968; Murphy 1937).
9. Speaking of self-love, Fromm (1956) added, "It is true that selfish persons are incapable of loving others, but they are not capable of loving themselves either" (p. 61). The stance taken by Rubin (1997), among

others, represents a gross misreading of analysis. He writes, "It is not surprising that psychoanalysis lacks a nuanced and compelling account of emotional intimacy among egalitarian subjects. For how could there be an adequate account of intimacy when the other is seen mostly it terms of what it does (or does not do) for the self?" (p. 85). This omits nearly the whole of object relations theory, object love, and substitutes not only narcissism for the whole, but pathological narcissism at that.

10. These issues are complicated by the diversity of meanings and applications of the term *narcissism*. See the review of usages by Pulver (1970) and Moore (1975).

CHAPTER 8. OBJECT LOVE AND ALTRUISM

1. The case can be made that libido, in contrast, is never freely given, but is always passive and reactive.

2. Fromm (1956) stressed the active character of love: "Love is an activity, not a passive affect; . . . In the most general way, the active character of love can be described by stating that love is primarily *giving*, not receiving" (p. 22, italics in original). But for productive characters giving, rather than impoverishment, is experienced as wealth, strength, power, and heightened vitality that leads to joy and self-enrichment.

3. Fromm (1956) added: "Care and concern imply another aspect of love; that of *responsibility*. Today responsibility is often meant to denote duty, something imposed upon one from the outside. But responsibility, in its true sense, is an entirely voluntary act; it is my response to the needs, expressed or unexpressed, of another human being" (pp. 27–28).

4. Fletcher (1967) erected the love commandment into the centerpiece and all-encompassing criterion of ethical goodness and correctness. His position has been subjected to stringent questioning and criticism by other ethicists and moral theologians. See Cox (1968).

5. This is very different from the sense of Eros proposed by Freud (1920a) in opposition to Thanatos—as a fundamental instinctual drive toward greater unity and integration at increasing levels of complexity.

6. Fromm (1956) warned that responsibility undertaken out of a sense of duty or even paternalistic concern can deteriorate into domination or possessiveness, unless tempered by respect.

7. Brotherly love applies without prejudice to all fellow humans. Love for all men is love for all fellow humans—the generic terms *men* or *mankind* are inclusive of all humans regardless of gender.

8. Hamilton (1963, 1964) described "inclusive fitness" whereby individual reproductive success could be favored by self-sacrifice insofar as sacrifice promotes survival of genetic material in future generations. This became the basis for kin altruism benefiting the kin group. See also Badcock (1986).

9. Disconnection of the themes of feminine self-sacrifice for the sake of relationships was initiated among analysts by Blum (1976a) for whom apparent feminine masochism was related to feminine ego-ideals and correlative value systems. The theme was elaborated by Gilligan (1977, 1982) and others.

10. Personality characteristics may play a role as well. Schwartz and his colleagues (1969) found that n-Achievement related positively to not cheating and negatively to helpfulness, and conversely n-Affiliation related positively to helpfulness and neutrally to cheating—cheating serving as a mode of self-interest and helping as a mode of other-interest.

11. See also Mk (12: 30–31) and Lk (10: 26–28).

12. The Christian format is entirely consistent with the Judaic tradition. Erikson (1964) cited Rabbi Hillel, who was once challenged by an unbeliever to speak the whole truth of the Torah while standing on one foot. The rabbi replied, "What is hateful to yourself, do not to your fellow man. That is the whole of the Torah and the rest is but commentary" (p. 243).

13. Hallett (1989) categorized six incompatible versions of love of neighbor—self-preference, parity, other-preference, self-subordination, self-forgetfulness, and self-denial.

14. Freud's targeting views common among Christians left at least some Christian ethical thinkers unscathed. Aquinas (1941), for example, maintained that love of neighbor included love of self and that universal love was impossible if it implied equal love for all (ST II-IIae, 25, iv, viii); also that we ought to love those near and dear to us more than others (ST, II-IIae, 26, vi). Freud and the Angelic Doctor would find common ground at least to this extent.

15. It has been argued, since Darwin (1872) that man is by nature disposed to altruism, that is, he is naturally attuned to group loyalty and sensitive and responsive to the social expectations and needs of his fellow men. See Campbell (1965) and Hamilton (1971). This perspective is also congruent with sociobiological perspectives (Wilson 1975). But these biological components enter into interaction with environmental and social determinants to produce a final result (Campbell 1975). Psychoanalysis is more concerned with certain subcategories of the latter, but not to disparagement or disregard of the former.

16. Cited in E. L. Freud (1975, p. 364, letter 217).

17. Lacan (1992) noted this aspect of Freud's thinking; referring to Matthew's Gospel, he observed: "Then after that there is the statement, 'Thou shalt love thy neighbor as thyself.' That's the commandment that appropriately enough, given its obvious relevance, is the terminal point of *Civilization and Its Discontents*; it is the ideal end to which his investigation by necessity leads him—Freud never held back from anything that offered itself to his examination" (p. 96).

18. A similar position regarding love of self and other was proposed by Fromm (1955):

> *Love is union* with somebody, or something, outside oneself, *under the condition of retaining the separateness and integrity of one's own self.* It is an experience of sharing, of communion, which permits the full unfolding of one's own inner activity. The experience of love does away with the necessity of illusions. There is no need to inflate the image of the other person, or of myself, since the reality of active sharing and loving permits me to transcend my individualized existence, and at the same time to experience myself as the bearer of the active powers which constitute the act of loving. (pp. 31–32, italics in original)

CHAPTER 9. ETHICAL DECISION-MAKING AND SELF-DECEPTION

1. Distinction of the action itself from the preceding decision process is essential. Intentions, decisions, choices are acts of intellect and will that precede and lead to actual doing, regardless of what capacity does the doing—psychic or motoric. The question remains as to what in the sequence is to be regarded as action and what as consequence and where to draw the line. The distinction is required to keep formalist theories judging actions by ethical rules separate from utilitarian theories judging by consequences. See Oldenquist (1967) and the discussion in chapter 2. Moreover, to be morally relevant, a psychological theory requires a decision process that is at least action-guiding (A. O. Rorty 1988b).

2. Deciding and choosing go together, but with shades of implication. They are sometimes synonymous in usage, but in many contexts choosing may be associated more with action and deciding with intentionality. See Oldenquist (1967); Rangell (1963b) also touches on this question.

3. I will take the liberty of modifying some of Rangell's formulations to fit with the theory of dynamic motivation and agency of the self I am proposing.

4. Level of moral development may also play a role. Holland (1976) found that ethical essays within one level higher or lower than the recipient's moral stage, as defined by Kohlberg's (1969) rating scale, had greater persuasive effect on moral judgment.

5. See also Rangell (1963b, 1969d, 1971, 1987, 1989).

6. Bursztajn and his colleagues (1981) have discussed the probabilistic approach to decision-making in uncertain circumstances. Their discussion treats of medical decisions, but the principles are also applicable to ethical decision-making in terms of the so-called probabilistic paradigm.

7. Objection has been raised that if choices are actions and all actions are preceded by choices, this leads to an infinite regress. To the contrary, choice is an action of the will as a function of the self-as-agent, which acts as originating agent of the act of choice. Preceding acts are in the order of intention (ideas, motives) and do not play a causative role as efficient causes of the act in the order of execution. This seems preferable to disqualifying choice as an action, which would introduce other inconsistencies.

8. This process is also subject to the reality principle, leading to the question of whether the evaluation is objective or not or in what degree. Ewing (1962) noted that sources of error are multiple: one can even avoid facts in order to bypass a disagreeable duty or obligation. Not only do motives to distort matters of fact obtain, but judgments are made more in terms of individual psychic reality than actual reality.

9. This conception is reinforced by emergent views of conscious and unconscious mental processing in terms of reciprocal synergism rather than in opposition across repression barriers (Dennett 1991; Eagle 1987). Dennett envisions specialist modules processing information unconsciously and selectively finding expression in the global working space of consciousness. As Migone and Liotti (1998) put it, "people can unconsciously think, test reality and carry out plans, which is highly congruent with the view we get from the cognitive theorists' conception of unconscious 'specialists' working in synergism and in continuous exchange with the conscious, higher-order mental process" (p. 1088).

10. These variations on the conflict theme intersect to a degree with Kris's (1985, 1988) discussion of divergent and convergent conflicts.

11. See my discussion of Hartmann's theory of action in Meissner (1986a).

12. In locating the source of agency in the ego Rangell makes the ego an independent source of action, as if it were a second source of action

separate from the person. In my view, there is only one agent, the self in its role as self-as-agent; the ego is not a separate entity or agency— it is nothing more than the self acting in ego-terms and in the manner of ego-functions. There is only one real agent—the self, myself, me— and no other. Otherwise, our theory is open to issues of reification, misplaced concreteness, and the artificial division of the human agent that has given rise to the homuncular diversion. See my discussion of these issues in Meissner (1993, 1996a, 1999d,e, 2000e,f,g,h).

13. The theory advanced here regards choice as an action of will leading to, but not synonymous with, actually doing one thing rather than another. We can choose in advance to do something later; this is not in my view the same as deciding in advance—deciding belongs more to intellect, choosing more to will; even in advance, deciding precedes choosing. The decision process precedes and leads to choice, and choice to action. *E contra*, see Oldenquist (1967).

14. An obvious and perhaps unnecessary comment—"will" is another theoretical construct, like ego or superego; we do not intend a preexisting and separate entity, the will, possessing degrees of power and/or weakness. We are conceptualizing a function of the self-as-agent with discriminable and specific qualities and functions that we attribute descriptively to the ego as a substructal organization of the self-system. When these functions are consistently, effectively, and firmly performed, we can speak of strength of will or willpower.

15. Wilshire (1988) called attention to the disparity between verbalizable intellection and perception, an incoherence greatly facilitating self-deception by concealing one portion of experience from another. This is particularly so in perceptual experience of one's own body; see Straus's experiment (1969).

16. This does not argue against conscious awareness of contrary propositions, as opposed to contradictory.

17. Philosophers tend to resist any appeal to unconscious beliefs. See McLaughlin (1988). At the same time, Mclaughlin holds out the possibility that self-deception is possible if and when one of a set of contradictory beliefs is accessible and the other is not. The distinction between an inaccessible belief and an unconscious belief escapes me.

18. Some would dispense with any idea of belief based on desire, defining belief as based on evidence only; see Price (1973).

19. Sartre's dismissal of unconscious processes and insistence that all knowing is consciousness of knowing are essential to his project regarding bad faith. Bad faith seems to have been Sartre's rendition of self-deception, defined as consciously believing something that at the same time one consciously disbelieves. See Wood's (1988) discussion of this issue.

CHAPTER 10. RESPONSIBILITY

1. Szasz advocated an individualistic ethics, in which the individual was seen as autonomous and the sole responsible agent for his own actions. On these terms, forcible treatment violates the assumption of unconditional autonomy (Laor 1984; Szasz 1958, 1961). Regardless of diagnosis, the individual should be held unconditionally responsible for his actions (Szasz 1963, 1974).
2. It is worth keeping in mind that legal and social systems have different ways of determining personal or corporate agency and accordingly personal or corporate liability. A person may be held to legal responsibility when subjective responsibility is minimal, and vice versa. An admirable statement of the mingling and disparity of ethical meaning and legal adjudication can be found in Forer (1980).
3. Conn (1981) remarked, "As such, responsibility is rooted in, and symbolizes, the discovery that . . . one can only be true to one's self insofar—and just insofar—as one is true to others—insofar, that is, as one responds to the *values* in each human situation in a manner that is at once free and creative, critical and fitting" (pp. 5–6).
4. Russell (1910) argued that responsibility, assignment of praise or blame, was a matter of choice, praise or blame of choosing rightly or wrongly; responsibility was thus not destroyed by determinism.
5. I would note that this concept differs from the concept of self as an aggregate of relatively autonomous subsystems advocated by Rorty (1988b). Her subsystems enjoy their own autonomous agency so that her "self" becomes an integration of fragmented autonomies exerting their jurisdiction independently of the jurisdiction of other subsystems; the self-as-agent (Meissner 1993), however, envisions only one agent, the self, synonymous with the person himself (Meissner 2000e). *Entia non multiplicanda!*
6. Heidegger (1962) addressed these issues in terms of *Sorge* (care), a basic constituent of human existence giving rise to desire and will. Willing and wishing would be impossible without a foundation in care, and conversely, if we really and authentically care, we cannot avoid wishing and willing.
7. On this question, see the discussion of Madden (1957).
8. See Fingarette (1955) and Madden (1957) on taking responsibility in analysis or therapy. My own discussion of the place of responsibility in analysis comes to similar conclusions; see Meissner (1996b).
9. See my further discussion of the role of neutrality in Meissner (1996b, 1998a).
10. Unconscious motives can undermine responsibility, or can promote it by defensive responses. Some clinical cases involving strong commit-

ment to responsibility and duty result from reaction-formations coun-
tering underlying motives involving envy, competitive hostility, and
sadomasochistic impulses.

11. As Rorty (1988b) noted, conditions establishing one as a responsible
agent are connected to personal identity, so that responsibility and
whatever constitutes personal agency are intertwined.

12. Some analysts tend to make responsibility a function of superego, but
in a qualified sense. Tyson (1996) cites Loewald as attributing a capacity for self-responsibility to superego (Loewald 1979): "Self-responsibility means the existence not simply of a guilt-producing, punishing
superego, a superego that acts after the fact, but also of a superego that
insures compliance with internalized rules" (p. 183). This formulation
appeals to a form of superego autonomy that connotes integration, in
my view, with relatively autonomous ego-functions. Moral judgment
and the judgment of responsibility involve conjoined ego- and superego-functions, both operating in virtue of the agency of the self.

CHAPTER 11. SUPEREGO AND MORAL DEVELOPMENT

1. In my view, superego is a substructure of the self so that any agency
attributed to the superego is synonymously agency of the self operating in superego-mode. I imply no multiplication of entities or agencies.
See my previous discussions of these considerations in Meissner (1993,
2000e,h,i,j).

2. A good synthetic review of the classic theory of the superego can be
found in Meissner (2000b). See also my reconsideration of oedipal
development (Meissner 1986b).

3. This tendency was clearly formulated by Piers and Singer (1953) who
distinguished between guilt and shame—guilt reflected a tension
between ego and superego, shame a tension between ego and ego-ideal.

4. This question, along with the question of locating identifications in ego
versus superego, are somewhat alleviated by a revised metapsychology
allocating agency to the self-system (Meissner 1993). In that perspective ego is a mental construct representing the agency of the self acting
in an ego modality; likewise the superego is a construct representing
action of the self in a superego mode. As constructs, they cannot be
conceived as separate or independent sources of agency.

5. Nietzsche (1887) wrote:

    The formidable bulwarks by means of which the polity pro-
    tected itself against the ancient instincts of freedom (punishment
    was one of the strongest of these bulwarks) caused those wild,

extravagant instincts to turn in upon men. Hostility, cruelty, the delight in persecution, raids, excitement, destruction all turned against their begetter. Lacking external enemies and resistances, and confined within an oppressive narrowness and regularity, man began rending, persecuted, terrifying himself, like a wild beast hurling itself against the bars of its cage. (p. 218)

6. See also Freud (1933a).
7. See also the extensive discussions of feminine development in Blum (1976b)
8. A similar appraisal is rendered by Schafer (1992).
9. Mahler's (Mahler, Pine, and Bergman 1975) work also suggested development of superego precursors, especially in the resolution of rapprochement conflicts (McDevitt 1979). Buchsbaum and Emde (1990) have also traced emergence of moral components in relation to the affective quality of the mother-child relation in years one-to-three. Studying play narratives, they ask: "Are 36-month-olds competent to represent internalized moral themes? The clear and resounding answer is yes. Children gave meaningful responses to story items probing for empathic, prosocial responses, adherence to rules, and, most dramatically, to a moral dilemma" (p. 140).
10. I would call attention in this regard to my discussion of the integration of the body self, and its relations to both the physical body and the body image (Meissner 1997, 1998b,c,d), especially with reference to the body self and self-object differentiation in pregnancy (Meissner 1998b).
11. The original concept of the significance of the auditory sphere in relation to the development of language for superego development came from Isakower (1939).
12. See also Gillman (1982) on this point.
13. Erikson (1950, 1956) envisioned a similar dynamic in terms of the psychosocial crisis of trust.
14. J. H. Smith (1986) noted reasons why in the constitution of self and object, badness is associated with the self and goodness with the object. Paradoxically, he observed, "the intensity of this coloration of the self as bad and the object—the mother—as good is intensified to the extent that mothering is inadequate" (p. 69).
15. R. J. Campbell (1971) noted in this regard, "Many parents indeed have clinically obvious superego defects, and the child of such parents is likely to develop a superego that will reflect those defects" (p. 86).
16. Goodenough's (1930) early studies of the effects of parental discipline found a greater incidence of rebellious outbursts and resentment in children whose parents were inconsistent in disciplining, and con-

cluded with an old adage: "Self-control in the parents is after all the best guarantee of self-control in the child," that might receive analytic endorsement.

17. It should be noted that internalization as a learning phenomenon is not the same as internalization as conceived psychoanalytically. Sears, Macoby, and Levin (1957) appeal to identification in the formation of conscience, but this a form of learning differing from analytic identification (see Meissner 1974a,b).

18. A. Freud (1965) designated the mother as the child's "first external legislator" (p. 168).

19. These distinctions are implicit in the differentiation between introjection and identification as forms of internalization. See my discussions in Meissner (1970b, 1971, 1972, 1981)

CHAPTER 12. SUPEREGO FUNCTIONS AND CONSCIENCE

1. Klass (1978), in reviewing experimental evidence for guilt-reduction, concluded that evidence does not offer much support for showing that these reactions actually do reduce guilt. Methodological difficulties suggest that clinical impressions may have to carry their own weight without support from experiment.

2. Campbell (1971) offered a complementary listing of superego functions in adult life, including regulation of self-esteem, guilt feelings, moral masochism, the syndrome of the criminal from a sense of guilt, asceticism, some types of delinquency, and contributions of neurotic or psychotic symptomatology.

3. Nunberg (1932) made the case for the superego's role in reality-testing, arguing that superego supervised the ego's perceptions, evaluating recognition of reality and sanctioning it. A more contemporary view would assign such cognitive functions to the ego, whose cognitive processing takes place on more than one level, thus obviating the need for splitting of functions. Loewenstein (1966) held a similar view, but if the formula had any validity, it was in response to value systems (Esman 1972).

4. Such responses to superego assault become characterological in socalled masochistic characters. Flugel (1945) described this form of character pathology in the character Arkad in Dostoevsky's *Raw Youth* (1875), who says of himself:

Strange to say, I always had, perhaps from my earliest childhood, one characteristic: if I were ill treated, absolutely wronged and insulted to the last degree, I always showed at once an irresistible desire to submit passively to the insult, and even to accept more than my assailant wanted to inflict on me, as though I would say: "All right, you have humiliated me, so I will humiliate myself even more; look and enjoy it." (p. 80)

5. Superego sadism directed against the self can also find expression in forms of ascetical practice, even when based on sincere and devoted religious motivation. See Flugel's (1945) extended discussion of variants of asceticism and their relation to masochistic themes.

6. See my further discussion of the uses of humor in psychoanalytic therapy (Meissner 1999c).

7. Kafka (1990) makes a point of the role of superego in buffering effects of trauma and salvaging self-esteem—I would add that such effects are rarely simply superego effects but require integration of ego and superego. However, Kafka regards superego as *the* agent of morality.

8. These vicissitudes of the mother-child relation are particularly relevant to the rapprochement crisis (Mahler, Pine, and Bergman 1975). Observers of toddler behavior have noted patterns of identification related to resolution of the rapprochement crisis (Bergman and Fahey 1996; Mahler and McDevitt 1982). See also Furer (1967) and Arlow (1982).

9. See the evaluation of Gilligan's approach in Rosen and Zickler (1996).

10. This is more-or-less synonymous with Broad's (1940) wider sense of "conscience," which he distinguished from more particular obligations, whether teleological (increasing the good in the world) or non-teleological (keeping promises). Ryle (1940) followed a narrower sense by which conscience involves applying moral convictions in the face of temptation. R. Rorty (1991) appeals to conscience as the source of civic virtue and the claim to human dignity and rights.

11. Perry (1926) referred to this as the "imperious will," analogous to the authoritarian conscience.

12. Freud was not unaware of the anticipatory role of conscience, but attributed it to ego as an intellective activity endeavoring to calculate consequences of a proposed line of future conduct (1940). Wilder (1973) modified Freud's view by postulating superego regulation of pain-pleasure, also in the future. I would attribute this function not simply to ego, but to ego and superego functioning integratedly.

13. We need to consider the issue of antecedent or consequent to what. McGuire (1961), for example, regarded shame and guilt appropriately as always consequent to moral judgment; but, consistent with the present distinction, this would be antecedent to the moral act itself.

14. In my terms, it is the reaction of the self. See Meissner (1986c, 1993).
15. Fromm (1947) noted that although these forms of conscience can be radically distinguished, they can exist in combined forms in most people. Fromm (1955) also commented on derivation of a more developed conscience from parental figures—"the positive aspects of the patriarchal complex are reason, discipline, conscience and individualism; the negative aspects are hierarchy, oppression, inequality, submission. . . . But there is not only a *fatherly* but also a *motherly conscience;* there is a voice which tells us to do our duty, and a voice which tells us to love and to forgive—others as well as ourselves" (p. 47).
16. This engages the issue of responsibility—what I can be held responsible for and what not, and in what sense. See the discussion of responsibility in chapter 10.
17. Renik (1993) made the case that subjectivity in human affairs is universal and irreducible. The same argument has appropriate application to judgments of conscience. However, the hegemony of subjectivity does not rule out forms and degrees of objectivity. See Cavell's (1998) objections to Renik's epistemology and my own exploration of related issues in Meissner (2000d, 2001).
18. Odier (1943) distinguished genuine from false or pseudomoral conscience. Psychoanalytic insights into superego functions have contributed to increasing acknowledgment of a level of infantile morality along with mature conscience in adults. The differentiation of superego from conscience was also endorsed by Hunter (1963) and Jones (1966). Garnett (1965) also distinguished critical from traditional conscience, the former corresponding to superego or authoritarian conscience and the latter to moral or humanistic conscience. Glaser (1971) discussed the distinction of superego and conscience within a moral theological perspective. Some distinguish conscience as conscious and superego as unconscious (R. J. Campbell 1971; Smith 1969). Superego does operate more on an unconscious than a conscious level, and conscience more on a conscious than unconscious level, but the dichotomy is too stark. I would prefer a view of both operating, to varying degrees and in varying contexts, on both conscious and unconscious terms. For example, the ethical decision process may take place on an unconscious or preconscious level. Many analysts have recognized conscience without distinguishing it from superego.
19. Attempts to define such terms, especially after G. E. Moore's (1903) critique of the concept of "good," have been unsatisfactory. Similarly *ought* is a basic term that cannot be analyzed or defined in any other terms, but whose meaning is rooted in our experience (Ewing 1962)—even if we cannot define it, we still know what it means.

20. Insistence on rules as central to understanding morality is common—see Wright (1971), for example—but this may be a kantian residue and does not reflect the full scope of ethical reflection.

21. Beres (1966) distinguished a "sense of guilt" from guilt feelings. The latter would belong to superego, the former implying a more complex moral assessment and judgment based on superego and ego acting in concert. On the integration of ego, superego, and id in guilt, see Stein's (1972) comments.

22. Buber (1965) charged Freud with denying real guilt, but the difference may be more a matter of emphasis. Freud disavowed the "higher" moral concerns in favor of unconscious guilt largely connected with infantile dynamics. He never denied a realm of guilt beyond the neurotic. His comments distinguishing neurotic guilt from criminal guilt (1906) also suggest differentiation of real from unconscious and fantasy guilt. See Lewis (1947), Wallace (1986b), and Paul (1947).

23. Such consciences may also have an egoistic bent, distinct from the implicit altruism of the humanistic conscience. Their guilt may show more concern for self-failure or narcissistic self-depletion than real concern for any pain or injury caused to others (Deigh 1984).

24. Remorse would only seem possible when we have done injury to someone we care about, love, or feel responsibility toward (Deigh 1984). This aspect of Klein's depressive position can have anticipatory links to altruism and to a humanistic conscience.

25. These descriptive differentiations between authoritarian and humanistic consciences tend to parallel the differences noted previously (chapter 11 and in this chapter) between male and female superegos; for experimental data supporting this association developmentally see Hoffman (1975).

26. Pace Lamb (1983) who regards shame as always conscious and guilt as not necessarily so.

CHAPTER 13. CHARACTER AND VIRTUE

1. I insist on integration of values, virtues, and vices as constitutive of psychoanalytic concepts of character, and as bridging concepts between analytic perspectives and ethical concerns.

2. Terms like *stable* or *enduring* have only relative connotation. While there are continuities in development from childhood to adulthood, there are also discontinuities. Changes in character are common during adolescence, and while some adult patients report similarities in themselves from childhood, others observe how much they have changed.

As Abrams (1992) put it, "Character traits abide over time—more or less, yes and no" (p. 257).

3. Baudry (in Panel 1983) questioned whether there was "a nonphenomenological inner organization corresponding to the outer façade which we can identify as a structure on a somewhat different plane from that of the ego, id, and superego?" (p. 213). My appeal to a supraordinate concept of the self may provide one possible answer.

4. For a suggestive study of the influence of culture on character structure, possibly along lines suggested by Fromm, see Draguns's (1974) discussion of the influence of the Protestant ethic.

5. Rieff (1959) pointed out the tautology in Fromm's view: "And here the whole system of neo-Freudian tautologies is exposed. See Fromm, *Man for Himself* (1947, p. 49): "The mature, productive, rational person will choose a system [of belief] which permits him to be mature, productive, rational" (p. 60).

6. Questions regarding classification and definition of character and character traits remain in flux. Current views lean preferentially toward an empirical approach, as exemplified in Schlesinger (1992) and McLean (1992), keeping lines of inquiry open rather than foreclosing further inquiry (Abrams 1992).

7. The distinction is similar to that between authoritarian versus humanistic conscience (see chapter 12).

8. Boesky (in Panel 1983) challenged Baudry's view of character as supraordinate and related to the ego, on the basis of conflicts in deriving traits from each of the three major functional systems. Reconciliation of character as supraordinate with the tripartite entities was impossible, he thought, because they occupy totally different frames of reference. In my view, that knife cuts both ways. It is precisely differences in frame of reference that call for different supraordinate sets of concepts since the tripartite entities disparately fall short of encompassing the data. This perspective remains controversial, but at the same time, accepting Boesky's comments on the difficulties of developing a character typology, character traits are used extensively in the descriptive typology of DSM-III, III-R, and IV, especially in area II personality disorders.

9. See my discussion of identity and its relation to the concept of the self in Meissner (2000e).

10. Freud paid little or no attention to them; the only reference to "virtue" in the index of the *Standard Edition* is to the *Three Essays on the Theory of Sexuality* (1905c) where Freud remarked, "The multifariously perverse sexual disposition of childhood can accordingly be regarded as the source of a number of our virtues, in so far as through reaction-formation it stimulates their development" (p. 239).

11. The cardinal virtues were originally stoic in inspiration (Long and Sedley 1987), and have persisted in Western philosophical tradition ever since.

12. See Rawls's (1971) view of distributive justice as pertaining to what the nonaltruistic individual, even though motivated by self-interest, would choose for society. Difficulties and controversies over Rawls's theory are discussed in Barry (1973), especially his view of justice as fairness. For a somewhat different approach, see Rescher (1966).

CHAPTER 14. VALUES

1. These basic distinctions are followed by Flugel (1945) and Ramzy (1972) among other analysts.

2. See also Macklin (1973), who admits that "the distinction is exceedingly difficult to maintain in a rigorous way, both in the explication of psychoanalytic concepts and in the application of those concepts to persons in identifying and treating mental illness" (p. 133). See also M. B. Smith's (1980) related comments.

3. I regard values as subjective in that they constitute elements in the formation of the subjective self and as an integal component of the ethical agent; this does not gainsay a degree of objectivity in the reference of values in relation to real contexts of decision and action. A good example of dialogue between psychotherapist and ethicist can be found in Egenter and Matussek (1967).

4. Schafer (1994) also recognizes values in psychoanalysis that reflect the power of cultural conventions and cannot be discarded without violence to the nature of analysis. Schafer (1974) had previously noted an implicit evolutionary value-system in Freud's thinking, a brand of natural law ethics. Person (1982) also argued that no cultural enterprise, including psychoanalysis, can be value-free, noting particularly the value-bias in Freud's views of feminine sexuality and psychology. See Blum's (1976a) proposals regarding the feminine ego-ideal, and Guttman's (1983) discussion of values related to mothering. On differences in male-female value-systems, see Rokeach (1973).

5. In *The Uncommitted* (1965) and in *Young Radicals* (1968) Keniston provided a series of studies documenting the adolescent struggles over identity and the assimilation of values.

6. Analysts have generally acknowledged the motivational aspect of values. See Greenbaum (1980).

7. This would correspond to Winnicott's (1960) "true self."

8. Unconscious intentionality has been a stumbling block for value theorists, especially Perry (1926).

References

Abel, D. C. 1989. *Freud on Instinct and Morality*. Albany: State University of New York Press.

Abrams, S. 1992. Confronting dilemmas in the study of character. *Psychoan. Study Child*, 47: 253–262.

Adler, M. 1958–1961. *The Idea of Freedom*. 2 vols. New York: Doubleday.

Aichhorn, A. 1925. *Wayward Youth*. New York: Viking, 1935.

Aquinas, T. 1945. *Basic Writings of Saint Thomas Aquinas*. 2 vols. ed. A. C. Pegis. New York: Random House.

Arieti, S. 1972. Volition and value: a study based on catatonic schizophrenia. In *Moral Values and the Superego Concept in Psychoan.*, ed. S. C. Post. New York: International Universities Press, 275–288.

Arlow, J. A. 1959. Psychoanalysis as scientific method. In *Psychoanalysis, Scientific Method, and Philosophy*, ed. S. Hook. New York: New York University Press, 201–211.

———. 1982. Problems of the superego concept. *Psychoan. Study Child*, 37: 229–244.

———., and Brenner, C. 1964. *Psychoanalytic Concepts and the Structural Theory*. New York: International Universities Press.

Arnold, M. B. 1960. *Emotion and Personality*. 2 vols. New York: Columbia University Press.

Aronfreed, J. 1961. The nature, variety, and social patterning of moral responses to transgression. *J. Abn. Soc. Psychol.*, 63: 223–240.

———. 1968. *Conduct and Conscience: The Socialization of Internalized Control over Behavior*. New York: Academic.

Aronson, E., and Mettee, D. R. 1968. Dishonest behaviour as a function of differential levels of induced self-esteem. *J. Pers. Soc. Psychol.*, 9: 121–127.

Austin, J. L. 1970. A plea for excuses. In *J. L.Austin: Philosophical Papers*, eds. J. O. Urmson and G. J. Warnock. London: Oxford University Press, 175–294.

Badcock, C. R. 1986. *The Problem of Altruism.* New York: Blackwell.

Barry, B. 1973. *The Liberal Theory of Justice.* Oxford: Clarendon Press.

Barton, A. H. 1962. Measuring the values of individuals. In *Review of Recent Research Bearing on Religious and Character Formations.* [*Relig. Educ.*, Suppl.]: 82–97.

Basch, M. F. 1979. An operational definition of the "self." Paper presented at the Boston Psychoanalytic Society and Institute, 16 November 1979.

Baudry, F. 1984. Character: a concept in search of an identity. *J. Amer. Psychoan. Assn.*, 32: 455–477.

———. 1989. Character, character type, and character organization. *J. Amer. Psychoan. Assn.*, 37: 655–686.

Benfari, R., and Calogeras, R. C. 1968. Levels of cognition and conscience typologies. *J. Proj. Techniques and Personal Assessment*, 32: 466–474.

Benjamin, J. 1988. *Bonds of Love.* New York: Pantheon Books.

Beres, D. 1966. Superego and depression. In *Psychoanalysis—A General Psychology*, eds. R. M. Loewenstein, L. M. Newman, M. Schur, and A. J. Solnit. New York: Int. Universities Press, 479–498.

Bieber, I. 1972. Morality and Freud's concept of the superego. In *Moral Values and the Superego Concept in Psychoanalysis,* ed. S.C. Post. New York: International Universities Press, 126–143.

Blasi, A. 1980. Bridging moral cognition and moral action: a critical review of the literature. *Psychol. Bull.*, 88: 1–45.

Blum, H. P. 1976a. Masochism, the ego ideal, and the psychology of women. *J. Amer. Psychoan. Assn.*, 24 [Suppl.]: 157–191.

———. ed. 1976b. Female Psychology. *J. Amer. Psychoan. Assn.*, 24 [Suppl.].

Bornstein, B. 1951. On latency. *Psychoan. Study Child*, 6: 279–285.

Bourke, V. J. 1964. *Will in Western Thought: An Historico-Critical Survey.* New York: Sheed and Ward.

Bowman, M. R. 1996. On the idea of natural science as a resistance to psychoanalysis. *Psychoan. Contemp. Thought*, 19: 371–402.

Bradley, F. H. 1951. *Ethical Studies: Selected Essays.* New York: Liberal Arts Press.

Brakel, L. A. W., and Snodgrass, M. 1998. From the brain, the cognitive laboratory, and the couch. *J. Amer. Psychoan. Assn.*, 46: 897–920.

Brandt, R. B. 1967. Hedonism. In *The Encyclopedia of Philosophy.* Vol. 3. ed. P. Edwards. New York: Macmillan, 432–435.

Breen, H. J. 1986. A psychoanalytic approach to ethics. *J. Amer. Acad. Psychoan.*, 14: 255–275.

Brenner, C. 1982. *The Mind in Conflict.* New York: International University Press.

Bretall, R., ed. 1946. *A Kierkegaard Anthology.* Princeton, NJ: Princeton University Press, 1973.

Breuer, J., and Freud, S. 1893–1895. Studies on hysteria. *Standard Edition* 2.

Brickman, A. S. 1983. Pre-oedipal development of the superego. *Int. J. Psychoan.*, 64: 83–92.

Brierly, M. 1951. *Trends in Psychoanalysis.* London: Hogarth Press.

Brissett, D., and Oldenburg, R. 1982. Friendship: an exploration and appreciation of ambiguity. *Psychiatry*, 45: 325–335.

Broad, C. D. 1940. Conscience and conscientious action. In *Conscience*, eds. J. Donnelly and L. Lyons. New York: Alba House, 1973, 5–23.

Buber, M. 1958. *I and Thou.* 2d ed. New York: C. Scribner's Sons.

———. 1965. *The Knowledge of Man.* New York: Harper.

Buchsbaum, H. K., and Emde, R. N. 1990. Play narratives in 36-month-old children: early moral development and family relationships. *Psychoan. Study Child*, 45: 129–156.

Buie, D. H., Meissner, W. W., Rizzuto, A.-M., and Sashin, J. I. 1983. Aggression in the psychoanalytic situation. *Int. Rev. Psychoan.*, 10: 159–170.

———., ———., and Rizzuto, A.-M. 1996. The role of aggression in sado-masochism. *Canadian J. Psychoan.*, 4: 1–27.

Bultmann, R. 1958. *Jesus and the Word.* New York: C. Scribner's Sons.

Bursztajn, H., Feinbloom, R. I., Hamm, R. M., and Brodsky, A. 1981. *Medical Choices, Medical Chances: How Patients, Families, and Physicians Can Cope with Uncertainty.* New York: Dell Publishing.

Campbell, D. T. 1965. Ethnocentric and other altruistic motives. In *Nebraska Symposium on Motivation: 1965*, ed. D. Levine. Lincoln: University of Nebraska Press.

———. 1975. On the conflicts between biological and social evolution and between psychology and moral tradition. *Amer. Psychologist*, 30: 1103–1126.

Campbell, R. J. 1971. Superego and conscience. In *Conscience: Its Freedom and Limitations*, ed. W. C. Bier, S. J. New York: Fordham University Press, 82–91.

Cavell, M. 1998. Brief communication: in response to Owen Renik's "The analyst's subjectivity and the analyst's objectivity." *Int. J. Psychoan.*, 79: 1195–1202.

Chasseguet-Smirgel, J. 1975. *The Ego Ideal: A Psychoanalytic Essay on the Malady of the Ideal.* New York: Norton, 1985.

Chomsky, N. 1959. Review of *Verbal Behavior* by B. F. Skinner. *Language*, 35: 26–58.

Comfort, A. 1972. Review of *Beyond Freedom and Dignity* by B. F. Skinner. *The Human Context*, 4: 446–455.

Compton, A. 1983. The current status of the psychoanalytic theory of instinctual drives. 2. The relation of the drive concept to structures, regulatory principles, and objects. *Psychoan. Quart.*, 52: 402–426.

Conn, W. E. 1981. *Conscience: Development and Self-Transcendence.* Birmingham: Religious Education Press.

Cox, H., ed. 1968. *The Situation Ethics Debate.* Philadelphia: Westminster Press.

Darwin, C. 1872. *The Expression of the Emotions in Animals and Man.* Chicago: University of Chicago Press, 1965.

Deigh, J. 1984. Remarks on some difficulties in Freud's theory of moral development. *Int. Rev. Psychoan.*, 11: 207–225.

Dennett, D. C. 1991. *Consciousness Explained.* Boston: Little, Brown.

Dewey, J. 1920. *Reconstruction in Philosophy.* New York: Holt.

———. 1922. *Human Nature and Conduct.* New York: Holt.

———. 1929. *The Quest for Certainty.* New York: Minton, Balch.

———. 1939. *Theory of Valuation.* Chicago: University Chicago Press.

Dineen, S. J., J. A. 1971. Freedom of conscience in philosophical perspective. In *Conscience: Its Freedom and Limitations*, ed. W. C. Bier, S. J. New York: Fordham University Press, 101–106.

Dodd, C. H. 1951. *Gospel and Law.* New York: Columbia University Press.

Doi, T. 1989. The concept of *amae* and its psychoanalytic implications. *Int. Rev. Psychoan.*, 16: 349–354.

Donnellan, K. S. 1967. Reasons and causes. In *The Encyclopedia of Philosophy*. Vol. 7. ed. P. Edwards, New York: Macmillan, 85–88.

Dostoevsky, F. 1875. *A Raw Youth.* New York: Dell Publishing, 1961.

Doty, S. C. 1995. *Poesis/Noesis*: the postmodern question of the ethical. *Adducere II*. Denver: Regis University Press, 109–122.

Draguns, J. G. 1974. Values reflected in psychopathology: the case of the protestant ethic. *Ethos*, 2: 115–136.

Eagle, M. N. 1987. The psychoanalytic and the cognitive unconscious. In *Theories of the Unconscious and Theories of the Self*, ed. R. Stern. Hillsdale, NJ: Analytic Press, 155–189.

Eckardt, M. H. 1996. Fromm's humanistic ethics and the role of the prophet. In *A Prophetic Analyst: Erich Fromm's Contributions to Psychoanalysis*, eds. M. Cortina and M. Maccoby. Northvale, NJ: Jason Aronson, 151–165.

Egenter, R., and Matussek, P. 1967. *Moral Problems and Mental Health.* New York: Alba House.

Eisnitz, A. J. 1974. On the metapsychology of narcissistic pathology. *J. Amer. Psychoan. Assn.*, 22: 279–291.

Emde, R. N. 1992. Individual meaning and increasing complexity: contributions of Sigmund Freud and René Spitz to developmental psychology. *Dev. Psychol.*, 28: 347–359.

———, Johnson, W. F., and Esterbrooks, M. A. 1988. The do's and don'ts of early moral development: psychoanalytic tradition and current research. In *The Emergence of Morality,* eds. J. Kagan and S. Lamb. Chicago: University of Chicago Press, 245–277.

Erikson, E. H. 1950. *Childhood and Society.* Rev. ed. New York: Norton, 1963.

———. 1956. The problem of ego identity. *J. Amer. Psychoan. Assn.,* 4: 56–121.

———. 1959. *Identity and the Life Cycle.* New York: International Universities Press [Psychol. Issues, Monogr. 1].

———. 1964. *Insight and Responsibility.* New York: Norton.

———. 1969. *Gandhi's Truth: On the Origins of Militant Non-Violence.* New York: Norton.

Erwin, E. 1988. Psychoanalysis and self-deception. In *Perspectives on Self-Deception,* eds. B. P. McLaughlin and A. O. Rorty. Berkeley: University of California Press, 228–245.

Esman, A. H. 1972. Adolescence and the consolidation of values. In *Moral Values and the Superego Concept in Psychoanalysis,* ed. S. C. Post. New York: International Universities Press, 87–100.

———. 1985. Neglected classics. *Psychoan. Quart.,* 54: 66–69.

Ewing, A. C. 1947. Different meanings of "good"and "ought." In *Readings in Ethical Theory,* eds. W. Sellars and J. Hospers. New York: Appleton-Century-Crofts, 1952, 210–230.

———. 1962. *Ethics.* New York: Collier Books.

Falk, W. D. 1947–1948. "Ought" and motivation. In *Readings in Ethical Theory,* eds. W. Sellars and J. Hospers. New York: Appleton-Century-Crofts, 1952, 492–510.

Farber, L. 1966. *The Ways of the Will: Essays toward a Psychology and Psychopathology of Will.* New York: Basic.

Federn, P. 1952. *Ego Psychology and the Psychoses.* New York: Basic.

Fenichel, O. 1945. *The Psychoanalytic Theory of Neurosis.* New York: Norton.

Fenichel, O. 1954. *The Collected Papers of Otto Fenichel.* 2d series. New York: David Lewis.

Ferenczi, S. 1924. *Thalassa: A Theory of Genitality.* New York: Norton, 1968.

———. 1925. Psycho-analysis of sexual habits. In *Further Contributions to the Theory and Technique of Psycho-Analysis.* London: Hogarth Press, 1927.

Fingarette, H. 1955. Psychoanalytic perspectives on moral guilt and responsibility: a re-evaluation. *Phil. Phenomenol. Res.,* 16: 18–36.

Fisher, A. 1961. Freud and the image of man. In *Foundations for a Psychology of Grace,* ed. W. W. Meissner, S. J. Glen Rock, NJ: Paulist Press, 1966, 124–152.

Fletcher, J. 1967. *Moral Responsibility: Situation Ethics at Work.* Philadelphia: Westminster Press.

Flugel, J. C. 1945. *Man, Morals and Society*. New York: International Universities Press.

Forer, L. G. 1980. Moral failures of the legal system. *Bull. Menninger Clin.*, 44: 457–481.

Frank, C., and Weiss, H. 1996. The origins of disquieting discoveries by Melanie Klein: the possible significance of the case of 'Erna.' *Int. J. Psychoan.*, 77: 1101–1126.

Freud, A. 1937. *The Ego and the Mechinisms of Defense*. In *The Writings of Anna Freud*. Vol. 2. Rev. ed. New York: International Universities Press, 1966.

———. 1965. *Normality and Pathology in Childhood: Assessments of Development*. In *The Writings of Anna Freud*. Vol. 6. New York: International Universities Press, 1973.

———. 1967. About losing and being lost. *Psychoan. Study Child*, 22: 9–19.

Freud, E. L. ed. 1975. *Letters of Sigmund Freud*. New York: Basic.

Freud, S. 1891. *On Aphasia*. New York: International Universities Press, 1953.

———. 1950 [1892–1899]. Extracts from the Fliess papers. *Standard Edition* 1: 173–280.

———. 1894. The neuro-psychoses of defence. *Standard Edition* 3: 41–68.

———. 1895. Project for a scientific psychology. *Standard Edition* 1: 281–397.

———. 1896. Further remarks on the defense neuro-psychoses. *Standard Edition* 3: 157–185.

———. 1900. The interpretation of dreams. *Standard Edition* 4 and 5.

———. 1901. The psychopathology of everyday life. *Standard Edition* 6.

———. 1905a. Fragment of an analysis of a case of hysteria. *Standard Edition* 7: 1–122.

———. 1905b. On psychotherapy. *Standard Edition* 7: 255–268.

———. 1905c. Three essays on the theory of sexuality. *Standard Edition* 7: 123–245.

———. 1906. Psycho-analysis and the establishment of the facts in legal proceedings. *Standard Edition* 9: 103–114.

———. 1907. Obsessive actions and religious practices. *Standard Edition* 9: 115–127.

———. 1908a. Character and anal erotism. *Standard Edition* 9: 167–175.

———. 1908b. Creative writers and day-dreaming. *Standard Edition* 9: 141–153.

———. 1909a. Analysis of a phobia in a five-year-old boy. *Standard Edition* 10: 1–149.

———. 1909b. Five lectures on psychoanalysis. *Standard Edition* 11: 1–55.

————. 1909c. Notes upon a case of obsessional neurosis. *Standard Edition* 10: 151–320.

————. 1910a. Five lectures on psychoanalysis. *Standard Edition* 11: 1–55.

————. 1910b. Leonardo da Vinci and a memory of his childhood. *Standard Edition* 11: 57–137.

————. 1911. Psychoanalytic notes on an autobiographical account of a case of paranoia (dementia paranoides). *Standard Edition* 12: 1–82.

————. 1912a. The dynamics of transference. *Standard Edition* 12: 97–108.

————. 1912b. Recommendations to physicians practising psychoanalysis. *Standard Edition* 12: 109–120.

————. 1912c. On the universal tendency to debasement in the sphere of love. *Standard Edition* 11: 179–190.

————. 1913b. Totem and taboo. *Standard Edition* 13: vii–162.

————. 1914a. On narcissism: an introduction. *Standard Edition* 14: 67–102.

————. 1914b. Remembering, repeating and working-though. *Standard Edition* 12: 145–156.

————. 1915a. Instincts and their vicissitudes. *Standard Edition* 14: 109–140.

————. 1915b. Observations on transference love. *Standard Edition* 12: 157–171.

————. 1915c. Thoughts for the times on war and death. *Standard Edition* 14: 273–302.

————. 1916. Some character-types met with in psychoanalytic work. *Standard Edition* 14: 309–333.

————. 1916–1917. Introductory lectures on psychoanalysis. *Standard Edition* 15, 16.

————. 1917. Mourning and melancholia. *Standard Edition* 14: 237–260.

————. 1919a. 'A child is being beaten': a contribution to the study of the origin of sexual perversion. *Standard Edition* 17: 175–204.

————. 1919b. The "uncanny." *Standard Edition* 17: 217–256.

————. 1920a. Beyond the pleasure principle. *Standard Edition* 18: 1–64.

————. 1920b. The psychogenesis of a case of homosexuality in a woman. *Standard Edition* 18: 145–172.

————. 1921a. Group psychology and the analysis of the ego. *Standard Edition* 18: 65–143.

————. 1921b. Preface to J. J. Putnam's *Adresses on Psycho-analysis*. *Standard Edition* 18: 269–270.

————. 1923a. The ego and the id. *Standard Edition* 19: 1–66.

————. 1923b. Joseph Popper-Lynkeus and the theory of dreams. *Standard Edition* 19: 259–263.

———. 1923c. Two encyclopedia articles. *Standard Edition* 18: 233–259.

———. 1924a. The dissolution of the Oedipus complex. *Standard Edition* 19: 171–179.

———. 1924b. The economic problem of masochism. *Standard Edition* 19: 155–170.

———. 1924c [1923]. A short account of psychoanalysis. *Standard Edition* 19: 189–209.

———. 1925a [1924]. The resistances to psychoanalysis. *Standard Edition* 19: 211–224.

———. 1925b. Some additional notes on dream-interpretation as a whole. *Standard Edition* 19: 123–138.

———. 1925c. Some psychical consequences of the anatomical distinction between the sexes. *Standard Edition* 19: 241–258.

———. 1926. Inhibitions, symptoms and anxiety. *Standard Edition* 20: 75–175.

———. 1927a. The future of an illusion. *Standard Edition* 21: 1–56.

———. 1927b. Humour. *Standard Edition* 21; 159–166.

———. 1930. Civilization and its discontents. *Standard Edition* 21: 57–145.

———. 1932. The acquisition and control of fire. *Standard Edition* 22: 183–193.

———. 1933a. New introductory lectures. *Standard Edition* 22: 1–182.

———. 1933b. Why war? *Standard Edition* 22: 195–215.

———. 1937. Analysis terminable and interminable. *Standard Edition* 23: 209–253.

———. 1939. Moses and monotheism. *Standard Edition* 23: 1–137.

———. 1940. An outline of psychoanalysis. *Standard Edition* 23: 141–209.

Friedman, L. 1956. Psychoanalysis and the foundation of ethics. *J. of Philosophy*, 53: 15–20.

Fromm, E. 1941. *Escape from Freedom*. New York: Holt.

———. 1947. *Man for Himself: An Inquiry into the Psychology of Ethics*. New York: Holt.

———. 1955. *The Sane Society*. New York: Rinehart.

———. 1956. *The Art of Loving*. New York: Harper.

Furer, M. 1967. Some developmental aspects of the superego. *Int. J. Psychoan.*, 48: 277–280.

———. 1972. The history of the superego concept in psychoanalysis: a review of the literature. In *Moral Values and the Superego Concept in Psychoanalysis*, ed. S. C. Post. New York: International Universities Press, 11–62.

Furman, E. 1982. Mothers have to be there to be left. *Psychoan. Study Child*, 37: 15–28.

———. 1992. *Toddlers and Their Mothers*. Madison, CT: International Universities Press.

———. 1994. Early aspects of mothering: what makes it so hard to be there to be left. *J. Child Psychother.*, 20: 149–164.

———. 1996. On motherhood. *J. Amer. Psychoan. Assn.*, 44 (Suppl.): 429–447.

Fuss, P. 1963–1964. Conscience. In *Conscience*, eds. J. Donnelly and L. Lyons. New York: Alba House, 1973, 35–50.

Garnett, A. C. 1965. Conscience and conscientiousness. In *Conscience*, eds. J. Donnelly and L. Lyons. New York: Alba House, 1973, 205–220.

Gay, P. 1988. *Freud: A Life for Our Times*. New York: Norton.

Gaylin, W. 1974. On the borders of persuasion: a psychoanalytic look at coercion. *Psychiatry*, 37: 1–9.

Gedo, J. E. 1983. *Portraits of the Artist: Psychoanalysis of Creativity and Its Vicissitudes*. New York: Guilford.

———., and Gedo, M.M. 1992. *Perspectives on Creativity: The Biographical Method*. Norwood, NJ: Ablex Publishing Co.

Gilligan, C. 1977. In a different voice: women's conception of the self and of morality. *Harvard Educ. Rev.*, 47: 481–517.

———. 1980. The effects of social institutions on the moral development of children and adolescents. *Bull. Menninger Clin.*, 44: 498–523.

———. 1982. *In a Different Voice: Psychological Theory and Women's Development*. Cambridge: Harvard University Press.

Gillman, R. 1982. Preoedipal and early oedipal components of the superego. *Psychoan. Study Child*, 37: 273–281.

Giovacchini, P. L. 1980. Sanity and the quest for values. *Bull. Menninger Clin.*, 44: 562–583.

Glaser, S. J., J. W. 1971. Conscience and superego: a key distinction. *Theol. Stud.*, 32: 30–47.

Goodenough, F. L. 1930. *Anger in Young Children*. Minneapolis: University of Minnesota Press.

Granrose, J. T. 1970. The authority to conscience. In *Conscience*, eds. J. Donnelly and L. Lyons. New York: Alba House, 1973, 221–235.

Greenacre, P. 1945. Conscience in the psychopath. *Amer. J. Orthopsychiat.*, 15: 495–509.

———. 1948. Anatomical structure and superego development. *Amer. J. Orthopsychiat.*, 18: 636–648.

Greenbaum, H. 1980. Human values and psychoanalysis. *J. Amer. Acad. Psychoan.*, 8: 353–368.

Gregory, I. 1975. Psycho-analysis, human nature and human conduct. In *Nature and Conduct*, ed. R. S. Peters. New York: St. Martin's, 99–120.

Grinberg, L. 1964. Two kinds of guilt—their relations with normal and pathological aspects of mourning. *Int. J. Psychoan.*, 45: 366–372.

Grossman, W. I. 1992. Hierarchies, boundaries, and representation in the Freudian model of mental organization. *J. Amer. Psychoan. Assn.*, 40: 27–62.

Grunberger, B. 1971. *Narcissism: Psychoanalytic Essays*. New York: International Universities Press, 1979.

Gutkin, D. C. 1973. An analysis of the concept of moral intentionality. *Human Dev.*, 16: 371–381.

Guttman, H. A. 1983. Autonomy and motherhood. *Psychiatry*, 46: 230–235.

Hale Jr., N. G. ed. 1971. *James Jackson Putnam and Psychoanalysis*. Cambridge: Harvard University Press.

Hallett, G. 1989. *Christian Neighbor-Love: An Assessment of Six Rival Versions*. Washington, DC: Georgetown University Press.

Hamilton, W. D. 1963. The evolution of altruistic behavior. *Amer. Naturalist*, 97: 354–356.

———. 1964. The genetic evolution of social behavior. *J. Theor. Biol.*, 12 12–45.

———. 1971. Selection of selfish and altruistic behavior in some extreme models. In *Man and Beast: Comparative Social Behavior*, eds. J. F. Eisenberg, and W. S. Dillon. Washington, DC: Smithsonan Institute Press.

Hampshire, S. 1959. *Thought in Action*. London: Chatto and Windus.

Hanly, C. 1979. *Existentialism and Psychoanalysis*. New York: International Universities Press.

Hare, R. M. 1964. *The Language of Morals*. New York: Oxford University Press.

Hartmann, E. 1966. The psychophysiology of free will: an example of vertical research. In *Psychoanalysis—A General Psychology*, eds. R. M. Loewenstein, L. M. Newman, M. Schur, and A. J. Solnit. New York: International Universities Press, 521–536.

Hartmann, H. 1939. *Ego Psychology and the Problem of Adaptation*. New York: International Universities Press, 1958.

———. 1947. On rational and irrational action. In *Essays on Ego Psychology*. New York: International Universities Press, 1964, 37–68.

———. 1950. Comments on the psychoanalytic theory of the ego. In *Essays on Ego Psychology*. New York: International Universities Press, 1964, 115–141.

———. 1960. *Moral Values in Psychoanalysis*. New York: International University Press.

———., and Loewenstein, R. M. 1962. Notes on the superego. *Psychoan. Study Child*, 17: 42–81.

Hartshorne, H., and May, M. A. 1928–1930. *Studies in the Nature of Character. Vol. 1: Studies in Deceit; Vol. 2: Studies in Service and Self-*

control; Vol. 3: *Studies in Organization of Character*. New York: Macmillan.

Havighurst, R. J., Robinson, M. Z., and Dorr, M. 1946. The development of the ideal self in childhood and adolescence. *J. Educ. Res.*, 40: 241–257.

Hegeman, E. 1994. Worldview as cultural parataxis. *Contemp. Psychoan.*, 30: 424–441.

Heidegger, M. 1962. *Being and Time*. New York: Harper and Row.

Heimann, P. 1952. Certain functions of introjection and projection in early infancy. In *Developments in Psycho-Analysis*, ed. J. Riviere. London: Hogarth Press, 122–168.

Hiltner, S. 1980. Moral development as paradox. *Bull. Menninger Clin.*, 44: 441–456.

Hoffman, M. L. 1970. Conscience, personality, and socialization techniques. *Human Dev.*, 13: 90–126.

———. 1971. Identification and conscience development. *Child Dev.*, 42: 1071–1082.

———. 1975. Sex differences in moral internalization and values. *J. Pers. Soc. Psychol.*, 32: 720–729.

———. 1981. Is altruism part of human nature? *J. Pers. Soc. Psychol.*, 40: 121–137.

Hogan, R. 1970. A dimension of moral judgment. *J. Consult. Clin. Psychol.*, 35; 205–212.

———. 1973. Moral conduct and moral character: a psychological perspective. *Psychol. Bull.*, 79: 217–232.

Holder, A. 1982. Preoedipal contributions to the superego. *Psychoan. Study Child*, 37: 245–272.

Holland, M. F. 1976. Effects of moral maturity and essay structure on moral persuasion. *J. Pers.*, 44: 449–466.

Holstein, C. B. 1976. Irreversible, stepwise sequence in the development of moral judgment: a longitudinal study of males and females. *Child Dev.* 47: 51–61.

Holt, R. R. 1965. A Review of some of Freud's biological assumptions and their influence on his theories. In *Psychoanalysis and Current Biological Thought*. eds. N. S. Greenfield and W. C. Lewis. Madison: University Wisconsin Press, 93–124.

———. 1972. Freud's mechanistic and humanistic images of man. *Psychoan. Contemp. Sci.*, 1: 3–24.

———. 1976. Drive or wish? A reconsideration of the psychoanalytic theory of motivation. In *Psychology versus Metapsychology. Psychoanalytic Essays in Memory of George S. Klein*. New York: International Universities Press, 158–197 [Psychol. Issues, Monogr. 36].

Home, H. J. 1966. The concept of mind. *Int. J. Psychoan.*, 47: 42–49.

Horney, K. 1924. On the genesis of the castration complex in women. *Int. J. Psychoan.*, 5: 50–65.

———. 1950. *Neurosis and Human Growth*. New York: Norton.

Hospers, J. 1950. Free will and psychoanalysis. In *Readings in Ethical Theory*, eds. W. Sellars and J. Hospers. New York: Appleton-Century-Crofts, 1952, 560–575.

Hunter, J. F. M. 1963. Conscience. In *Conscience*, eds. J. Donnelly and L. Lyons. New York: Alba House, 1973, 55–84.

Isakower, O. 1939. On the exceptional position of the auditory sphere. *Int. J. Psychoan.*, 20: 340–348.

Jacobson, E. 1937. Wege der weiblichen Uber-Ich-Bildung. *Int. Z. für Psychan.*, 23: 402–412.

———. 1964. *The Self and the Object World*. New York: International Universities Press.

———. 1976. Ways of superego formation and the castration complex. *Psychoan. Quart.*, 45: 525–538.

James, W. 1890. *The Principles of Psychology*. 2 vols. New York: Dover, 1950.

———. 1891. The moral philosopher and the moral life. In *Essays on Faith and Morals*. New York: Meridian Books, 1962, 185–205.

Johnson, A. M. 1949. Sanctions for superego lacunae of adolescents. In *Searchlights on Delinquency*, ed. K. Eissler. New York: International Universities Press, 225–245.

———., and Szurek, S. A. 1952. The genesis of antisocial acting out in children and adults. *Psychoan. Quart.*, 21: 323–343.

Johnston, M. 1988. Self-deception and the nature of mind. In *Perspectives on Self-Deception*, eds. B. P. McLaughlin and A. O. Rorty. Berkeley: University of California Press, 63–91.

Jones, D. H. 1966. Freud's theory of moral conscience. In *Conscience*, eds. J. Donnelly and L. Lyons. New York: Alba House, 1973, 85–114.

Joseph, E. D. 1987. The consciousness of being conscious. *J. Amer. Psychoan. Assn.*, 35: 5–22.

Kafka, E. 1990. The uses of moral ideas in the mastery of trauma and in adaptation, and the concept of superego severity. *Psychoan. Quart.*, 59: 249–269.

Kant, I. 1781. *Critique of Pure Reason*. Garden City, NY: Doubleday, Anchor Books, 1966.

Keniston, K. 1965. *The Uncommitted: Alienated Youth in American Society*. New York: Dell Publishing Co.

———. 1968. *Young Radicals: Notes on Committed Youth*. New York: Harcourt, Brace and World.

Kennedy, H., and Yorke, C. 1982. Steps from outer to inner conflict viewed as superego precursors. *Psychoan. Study Child*, 37: 221–228.

Kenny, A. 1975. *Will, Freedom and Power*. Oxford: Basil Blackwell.

Kernberg, O. F. 1976. *Object Relations and Clinical Psychoanalysis*. New York: Jason Aronson.

———. 1996. The importance of diagnosis in facilitating the therapeutic action of psychodynamic psychotherapy of an adolescent. In *Understanding Therapeutic Action: Psychodynamic Concepts of Cure*, ed. L. E. Lifson. Hillsdale, NJ: Analytic Press, 51–68.

King, R. H. 1986. Self-realization and solidarity: Rorty and the judging self. In *Pragmatism's Freud: The Moral Disposition of Psychoanalysis*, eds. J. H. Smith and W. Kerrigan. Baltimore, MD: Johns Hopkins University Press, 28–51.

Kitayama, O. 1991. The wounded caretaker and guilt. *Int. Rev. Psychoan.*, 18: 229–238.

Klass, E. T. 1978. Psychological effects of immoral actions: the experimental evidence. *Psychol. Bull.*, 85: 756–771.

Klein, G. S. 1967. Peremptory ideation: structure and force in motivated ideas. In *Motives and Thought: Psychoanalytic Essays in Honor of David Rapaport*, ed. R. R. Holt. New York: International Universities Press, 80–128. [Psychol. Issues, Monogr. 18/19]

———. 1976a. Freud's two theories of sexuality. In *Psychology versus Metapsychology: Psychoanalytic Essays in Memory of George S. Klein*, eds. M.M. Gill and P.S. Holzman. New York: International Universities Press, 14–70 [Psychol. Issues, Monogr. 36].

———. 1976b. *Psychoanalytic Theory: An Exploration of Essentials*. New York: International Universities Press.

Kluckhohn, C. et al. 1962. Values and value-orientations in the theory of action: an exploration in definition and classification. In *Toward a General Theory of Action*, eds. T. Parsons and E. A. Shils. New York: Harper, 388–433.

Knapp, P. H. 1966. Libido: a latter-day look. *J. Nerv. Ment. Dis.*, 142: 395–417.

Knight, R. P. 1946. Determinism, "freedom" and psychotherapy. In *Psychoanalytic Psychiatry and Psychology*, ed. R. P. Knight. New York: International Universities Press, 365–381.

Kohlberg, L. 1964. Development of moral character and moral ideology. In *Rev. Child Dev. Res.* Vol. 1, eds. M. L. Hoffman and L. W. Hoffman. New York: Russell Sage Foundation.

———. 1969. Stage and sequence: the cognitive-developmental approach to socialization. In *Handbook of Socialization Theory and Research*, ed. D. A. Goslin. Chicago: Rand McNally.

──────. 1981. *The Philosophy of Moral Development*. San Francisco: Harper.

──────. 1984. *The Psychology of Moral Development*. San Francisco: Harper.

──────., and Kramer, R. 1969. Continuities and discontinuities in childhood and adult moral development. *Human Development*, 12: 93–120.

Kohut, H. 1966. Forms and transformations of narcissism. *J. Amer. Psychoan. Assn.*, 14: 243–272.

──────. 1971. *The Analysis of the Self*. New York: International Universities Press.

Kovel, J. 1982. Values, interests, and psychotherapy. *Amer. J. Psychoan.*, 42: 109–119.

Kramer, P. 1958. Note on one of the preoedipal roots of the superego. *J. Amer. Psychoan. Assn.*, 6: 38–46.

Kramer, S., and Rudolph, J. 1980. The latency stage. In *The Course of Life: Psychoanalytic Contributions Toward Understanding Personality Development. Vol. 2. Latency, Adolescence, and Youth*, eds. G. Pollock and S. Greenspan. Washington, DC: U.S. Government Printing Office, 109–119.

Krebs, D. L. 1970. Altruism—an examination of the concept and a review of the literature. *Psychol. Bull.*, 78: 258–302.

Kris, A. O. 1982. *Free Association: Method and Process*. New Haven, CT: Yale University Press.

──────. 1985. Resistance in convergent and in divergent conflicts. *Psychoan. Quart.*, 54: 537–568.

──────. 1988. Some clinical applications of the distinction between divergent and convergent conflicts. *Int. J. Psychoan.*, 69: 431–441.

Kris, E. 1952. *Psychoanalytic Explorations in Art*. New York: Schoken Books.

Lacan, J. 1927. *Ecrits: A Selection*. New York: Norton.

──────. 1992. *The Seminar of Jacques Lacan. Book 7: The Ethics of Psychoanalysis 1959–1960*, ed. J.-A. Miller. New York: Norton.

Lamb, R. E. 1983. Guilt, shame, and morality. *Phil. Phenomenol. Res.*, 43: 329–346.

Lampl-deGroot, J. 1962. Ego ideal and superego. *Psychoan. Study Child*, 17: 94–106.

──────. 1963. Symptom formation and character formation. *Int. J. Psychoan.*, 44: 1–11.

Laor, N. 1984. Common sense ethics and psychiatry. *Psychiatry*, 47: 135–150.

Laplanche, J., and Pontalis, J.-B. 1973. *The Language of Psychoanalysis*. New York: Norton.

Lasch, C. 1979. *The Culture of Narcissism.* New York: Norton.

Laufer, M. 1964. Ego ideal and pseudo ego ideal in adolescence. *Psychoan. Study Child,* 19: 196–221.

Leavy, S. A. 1994. Erich Fromm on psychoanalysis and ethics. *Contemp. Psychoan.,* 30: 442–445.

———. 1996a. Against "narcissism." *Psychoan. Contemp. Thought,* 19: 403–424.

———. 1996b. Review of J.-A. Miller ed. *The Seminar of Jacques Lacan: Book 7. The Ethics of Psychoanalysis 1992. J. Amer. Psychoan. Assn.,* 44: 1276–1281.

Levin, S. 1967. Some metapsychological considerationson the differentiation between shame and guilt. *Int. J. Psychoan.,* 48: 267–276.

Lewis, H. D. 1947. Guilt and freedom. In *Readings in Ethical Theory,* eds. W. Sellars and J. Hospers. New York: Appleton-Century-Crofts, 1952, 597–620.

Lewy, E. 1961. Responsibility, free will, and ego psychology. *Int. J. Psychoan.,* 42: 260–270.

Libet, B., Wright, E., and Gleason, C. 1982. Readiness potentials preceding unrestricted "spontaneous" vs. pre-planned voluntary acts. *Electroenceph. Clin. Neurophysiol.,* 54: 322–335.

———., Wright, E., Gleason, C., and Pearl, D. 1983. Time of conscious intention to act in relation to onset of cerebral activities readiness potential; the unconscious initiation of a freely voluntary act. *Brain,* 106: 623–642.

Lichtenberg, J. 1989. *Psychoanalysis and Motivation.* Hillsdale, NJ: Analytic Press.

Lively, E., Dinitz, S., and Reckless, W. 1962. Self concept as a predictor of juvenile delinquency. *Amer. J. Orthopsychiat.,* 32: 159–168.

Loewald, H. W. 1979. The waning of the Oedipus complex. In *Papers on Psychoanalysis.* New Haven, CT: Yale University Press, 1980., 384–404.

Loewenstein, R. M. 1966. On the theory of the superego: a discussion. In *Psychoanalysis—A General Psychology,* eds. R. M. Loewenstein, L. M. Newman, M. Schur, and A. J. Solnit. New York: International Universities Press, 298–314.

London, P., and Bower, R. K. 1968. Altruism, extraversion, and mental illness. *J. Soc. Psychol.,* 76: 19–30.

Long, A. A., and Sedley, D. N. 1987. *The Hellenistic Philosophers.* Vol. 1. Cambridge: Cambridge University Press.

Macklin, R. 1973. Values in psychoanalysis and psychotherapy: a survey and analysis. *Amer. J. Psychoan.,* 33: 133–150.

Madden, E. H. 1957. Psychoanalysis and moral judgeability. *Phil. Phenomenol. Res.,* 18: 68–79.

Mahler, M. S., and McDevitt, J. B. 1982. Thoughts on the emergence of the sense of self, with particular emphasis on the body self. *J. Amer. Psychoan. Assn.*, 30: 827–848.

Mahler, M. S., Pine, F., and Bergman, A. 1975. *The Psychological Birth of the Human Infant: Symbiosis and Individuation*. New York: Basic.

Mannarino, A. P. 1976. Friendship patterns and altruistic behavior in preadolescent males. *Dev. Psychol.*, 2: 555–556.

———. 1979. The relationship between friendship and altruism in preadolescent girls. *Psychiatry*, 42:280–284.

May, R. 1953. *Man's Search for Himself*. New York: New American Library, 1967.

———. 1969. *Love and Will*. New York: Norton.

McCarthy, D. 1971. Development of the normal conscience. In *Conscience: Its Freedom and Limitations*. ed. W. C. Bier, S. J. New York: Fordham University Press, 39–61.

McDevitt, J. B. 1979. The role of internalization in the development of object relations during the separation-individuation phase. *J. Amer. Psychoan. Assn.*, 27: 327–344.

McGuire, M. C. 1961. On conscience. In *Conscience*, eds. J. Donnelly and L. Lyons. New York: Alba House, 1973, 145–157.

McIntosh, D. 1993. Cathexes and their objects in the thought of Sigmund Freud. *J. Amer. Psychoan. Assn.*, 41: 679–709.

McKeon, R., ed. 1941. Ethica Nichomachea. *The Basic Works of Aristotle*. New York: Random, 935–1112.

McLaughlin, B. P. 1988. Exploring the possibility of self-deception in belief. In *Perspectives on Self-Deception*, eds. B. P. McLaughlin and A. O. Rorty. Berkeley: University of California Press, 29–62.

McLean, D. 1992. Maturational and experiential components of character formation. *Psychoan. Study Child*, 47: 235–252.

Meissner, S. J., W. W. 1970a. Erikson's truth: the search for ethical identity. *Theol. Stud.*, 31: 310–319.

———. 1970b. Notes on identification. 1. Origins in Freud. *Psychoan. Quart.*, 39: 563–589.

———. 1971. Notes on identification. 2. Clarification of related concepts. *Psychoan. Quart.*, 40: 277–302.

———. 1972. Notes on identification. 3. The concept of identification. *Psychoan. Quart.*, 41: 224–260.

———. 1974a. Differentiation and integration of learning and identification in the developmental process. *Ann. Psychoan.*, 2: 181–196.

———. 1974b. The role of imitative social learning in identificatory processes. *J. Amer. Psychoan. Assn.*, 22: 512–536.

———. 1978a. *The Paranoid Process*. New York: Jason Aronson.

———. 1978b. Psychoanalytic aspects of religious experience. *Ann. Psychoan.*, 6: 103–141.

———. 1981. *Internalization in Psychoanalysis*. New York: International Universities Press [Psychol. Issues, Monogr. 50].

———. 1983. Values in the psychoanalytic situation. *Psychoan. Inq.*, 3: 577–598.

———. 1984a. *The Borderline Spectrum: Differential Diagnosis and Developmental Issues*. New York: Jason Aronson.

———. 1984b. The cult phenomenon: psychoanalytic perspective. *Psychoan. Study Soc.*, 10: 91–111.

———. 1984c. *Psychoanalysis and Religious Experience*. New Haven, CT: Yale University Press.

———. 1985a. A case of phallic-narcissistic personality. *J. Amer. Psychoan. Assn.*, 33: 437–469.

———. 1985b. Psychoanalysis: the dilemma of science and humanism. *Psychoan. Inq.*, 5: 471–498.

———. 1986a. Some notes on Hartmann's ego psychology and the psycholgy of the self. *Psychoan. Inq.*, 6: 499–521.

———. 1986b. The Oedipus complex and the paranoid process. *Ann. Psychoan.*, 14: 221–243.

———. 1986c. Can psychoanalysis find its self? *J. Amer. Psychoan. Assn.*, 34: 379–400.

———. 1986d. *Psychotherapy and the Paranoid Process*. New York: Jason Aronson, 1994.

———. 1988a. The cult phenomenon and the paranoid process. *Psychoan. Study Soc.*, 12: 69–95.

———. 1988b. *Treatment of Patients in the Borderline Spectrum*. Northvale, NJ: Jason Aronson, 1995.

———. 1989. A note on psychoanalytic facts. *Psychoan. Inq.*, 9: 193–219.

———. 1991a. Aggression in phobic states. *Psychoan. Inq.*, 11: 261–283.

———. 1991b. *What Is Effective in Psychoanalytic Therapy: The Move from Interpretation to Relation*. Northvale, NJ: Jason Aronson.

———. 1992a. The concept of the therapeutic alliance. *J. Amer. Psychoan. Assn.*, 40: 1059–1087.

———. 1992b. *Ignatius of Loyola: The Psychology of a Saint*. New Haven, CT: Yale University Press.

———. 1993. Self-as-agent in psychoanalysis. *Psychoan. Contemp. Thought*, 16: 459–495.

———. 1995a. The economic principle in psychoanalysis. 1. Economics without energetics. *Psychoan. Contemp. Thought*, 18: 197–226.

———. 1995b. The economic principle in psychoanalysis. 2. Regulatory principles. *Psychoan. Contemp. Thought*, 18: 227–259.

———. 1995c. The economic principle in psychoanalysis. 3. Motivational principles. *Psychoan. Contemp. Thought*, 18: 261–292.

———. 1995d. *Thy Kingdom Come: Psychoanalytic Perspectives on the Messiah and the Millennium*. Kansas City, MO: Sheed and Ward.

———. 1996a. The self-as-object in psychoanalysis. *Psychoan. Contemp. Thought*, 19: 425–459.

———. 1996b. *The Therapeutic Alliance*, New Haven, CT: Yale University Press.

———. 1997. The self and the body. 1. The body-self and the body image. *Psychoan. Contemp. Thought*, 20: 419–448.

———. 1998a. Neutrality, abstinence, and the therapeutic alliance. *J. Amer. Psychoan. Assn.*, 46: 1089–1128.

———. 1998b. The self and the body. 2. The embodied self—self vs. non-self. *Psychoan. Contemp. Thought*, 21: 85–111.

———. 1998c. The self and the body. 3. The body image in clinical perspective. *Psychoan. Contemp. Thought*, 21: 113–146.

———. 1998d. The self and the body. 4. The body on the couch. *Psychoan. Contemp. Thought*, 21: 277–300.

———. 1999a. The dynamic principle in psychoanalysis. 1. The classic theory reconsidered. *Psychoan. Contemp. Thought*, 22: 3–40.

———. 1999b. The dynamic principle in psychoanalysis. 2. Toward a revised theory of motivation. *Psychoan. Contemp. Thought*, 22: 41–83.

———. 1999c. Humor is a funny thing: dimensions of the therapeutic relationship. In *Humor and Psyche: Psychoanalytic Perspectives*, ed. J. W. Barron. Hillsdale, NJ: Analytic Press, 131–158.

———. 1999d. The self-as-subject in psychoanalysis. 1. The nature of subjectivity. *Psychoan. Contemp. Thought*, 22: 155–201.

———. 1999e. The self-as-subject in psychoanalysis. 2. The subject in analysis. *Psychoan. Contemp. Thought*, 22: 383–428.

———. 2000a. *The Cultic Origins of Christianity: The Dynamics of Religious Development*. Collegeville, MN: Liturgical Press.

———. 2000b. *Freud and Psychoanalysis*. Notre Dame, IN: University of Notre Dame Press.

———. 2000c. The many faces of analytic interaction. *Psychoan. Psychol.*, 17: 512–546.

———. 2000d. Reflections on psychic reality. *Int. J. Psychoan.*, 81: 1117–1138.

———. 2000e. The self-as-person in psychoanalysis. *Psychoan. Contemp. Thought*, 23: 479–523.

———. 2000f. The self-as-relational in psychoanalysis. 1. Relational aspects of the self. *Psychoan. Contemp. Thought*, 23: 177–204.

————. 2000g. The self-as-relational in psychoanalysis. 2. The self as related within the analytic process. *Psychoan. Contemp. Thought*, 23: 205–247.

————. 2000h. The self as structural. *Psychoan. Contemp. Thought*, 23: 373–416.

————. 2000i. The structural principle in psychoanalysis. 1. The meaning of structure. *Psychoan. Contemp. Thought*, 23: 283–330.

————. 2000j. The structural principle in psychoanalysis. 2. Structure formation and structural change. *Psychoan. Contemp. Thought*, 23: 331–371.

————. 2001. Psychic reality in the psychoanalytic process. *J. Amer. Psychoan. Assn.*, 49: 855–890.

————. 2003. *The Therapeutic Alliance: A Vital Elelment in Clinical Practice*. Northvale, NJ: Jason Aronson.

————. in press. Friendship as a religious theme: psychoanalytic reflections.

————., Rizzuto, A.-M., Sashin, J., and Buie, D. H. 1987. A view of aggression in phobic states. *Psychoan. Quart.*, 56: 452–476.

Mendel, W. M. 1968. Responsibility in health, illness, and treatment. *Arch. Gen. Psychiat.*, 18: 697–705.

Meng, H., and Freud, E. L. eds. 1963. *Psychoanalysis and Faith: The Letters of Sigmund Freud and Oskar Pfister*. New York: Basic.

Menninger, K. 1973. *Whatever Became of Sin?* New York: Bantam Books, 1978.

Migone, P., and Liotti, G. 1998. Psychoanalysis and cognitive-evolutionary psychology: an attempt at integration. *Int. J. Psychoan.*, 79: 1071–1095.

Milgram, S. 1975. *Obedience to Authority: An Experimental View*. New York: Harper.

Miller, A. 1979. Depression and grandiosity as related forms of narcissistic disturbances. *Int. Rev. Psychoan.*, 6: 61–76.

Miller, S. B. 1989. Shame as an impetus to the creation of conscience. *Int. J. Psychoan.*, 70: 231–243.

Milrod, D. 1990. The ego ideal. *Psychoan. Study Child*, 45: 43–60.

Mitchell, J. J. 1975a. Moral dilemmas of early adolescence. *Adolescence*, 10: 442–446.

————. 1975b. Moral growth during adolescence. *Adolescence*, 10: 221–226.

Mitchell, S. A. 1993. *Hope and Dread in Psychoanalysis*. New York: Basic.

Money-Kyrle, R. E. 1952. Psychoanalysis and ethics. *Int. J. Psychoanal.*, 33: 225–234.

————. 1955. The anthropological and the psychoanalytic concept of the norm. *Psychoan. Soc. Sci.*, 4: 51–60.

———. 1961. *Man's Picture of His World.* New York: International Universities Press.

Moore, B. E. 1975. Toward a clarification of the concept of narcissism. *Psychoan. Study Child,* 30: 243–276.

———, and Fine, B. D. eds. 1990. *Psychoanalytic Terms and Comcepts.* New Haven, CT: Amer. Psychoanal. Assn. and Yale University Press.

Moore, G. E. 1903. *Principia Ethica.* London: Cambridge University Press, 1962.

———. 1912. *Ethics.* London: Oxford University Press, 1965.

Moran, F. M. 1993. *Subject and Agency in Psychoanalysis: Which Is to Be Master?* New York: New York University Press.

Morrison, A. P. 1989. *Shame: The Underside of Narcissism.* Hillsdale, NJ: Analytic Press.

Muller, J. P., and Richardson, W. J. 1982. *Lacan and Language: A Reader's Guide to* Écrits. New York: International Universities Press.

Murphy, L. B. 1937. *Social Behavior in Child Personality.* New York: Columbia University Press.

Murray, J. M. 1964. Narcissism and the ego ideal. *J. Amer. Psychoan. Assn.,* 12: 477–511.

Muslin, H. L. 1972. The superego in women. In *Moral Values and the Superego Concept in Psychoanalysis,* ed. S. C. Post. New York: International Universities Press, 101–125.

Naranjo, C. 1982. On puritanical character. *Amer. J. Psychoan.,* 42: 143–148.

Nass, M. L. 1966. The superego and moral development in the theories of Freud and Piaget. *Psychoan. Study Child,* 15: 51–68.

Neville, R. 1972. The limits of freedom and technologies of behaviour control. *The Human Context,* 4: 433–446.

Niebuhr, H. R. 1963. *The Responsible Self.* New York: Harper.

Nietzsche, F. W. 1887. "Guilt," "Bad conscience," and related matters. In *The Birth of Tragedy and the Geneology of Morals.* Garden City, NY: Doubleday, 1956, 189–230.

Novey, S. 1955. The role of the superego and ego-ideal in character formation. In *Readings in Psychoanalytic Psychology,* ed. M. Levitt. New York: Appleton-Century-Crofts, 1959, 114–123.

Nowell-Smith, P. H. 1954. The value of conscientiousness. In *Conscience,* eds. J. Donnelly and L. Lyons. New York: Alba House, 1973, 197–204.

Nunberg, H. 1932. *The Principles of Psychoanalysis.* New York: International Universities Press, 1955.

Odier, C. 1943. *Les deux sources consciente et unconsciente de la vie morale.* Neuchatel, Switzerland: Editions de la Baconniere, 1968.

Oldenquist, A. 1967. Choosing, deciding, and doing. In *The Encyclopedia of Philosophy.* Vol. 2. ed. P. Edwards. New York: Macmillan, 96–104.

O'Shaughnessy, B. 1980. *The Will: A Dual Aspect Theory.* 2 vols. Cambridge: Cambridge University Press.

Ottenheimer, L. 1972. Some considerations on moral values and psychoanalysis. In *Moral Values and the Superego Concept in Psychoanalysis,* ed. S. C. Post. New York: International Universities Press, 240–243.

Panel 1983. Theory of character. Reported by S. Abend. *J. Amer. Psychoan. Assn.,* 31: 211–224.

Parens, H. 1990. On the girl's psychosexual devleopment: reconsiderations suggested from direct observation. *J. Amer. Psychoan. Assn.,* 38: 743–772.

Pattison, E. M. 1968. Ego morality: an emerging psychotherapeutic concept. *Psychoan. Rev.,* 56: 187–222.

Paul, G. A. 1947. H. D. Lewis on the problem of guilt. In *Readings in Ethical Theory,* eds. W. Sellars and J. Hospers. New York: Appleton-Century-Crofts, 1952, 621–628.

Perry, R. B. 1926. *General Theory of Value.* Cambridge: Harvard University Press, 1967.

Person, E. S. 1982. The influence of values in psychoanalysis: the case of female psychology. *Psychiatry Update,* Vol. 2: 36–50.

Piaget, J. 1932. *The Moral Judgment Child.* New York: Harcourt, Brace and World.

Piers, G., and Singer, M. B. 1953. *Shame and Guilt: A Psychoanalytic and a Cultural Study.* Springfield, IL: Thomas.

Plé, A. 1964a. Moral acts and the pseudo-morality of the unconscious. In *Cross Currents of Psychiatry and Catholic Morality,* eds. W. Birmingham and J. E. Cunneen. New York: Pantheon Books, 152–193.

———. 1964b. St. Thomas and the psychology of Freud. In *Cross Currents of Psychiatry and Catholic Morality,* eds. W. Birmingham and J. E. Cunneen. New York: Pantheon Books, 84–109.

Pollock, G. H. 1989. *The Mourning-Liberation Process.* 2 vols. Madison, CT: International Universities Press.

Post, S. C. 1972. Editor's foreword. In *Moral Values and the Superego Concept in Psychoanalysis,* ed. S. C. Post. New York: International Universities Press, 1–8.

Power, D. G. 2000. On trying something new: effort and practice in psychoanalytic change. *Psychoan. Quart.,* 69: 493–526.

Price, H. H. 1973. *Perception.* London: Methuen.

Pulver, S. 1970. Narcissism: the term and the concept. *J. Amer. Psychoan. Assn.,* 18: 319–341.

Radke-Yarrow, M., Zahn-Waxler, C., and Chapman, M. 1983. Children's prosocial dispositions and behavior. In *Handbook of Child Psychology, Vol. 4: Socialization, Personality, and Social Development.* 4th ed. eds. P. H. Mussen and E. M. Hetherington. New York: Wiley, 470–545.

Ramzy, I. 1965. The place of values in psychoanalysis. *Int. J. Psychoan.*, 46: 97–106.

———. 1972. The place of values in psychoanalytic theory, practice and training. In *Moral Values and the Superego Concept in Psychoanalysis*, ed. S. C. Post. New York: International Universities Press, 205–225.

Rangell, L. 1963a. On friendship. *J. Amer. Psychoan. Assn.*, 11: 3–54.

———. 1963b. Structural problems in intrapsychic conflict. *Psychoan. Study Child*, 18: 103–138.

———. 1969a. Choice-conflict and the decision-making function of the ego: a psychoanalytic contribution to decision theory. *Int. J. Psychoan.*, 50: 599–602.

———. 1969b. Closing remarks of the author. *Int. J. Psychoan.*, 51: 195–209.

———. 1969c. The intrapsychic process and its analysis—a recent line of thought and its clinical analysis. *Int. J. Psychoan.*, 50: 65–77.

———. 1969d. Introductory remarks of the author. *Int. J. Psychoan.*, 51: 195–209.

———. 1971. The decision-making process: a contribution from psychoanalysis. *Psychoan. Study Child*, 26: 425–452.

———. 1974. A psychoanalytic perspective leading currently to the syndrome of the compromise of integrity. *Int. J. Psychoan.*, 55: 3–12.

———. 1981. From insight to change. *J. Amer. Psychoan. Assn.*, 29: 119–141.

———. 1986. The executive functions of the ego: an extension of the concept of ego autonomy. *Psychoan. Study Child*, 41: 1–37.

———. 1987. A core process in psychoanalytic treatment. *Psychoan. Quart.*, 66: 222–249.

———. 1989. Action theory within the structural view. *Int. J. Psychoan.*, 70: 189–203.

Rank, O. 1936. *Will Therapy*. New York: Knopf.

Rapaport, D. 1953. Some metapsychological considerations concerning activity and passivity. In *The Collected Papers of David Rapaport*, ed. M. M. Gill. New York: Basic, 1967, 530–568.

———. 1957. A theoretical analysis of the superego concept. In *The Collected Papers of David Rapaport*, ed. M. M. Gill. New York: Basic, 1967, 685–709.

———. 1958. A theory of ego autonomy: a generalization. In *The Collected Papers of David Rapaport*, ed. M. M. Gill. New York: Basic, 1967, 722–744.

———. 1960. On the psychoanalytic theory of motivation. In *The Collected Papers of David Rapaport*, ed. M. M. Gill. New York: Basic, 1967, 853–915.

Raphling, D. 1996. The interpretation of daydreams, 1. *J. Amer. Psychoan. Assn.*, 44: 533–547.

Rawls, J. 1971. *A Theory of Justice.* Cambridge: Harvard University Press.

Reich, A. 1953. Narcissistic object choice in women. *J. Amer. Psychoan. Assn.*, 1: 22–44.

———. 1954. Early identifications as archaic elements in the superego. *J. of the Amer. Psychoan. Assn.*, 2: 218–238.

———. 1960. Pathological forms of self-esteem regulation. *Psychoan. Study Child*, 15: 215–232.

Renik, O. 1993. Analytic interaction: conceptualizing technique in light of the analyst's irreducible subjectivity. *Psychoan. Quart.*, 62: 553–571.

———. 1998. The analyst's subjectivity and the analyst's objectivity. *Int. J. Psychoan.*, 79: 487–497.

Rescher, N. 1966. *Distributive Justice: A Constructive Critique of the Utilitarian Theory of Distribution.* Indianapolis, IN: Bobbs-Merrill.

Rest, J. R. 1980. Understanding the possibilities and conditions of cooperation. *Bull. Menninger Clin.*, 44: 524–561.

Rice, P .B. 1947. Definitions in value theory. *J. Phil.*, 44: 57–67.

Ricoeur, P. 1970. *Freud and Philosophy: An Essay on Interpretation.* New Haven, CT: Yale University Press.

———. 1981. *Hermeneutics and the Human Sciences: Essays on Language, Action, and Interpretation.* New York: Cambridge University Press.

Rieff, P. 1959. *Freud: The Mind of the Moralist.* New York: Doubleday, Anchor Book, 1961.

———. 1968. *The Triumph of the Therapeutic: Uses of Faith After Freud.* New York: Harper.

Ring, K., Wallston, K., and Corey, M. 1970. Mode of debriefing as a factor affecting subjective reactions to a Milgram-type obedience situation. *Representative Res. Soc. Psychol.*, 1: 67–85.

Ritvo, S. 1972. Outcome of predictions on superego formation: longitudinal observations. In *Moral Values and the Superego Concept in Psychoanalysis*, ed. S. C. Post. New York: International Universities Press, 74–86.

———., and Solnit, A. J. 1958. Influences of early mother-child interaction on identification processes. *Psychoan. Study Child*, 13: 64–85.

Rizzuto, A.-M., Meissner, S. J., W. W., and Buie, D. H. in press. *A New Theory of Aggression: Drive vs. Motive.* New York: Brunner-Routledge.

Rizzuto, A.-M., Sashin, J. I., Buie, D. H., and Meissner, S. J., W. W. 1993. A revised theory of aggression. *Psychoan. Rev.*, 80: 29–54.

Robbins, M. 1996. Nature, nurture, and core gender identity. *J. Amer. Psychoan. Assn.*, 44 [Suppl.]: 93–117.

Rochlin, G. 1961. The dread of abandonment: a contribution to the etiology of the loss complex and to depression. *Psychoan. Study Child*, 16: 451–470.

————. 1965. *Griefs and Discontents: The Forces of Change*. Boston: Little, Brown.

————. 1973. *Man's Aggression: The Defense of the Self*. Boston: Gambit Press.

Rokeach, M. 1973. *The Nature of Human Values*. New York: Free Press.

Rorty, A. O. 1988a. The deceptive self: liars, layeers, and lairs. In *Perspectives on Self-Deception*, eds. B. P. McLaughlin and A. O. Rorty. Berkeley: University of California Press, 11–28.

————. 1988b. *Mind in Action: Essays in the Philosophy of Mind*. Boston: Beacon.

Rorty, R. 1979. *Philosophy and the Mirror of Nature*. Princeton, NJ: Princeton University Press.

————. 1986. Freud and moral reflection. In *Pragmatism's Freud: The Moral Disposition of Psychoanalysis*, eds. J. H. Smith and W. Kerrigan. Baltimore, MD: Johns Hopkins University Press, 1–27.

————. 1991. *Objectivity, Relativism, and Truth: Philosophical Papers*. Vol. 1. Cambridge: Cambridge University Press.

Rosen, H., and Zickler, E. 1996. Feminist psychoanalytic theory: American and French reactions to Freud. *J. Amer. Psychoan. Assn.*, 44 [Suppl.]: 71–92.

Rosenblatt, A. D., and Thickstun, J. T. 1970. A study of the concept of psychic energy. *Int. J. Psychoan.*, 51: 265–278.

————., and Thickstun, J. T. 1977a. Energy, information, and motivation: a revision of psychoanalytic theory. *J. Amer. Psychoan. Assn.*, 25: 537–558.

————, and Thickstun, J. T. 1977b. *Modern Psychoanalytic Concepts in a General Psychology*. New York: International Universities Press [Psychol. Issues, Monogr. 42/43].

Rubenstein, B. 1967. Explanation and mere description: a metascientific examination of certain aspects of the psychoanalytic theory of motivation. In *Motives and Thought: Psychoanalytic Essays in Honor of David Rapaport*, ed. R. R. Holt. New York: International Universities Press, 29–77 [Psychol. Issues, Monogr. 18/19].

Rubin, J. B. 1997. Psychoanalysis is self-centered. In *Soul on the Couch: Spirituality, Religion, and Morality in Contemporary Psychoanalysis*, eds. C. Spezzano and G. J. Gargiulo. Hillsdale, NJ: Analytic Press, 79–108.

Russell, B. 1910. The elements of ethics. In *Readings in Ethical Theory*, eds. W. Sellars, and J. Hospers. New York: Appleton-Century-Crofts, 1952, 1–32.

Ryle, G. 1940. Conscience and moral convictions. In *Conscience*, eds. J. Donnelly and L. Lyons. New York: Alba House, 1973, 25–34.

Sandler, J. 1960. On the concept of superego. *Psychoan. Study Child*, 15: 128–162.

———., and Freud, A. 1985. *The Analysis of Defense: The Ego and the Mechanisms of Defense Revisited*. New York: International Universities Press.

———., Holder, A., and Meers, D. 1963. The ego ideal and the ideal self. *Psychoan. Study Child*, 18: 139–158.

Sartre, J. P. 1965. *Being and Nothingness: An Essay in Phenomenological Ontology*. New York: Citadel Press.

Schafer, R. 1960. The loving and beloved superego in Freud's structural theory. *Psychoan. Study Child*, 15: 163–188.

———. 1968. *Aspects of Internalization*. New York: International Universities Press.

———. 1974. Problems in Freud's psychology of women. *J. Amer. Psychoan. Assn.*, 22: 459–485.

———. 1976. *A New Language for Psychoanalysis*. New Haven, CT: Yale University Press.

———. 1992. *Retelling a Life: Narration and Dialogue in Psychoanalysis*. New York: Basic.

———. 1994. Revisiting classics: an essay on Heinz Hartmann's 'Psychoanalysis and moral values.' *Psychoan. Inq.*, 17: 251–286.

Schlesinger, H. J. 1992. What does psychoanalysis have to contribute to the understanding of character? *Psychoan. Study Child*, 47: 225–234.

Schur, M. 1966. *The Id and the Regulatory Principles of Mental Functioning*. New York: International Universities Press.

Schwartz, S. H., and Bilsky, W. 1987. Toward a universal psychological structure of human values. *J. Pers. Soc. Psychol.*, 53: 550–562.

———., Feldman, K. A., Brown, M. E., and Heingartner, A. 1969. Some personality correlates of conduct in two situations of moral conflict. *J. Pers.*, 37: 41–57.

Schwartz, W. 1984. The two concepts of action and responsibility in psychoanalysis. *J. Amer. Psychoan. Assn.*, 32: 557–572.

Sears, R. R., Maccoby, E. E., and Levin, H. 1957. *Patterns of Child Rearing*. Evanston, IL: Row, Peterson.

Seelig, B. J., and Rosof, L. S. 2001. Normal and pathological altruism. *J. Amer. Psychoan. Assn.*, 49: 933–959.

Shapiro, D. 1970. Motivation and action in psychoanalytic psychiatry. *Psychiatry*, 33: 329–343.

Sherwood, M. 1969. *The Logic of Explanation in Psychoanalysis*. New York: Academic.

Simons, R. C. 1987. Psychoanalytic contributions to psychiatric nosology: forms of masochistic behavior. *J. Amer. Psychoan. Assn.*, 35: 583–608.

350   *References*

Smith, J. H. 1986. Primitive guilt. In *Pragmatism's Freud: The Moral Disposition of Psychoanalysis*, eds. J. H. Smith and W. Kerrigan. Baltimore: Johns Hopkins University Press, 52–78.

———., and Kerrigan, W. 1986. Introduction. In *Pragmatism's Freud: The Moral Disposition of Psychoanalysis*, eds. J. H. Smith and W. Kerrigan. Baltimore: Johns Hopkins University Press, ix–xxi.

Smith, M. B. 1969. *Social Psychology and Human Values*. Chicago: Aldine Publishing Company.

———. 1980. Attitudes, values, and selfhood. In *Nebraska Symposium on Motivation 1979*, eds. H. E. Howe Jr. and M. M. Page. Lincoln: University of Nebraska Press, 305–350.

Spiegel, L. A. 1966. Affects in relation to self and object: a model for the derivation of desire, longing, pain, anxiety, humiliation, and shame. *Psychoan. Study Child*, 21: 69–92.

Spitz, R. 1958. On the genesis of superego components. *Psychoan. Study Child*, 13: 375–404.

Stein, M. H. 1972. A Clinical illustration of a "moral" problem in psychoanalysis. In *Moral Values and the Superego Concept in Psychoanalysis*, ed. S. C. Post. New York: International Universities Press, 226–239.

Steiner, R. 1995. Hermeneutics or Hermes-mess? *Int. J. Psychoan.*, 76: 435–445.

Steingart, I. 1969. On self, character, and the development of a psychic apparatus. *Psychoan. Study Child*, 24: 271–306.

Stern, D. N. 1985. *The Interpersonal World of the Infant*. New York: Basic.

Stout, A. E. 1936–1937. Free will and responsibility. In *Readings in Ethical Theory*, eds. W. Sellars and J. Hospers. New York: Appleton-Century-Crofts, 1952, 537–548.

Strachey, J. 1934. The nature of the therapeutic action of psychoanalysis. *Int. J. Psychoan.*, 15: 127–159.

Straus, E. W. 1969. Embodiment and excarnation. In *Toward a Unity of Knowledge*, ed. M. Grene. New York: International Universities Press, 217–250 [Psychol. Issues, Monogr. 22].

Svrakic, D. M. 1986. On narcissistic ethics. *Amer. J. Psychoan.*, 46: 55–61.

Szasz, T. S. 1958. Men and machines. *Brit. J. Phil. Sci.*, 3: 310–317.

———. 1961. *The Myth of Mental Illness*. Rev. ed. New York: Harper, 1974.

———. 1963. *Law, Liberty, and Psychiatry*. New York: Macmillan.

———. 1974. *The Ethics of Psychoanalysis*. New York: Basic Books.

Taylor, R. 1967. Determinism. In *The Encyclopedia of Philosophy*, ed. P. Edwards. Vol. 2. New York: Macmillan, 359–373.

Ticho, E. 1972. The development of superego autonomy. *Psychoan. Rev.*, 59: 217–233.

Tillich, P. 1955. *The Courage to Be.* New Haven, CT: Yale University Press.

Tomkins, S. S. 1962. *Affect, Imagery, Consciousness.* Vol 1. New York: Springer.

———. 1970. Affects as the primary motivational system. In *Feelings and Emotions: The Loyola Symposium*, ed. M. B. Arnold. New York: Academic, 101–110.

Tov-Ruach, L. 1988. Freud on unconscious affects, mourning, and the erotic mind. In *Perspectives on Self-Deception*, eds. B. P. McLaughlin and A. O. Rorty. Berkeley: University of California Press, 246–263.

Trivers, R. L. 1971. The evolution of reciprocal altruism. *Quart. Rev. Biology*, 46 35–57.

Turiel, E. 1976. A comparative analysis of moral knowledge and moral judgment in males and females. *J. Pers.*, 44: 195–208.

Tyson, P. 1996. Object relations, affect management, and psychic structure formation. *Psychoan. Study Child*, 51: 172–189.

Ury, C. 1997. The shadow of object love: reconstructing Freud's theory of preoedipal guilt. *Psychoan. Quart.*, 66: 34–61.

Vacek, S. J., E. C. 1994. *Love, Human and Divine: The Heart of Christian Ethics.* Washington, DC: Georgetown University Press.

Vaillant, G. 1977. *Adaptation to Life.* Boston: Little, Brown.

Valenstein, A. F. 1972. The earliest mother-child relationship and the development of the superego. In *Moral Values and the Superego Concept in Psychoanalysis*, ed. S. C. Post. New York: International Universities Press, 63–71.

Vivas, E. 1963. *The Moral Life and the Ethical Life.* Chicago: Regnery.

Volkan, V. D. 1988. *The Need to Have Enemies and Allies.* Northvale, NJ: Jason Aronson.

Waelder, R. 1936a. The principle of multiple function: observations on over-determination. *Psychoan. Quart.*, 5: 45–62.

———. 1936b. Problems of freedom in psychoanalysis, and of reality testing. *Int. J. Psychoan.*, 17: 89–108.

Walker, L. J. 1984. Sex differences in the development of moral reasoning: a critical review. *Child Dev.*, 55: 677–691.

Wallace, E. R. 1985. *Historiography and Causation in Psychoanalysis: An Essay on Psychoanalysis and Historical Epistemology.* Hillsdale, NJ: Analytic Press.

———. 1986a. Determinism, possibility, and ethics. *J. Amer. Psychoan. Assn.*, 34: 933–974.

———. 1986b. Freud as ethicist. In *Freud: Appraisals and Reappraisals*, ed. P. Stepansky. Hillsdale, NJ: Analytic Press, 83–141.

———. 1995. Review of *Psychoanalysis and Ethics* by Ernest Wallwork. *J. Amer. Psychoan. Assn.*, 43: 1221–1229.

Wallerstein, R. S. 1992. *The Common Ground of Psychoanalysis*. Northvale, NJ: Jason Aronson.

Wallington, S. A. 1973. Consequences of transgression. *J. Pers. Soc. Psychol.*, 28: 1–7.

Wallwork, E. 1991. *Psychoanalysis and Ethics*. New Haven, CT: Yale University Press.

Weisman, A. D. 1965. *The Existential Core of Psychoanalysis: Reality Sense and Responsibility*. Boston: Little, Brown.

Wheelis, A. 1956. Will and psychoanalysis. *J. Amer. Psychoan. Assn.*, 4: 285–303.

White, R. W. 1959. Motivation reconsidered: the concept of competence. *Psychol. Rev.*, 66: 297–333.

———. 1960. Competence and the psychosexual stages of development. In *Nebraska Symposium on Motivation*, ed. M. R. Jones. Lincoln: University of Nebraska Press, 97–141.

———. 1963. *Ego and Reality in Psychoanalytic Theory*. New York: International Universities Press [Psychol. Issues, Monogr. 11].

White, S. L. 1988. Self-deception and responsibility for the self. In *Perspectives on Self-Deception*, eds. B. P. McLaughlin and A. O. Rorty. Berkeley: University of California Press, 450–484.

Whiting, J. W. M. 1959. Sorcery, sin, and the superego. In *Nebraska Symposium on Motivation*, ed. M. R. Jones. Lincoln: University of Nebraska Press, 174–195.

———., and Child, I. L. 1953. *Child Training and Personality: A Cross-cultural Study*. New Haven, CT: Yale University Press.

Wilder, J. 1973. Values and the psychology of the superego. *Amer. J. Psychotherapy*, 27: 187–203.

Wilshire, B. 1988. Mimetic engulfment and self-deception. In *Perspectives on Self-Deception*, eds. B. P. McLaughlin and A. O. Rorty. Berkeley: University of California Press, 390–404.

Wilson, E. O. 1975. *Sociobiology: The New Synthesis*. Cambridge: Harvard University Press.

Winnicott, D. W. 1960a. Ego distortion in terms of true and false self. In *The Maturational Processes and the Facilitating Environment: Studies in the Theory of Emotional Development*. New York: International Universities Press, 1965, 140–152.

———. 1960b. The theory of the parent-infant relationship. In *The Maturational Processes and the Facilitating Environment: Studies in the Theory of Emotional Development*. New York: International Universities Press, 1965, 37–55.

———. 1963. Morals and education. In *The Maturational Processes and the Facilitating Environment: Studies in the Theory of Emotional*

Development. New York: International Universities Press, 1965, 93–105.

———. *Psycho-Analytic Explorations*. ed. C. Winnicott, R. Shepherd, and M. Davis. Cambridge: Harvard University Press.

Wolf, A. 1972. Morality and the population explosion. In *Moral Values and the Superego Concept in Psychoanalysis*, ed. S. C. Post. New York: International Universities Press, 472–490.

Wood, A. W. 1988. Self-deception and bad faith. In *Perspectives on Self-Deception*, eds. B. P. McLaughlin and A. O. Rorty. Berkeley: University of California Press, 207–227.

Wright, D. 1971. *The Psychology of Moral Behaviour*. Middlesex, England: Penguin Books.

Wurmser, L. 1978. *The Hidden Dimension*. New York: Jason Aronson.

Zahn-Waxler, C., and Radke-Yarrow, M. 1982. The development of altruism: alternative research strategies. In *The Development of Prosocial Behavior*, ed. N. Eisenberg. New York: Academic, 109–137.

Zetzel, E. 1964. Symptom formation and character formation. *Int. J. Psychoan.*, 45: 151–154.

Zinberg, N. 1972. Value conflict and the psychoanalyst's role. In *Moral Values and the Superego Concept in Psychoan.*, ed. S. C. Post. New York: International Universities Press, 169–196.

Index of Names

Subject Index

authority, 230, 233, 236, 252, 253,
255–257, 262, 263, 269; authoritarian
submission, 21; irrational, 14, 268, 269;
moral, 257; parental, 219, 221, 227–230,
235, 237, 262, 265; rational, 14
autonomy, 2, 10, 13, 23, 25, 35, 53, 54, 70,
81, 91, 92, 102, 105, 106, 107, 109, 110,
150, 184, 189, 190, 196, 198–200, 202,
215, 220, 234, 250, 268, 271, 293, 301,
305, 307, 315; functional, 106; personal,
200, 257; secondary, 106

bad, badness, 49, 118, 180, 182, 201, 206,
212, 219, 228, 231, 251, 252–254, 258,
259, 261, 265, 268, 273–275, 286, 287,
289, 302, 317
bad faith, 193, 314
belief(s), 187–190, 193, 247, 281, 314;
unconscious, 314
benevolence, 31, 171, 252, 270
bipolar affective states, 109; manic phase,
109
bisexuality, 6, 223
borderline, 109; higher order, 109; lower
order, 109

capacity(ies), 69, 76, 79, 80, 86, 90, 91, 98,
101, 198, 202; for action, 70
care, caring, 151, 152, 155, 159, 224, 249,
250, 274, 294, 310, 315
categorical imperative, 32, 34, 35, 37, 47,
81
causality, causes, 55–57, 60, 76, 87–89, 98,
99, 202, 301, 302; efficient, 84, 86–89,
100–102, 202, 301, 302, 313; final, 84,
86, 88, 100, 101, 102, 202, 302; linear,
302; psychic, 54, 57, 59, 97, 301
chance, 98
character, 13, 14, 16, 17, 79, 91, 96, 156,
161, 195, 230, 267–284, 290, 321, 322;
antisocial, 270; authoritarian, 14, 268,
269; bad, 267; depressive, 137; disorders,
296; ethical, 133, 273, 291; exploitative,
268; formation, 6, 58, 229, 267, 268,
271–273, 276; good, 267; hoarding, 268;
infantile, 195; marketing, 268; masochistic, 318; moral, 17, 21, 75, 255, 268,
291; narcissistic, 137; neurotic, 117;
pathology, 7, 13, 270–271, 318; productive, 268, 310; psychology of, 267–268;
puritanical, 270; receptive, 268; structure,

58, 283, 292, 294, 322; traits, 185, 195,
222, 268–271, 273–275, 322
charity, 152, 167, 169
choice (choosing), 33, 48, 54, 73, 76, 78,
81, 82, 84–87, 93, 96, 97, 98, 100, 98,
100, 102–104, 106–109, 111, 121, 124,
138, 156, 177, 178, 181, 182, 184–186,
189, 192, 194, 196, 197, 200, 201–203,
205, 206, 208, 210, 212–214, 215, 216,
249, 253, 254, 256–258, 260, 264, 276,
279–281, 284–288, 292, 295, 301,
304–307, 312–315; conflicts of, 182–183;
ethical, 285; free, 54, 81, 95, 99, 202,
215, 306; moral, 75; responsible, 132;
unconscious, 185–186
civilization, 19, 30, 219, 253, 262, 263
clinical theory, 2
coma, 108; comatose states, 111
competence, 71, 120, 141, 215, 233, 237, 274
compliance, 305
compromise, 88, 204, 254, 278, 284, 301
concupiscence, 170
conflict(s), 18, 19, 62, 79, 80, 92, 110, 179,
181–184, 186, 188, 190, 194, 198, 199,
205, 217, 223, 230, 231, 233–235, 239,
250, 254, 260, 265, 267, 276, 280, 284,
286, 294, 304, 313; aggressive, 297; anal,
225; convergent, 313; divergent, 313;
instinctual, 298; intersystemic, 182, 189;
intrasystemic, 182, 189, 242; libidinal,
297; moral, 124; narcissistic, 297; neurotic, 218, 246, 296; oedipal, 221, 235;
unconscious, 9, 205
conformity, 219, 232, 234, 242, 256, 259
conscience, 2, 5–7, 12–14, 18, 28, 30, 31,
33–35, 37, 42, 43, 46, 57, 64, 75, 112,
127, 201, 218, 219, 221, 222, 225, 227,
229, 230, 234, 235, 241, 266–269,
272279, 288, 290, 292, 296, 318–321;
antecedent, 253, 258, 259, 319; authoritarian, 255, 263, 319–322; consequent, 253,
258, 259; ethics of, 213, 272; humanistic,
255, 263, 320–322; as moral guide, 12;
neurotic, 243; objective, 256–257; pseudomoral, 320; subjective, 256–257
conscious, consciousness, 75, 83, 87, 108,
111, 114, 116, 140, 179, 182, 183, 190,
200, 209, 211, 228, 238, 295, 302, 303,
306, 313, 314; moral, 253, 261; self-consciousness, 112, 190, 191, 217
constancy, principle of, 63

drugs, amphetamines, 110; hallucinogenic, 110; LSD, 110
duty, 32, 33, 34, 35, 37, 38, 40, 45, 117, 119, 167, 177, 196, 201, 206, 207, 210, 213, 229, 261–262, 290, 300, 310, 313, 316, 320
dynamic hypothesis, 2, 83

economic explanation, 3
effectance, 71
ego, 16, 18, 31, 73, 75, 76, 79, 80, 93, 96, 99, 106, 107, 109, 111, 120, 121, 133, 137, 140, 141, 142, 148, 150, 177, 178, 179, 181, 182, 184, 189, 190, 191, 195, 202, 212, 215, 217, 218, 221, 222, 223, 229, 230, 233, 235, 241, 242, 244, 245, 246, 247, 259, 262, 267, 268, 271, 272, 274, 280, 293, 296, 297, 298, 300, 304, 305, 307, 309, 313, 314, 318, 319, 322; autonomous, autonomy, 196, 274, 296, 302, 306; capacities, 220, 241, 248, 258; development, 23, 227; energy, 88; formation, 224; functions, functioning, 30, 182, 183–184, 192, 214, 219, 246, 254, 258, 259, 269, 270, 277, 288, 295, 296, 297, 302, 303, 306, 314, 316: deliberating, 96, regulating, 96; psychology, 11, 16, 121, 268; regulation, 13; strength, 79, 184, 185, 260, 261, 274; structure, 297
egoism, 131, 148–150, 163, 166, 172, 175; egoistic traits, 162; egoistic motives, 163, 192, 281
empathy, 153, 163, 231, 250, 270, 271, 272, 294
energy, 57, 302, 303; psychic, 58
energic models, 3; closed-system, 143, 174
envy, 136, 146, 192, 238, 316; penis envy, 223, 226
epigenetic schema, 24
Eros, 10, 11, 30, 129, 172, 310
Erikson, *Childhood and Society,* 23
ethics, 2, 4, 5, 23, 112, 125, 185, 203, 253, 263, 288, 292, 293, 294, 299; authoritarian, 14; ethical action, 145, 217, 273, 285, 294, 296; ethical agency, agent, 42, 53, 73, 202, 270, 273, 274, 281, 285, 323; ethical attitudes, 6, 180; ethical behavior, 12, 17, 50, 112, 147, 148, 164, 166, 172, 256, 270, 300; ethical decision, 13, 112, 185, 233, 260, 266; ethical dilemmas, 182, 189; ethical dynamism,

24; ethical facts, 44; ethical ideals, 40; ethical issues, 11, 132, 244, 246, 259; ethical judgment, 9, 36, 40, 42, 125, 180, 214, 217, 234, 245, 246, 248, 252, 266, 288, 292, 295, 300; ethical maturity, 9, 234, 236, 254, 260; ethical neutrality, 9, 16, 17, 285; ethical perspectives, vii, 125, 146; ethical principles, 10, 32, 40, 42, 125, 144, 156, 254, 255; ethical reflection, 38, 45, 182, 217, 262, 321; ethical rules, 23; ethical sense, 23, 25, 258, 292; ethical standards, 288, 289, 294; ethical systems, 27–52, 146; ethical theory, 15, 28–52, 111, 119, 294: analytic, 43–47, axiology, 29, 49–50, cognitive, 28, deontology, 29, existential, 47–49, formalism, 29, 31–35. Hedonistic, 15, 28. Intuitionist, 28, 29–31, 46, metaphysical, 28, naturalist, 28, 38–43, noncognitive, 28, pragmatist, 28, utilitarian, 28, 36–38, 45, 114, 122, 252: egotistic, 36, universal, 36; of conscience, 213, 272; of responsibility, 213, 214, 272; ethical view of human nature, 25; freudian, 1; humanistic, 14
evil, 5, 39, 40, 45, 49, 64, 83, 93, 127, 128, 131, 134, 144, 170, 171, 185, 194, 211, 212, 238, 243, 245, 252, 253, 254, 261, 265, 270, 275, 280, 286, 294; Garden of, 128
evolution, 39
execution, order of, 313

false-self, 22; conformity, 22
fantasies, 63, 76, 89, 199, 211, 221, 225, 242, 243, 258, 262, 264, 278, 286; beating 225, 245; grandiose, 137; narcissistic, 139, 225; sadistic, 225; unconscious, 88, 179
femininity, 223, 229, 250
fidelity, 274, 294
finality, 88, 92
forgiveness, 248, 264, 293, 320
free association, 55, 85, 103, 107
free, freedom, 13, 20, 27, 33, 35, 47, 48, 49, 54, 75, 76, 80, 91, 95–112, 148, 153, 173, 177, 198, 200, 202, 204, 205, 214–217, 248, 251, 259, 260, 261, 268, 295, 301, 304, 305, 306, 307, 316; freedom for, 106; freedom from, 13, 106; freedom to, 13; in Freud, 95–97; limits of, 108–111; meaning of, 101–105; negative